FREDRIC MARCH:

A CONSUMMATE ACTOR

BY CHARLES TRANBERG

FREDRIC MARCH: A CONSUMMATE ACTOR
©2013 CHARLES TRANBERG

Published in the USA by:

BEARMANOR MEDIA
P.O. BOX 71426
ALBANY, GEORGIA 31708
www.BearManorMedia.com

ISBN-10: 1-59393-745-8 (alk. paper)
ISBN-13: 978-1-59393-745-4 (alk. paper)

DESIGN AND LAYOUT: VALERIE THOMPSON

TABLE OF CONTENTS

INTRODUCTION

When I told people that I was planning to write a book about Fredric March, I had two questions that were asked of me with the most frequency:

1)   Why Fredric March?

2)   Who is Fredric March? (This was asked of me mostly by those under the age of forty.)

At one time, Fredric March was one of the most sought after and successful stars in motion pictures. He was considered by audiences and his peers to be one of the very finest actors of his time. He appeared in films that were, on the whole, critically acclaimed. He was nominated five times for Best Actor by the Academy of Motion Pictures Arts and Sciences (AMPAS); he won the Oscar twice (in 1932 and 1947). He made more than seventy films over a period of forty-four years from 1929-1973. He was among the first major stars to buck the contract system, and by the mid-1930s he was making films for a variety of studios without the constraints of a long-term studio contact. When he decided he wanted to make his mark on the Broadway stage he found acclaim in such prestigious and long-running productions as *The American Way, The Skin of Our Teeth, A Bell for Adano* and, most significantly, *A Long Day's Journey Into Night.* Along the way, he won Two Tony Awards, including the very first Tony given for an actor in the Theater. He worked with some of the best and most inventive directors of his day: Dorothy Arzner, Rouben Mamoulian, Cecil B. DeMille, Mitchell Leisen, Howard Hawks, John Ford, William Wellman, George Cukor, William Wyler, Elia Kazan, Stanley Kramer, and John Frankenheimer.

March gave memorable performances in dozens of important/ classic films:

He starred in one of the first films to inspire the screwball comedy genre, *Laughter* (1930); he was the screen's best impersonator of John Barrymore in *The Royal Family of Broadway* (1930); he won his first Oscar for his stunning duel role as *Dr. Jekyll and Mr. Hyde* (1931); he was a war hero at odds with killing in *The Eagle and the Hawk* (1933); and he made an alluring and sympathetic 'Death' in *Death Takes a Holiday* (1934).

For many years he was the definitive Jean Valjean in *Les Miserables* (1935); he gave one of his finest performances as Norman Maine in the original *A Star is Born* (1937); he kept up with Carole Lombard knocks and all in the rollicking *Nothing Sacred* (1937); he starred as a Midwestern pastor in the superb piece of Americana that is *One Foot in Heaven* (1941); he brought Mark Twain to life in *The Adventures of Mark Twain* (1944); and he and Myrna Loy epitomized mature love in *The Best Years of Our Lives* (1946).

He finally got to play Willy Loman (he had been offered the stage role, but turned it down) in *Death of a Salesman* (1951); he stood his ground against Humphrey Bogart in *The Desperate Hours* (1955); he gave a vivid portrait of May-December romance opposite Kim Novak in *Middle of the Night* (1959); he was a blustery William Jennings Bryan opposite Spencer Tracy's Clarence Darrow in *Inherit the Wind* (1960); he played the liberal minded president of the United States going toe to toe against a military coup in *Seven Days in May* (1964); and he made a deeply affecting Harry Hope in *The Iceman Cometh* (1973), his final film.

Ephraim Katz, in his book *The Film Encyclopedia*, wrote that March, "…emerged as one of Hollywood's subtlest and most sensitive actors, a performer of considerable range with an intuitive grasp of the specific requirements of screen acting, where the slightest nuance of facial expression can be magnified to great advantage."

I think the above answers part of the question, 'Why Fredric March?' The other part of the equation is that despite these many accomplishments, Fredric March isn't usually counted among the legendary stars of the Golden Age of Hollywood. His film work isn't as fondly recalled as that of his contemporaries. A case in point is that in 1999, the American Film Institute (AFI) compiled a list of the "50 Greatest Screen Legends." The name Fredric March doesn't appear on the list. Contrast this with a 1955 poll of top stars, directors, and producers that named March as "The Screen's best Actor." (The runners up were Marlon Brando, who was at the zenith of his *Streetcar Named Desire* and *On the Waterfront* popularity, William Holden, Ronald Colman, and Spencer Tracy.) Furthermore, the AFI also compiled a list (in 1998) of the 100 Best American Films—and the list includes only one March title (William Wyler's superb ensemble *The Best Years of Our Lives*). There are films that are recognizable as John Wayne films, Humphrey Bogart films, or Cary Grant films, but there is no collection of films that are well-known as Fredric March films. He is an actor first and a personality second—if at all. This is both his glory and his curse. For it's the personality-stars who have managed, on the whole, to survive the test of time.

Unlike some of the screen's great legends, and Fredric March contemporaries, March didn't establish a recognizable screen persona that he carried from film to film and that was identified solely with him. Film biographer and historian David Thomson wrote of March in his *Biographical Dictionary of Film*:

> *March is a good instance of the durable leading man, much relied upon by major studios, but never a star who dominated audiences…yet he gave moments that are hard to forget.*

Another film historian, David Shipman, wrote of March:

> *He is normally quietly excellent, seldom memorable and less affectionately regarded than the other two actors who twice won Best Actor Oscars, Spencer Tracy and Gary Cooper. He did go through a spell of being a very romantic leading man, but for most of his career he has been a dedicated no-nonsense actor, authoritative and reliable; if you look at publicity stills of March you will find them more direct, less affected, than those of any other leading star: he does not pose. He is direct. And he managed to be in an above-average number of good movies.*

> *Yet March is an actor who cries out to be rediscovered. His*

body of work and consistently fine performances (though at times there is an element of the ham in him, as he well knew, and he told more than one director to be sure and tone him down) deserve a new generation of recognition.

The literary, film and stage critic John Simon wrote five years after March's death in Esquire:

> *Whether in romantic leads or modern dress, March was easily, manfully in command. He made the transition from juvenile to leading man to character actor with elegant facility and was just as good in the lower and middle class world of The Best Years of Our Lives as in the uppermost reaches of Executive Suite.*

This book I hope also gives a glimpse of the private man. The Midwestern boy who grew up to be a great actor and yet never really lost the common touch. He was married twice. His first brief marriage was something he never spoke about and, in fact, few people outside of very close friends and family ever knew he had been married prior to his long-running marriage to actress Florence Eldridge.

Florence Eldridge was an important part of the life of Fredric March. Not only was she his spouse of nearly forty-seven years, but she was often his partner in several different acting endeavors. They made nine films together (probably *Inherit the Wind* is the best known, where she plays his onscreen wife), but most memorably they worked together on the stage, including three landmark plays: *The American Way, The Skin of Our Teeth,* and *Long Day's Journey Into Night.* On the screen she was never his equal, but on the stage they were partners through and through.

Offscreen they were good, concerned citizens. Some would call them 'do-gooders,' and they believed in the liberal populism of Franklin Roosevelt and stood up against fascism, racism, and a variety of other isms, but still got tarred and feathered by some who thought they were soft on communism. Unlike some of those who were attacked as Communists when, in fact, they were nothing more than well-meaning liberals, the Marches fought back. They were not going to have their Americanism challenged by anybody.

Publicly, the March marriage was considered one of the most rock solid in show business—and in many ways it was. There was never a hint of scandal about either Fredric March or Florence Eldridge in the press. It's clear that there was a deep devotion and love between them. March was often solicitous of Florence, who early on was a bigger star than he was, but since their marriage she allowed her career to take a distinct back seat. On two big occasions he told theater producers he wouldn't do a play unless Florence was cast opposite him: *The Skin of Our Teeth* and *Long Day's Journey Into Night.* His judgment proved sound. Yet this same solicitous, loving, and devoted husband acquired a reputation within the industry as one of the most lecherous womanizers around. It was said there was not a fanny safe from the groping fingers of 'Freddie' March. Yet for all the fanny pinching, inappropriate touching, and juvenile attempts at seduction, there doesn't appear to be any evidence that any other woman took a place in the heart of Fredric March—other than Florence Eldridge.

Finally my thanks to the following people for their help with this book:

LISA BURKS, a wonderful, kind-hearted lady who always looks out for our four-legged friends. She is also a very fine film historian and researcher. I want to thank her for the time she spent at the Academy of Motion Pictures Arts and Sciences (AMPAS) library providing me with material from the Gladys Hall Papers, George Cukor Papers, and Martin Ritt Papers, all of which included material never before published.

THE STAFF OF THE WISCONSIN STATE HISTORICAL SOCIETY ARCHIVES, in my hometown of Madison, Wisconsin. One of the finest archives in the country, with a staff of talented and caring professionals who are always helpful and considerate. Not only does the WSHSA hold the papers of Fredric March but also of several other producers, directors, and stars who were associated with the career of Fredric March. I truly enjoyed working in the archives again.

ACTOR BRADFORD DILLMAN, who came to know Fredric March and Florence Eldridge when he was cast as the youngest son in the landmark Broadway production of *Long Day's Journey Into Night.* He also worked with March in March's final film, *The Iceman Cometh,* made at a time when March was in seriously declining health. Mr. Dillman offered great insight into these projects as well as the personalities of Fredric March and Florence Eldridge.

WENDY FINN—Who has done a fantastic job of editing this book, Thank you for such a professional job.

VALERIE THOMPSON—The best book designer I've ever had the good fortune of working with. Thank you for the terrific job (as always).

GARY McFALL—A good friend who, as he had on my last two books, scanned the pictures that are included this book. I appreciate your help and friendship.

SCOTT O'BRIEN—A terrific film writer and biographer whose books on Kay Francis, Virginia Bruce, and Ann Harding are among the best film biographies I've had the pleasure to read. I thank you for your support and help with comments and photographs.

BEN OHMART—Thank you for continuing to publish books about a bygone era that deserves to be remembered.

Finally, this is my seventh book, and I want to thank all of those who have supported my work over the years. I hope you will enjoy this effort too.

CHARLES TRANBERG
MADISON, WISCONSIN
APRIL 30, 2013

CHAPTER ONE
1897–1914

The baby who grew up to be Fredric March was born in Racine, Wisconsin. Among the things that Wisconsin has, over the years, been known for are its breweries, cheeses, lush farm land, and progressive politics. It wouldn't be an exaggeration to add that the state has also produced more than its share of talented people who excelled on the stage and screen: Spencer Tracy, Fred MacMurray, Hattie McDaniel, Don Ameche, Dennis Morgan, Jack Carson, Orson Welles, Alfred Lunt, Ellen Corby, as well as the directors Howard Hawks and Nicholas Ray—just to name a few.

Located in the southeastern part of the state, Racine derived its name from the French word "root" and is located on the shore of Lake Michigan. The mouth of the nearly forty-four-mile Root River empties into Lake Michigan from Racine. Racine is located in the center between two great American cities: Milwaukee, only thirty miles to the east, and Chicago, just under sixty miles to the south. Racine was a sizable city for its time with a population approaching 30,000—the fifth largest in the state. Despite this, March considered himself a country boy at heart. "You see I was born in Racine, Wisconsin," he once said, "and compared to a cosmopolitan city, like New York, that was the country. As a boy I did all the things that country boys traditionally do, or did."

March was born on August 31, 1897, and given the name Ernest Frederick McIntyre Bickel—Fred for short. He was the last of four children born to John and Cora Bickel. His father was thirty-eight years old at the time of his birth, and his mother, whose maiden name was Marcher, was thirty-four. His siblings were between five and ten years older than Fred. (The oldest was Harold, born in

1887, followed by sister Rosina, born in 1889.) The sibling closest to Fred was the one closest to his age: John (who went by Jack to differentiate himself from his father) was five years older than Fred.

Fred's grandparents on his paternal side were both born in Germany and had emigrated to the small Wisconsin village of Caledonia, and then, when their son John was fourteen, they moved to the nearby city of Racine. Meanwhile, his maternal grandfather, Thomas, emigrated to the United States from England, and his grandmother, Samantha, was born in New York. Eventually they settled in Onarga, Illinois, before making their way to Racine as well. John and Cora met in 1884, and then they married in Racine on January 23, 1886.

Fred would later recall his as a "swell family." He would describe his mother as "gay, charming, (and) very naïve. We kidded her and adored her." She also had a love of literature and poetry, which she instilled into each of her children. His father was a pillar of the community. He was in the wholesale hardware business and was an elder in the Presbyterian Church. March recalled his father as being a man of "wise understanding and tolerance (and) such humor." Fred's earliest recollection was of eating cookies his Grandmother Marcher made "munching them comfortably beside the big bed in which my grandfather lay ill."

Shortly after Fred's birth, the family moved into the large two-story Victorian house that Cora's parents lived in, located at 1635 College Avenue, a tree-lined street that had been paved the summer of March's birth with red brick and stone—as a portion of this block continues to be to this day. Grandfather Marcher had died shortly beforehand, and the family made the move in part to keep grandmother Marcher company.

Because of the Root River and Lake Michigan, swimming and other water sports were always a big source of entertainment. Swimming in the summer and ice skating in the winter. Growing up, Fred and his friends could be a mischievous lot. They would steal lumber from houses that were under construction so that they could build rafts. They also liked to steal vegetables from neighbors' gardens and make it look as if the culprits were rabbits or some other animal.

But their petty theft eventually caught up with them when they attempted to steal watermelons from a garden just outside of Racine. "We sneaked from our homes after supper," March later recalled, "congregated, and made a foray on the melon-patch of a farmer. As we left, laden with melons, his son saw us and gave chase, shouting terrible threats…Desperately, we dropped the melons as we ran, but he caught us, shook us, and cuffed us individually…paralyzed with fright, we promised to bring him money for the melons the next morning." The boys were told that they had to come up with seventy-five cents or else the police would be informed. While it doesn't seem like a lot today, in that day and age, seventy-five cents was close to ten dollars in today's currency. None of the boys had the money to pay for the melons.

March recalled a "dreadful, sleepless night" followed by the realization that he had no choice; he had to go to his father. While his father acknowledged that what the boys did was "silly and not nice," he would pay the farmer but he would also speak with his lawyer. Mr. Bickel's attorney told him that while what the boys did was considered a felony—the farmer's son had compounded the felony by setting a price for stolen goods. Mr. Bickel apologized to the farmer on behalf of his son and his friends, and paid for the melons, but also let the farmer know that his son was guilty of compounding the felony. "My father was practically a god from then on," March said.

John Bickel expected his children to learn the value of a dollar. "Security is what I have always wanted beyond and above all else," March later said. "An heritage, no doubt, from my businessman father…always a sound, substantial man who knew the value of a dollar and the greater value of a dollar put away." Young Fred was given a fifty-cent-per-week allowance, and was then expected to deposit twenty-five or thirty-five cents of it into a savings account at the local bank.

As he grew older, Fred didn't expect to simply depend on his father's weekly allowances for money. He took on odd jobs, including mowing lawns in the summer and shoveling snow in the winter. "I liked keeping tidy accounts of all my earnings and expenditures," he later said—a practice he continued well into adulthood.

Due to the encouragement of his mother, who was a former school teacher, Fred became an avid reader, though he maintained that he didn't read "respectable literature," but rather enjoyed the rags to riches stories of Horatio Alger and those mischievous Rover Boys. He had an inquisitive mind and avid imagination. He developed a gift for mimicry and would spend hours studying people—strangers or friends alike—and then do an accurate impersonation. "He always imitated the people with whom he came into contact throughout the day," his mother later said, "and it was always in a kindly manner," or so she hoped. Friends could recall that at times he could be quite malicious in his very accurate impersonations, though he tried to avoid being caught doing so by his parents—and the person he was impersonating.

He liked to dramatize some of the stories he read, on a makeshift stage built in the family barn—which boarded a lone pony—behind the house on College Avenue. He had a group of friends who were nicknamed "The College Avenue Gang," (including Vinnie Hood, Charlie Carpenter, Jimmy Huguenin, Vernon Crane and Jack Ramsey) who participated with him in amateur theatrics and other activities. "I remember I always wanted to be the boss," March later said. "Well, after all, it's my own father's barn, I guess."

He was a good student, and popular with his peers and teachers alike. He became the president of his class in his final year of grammar school. By this time, he was often invited by his teachers to recite—something he loved to do because it allowed him to be in the limelight. "My one and only distinguishing feature was a revolting one," he later said. "I recited. I couldn't be kept from reciting. You know the occasions—church bazaars, school entertainments, Sunday school parties. I wasn't precocious. Just plain obnoxious." In high school, he became particularly adept at oratory. "I developed a repertoire of all the old war-horses like 'Touissant L'Overture.' And I harangued with such heat that I was one of the regular stars of school and Sunday school entertainment."

Fred entered the state oratorical contest in 1911, at age fourteen. He won the local contest and went on to represent Racine at the state tournament in Sheboygan, where he delivered portions of Spartacus's "Address to the Gladiators." He came in third. "Never was there such indignation and astonishment as seethed in my soul then," March recalled. "I couldn't understand it. I had always been the star boy at home and this sudden downfall was humiliating. One of the judges tried to console me—'Well, you know, you're still in short pants.' I was enraged. Now maybe my parents would see their folly and buy me long pants!"

The following year he entered again, and once more went to the state championship representing Racine. This time the contest was held in Tomahawk, Wisconsin—some 250 miles away. Fred was accompanied by the high school principal and his wife. This time his recitation was Henry Grattan's "Invective against Corry." "This was something a little different," he recalled. "It was a dramatic, human-sounding speech—genuinely arresting." This time he won— and he wore long pants. Fred received a gold medal and state wide recognition. His school newspaper wrote, "There is a young fellow named Bickel, who before each oration eats a pickle, though in stature he's small he makes them all fall, when he shows them his medal of nickel."

In the summer of 1912, while she was away, Fred wrote his mother a series of letters in which he wrote about nothing too important but gave an idea of the idyllic and serene summer that a carefree and well-adjusted fourteen-year-old was enjoying. Here are a few excerpts:

Sunday, June 23, 1912:

Jack and I came home to a fine dinner yesterday and then went out to a double header (2 games) in the afternoon. Racine won the 1st 7-1 but lost what should have been theirs in the 2nd 3-2...This morning Jack and I both went to church and I stayed to Sunday School. The veal was fine at noon and the rest of the dinner also. Aunt Hattie, Uncle Gene, Marion...all came down. Marion and Jack made some fudge and we sat and read or talked until Jack went down to fill an invitation to dinner at Jack Davies. The other folks went home shortly and I got Grandma some tea...she seemed to be feeling very good. We did the dishes and now she is in her room...I hope this note will relieve your mind, for everything is fine and dandy. With much love from Fred.

July 5, 1912

Everything is going along fine here. My! But I'm sorry I didn't write you more regularly... Gee but I had a big day yesterday. Got up about 4 o'clock and saw Ringling's Circus come in. Then Maynard Miller picked us up in his auto and took us down to see the Journal News Motorcycle Reliability Race. When I got home I shot some firecrackers and then rode over to 12th and Herrick and saw the circus tents... Met Marion, Jack, Aunt Hattie and Uncle Gene going down town to see parade... The Hood's invited us to sit in the shirt factory there kitty corner from (the) grocery. We waited til about 1 o'clock and finally saw the parade. Then we went home to dinner and Jack, Uncle Gene and I went out and saw Racine win a double header from Aurora (IL). Then supper... stayed home in the evening. I shot off a few more firecrackers and then went to bed and fell right asleep. Woke up this a.m and found my light burning and curtains still down. Gee! I bet our gas bill will be high. I must have just crawled in and fell asleep without thinking...

July 11, 1912

Don't know of any special news, but that you might like to know that all is going along fine here. I have my diary in front of me so I guess you can get a little idea of what is happening... (on) 7th Sun Harold, Jack and I went to church. Put about 40 cents in collection offering together... Rode to Eagle Lake with Phil and his folks in P.M. just 'looked around.' Rode on new 'pay as you enter' cars (streetcars) for 1st time... Broke Grandma's saucer washing dishes in the evening. 8th: Jack, Phil, Jim and I went to Orpheum in Jack's car... 9th: Just loafed and stuck around all day. Had big storm in eve. 10th: Swede and I sold a case of pop in A.M. (for) 25 cents apiece... Saw Racine lose 2-1 in P.M... Transplanted some of those plants which were in front of the hedge to behind the hedge. Cut... branches from peach trees and bustled the sweet peas. Also dug little trenches along the sidewalk and cut the lawn...

Of all of his siblings, the one that Fred was closest to was the one who was closest in age to him, Jack. By March of 1913, Jack was a student at the University of Wisconsin in Madison and had just turned twenty-one when Fred (now fifteen) sent him the following letter and demonstrates that he wasn't afraid to give his own opinion on an important college decision that Jack was considering:

> *Dear Jack:*
> *Kindly forgive and forget my not writing you before, especially at the time when you reached your majority.* **Many of 'em!** *...Pop was in bed yesterday with a little grippe and cold; but is up and at work today. Only troubled with a little back-ache now...Mr. Edwards, a Milwaukee man, invited me to speak at the Westminster Pres(byterian) Church Mil., (March 18) but I politely refused after due consideration. Don't know whether you knew that I saw Maude Adam's in "Peter Pan" last month or not. Sat in pit (50 cents.* **Gee** *it was* **fine**. *I read your letter received by Harold to-day and, altho you may not have known it, have been very earnestly watching proceeds as much as possible between you and fraternities. It may not seem to be any of my business, and I hope you will not get sore, but I (hope) that my opinion might help a little...I hope you will not consider anything but Alpha Delt. I know just about what Harold has told you—to use your own judgment. That's all right, too. But looking at it in another way— If I ever get as far as you are, and have to decide between two fraternities, yours and Harold's, you can readily see it might be a little hard. That may seem selfish, and perhaps is not much of a point, but some way, I don't know why, I* **hope** *you will go Alpha Delt. You may think because Harold has made us have such a high opinion of A.D. that I think there are no others. I realize and understand Harold's praises and think I know pretty well how these other fraternities rank. But if you get a 'bid' from Psi U and Delta Tan, as you most likely will, I certainly hope with all my heart that you will receive and* **accept** *one from Alpha Delta Phi. With lots of love from your kid brother.*
> *Fred*

Seeing Maude Adams, one of the most prominent and admired

actresses of the day, in *Peter Pan*, left a great impression on Fred. He later called it his "first real glimpse of theater" and spoke of his "excitement, recognizing its quality as something different from anything I had ever seen, as something I had never known existed."

By his senior year of high school (1913-1914), Fred was thinking about his future. He had certainly made a good impression academically and socially. He was elected senior class president, and decided to give school dramatics a chance and got the second lead in the senior class play *The Country Chairman*. He also had a steady girlfriend, Julia Burns. His high school senior year book put the following caption under Julia's picture, "Julia likes pickles. That's why she likes Bickels." While under Fred's picture is the caption, "He oft hath 'burned' the midnight oil, but never, I aver, in toil." Fred graduated from Racine High School on June 18, 1914. He was just over two months shy of his seventeenth birthday (he had started school early—at age four).

Fred thought he'd be attending the University of Wisconsin in Madison, like his brothers Harold and Jack. However, times were tough and had taken a toll on John Bickel's business affairs. The bank that John's business dealt with failed, which caused the business to lose a lot of money. "We weren't really poor, but it meant a cessation of the little extra comforts and indulgences we had been accustomed to," March later said. It may also have made it more difficult for his father to support yet another son in college. Fred told his father that was fine—he was willing to wait a couple of years and, in the meanwhile, earn some money of his own. With his father's assistance, he got a job as a drafts man at another local bank.

CHAPTER TWO
1916–1924

Fred worked in the bank for two years—a period he would call "wholly uneventful." He continued to date his high school sweetheart, June, but they eventually drifted apart when she wanted to become serious and he didn't. He also taught a Sunday school class and attended the theater regularly in his spare time.

Finally, at the end of two years, his father decided that he could now afford to help Fred go to college. "Following in my brothers' footsteps, I went to the University of Wisconsin, and following my oldest brother's advice, I took commerce," he later said. Madison, the home of the University of Wisconsin and the seat of government for the state, was just over 100 miles from Racine. Situated about a mile and a half from the State Capitol building at the end of State Street and sitting on Bascomb Hill, the University was considered one of the finest in the country—certainly the finest university in the middle west.

In his freshman year, and in addition to his other studies, Fred got involved in debate. This he later regretted. "I was rotten! That may have been an omen of my future, a flair for reading someone else's lines but no ability to create my own." He also conceded that any plans he might have had about becoming a lawyer were also stymied. He reasoned that if he couldn't think on his feet during a debate, then he certainly couldn't before a jury. This he thought left no other choice for him—commerce and banking. "So I supposed I could probably be a banker," he recalled. "Of course, when I thought of it, it was always by that title—never as 'bank clerk.'"

Oratory—called declamatory in college—was still an activity that Fred excelled in. Fred won the right to compete against nine other freshmen representing various campus literary societies in a declamatory contest. On March 8, 1917, he competed and won— receiving a gold medal and mention in the campus newspaper, *The Daily Cardinal,* for having "a rich oratorical voice accompanied by perfect platform poise."

Like his two brothers, Harold and Jack, Fred pledged to the Alpha Delta Phi fraternity. To help earn spending money and ease the burden on his father, Fred waited tables in the fraternity house and also sold apples and Hershey bars to his fraternity brothers. March was a good student and excelled in his studies, and he was rewarded by being selected, along with four other students, as one of the most promising and likely to succeed young men by an eastern bank that was scouting around for exceptional talent.

In his spare time he joined a dramatic society, "The Edwin Booth Group," which was one of two dramatic clubs on campus. One classmate later wrote that "even though Freddie took part in the annual 'Edwin Booth' production, he was never pointed out as having special histrionic ability. True, he was good looking and did right well, but many of the other members had the same qualifications."

But Fred didn't spend all his time on extracurricular activities. He was very good at planning his day. He had a set time when he would get up in the morning and kept to it even if it meant getting just a few hours of sleep. He allocated a certain amount of time each day for study, campus activities, and exercise and recreation. "Fred accomplished such an enormous lot of things," one of his fraternity brothers later said, "just because he planned his day."

It was through a fellow fraternity brother that Fred met the woman he would date for much of his college years: Aline Ellis. Aline came from a wealthy Indiana family and was described by one of her sorority sisters as having "very black hair (which) accentuated the clearness of her skin and formed a decided simi-frame for her regular features. She dressed very well and knew how to wear her clothes...used practically no makeup, never wore electric colors, and yet she was the kind of person once notices and remembers. Her unusually large dark eyes had something to do with this; they were fascinating, but seemed to be always sad, she had a well-shaped hand, long pointed fingers...quiet thoughtful disposition..."

While at the UW, Aline majored in letters and science, and was active in the women's sorority dramatic club, Twelfth Night, it was probably due to their mutual interest in campus dramatics that Aline and Fred initially connected. While they attended the UW, Fred and Aline became engaged, which didn't please Aline's wealthy family, particularly her mother, who felt that Fred was below her station in life.

Fred was attending college when the United States, which for three years maintained neutrality in the European war, finally entered on the side of the Allies in the spring of 1917. During his time at the UW, Fred had been active in the Universities Corp of Cadets where he finally advanced to the rank of First Sergeant in November of 1917. Several of his friends were looking into joining the war effort, and after final exams in the spring of 1918, Fred wanted to do his bit as well, and wanted to apply as an officer with the Field Artillery Central Officers Training School. Later, Fred conceded that one of the reasons why he wanted to get into the war effort was because he had "become engaged to a nice girl co-ed and probably in the back of my mind was a desire to impress her with my maturity and gallantry." He spent a month at Fort Sheridan in Illinois (June 3-July 3, 1918), a preliminary training camp for infantry officers. March later related what followed:

> Then my oldest brother (Harold) advised me to get into the artillery. Respecting his judgment in this as I had in the matter of taking commerce at college, I went down to Camp Zachary Taylor (located in Louisville, Kentucky) where he was aide to General Austin. After three months, I got my commission as second lieutenant in the artillery. But instead of going overseas, I was retained as an instructor of equestrianism. Heaven knows why, because up to that time my only riding had been done on the fat, indolent pony we had as children. Anyway, after serving a period there, during which time the Armistice was declared and all hopes of covering myself with military glory went glimmering, I was sent to Fort Sill, Oklahoma, to the School of Fire there. It was the most interesting base I was in, patterned after the Napoleonic School of Fire. I was discharged in February 1919.

Fred soon returned to the UW to continue his college education and was reunited with Aline, who had served as an army nurse for six months during the war. In between studies, he and his friend Chuck Carpenter teamed up to present shows for the amusement of their fellow students, with Chuck playing the piano and Fred playing straight man for him. The act was so popular with their classmates that they decided to team up with a vaudeville act of sorts, called Carpenter and Bickel. They entered a college competition and came in third place. "It was a grand act," one classmate recalled years later. "Chuck was one of the campus funny boys and Bickel had swell stage presence, also poise and popularity. The act was big stuff in those days."

Next, Fred auditioned for the romantic male lead in the junior class production of Edmond Rostand's comedy *The Romancers* (which would later be updated and become very popular as the off-Broadway musical *The Fantastiks*). His good looks and dramatic ability won him the lead as well as his first review as a dramatic performer in *The Daily Cardinal*, "Fred Bickel was burdened with a wordy part but came through well...subtle, sly humor fits Bickel well."

In his senior year, Fred, as he had in grade school and then high school, ran for senior class president. To the surprise of virtually nobody, Fred won. The great achievement of "The Bickel Administration" was the launching of a fund-raising campaign among students—as opposed to only alumni—to build a student union. About half of UW students became 'life members' of the student union fund by donating fifty dollars—an impressive achievement. (The UW Student Memorial Union was completed in 1928. It is located just off of Library Mall and across the street from the impressive State Historical Society building, and continues to be a popular student activity center overlooking Lake Mendota.)

In the spring of 1920, Fred was nominated for a banking scholarship. "Frank Vanderlip of the National City Bank in New York was launching an experiment which was to take a number of college boys and train them, as apprentices and students in the main branch, for work in the foreign branches," Fred later related. "It sounded romantic." With his background working at the Racine bank and his good grades in a tough major—commerce—Fred was one of the winners of the scholarship. He would leave for New York shortly after graduation.

Then there was the question of Aline. Fred knew that her family disapproved of him, but if he could succeed and become a prominent banker—perhaps in some exotic foreign locale—it might make them better accept him, and he could provide a decent living for her. Fred wanted to marry Aline and take her to New York with him. However, Aline's family disapproved of this plan and wanted her to return to Indiana. Aline apparently backed her family up and told Fred that they should put off marriage until he made a success of himself in business. Fred was crestfallen, but was willing to abide by her decision.

Fred graduated from College on June 12, 1920. He returned to Racine to pack and spend a few days with his family, before leaving for New York for what promised to be a new beginning.

II

Fred arrived in New York in the summer of 1920. He got lodging in a rooming house in Brooklyn Heights, "overlooking all New York." As usual, he was diligent in his work. He worked in the bank during the day and studied by night. There was a postwar recession that was hurting profits and killing jobs. There was a shake-up at the bank, and a new man took over who Fred recalled wasn't as enthusiastic about the college apprenticeship program. "When I had been there seven or eight months, I grew discouraged," Fred later recalled. "None of us was being sent to foreign branches and I saw what was more likely to follow—a long apprenticeship with perhaps the final reward of becoming assistant cashier." A college friend, who was also in New York at this time, would tell writer Deborah C. Peterson, "his attitude toward life in general was different than in college; he was definitely bored by the routine of bank life."

Adding to his discouragement was a health scare, certainly more serious in 1921 than today—his appendix burst. "At noon, one day (at work), I suddenly fell over in the throes of acute pain," Fred recalled. "Friends took me to Brooklyn, my landlady sent for a doctor, and the doctor sent for an ambulance. I was to be operated on immediately." To try and distract him from the excruciating pain he was experiencing, his landlady, who had once been an actress, began telling him stories about her career in the theater. "I listened carelessly, but when I got to the hospital, I went under the anesthetic with those stories in my mind. And I woke up knowing I was going to be an actor—or else!" He was later to admit that this is probably something that subconsciously he had always wanted to do.

While convalescing from his surgery, which in those days meant staying in bed for several weeks, he devoured as many books he could on the theater. He still had not said anything to his parents, as he knew his family—particularly his father—would consider him a fool to give up a sure thing—a respectable career in banking—for what many in that day and age thought of as a frivolous waste of time. He knew, however, that he had to let Aline know his decision. However painful it may have been for her—and for Fred—she broke off the engagement. (Aline would go on to marry well—an important Indianapolis businessman. She would have children and travel a great deal, and she never spoke of Fred again—nor saw his movies once he was Fredric March.)

Some friends believed that Fred never got over Aline, using as evidence his questioning of whether she was attending the college reunions that Fred would later attend—she never did. But that is scant evidence that he never got over his love for her—after all he chose the theater over her.

Fred decided to give himself six months to prove himself—or at least get established in some way. He asked his bank to give him a six month leave of absence. He didn't state why he wanted the absence, such as 'I need to see if I can make it as an actor—but just in case I would like banking as a back-up.' However he put it, the request was granted. He then wrote a far more difficult letter to his parents back in Racine. "I cannot warm up to the banking business," he wrote them. "…It may all be out of my system in a year, and I promise you I will be as good a boy when I get through as I am now." They were bewildered but also strangely supportive. They told him to go for it—with the hope that he would get this acting bug out of his system.

Even though he had devoured those books on the theater, which had wetted his appetite for acting, he still didn't have the faintest idea of how he would go about becoming an established actor. It's not like he would open up a window and yell out, "I'm Fred Bickel and I am an actor!" and expect to be hired on the spot. Again, his landlady advised him of what to do. "I had some cheap pictures made—shirt open at the throat, two fingers contemplatively against the temple," he later recalled. He also began registering with agents. He checked out the telephone directory for agents' addresses and began leaving pictures with general information about him written on the back: height (5'11), weight (158), age (23), waist (32), shoe size (9.5) along with his address and phone number he could be reached. He also modestly wrote, "Will not pose in underwear."

After a few weeks, the phone finally did ring. An agent sent him—along with several others—to Paramount's Astoria Studios on Long Island for extra work. It was hardly what he wanted: "this fooling around in the low commerce of movies was distasteful to me. But I went along anyway, assuring myself that this was merely one of the exigencies of art." The film was *Paying the Piper* and its director was George Fitzmaurice, one of the most prominent directors of the day. March later recalled that he was "part of the mob and not very happy about it—until the pay checks were passed out and I discovered I had made $7.50. That was a horse of an entirely different hue...$7.50 a day—that made $45 a week—$180 a month! Movies were not so low after all." He continued to do extra work in films like *The Devil* (with George Arliss), *The Great Adventure* (with Lionel Barrymore), *The Education of Elizabeth* (with Billie Burke) and others he later couldn't recall.

It was while working on *The Education of Elizabeth* that Fred encountered a stroke of luck. He became reacquainted with a stage actor named David Cameron, who he had first met a couple of years earlier during his brief stint in the army. Fred told Cameron of his hopes and dreams, and Cameron told him to continue to pick up extra money in pictures but that he should also begin auditioning for parts on the stage. He also suggested that with his good looks, Fred could additionally supplement his income by posing for commercial ads. "So I switched from decorating the far backgrounds of movies to immortalizing cravats, shoes, shaving-cream and the like," Fred recollected years later. Among the illustrators he posed for were: Dean Cornwell, whose pictures adorned such publications as *Good Housekeeping, Redbook* and *Harper's Bizarre;* Howard Chandler Christy, famous for illustrating *The Christy Girl* and whose work appeared in such publications as *Scribner's & Colliers Weekly;* and Neysa McMein, who from 1923-1937 created all of *McCall's* covers.

Fred later came to believe his time as a model served him well in preparing him for his work as an actor. "Don't let anyone tell you that posing for artists is a sissy job," March later maintained. "I think my interlude of modeling was as good for me as those strenuous working-out exercises I heard about and was too lazy to take. Muscular control is necessary if you hope to get through one morning without falling off the stand. Standing straight and taut for two and three hours does a lot for coordination of the nervous system. What I'm getting at is it's darned hard work and doesn't deserve the stigma that is on it."

In the meanwhile, he was also trying to land jobs on the stage. Fred was called out for an audition for a new play that theater impresario David Belasco was producing. There were three hundred other hopeful actors waiting as well. One by one, the three hundred passed single file in front of Belasco, and in the end fifty were chosen to continue on—Fred was not one of them.

Fred was posing for Leon Gordon when Gordon asked him to pick up the tickets at a theater for the show that night. While he was doing this he ran into the agent who had sent him on his first job at Paramount Studios. He approached the agent and asked him point blank if he had anything for him. The agent sized him up for a moment and told him he might, and to go to the Belasco Theater as there were a couple of small parts not yet cast and "you might do for one of them." Off he went, and there he auditioned for the small part of Victor Hugo in *Deburau.* "No experience was very necessary and I looked near enough to their idea of Hugo to get by. So I was hired at $30 per week...in a Belasco production!"

On December 7, 1920, Fred Bickel of Racine, Wisconsin, made his professional stage debut at the Ford's Theater in Baltimore where *Deburau* had its first pre-Broadway try-out. On December 23, the play moved onto the Belasco Theater in New York. He was on

Broadway—it didn't matter that the part was a small one without any lines.

Fred would later say that *Deburau* and "my minor function in it was the finest training camp I could have possibly fallen into. They were very kind to me. At the first rehearsal…the director announced that those who wished would be welcome to watch the principals' rehearsals. Being green, I thought it was the thing to do and showed up punctually each day…the rest of the company, accustomed to the indifference of extras, were surprised and interested in my interest. The stage manager talked to me and I must have communicated my enthusiasm and earnestness to him. For, after that, I was also made third assistant stage manager and given two other bits to play besides Hugo. Later, I was made understudy."

Fred was in a whirlpool of excitement—and loved it. By day he still posed for commercial artists and by night he was at the theater performing in *Deburau*. "I think that was one of the happiest periods of my life. It was climaxed on the night when one of the principals was taken to the hospital for an emergency operation and I was shot into his place…I was still green enough not to be floored and Belasco was satisfied with my work. *That* was glory." The play enjoyed a successful run of 189 performances.

By this time, Fred had moved away from the Brooklyn boarding house and was living in an apartment in Manhattan near the theater district with three other young actors. He also decided he would take acting lessons. His teacher, Madame Alberti, was a famous teacher of mimicry, pantomime, and diction, and she taught at New York's prestigious American Academy of Dramatic Arts (AADA). "It was an invaluable investment—she taught me things I'd never have learned otherwise…a remarkable woman," Fred later recalled.

It was on his next production that Fred had his first important part on Broadway and would meet a man who would be a big part of his life and career as a friend and director for many years: John Cromwell. The Ohio born Cromwell had been a regular feature on the Broadway stage for over a decade by this time. He alternated between acting in plays and directing. The play that Cromwell offered Fred was *The Law Breaker*, a melodrama in four acts, in which he played the weak-willed son of a prominent banker. "It was the first part of substance I had and I was elated." The play was produced by William Brady, a prominent theatrical producer of the day. "At dress rehearsal, when we were rehearsing the curtain calls, Brady told me to come out...for a bow. In spite of my satisfaction with the part, I thought that was a little silly. But on opening night I actually got a hand." He also got his first mention in a review, "A remarkable unaffected performance...by Frederick Bickel." It was his new found friend Cromwell that suggested that the name Fredrick Bickel didn't quite have the right pizzazz for stage stardom and suggested he change it. For the time being he decided to leave it as it was.

Brady offered Fred a long-term contract at a good salary, but instead he decided he still had a lot to learn and thought that the best way to learn it would be as a member of a stock company. He signed on with a stock company in Dayton, Ohio, for twenty-nine weeks. "There I played, on the whole, pretty dumb juveniles," Fred later recalled. "But even that, in a stock company, is good training." He performed with the Brownell-Stork Company from April 2 to October 2, 1922. The *Dayton Journal* reviewed young Bickel in the stock production of the play *Enter Madame* and wrote, "Mr. Bickel shows promise that cannot be overlooked. " The following year he returned to Dayton and performed for three more months from July to October of 1923.

It was while in Dayton, that Fred met an actress named Ellis Baker. Ellis was the daughter of Edith Ellis, a playwright and director who operated a theater in Brooklyn. She was also the niece of actor Edward Ellis, probably best known as the murder victim and title character of the classic film *The Thin Man*. Ellis had been busy on the stage since the age of five. Ellis wasn't performing with the Brownell-Stork company but was visiting friends. According to Baker, what may have peaked Fred's romantic interest in her was the attention that one of his stage idols, John Barrymore, paid to her. She received a daily special delivery letter from Barrymore, who she had met while she was in a stock production in Atlantic City. On occasion, he would call her and send telegrams, so strong was his ardor for her. "That gave me a sort of 'Barrymore fixation,' I guess you might call it—because when I met Freddie later...I first fell for him because he looked like a young edition of Barrymore," Baker recalled years later.

Baker would remember Fred as "the most romantic man I've ever met before or since." She recalled him as being sweet, enthusiastic, and "terribly earnest about becoming a really good actor. Not just an actor, or even just a very highly paid actor—but a good actor." She and her mother took Fred under their wing and encouraged him to continue in stock because it was such a strong training ground for actors. Eventually Fred and Ellis became engaged, but their careers kept them apart for a good deal of time. However, Fred turned out to be a devoted letter writer and, according to Ellis, when she went abroad he arranged that she would receive a daily letter and some little present from him.

Meanwhile, Fred returned to New York, where he was cast in a play called *Zeno*. The play opened in Chicago where it broke house records before moving on to New York. It opened at the Forty-Eighth Street Theater on August 25, 1923, and didn't prove as wildly popular as it did in Chicago. It closed after a modest run of eighty-nine performances in early November of 1923. It was while he was performing in *Zeno* that John Cromwell signed Bickel to a ten year contract. Fred later said he signed with Cromwell—and for such a long-term contract—because he had "profound respect for his judgment and talent." But, just as it had earlier, Fred's last name—Bickel—bothered Cromwell, apparently he thought that Bickel had too much in common with pickle. Cromwell insisted that the name be changed—and this time Fred didn't object.

But, what was the name to be changed to? Ellis suggested that Fred use a combination of his middle name and her first name—McIntyre Ellis. While Fred was content to change his last name for stage purposes he was not too wild about changing his first name. He was too well-known and used to "Fred" or "Freddie." Finally, he decided that his first name would continue to be Frederick but the spelling would be altered slightly to the more phonetic form—Fredric. As for his last name, he thought about using his mother's maiden name—Marcher—Fredric Marcher, but finally decided to alter Marcher to the simpler March. Thus Fredric March was born.

On New Year's Day 1924, Fred sent the following message to agents and friends:

This is 1924,

I won't be Bickel anymore!
Fredric March is now my name,
Wishing everyone the same,
Happy New Year!

Fifty years later, when that little ditty was repeated to him, Fredric March moaned, "My God! How corny!"

CHAPTER THREE
1924–1927

The first time Fredric March appeared on Broadway (in May of 1924) was when he opened at the Ritz Theater in John Cromwell's production of *The Melody Man*, a comedy about a song plugger, which ran for fifty-six performances before closing towards the end of June. After the show closed, and prior to his next play for Cromwell, *Tarnish*, March made up his mind to ask Ellis to marry him. At the time, Ellis was performing in the Chicago production of *The Show Off*, and March would soon be in the windy city to open with *Tarnish*. When March arrived in Chicago he proposed to her and she accepted, and the two of them eloped to Milwaukee.

The next day, March surprised his parents in Racine with his new bride and found a distinctly frosty welcome. Cora Bickel didn't take to Ellis at all. First, she was a divorced woman—strike one! Second, she felt that Ellis was too self-centered—strike two! And finally, she wasn't at all like the gentle Aline, who the Bickel's all adored. His brother Jack's wife, Mary, also found Ellis's behavior to be strange to say the least. For instance, she would talk incessantly about Jack and Mary's dog but said not a word about their new baby. While not totally hiding her feelings, Cora did manage to arrange a tea in their honor. March got Ellis out of Racine as quickly as possible.

Back in Chicago, March played a young attorney in John Cromwell's production of *Tarnish*, which proved to be a solid success in the windy city. March was lauded for his performance by the critics, one of whom wrote that March would be "the talk of the loop and Michigan Blvd. before the week is told...he went straight under the skin of his part, into the flesh, bone and marrow."

Following its Chicago run, *Tarnish* went on to tour other Midwestern cities including Kansas City, Peoria, Indianapolis, Detroit, Cleveland, Pittsburgh, and Cincinnati—winning solid box office and enthusiastic reviews all along the way. In Detroit, the critic for the *Detroit News* wrote, "Mr. March is a handsome chap, whose features are not familiar to this reporter. He is not easy to forget. He has a way with him and he knows something about acting." His counterpart with the *Detroit Times* wrote, "Frederick (sic) March, as the young lover seems to me the shining light of the cast. He has the rugged good looks and the serious intensity that will take him safely out of the rank of juvenile parts before long." After playing in Toronto and then Baltimore, March's run in *Tarnished* finally ended on January 6, 1925.

Only three weeks later, with little time for Ellis, March was cast in a romantic melodrama about circus puppeteers titled *The Knife in the Wall*. The play opened in Providence, RI, on February 2, 1925, and again the critics were kind to March. One wrote that March's performance was so natural that it was almost as if he wasn't acting at all. At one point during the pre-Broadway run (in New Haven) the leading lady was replaced, and twenty-three-year-old Miriam Hopkins was cast opposite March for the first time—they would later go on to make three films together. March later said, "Little did she know that I would one day choke her to death in front of the camera in *Dr. Jekyll and Mr. Hyde*." (Another prominent name in the cast of is that of Dwight Frye, who would go on to win film immortality as Renfield opposite Bela Lugosi's *Dracula*.)

When *The Knife in the Wall* finally reached the Selwyn Theater in New York on March 9, 1925, it had a new title, *Puppets*. The next day, Alexander Woolcott wrote a review of *Puppets* for the *New York Sun* that is a tad on the negative side but found praise for "one scene…admirably realized by a young actor identified in the program as Frederick March, which sounds like a misprint, but then actors are so apt to sound like misprints." *Puppets* ran into April and concluded its run after a less than stellar fifty-four performances.

Shortly thereafter, March and Ellis went on a delayed honeymoon to Europe, which apparently didn't work out too well. There were arguments along the way. It was becoming increasingly evident that Ellis was becoming somewhat jealous of her husband's steady progress while her own career was largely stagnant. A telegram from John Cromwell brought March back home to begin rehearsals for a new play, *Harvest*. Set in a farmhouse in Michigan, and once again casting March as the juvenile, *Harvest* opened at the Belmont Theater in New York on September 19, 1925, and closed after a disastrous run of only nineteen performances. One critic wrote that "six or seven generally dull and uninteresting people sit around…boring themselves and all within earshot."

March then toured with a couple of other shows, which bombed quickly, before returning to Broadway in *The Half Caste*, set in Savaii, in the Samoan Islands, and cast him as yet another weak-willed juvenile—this one being a drunkard. The show opened at the National Theater on March 29, 1926, and had an unexceptional run of sixty-four performances—ending in May. While the play itself got negative reviews, March came out relatively well. The *New York Daily News* critic wrote, "Fredric March plays the juvenile lead with enthusiasm and some little skill," and the critic for the *Herald Tribune* wrote, "March, a good looking and temperamental youngster, impersonated the unlucky debauchee as well as possible."

Fortunately, March didn't have to worry about an upcoming job. The director of Elitch's Garden, a well-known and popular summer stock theater located outside Denver, Colorado, had seen his work in *The Half Caste* and was impressed with his looks and talent, and he believed him to be quite suitable as the company leading man for the upcoming 1926 summer season. With no other options on the table, and knowing the fine reputation that Elitch's Garden had, March signed on. He later noted that "anyone who was successful there (Elitch's Garden) had an excellent chance of getting better parts when he returned to New York."

Ellis also urged her husband to go to Denver. Being an actress herself, she understood the opportunities it might open for him and it did promise a steady income for the summer—always welcome news. Ellis later recalled that she received daily letters from March—as many as eighteen to twenty pages long—for the first few weeks he was in Denver. They were loving and touching, and all expressing how much he missed her. And then, she heard nothing for a week. She might have put that down to his being busy with the summer stock season, which meant learning lines for a different play every week. After a week of hearing nothing, she finally got a letter from March. The letter she received was highly impersonal and basically told her how well he was doing. Most importantly—for she had to re-read it to make sure—he didn't say anything about missing her.

Elitch's Garden was the country's oldest and most prestigious summer theater. Elitch's had been built in 1891 on the outskirts of Denver, Colorado, and in its background had a breathtaking view of mountain scenery. Close by there was an amusement park, and as the name of the place indicates, a striking flower garden. March was in awe of it. "I remember the first thing I did when I arrived in Denver, even before I unpacked my luggage, was to drive out to the Gardens and look around the place. I stood in the lobby and looked at the array of photographs. There were some great old actors represented there, and it was inspiring."

They did about a dozen productions during those three summer months and March was well paid for his work. As the leading man for the summer, he received $500 per week, which was the most money March had been paid up to that time. That meant for a twelve-week season March would bring home $6,000—a princely sum in 1926. It was hard work. There was a new play to be learned every week. The actors worked every day, seven days per week to deliver nine performances (two of the seven days, Wednesday and Saturday, had afternoon matinees).

It was while in Denver that March met his leading lady—an actress he certainly had heard of because she was already an established name in the theater—Florence Eldridge. "As far as I was concerned, heaven had descended right onto that stage," March later said.

II

Florence Eldridge was born Florence McKechnie in Brooklyn, New York, on September 5, 1901. The daughter of a newspaper editor, Florence was determined to be an actress. Pretty rather than beautiful, she had a keen mind and sharp intellect and enjoyed stimulating conversations about such topics as current events and books—she wasn't partial to small talk. Many people thought she lacked humor, but nevertheless found her to be a kind, if not exactly warm, person. She began working in musical-comedy but soon took on dramatic roles in stock. Her big break was working for the famous Manhattan Players of the Lyceum Theater of Rochester, New York, from 1917-1921. "I was pretty young then, and they asked me to take the big soprano part in a musical," she later recalled. "Why, I jumped at the chance! So we rehearsed for a few weeks and I was off to the races, quick as a wink." It was during her time with the Manhattan Players that a new assistant stage manager was brought in: George Cukor. The future Oscar-winning director "revolutionized the stage sets. He even went to museums, private homes and everywhere borrowing furniture and stuff to use," Eldridge recalled. Florence had a brief marriage to an older man, who was a dentist and apparently an alcoholic. She conceded in an interview that she had married not for love: "Shall we call it the animal spirits of youth."

Like March, Florence retained her first name while taking on a stage last name: Eldridge. Her experience in stock soon led to roles on the Broadway stage in productions for the prestigious Theater Guild. Among them was *Ambush* (1921, Garrick Theater), in which Florence played a grasping, immoral woman. One review called it "the finest American play of its sort." She then had a huge success in the popular comedy-thriller, *The Cat and the Canary* (1922, National Theater), in which she played the female lead. The critics loved it with one saying that the play was "more exciting than *The Bat*,"—a popular play of this type. She was: a married woman who becomes the obsession of a young swain in *The Love Habit* (1923, Bijou); a beautiful sorceress in *Bewitched* (1924, National Theater); and an amorous maid opposite Helen Hayes in *Young Blood* (1925, Ritz Theater). For this latter role she collected the best notices (even over Miss Hayes), with one critic writing that Eldridge performed with "real skill and power." More recently, she had gone on to great acclaim playing the role of Daisy in *The Great Gatsby* for more than one hundred performances. No doubt about it, Florence Eldridge was an authentic Broadway leading lady when she met Fredric March. She was also in her second season of summer stock at Elitch when March came aboard.

Though he had seen Florence's performance in *The Great Gatsby* and admired it tremendously, Denver was their first face to face introduction and March fell hard. "Denver is a beautiful place," March later said. "Beautiful places are romantic. So I had the aid of props by nature…Not that I needed props for my side of it. I'd have been romantic about Florence in Keokuk…But the props of clear moonlight, mountain ranges, sweet breezes and all that, helped my cause with her, I think."

Florence too was smitten. "There was just something about him that attracted me in the beginning and after I'd got to know him I discovered all those other things I adore," she later recalled. Among the other things she discovered about March that she came to adore was his sense of humor—perhaps because she was not naturally funny herself she took to somebody who could make her laugh. "It's a silly sort of humor that keeps you giggling all day long," she later said. "In most respects, it's exactly the same sort of humor you find in a child. He gets a kick out of the same things kids do." She liked his laid-back demeanor: "He's got the easiest going disposition I've ever come across in my life and it is a disposition that doesn't ruffle."

The chemistry they had off stage definitely helped on stage, as they became a very popular team that season. The first play presented was *The Swan* during the week of June 12. *The Swan* tells the story of a tutor who falls in love with a beautiful princess— naturally March and Eldridge had the leading roles. They received enthusiastic notices. "Fredric March, the new leading man…is smooth and finished, and his work, like that of the other players reflects keen appreciation and understanding of the role he portrays," wrote one critic. Florence's performance was called "inspiring and exemplary." It is worth noting that there were other familiar names in the Elitch stock company that summer including Beulah Bondi, Cora Witherspoon, and Douglas Dumbrille—all of who would go on to have top careers as character actors in films.

The following week, they presented *Love 'Em and Leave 'Em*, a modern comedy set in a boarding house, and once again the March and Eldridge team scored big. One review pointed out that Eldridge proved she can ". . . be something other than sweet." As for March: "You would never know Fredric March to be the same young man who played in *The Swan*. His voices, his movements, are changed to suit the role of the philandering youth who swerves between two sisters. Mr. March does not over play anything and the quality so very desirable and not found nearly often enough that of restraint, distinguished his performance last evening." And on it went that summer, with productions that included *Craig's Wife, The Poor Nut,* and *Liliom.*

There was one bit of controversy that season when March initially refused to act in *The Poor Nut*. The reason? Loyalty to his home state of Wisconsin, and particularly to the University of Wisconsin. The big scene of the comedy involves a relay race between students of Ohio University and the University of Wisconsin—with Wisconsin being defeated! Apparently March had no idea that this scene was included. He had begun rehearsals earlier in the week, and all went well until this scene turned up in the script. According to a contemporary newspaper account, March quietly put the script down and simply said, "I can't play this part." He then put out a statement, which read, "While I realize this is only a play, I do not feel I would be loyal to my university to appear in a role of a student of Ohio state who defeats his Wisconsin opponent, even in a stage production." Apparently there were some harried conferences with management explaining that he was also being very unfair to them. March did an about face and issued a new statement, "I feel that I would not be playing fair with the management, and despite my feeling for my college, I intend to make John Miller run as fast he can to win for Ohio. It's easily the best role I've had this summer."

As it turned out, March got a rave review for his performance in *The Poor Nut*, "There is something of Peter Pan and of Merton (of the Movies) about Fredric March and then again he seems to be very wise, and his performances are the kind that makes the audience observe closely every move he makes." While one can admire March's loyalty to his university, you have to wonder if this story is all together accurate. Certainly, March by this time was a professional actor who understood he was enacting a part. Somehow one gets the feeling that this hullabaloo was a carefully planned publicity gimmick.

There was one more controversy that season—and an all too real one: Ellis. After receiving little from March after his first couple of weeks in Denver and then receiving that rather dry letter speaking of the success he was enjoying but devoid of any emotion or longing for her, she was worried. She consulted her mother who urged her to go to Denver. She arrived in the middle of the season and she couldn't have mistaken the chemistry that March and his leading lady had for each other. But in a later interview, long after they had divorced, she never mentioned any inkling that anything was up between her husband and Florence. Instead she thought that March was getting too big-headed regarding the success he was enjoying. She decided to deflate that balloon. She began to minimize his success—after all it was only summer stock! In contrast, Florence was encouraging of March and consistently praised him and his talent. Ellis soon left for New York.

Following the end of the summer season, March returned to New York and Ellis in early September, just after his twenty-ninth birthday. He stayed for two days and then disappeared for a week. She had no idea where he was. They had made plans to see friends, but when these friends asked where her husband was she couldn't give them an answer. She made up a story that he had gone to Philadelphia to see a prize fight, but that fight was already over and done with and he still had not returned. When he did return home, he told Ellis he wanted a separation. Years later, Ellis recalled that March melodramatically told her, "A genius must live alone." He explained that his marriage and ambitions were not compatible. When she asked the obvious, "Are you in love with anybody else," March denied this to be the case. He gathered his things and moved out.

After a short while, March deputized his brother Jack to go and see Ellis and tell her that he wanted a divorce. At first she refused, hoping that he "would come to his senses." That was not what March wanted to hear, and soon he went to Mexico to obtain a divorce decree. Beaten, Ellis decided she had no choice but to begin divorce proceedings in the United States, as she was worried about the legality of a Mexican divorce. In return she was given $50 per month alimony, which was based on March's then income. (Even after March had gone on to Hollywood and became a big star and was receiving up to $100,000 per film, Ellis didn't reopen the case and ask for more money, stating that she considered the $50 per month "ample" for herself).

Later on, after March had married Florence Eldridge, most people (even friends) never knew that March had been previously married. Ellis Baker was never mentioned. With few exceptions no newspaper article ever spoke of her and certainly the Marches never would. The impression was that Florence was March's one and only wife and the love of his life. Only one article by Ellis herself in 1936 (in *Picture Play* magazine) spoke of this previous marriage. Even after that, few other articles brought this first marriage up. March who wrote his life story, a twenty-plus page article for *Screenland* magazine in 1932, doesn't mention a word about this marriage.

Meanwhile, March returned to the Broadway stage in December to portray a playboy—with Palm Beach tan and all—in *The Devil and the Cheese*. Though the play was a success (running from December 29, 1926, until May of 1927, for 157 performances) it was a critical bomb. Of most interest today is that the cast included Bela Lugosi and Dwight Frye, who were just four years away from working together in the horror classic *Dracula* for Universal.

The Devil and the Cheese is not the play that March had hoped he would be appearing in. When he returned to New York, he and Florence had hoped that they would be working together in a play on Broadway. They had both been selected for the leading roles in *The Proud Woman*, "This was to be my first honest-to-goodness lead on Broadway," March later told columnist Ed Sullivan. Of course, he also got to show-off in front of Florence. Rehearsals began, and after the sixth day March was dropped from the cast. There was a seven day provisional clause, and March was told they decided to go with another actor. "That was the toughest blow that ever hit me," March told Sullivan. Afterward, March and Florence went for a walk through Central Park, "I was trying to be nonchalant; she was attempting to be consoling," March recalled. "I was convinced that she would stop loving me immediately because I was a flop—I said to her 'Perhaps it's all for the best. Now I can have that operation for hemorrhoids.'" Remember it was his sense of humor that helped attract her. Career-wise, perhaps, it was for the best because *The Proud Woman* closed after only six performances and *The Devil and the Cheese* was a hit.

On May 30, 1927 (Decoration Day in the USA), just days after *The Devil and the Cheese* closed on Broadway, Fredric March and Florence Eldridge went to Mexico and were united in marriage. March had his wedding ring inscribed, "No more beyond thine eyes," from Edna St. Vincent Millay's *The Kings Henchmen*: "Now shall I look no more beyond thine eyes."

There was to be no real honeymoon. The Marches went almost immediately to Denver for another summer season with the Elitch Company. Originally, Florence was once again to be leading lady, but once management was informed that they were married, they decided to employ a new leading lady because they didn't feel that audiences would respond well to a married couple acting together (had they never heard of the Lunts?). That season began on June 11, 1927, and ran until the last week of August, and it involved March performing in such diverse plays as *Quality Street, Gentlemen Prefer Blondes, The Last of Mrs. Cheney,* and *The Cradle Snatchers*.

Once this obligation was completed, The Theater Guild employed the Marches to lead a repertoire company on a cross country tour— the first time the Guild had ever launched such a national tour. March later recalled:

> *Florence and I went on the road together...doing 'Arms and the Man,' 'Mr. Pim Passes By,' 'The Silver Cord,' and 'The Guardsman.' The plays themselves were fun, but the tour was badly managed. So very badly arranged that finally we were making train connections at four in the morning or arriving in a town two hours before curtain time. It was miserable.*

It was thirty weeks of misery, but at least they were together. A highlight, however, was in December, when the company arrived in Madison, Wisconsin, to present *Arms and the Man* at the Orpheum Theater. Many old college friends turned out.

In the midst of this misery, March was approached to play the part of Anthony Cavendish in the Broadway production of the new Edna Ferber and George S. Kaufman play *The Royal Family*, a thinly disguised parody of the Barrymores, with March approached to play the John Barrymore-like character, in part due to his resemblance to "The Great Profile." Unfortunately, due to his commitment to the Theater Guild tour, he had to turn this down—for now.

At the end of this 132-city tour, Lawrence Langer, the founder of the Theater Guild, welcomed the company back to New York and got an earful. "I have seldom met such a group of indignant, overworked people," Langer later wrote in his autobiography. Particularly irate were the Marches. "The verbal chastisement which I have received…at the hands of these two artists has taught me a lesson I will always remember."

Exhausted after thirty weeks of nonstop work and travel, the Marches took a little time off, bought a car, and decided to visit their families. While Florence was an actress—just as Ellis had been—the Bickels came to adore her. She was more down to earth than Ellis had been and seemed less egotistical. She didn't dominate every discussion and her repartee wasn't confined to show business. Above all, they could tell that she truly cared for their Fred—or as Florence, and practically everybody else (apart from his family), would now call him: Freddie.

In June, it was time to return to Denver, so March could begin a third season with the Elitch's Garden stock company. This time, they presented such plays as *Baby Cyclone, The Second Mrs. Tanqueray,* and *Saturday's Children.* In early August, an offer came for March to play Tony Cavendish in the west coast production of *The Royal Family.* The management conceded it was too good an opportunity for him to turn down, and with the season almost completed they agreed to release him.

Ethel Barrymore, the grande dame of the Barrymore family, threatened to sue. She felt the play was slanderous. Her attorney talked her out of it. For one reason, suing would bring more publicity and second, on the whole, the characters other than the Anthony/John character could not in any way be considered slanderous. Furthermore, John Barrymore himself was amused by it. In fact, if anybody had a grievance about *The Royal Family* it should have been Lionel, for he isn't represented in the play at all! Ethel reluctantly dropped the idea of legal action.

The character who really makes *The Royal Family* is Tony Cavendish, and he *is* a delicious caricature of John Barrymore. Yet Edna Ferber would say that Barrymore was "too improbable to copy from life."

Perhaps so, but March with his mastery of mimicry did little to disguise who he was lampooning—and the fun he had of doing it. He was theatrical to the core. He slid down banisters, disrobed, and in general exuded buoyancy and immense animal magnetism. No wonder Barrymore, then in his mid-forties and already beginning to show the consequences of alcoholism, didn't seem to mind.

For March, this was to be his star making role. "The experience was a tremendous one for me, and the effect on me...was very powerful. For a while, it was hard to break away from it. While I was in the play, my wife used to tell me I was being John Barrymore around the house."

The California run began in Santa Barbara on September 13, 1928, for two performances before moving on to San Francisco on September 16, for six weeks. The San Francisco reviews were excellent for March. "Fredric March...makes an enormous hit," wrote the critic for the *San Francisco Chronicle*.

The play then moved on to Los Angeles on October 29. The cast, including March, knew this would be an important engagement because it was in the backyard of the movie capital of the world: Hollywood. They understood that stars, directors, producers, and casting agents would be among those in the audience and that this could be their big break into pictures. Hollywood was then going through the transition from silent films to talkies, and the studios were on the lookout for talented and good-looking actors who could speak well.

Among those in the opening night audience was John Barrymore himself. "Fredric March played the fellow who was supposed to be me," he told reporters afterward. "He made me an utterly worthless, conceited hound, and he had my mannerisms, exaggerated but true to life." He went backstage to congratulate March "red faced from laughing, my hair tousled." When March heard the booming voice of Barrymore he nearly jumped out of the chair he was sitting. He didn't know for sure if the great actor was coming back to congratulate or condemn him. Luckily March could breathe a sigh of relief when Barrymore told him, "That's the greatest and funniest performance I ever saw."

Barrymore wasn't the only one in the audience who thought that March had done a great job and had star quality; casting agents for various studios were also bidding for his services. In the end, March decided it was time to settle down, set down roots with Florence, and give the picture business a try. He signed with Paramount Pictures on December 7, 1928, at $1,000 per week.

His father, still concerned about his career choice, wrote him, "Don't lose your reputation, Fred, money won't count at all then." March tried to assure him all would be well, and he responded, "Dad, many of the stories you hear are not true. They exaggerate out here. Besides, I'm too busy to notice."

CHAPTER FOUR
1929–1931

Paramount wasted little time utilizing Fredric March after signing him in December of 1928. His first film was released by the end of March of 1929, with his second film opening just a week later. In fact, from March of 1929 through October of 1931, seventeen films featuring Fredric March would be released. Paramount was determined that he would certainly earn his $1,000-per-week salary. He played everything from scholars, philanderers, sailors, alcoholics, lawyers, and playboys. His handsome features, striking profile, and stage-trained voice would help the studio bridge the gap between silent and sound films.

March entered pictures at just the right time, as the studio was adapting to 'talkies.' March was considered a likely leading man for several actresses making the transition from silent pictures to talkies (Clara Bow, Colleen Moore, Mary Brian, Nancy Carroll) as well as being ideally teamed with actresses who were relatively new to Hollywood and had a background in the theater (Ruth Chatterton, Ann Harding, Claudette Colbert).

In an interview with Hollywood columnist Gladys Hall, March spoke about his new status as a Hollywood actor:

I'm enormously interested in talking pictures. I don't know that I have any theories as yet. I've been asked what I do with my voice, how I 'get it across.' I don't know. Does one do things with their voice? I believe that I talk into the Mike as I talk into the ear of anyone attentive enough to listen to me. If I have any tricks I am not conscious of them. You do do things with the voice, of course. Emotion. Drama. Tragedy. Lighter things. But you do them naturally. I think I do.

It was a healthy attitude for the newcomer to have. So many silent actors took diction lessons, which made their speech sound particularly stagy with pronounced emphasis on vowels, that they didn't sound at all natural on film. This staginess would be a particular problem for many early films—March's included. Not only in the way some actors sounded but in the lack of movement in many early *motion* pictures. The microphone had to be stationary when hovering over the actors, which severely restricted movement.

March's debut film was *The Dummy* (released March 29, 1929), which was the first of two films he would make with Ruth Chatterton, an actress who had made her name on the Broadway stage in such plays as *Daddy Long Legs* and *Come Out of the Kitchen*. Chatterton was already thirty-six when she came to Hollywood the previous year, playing opposite Emil Jannings in the silent classic *Sins of the Father*. In *The Dummy*, March and Chatterton play an estranged couple whose little daughter is kidnapped. A youth, who works for the detective agency entrusted with rescuing her, feigns being mute to deliberately get abducted by the kidnappers in an effort to entrap them. Naturally, by the final scene the little girl is safe and the estranged couple is brought back together for the happy ending. Along with Chatterton and March, there is a superb supporting cast including Mickey Bennett (as the youth), ZaSu Pitts, John Cromwell (March's old friend from the theater), and two actors who would appear in several March films in the years to come—Eugene Pallette and Jack Oakie. Paramount had previously filmed *The Dummy* back in 1917 with Jack Pickford (brother of Mary) as the enterprising youth.

The *New York Times* reviewer wrote, "The antics of the people in *The Dummy* appeared to please an audience in the Paramount Theater on Saturday afternoon and even when the voices were as loud as that of a circus announcer, the spectators still remained interested in the story. Perhaps it was because the chief character on the screen was a boy and there were many youngsters in the theater." In fact, March isn't even mentioned in the review even though he is the nominal leading man. Chatterton too is largely overlooked and mentioned only in passing. Of this first film role, March remarked, "It's what you might term my 'break in' part. The studio gave me this role to get me used to working before a camera and also to get an idea as to how I looked on the screen."

March had better exposure in his second film, *The Wild Party* (released April 6, 1929). The primary reason for this has very little to do with Fredric March but a great deal to do with his leading lady, Clara Bow. Bow, the IT girl of the silent era, was making her talkie debut with *The Wild Party*, and audiences and critics alike were waiting to see if she passed the voice test or not.

Bow was petrified of what she would sound like on the screen. Her voice test was directed by the pioneering female director Dorothy Arzner, who would also direct *The Wild Party*. Bow wasn't pleased with the results and was increasingly nervous about how audiences would accept her voice. In fact it is OK. Her talkie introduction has her hauling a trunk into her college dorm room and then uttering "Just a working girl" in a charming, husky, and vaguely Bronx accent.

March is introduced in a funny scene where Bow's character is traveling by train to college and accidentally climbs into his sleeper berth. Clara doesn't realize she's in the wrong berth, thinking the covered up lump next to her is the girl she is sharing a berth with. She says, "Move over!" to give her some room. Only to have March in a (somewhat) seductive voice say, "So, who invited you in?" March flirts a bit with Clara much to her indignation. Later, she finds out that March is her new Anthropology instructor at the all-girl college. Of course all the girls think March is a dream boat.

Even though it's Clara Bow's sound debut, the film still uses a good deal of title cards and several silent sequences and voiceless close-ups. This may have been due to Bow's lack of confidence in the sound medium. Adolph Zukor, the Paramount Chairman, later said, "Her voice was actually quite good. But the unrestrained vitality, which had been her great asset, now was a curious handicap." She was inhibited by the 'mike,' which would dangle just out of camera range above her head. "We had quite a time in the beginning (with Bow)," Arzner later recalled, "because of the pantomime which she was accustomed to—then to have words to remember. (It) was very difficult for her." Bow developed a habit in which she allowed her gaze to travel upward towards the off-camera mike. This meant that Arzner had to cut scenes and do several different takes until she got over that habit. As for March, Arzner would recall him telling her,

"I always know when I'm doing a scene right by looking out at your face. Your face is my barometer."

Arzner was an innovator on this film. It was Arzner who had technicians rig a mike onto a fishing rod—creating the first boom microphone—which allowed the actors to move around more freely. Arzner was also an important early director for March. They would make four pictures together (not counting the all-star *Paramount on Parade*). Second unit director Arthur Jacobson later described Arzner as "a quiet woman" who "always wore dark glasses and mannish clothes...she never threw her weight around, but she knew her business, and I enjoyed working with her thoroughly." Even though directing was predominately a man's game, Arzner later maintained that she never had any problems working with men, "I never had any obstacles put in my way by the men in the business. They all tried to help me. Men actors never showed any prejudice against working with me. All the men who help—cameramen, who are so terribly important—assistants, property men, actors, everybody helped me." March later said of working with Arzner: ". . . never felt I was dealing with a woman—she was one of the guys."

March later said that he was lucky to have been cast in a Clara Bow picture at this stage in his career because she was still a hot commodity, and also because of interest in the film due to it being her sound debut. March later recalled Bow as "vital and gay." According to one of Bow's biographer's there may have even been a casual dalliance between them, as March had heard a great deal about Bow's uninhibited sex drive from a newly acquired friend: John Gilbert. According to the same biographers, March was acquiring a reputation around Paramount as "the best-looking young lech on the lot." But, while it isn't clear if they did have an affair, the reputation for having a roving eye for the ladies would follow March throughout his career, despite his evident devotion to Florence.

Clara Bow fans did come out in force to see *The Wild Party*. It did strong business in major cities around the country and broke house records in cities like Philadelphia and Providence. Many theaters in smaller towns and rural areas were not yet equipped with sound, so Paramount also released a silent version of the film. Critics rarely cared for Clara Bow, and her sound film debut got mostly negative notices from most of them. The *New York Times* critic wrote, "Miss Bow's voice is better than the narrative. It is not over-melodious in delivery, but it suits her personality." The review went on to say, "This production is intended for dwarfed intellects." Once again, March is not singled out by name.

March followed this with *The Studio Murder Mystery* (released June 1, 1929). He plays a philandering actor who is murdered. Florence, in the first of the seven films they would make together, plays his jealous wife—who has a big motive for committing the murder. The actual lead is Neil Hamilton, who had made a name for himself as a debonair silent screen star who, like Bow, was trying to adapt to sound. He has a theatrical, stage-trained voice of the type that early sound seemed to like, but Hamilton would survive and prosper as far as the 1960s when he would play Commissioner Gordon on the popular and campy *Batman* series. One other interesting side note is the presence in the film of Warner Oland, who plays the director—and another suspect. Oland would go on to film immortality as Charlie Chan in a series of enjoyable mysteries for 20th Century Fox. Of all the films of March's early career, this is the one that has the most feel of a "B" picture. That is not a put-down, because *The Studio Murder Mystery* with its behind the scenes action at a Hollywood studio is breezy good fun and highly enjoyable—a cracking good mystery.

The Studio Murder Mystery is Florence's first film, and she does have more to do in it than March. However, she would have a very uneven film career and could go for years without making one. She worked most often with her husband, both on screen and stage. A fine actress, Florence just didn't have what Katharine Hepburn would later call that "quality of personality" that makes one a star. While she would make an occasional film during these early years, most of her professional work was as a member of a stock company headed up by Edward Everett Horton, which worked out of a local Los Angeles theater. March's friend Ralph Bellamy, no admirer of Florence, later told Deborah C. Peterson, "Florence didn't hit it here (in Hollywood), ever. Nowhere near the rank that he was."

After three films, March had some definite opinions on the "talking picture business" and expressed them in an early newspaper article devoted to the fast-rising young actor. "It has been a great break for me that the people with whom I have been working with have been doing something almost as new to them as the whole picture business is to me," he related. "It must have been very tough on stage actors who came out here to try to work in silent pictures. One would feel like a rank amateur, I should think." He went on to describe how "every picture I have made has been the first talkie for its director," and described it as "the most interesting experience I have ever had." He gave a study of the techniques used by the three directors he had worked for up to that time:

> *Bob Milton with his stage experience was trying in The Dummy to smooth out the dialogue to make it clear, natural and intelligent. Dorothy Arzner remarked that the dialogue in talking pictures delayed the action and slowed the tempo. She was working for swiftness of movement. Frank Tuttle (The Studio Murder Mystery) strove for smoothness—to remove that jerkiness which had characterized all talkies up to that time.*

March indicted that observing directors at work convinced him that he eventually wanted to direct. "I began to act, because it was the thing I had to do. But, after all, you know, acting is a funny sort of job for a man. Make-up and all of that."

Paris Bound, his next film, is the story of a newly married couple who, when separated, are tempted by others. The husband (played by March) does have a rendezvous during a European trip, and the wife (Ann Harding) later finds out and considers divorcing him in Paris, so she can marry a young composer (played by Leslie Fenton, who later became a director of such films as *The Story of G.I. Joe* and March's 1944 anti-Nazi film *Tomorrow, The World!*).

The *New York Times* liked Harding's film debut, with Mordaunt Hall writing, "It is in fact a joyous relief to study the work of an actress in a motion picture who is so modulated in her talking and whose performance throughout is so different from other players." Hall found March "sympathetic and human." Overall he thought the film a "praiseworthy" adaptation of Barry's play.

Paris Bound gave March his best early showcase. At the time, he analyzed the film in a forthright and, in some ways, surprising way, given the fact that he was a married man.

Yes, I believe that the psychology of Paris Bound was correct,"
he told columnist Gladys Hall. "From the man's point of view, at
any rate. Under similar circumstances almost any man would do
what the man in the picture did. He would have had his little
affairs with 'the other woman.' He would have returned to his
wife without the slightest feeling that he had done her any injury
or harm to their love. Also without the slightest suspicion that she
might have heard about it. Men are like that.

Perhaps catching himself, he adds quickly:

I don't believe in matrimonial vacations. I am conservative,
perhaps old fashioned domestically speaking. I like being married.

One wonders, knowing today about his amorous reputation around
Paramount, if March was speaking about himself?

Jeanne Eagels was near the end of her tragically short life (she would
die before 1929 was out) when she and March starred together in
Jealousy (released September 13, 1929). March hadn't been the
original choice to costar opposite Eagels. He was brought in when
the voice test of the original leading man—British actor Anthony
Bushell—didn't pass muster. The film was shot at Paramount's New
York studio in Astoria where March would shoot several films over
the next few years. Eagels had been banned by Actor's Equity from
performing on the stage for well over a year, due to her inability to
appear for a performance due to her years of alcohol and drug
abuse. She decided to give movie acting a try, and early in 1929 had
a popular and critical success in the first film version of Somerset
Maugham's *The Letter.* (She would later be nominated posthumously
for an Academy Award for her work in this film.)

Jealousy is the story of a Paris shop owner (Eagels) who falls in
love with a struggling artist (March) and marries him. All the time,
she's carrying on an affair with the wealthy, and elderly, man who
set her up in business. The film attracted mixed notices. The *New
York Times* liked Eagels who is called "quite attractive" but didn't
think that March pulled off the role of a Parisian artist, "Mr. March
is hardly suited to his part," Mordaunt Hall sniffed. March later
summed up Eagels and the film this way, "Jeanne Eagels was

wonderful—even though *Jealousy*...was a stinker."

March's next film, *Footlight and Fools* (released November 8, 1929) teamed him with one of the brightest stars of the silent era, Colleen Moore. Moore had starred in such silent classics as *Flaming Youth* (A key 'flapper' film of the 1920s) *So Big, We Moderns, Ella Cinders, Lilac Time* (one of Gary Cooper's early showcases) and *Naughty but Nice*. The two great 'flapper' stars of the 1920s—that breed of independent, free-spirited women—were best epitomized by Clara Bow and Colleen Moore. Film biographer and historian Jeanine Basinger wrote, "Colleen Moore was perhaps a bigger star than Clara Bow, but she was not as big a personality...Moore became free and easy inside the frame of her own style." It is to Fredric March's credit and the studio's belief in him that they cast him as leading man opposite these two major stars in such a climactic year (1929) when both were nervously making the transition to sound. That Colleen Moore was still considered a major star is indicated in her salary for this seventy-minute film—a whopping $175,000 compared to $1,000 per week that March was paid.

Footlight and Fools—which is considered a lost film—tells the story of Betty Murphy, who under her stage name Fifi D'Auray, becomes a major musical star of the theater. For years, she has been in love with Jimmy, a reckless gambler (Raymond Hackett), but refuses to marry him until he makes something of his life. Enter a wealthy bachelor (March) who takes one look at Betty/Fifi and instantly falls for her. He connives a way to meet her but they butt heads. To make up, the March character finds a job for the gambler in a theater (as a bookkeeper). Naturally, money turns up missing, and all fingers point to Jimmy, who protests his innocence. Betty/Fifi believes in him and, to the consternation of the March character, marries him in a show of support. Gradually, however, the truth comes out that Jimmy was the culprit. Moore decides to divorce him but doesn't go running back to the decent March. In short, Moore's character is in the footlights (as Fifi, singing sensation) and is made a fool of by Jimmy.

The film can best be described as a musical melodrama. With sound a great curiosity, the studios began the first big vogue of the Hollywood musical in the late twenties, and five songs are included— "If I Can't Have You" (sung by Moore), "You Can't Believe My

Naughty Eyes," and "Pilly Pom Pom Plee." The film was heavily promoted as introducing "The NEW Colleen Moore!" The reviews were, on the whole, good. *Motion Picture* in its review thought, "*Footlights and Fools* indicates a new career for Moore in more sophisticated pictures." The *New York Times* said, "Colleen Moore pleases—her more serious acting is good." The *Los Angeles Times* thought there were "plenty of pleasant surprises in the film" including a singing Moore and a dashing March. The film went on to have an unspectacular run at the box office for Warner Brothers-First National, which March was loaned out to. As for Moore, she would appear in one more 1929 film and then be off the screen for three years until she returned in 1933 to play opposite Spencer Tracy in the superb *The Power and the Glory.* She then made three more films after that before retiring for good (at age thirty-five) in 1934. Not that she seemed to miss it—telling film historian John Kobal, "The adoration stopped about three years after I stopped making movies. I could walk down Broadway and nobody turned around—and I was delighted."

March's seventh and final film of 1929 teamed him with pretty Mary Brian in *The Marriage Playground* (released December 13, 1929). At twenty-three, Brian had already been a veteran of silent films since 1924 when she made a charming Wendy Darling in *Peter Pan.* She went on to play in more than twenty-five silent films in the years following, including *Paris at Midnight, High Hat,* and *Two Flaming Youths.* She had just recently starred as a New England school-marm-gone-west opposite Gary Cooper in the very successful *The Virginian.*

The Marriage Playground is based on Edith Wharton's novel "The Children," and tells the story of an American couple who leave their seven children behind as they go on a long and glittering tour of Europe. Judy (Mary Brian), the eldest, is put in charge. She soon meets another American tourist, Martin (March), who is on his way to Switzerland to join his fiancée. Up to now a solitary bachelor, Martin's life is given a new purpose as he interacts with Judy and her siblings—and he ends up staying on to help for several weeks before eventually leaving for Switzerland. Judy, who has fallen in love with him, soon follows. Martin is attracted to her spirit and devotion and falls in love too, and he proposes marriage. Together,

Martin and Judy will raise the other children together. March gives a very natural, likeable, and easy-going performance in this film in contrast to Mary Brian, who while likeable and pretty is stilted in that early talkies manner.

Paramount paid Wharton $25,000 for the film rights to the novel, and once they had it they made some drastic changes. Judy is fourteen in the novel, while in the film she is the more age-appropriate eighteen—you can't have a fourteen-year-old girl having a romance with an adult who is twice her age. Also in the novel, she is referred to as "Judith," while in the film she is the more modern "Judy." The younger children in the novel are all well-drawn characters with personalities of their own, while in the film they are all represented pretty much as scampy comic relief. (Another character providing comic relief is Lady Wrench, played by Kay Francis in one of her earliest film roles.) The ending is one of the most glaring of the changes. In the novel Martin is a kind but ineffectual man and, by the end, the family is scattered about. While the film delivers the happy ending of Martin and Judith marrying and keeping the children together, bringing up the children themselves—all is well in the world.

The Marriage Playground was probably March's best showcase of 1929, and was the film in which he got the most critical notice. *The New Movie Magazine* called it one of the best films of the year. The *New York Times* termed it an "intelligent production with well-woven strands of humor and sympathy, pathos, and an appealing romance." The leads were also lauded: "Frederic (sic) March and Mary Brian...are thoroughly believable in their roles." Edith Wharton biographer, Linda Costanzo Cahir, states that the film made an "unabashed...bid for audience popularity and commercial success" by lightening what was, on the whole, a dark novel. And yes, the film did register well at the box office.

March later said that it was the director of *The Marriage Playground*, Lothar Mendes, who gave him some of the best early advice he received on screen acting, "He said, 'Freddie, when I say 'camera,' all it means is relax.'"

March and his costar Ruth Chatterton had much more opportunity to shine in *Sarah and Son* (released March 14, 1930) than they did the prior year in *The Dummy*, and they made the most of it. Of course, it is more of a Ruth Chatterton picture than it is a Fredric March film—most of his pictures at this time were really vehicles for the leading ladies, with March offering solid and handsome support.

Sarah and Son is pure soap opera, about an impoverished house-keeper/vaudeville singer (Chatterton) whose abusive partner/husband leaves her—taking their son with him. He later sells the boy to a well-to-do family. As the years pass, the Chatterton character becomes a world-famous opera diva(!). Now, with money and influence behind her, she begins a search for the boy with the help of a lawyer (played by March) who, naturally, falls in love with her. Dorothy Arzner directs the Zoe Atkins script. Atkins was a Pulitzer-prize-winning playwright (RKO later bought her unproduced play *Morning Glory* for Katharine Hepburn) who would emerge as a top female screen writer during the thirties. Atkins would work with Arzner on three more pictures: *Anybody's Woman, Working Girl,* and *Christopher Strong,* resulting in a unique female director and female screenwriter collaboration.

The film is a rich showcase for Chatterton, as she plays an immigrant who goes from rags to riches, all the while keeping hope alive that she will one day be reunited with her lost son. It's a typically strong Arzner femme heroine—and one loaded with an abundance of sentiment—which is also one of the weaknesses of the film. For this performance Chatterton would earn an Oscar nomination as "Best Actress" of the year. March is equal to her, as he plays an attorney who begins working for the rich couple—who are also March's sister and brother-in-law—who bought the boy and raised him from the time he was a baby. His admiration for Chatterton changes his loyalties—and affections. Chatterton biographer Scott O'Brien summed up March's performance this way, "March brought a note of sanity to this film which I found a bit overwrought."

Despite the admirable performances, *Sarah and Son* seems static and stagy—with March and Chatterton both evoking the type of early sound line readings that emphasizes every letter and vowel in a slightly British, upper-crust way. The child actor (Philipp De Lacey) playing the lost son, who Sarah is eventually reunited with, is the kind of precious and precocious child actor that you sometimes long would get a swift kick in the rump.

Sarah and Son was a huge box office hit when it was released in 1930. It was also a big hit with most critics and appeared on several "best film" lists of the year. The *New York Times* felt *Sarah and Son* was "intelligently directed." The *Times* found Chatterton "splendid" and March "easy-going and natural." Overall, the review is good but with a minor reservation, "A little less attention to pathos and a little more attention to cheer would have made this an even better film than it is."

It was soon after the release of *Sarah and Son* that March's mother, Cora, died in Racine. March, naturally, came home for the funeral. The last time he had seen her had been the previous August, when he and Florence had taken a short trip to Racine so that Florence could meet some of his old school friends. When March came for the funeral, Cora's body was laid out in the parlor of the family home on College Street. While it wasn't announced in the papers that March was coming, it was, naturally, assumed that he would be. So, along with many of Cora's friends and family, the long lines outside the residence included those who didn't come to pay their respects to the deceased but came to view—and hopefully get the autograph of—the famous son. To keep these people out of the house, so as to allow in only those who truly did come to pay respects to Cora, March stood on the outdoor porch to greet these "mourners" and keep them away from entering. Such is the irony of fame.

Returning to Hollywood, March did his bit (playing a marine) in *Paramount on Parade* (released April 22, 1930), one of the best of the all-star studio extravaganzas of the early sound period. (MGM and Warner Brothers also produced such films.) Individual episodes were directed by top studio directors (including Dorothy Arzner, Edmund Goulding, Ernst Lubitch, Frank Tuttle and Edward Sutherland) and included performances by the studio contract roster, including stars like Maurice Chevalier, Clara Bow (singing the theme song from *True to the Navy*, which would also feature March later that year), Nancy Carroll, Ruth Chatterton, Evelyn Brent, William Powell, Kay Francis, Gary Cooper, George Bancroft, and on and on.

March was then third billed after George Bancroft and Mary Astor in *Ladies Love Brutes* (released May 15, 1930). Bancroft plays a rakish brute who has gone from rags to riches but still carries the rough edges of his early immigrant life. At a house party, the wealthy, married hostess (Astor—in her first sound film) takes a fancy to the brute, and an affair ensues. March is given the thankless role of her cuckold husband. Naturally, Astor is only playing with Bancroft and wouldn't think of having a future with him given his social inadequacies. *Ladies Love Brutes* is based on a play by Zoe Atkins and directed by Rowland V. Lee—a one-time actor who became a writer-director and proved particularly effective in the horror/fantasy genres with such films as *The Mysterious Dr. Fu Manchu, Zoo at Budapest, Son of Frankenstein* and *Tower of London.*

Bancroft became a leading man in the mid-1920s and found stardom in three films for director Josef von Sternberg, *Underworld, Docks of New York,* and *Thunderbolt,* for which Bancroft was nominated for an Oscar. But by the time of *Ladies Love Brutes,* his popularity was beginning to slip away while his ego remained inflated. Screenwriter Budd Schulberg would recall that on the set of one film when he was supposed to fall down after being shot, Bancroft refused to do so. When the director asked him why, Bancroft explained, "Just one bullet can't stop Bancroft!"

Astor and her husband Kenneth Hawks (the brother of director Howard Hawks) were personal friends of the Marches. Astor came relatively late to the sound field, and part of it was due to her nerves. For months, she couldn't or wouldn't allow herself to work. Finally, Florence stepped in to help. "Florence was very sympathetic and told me about a play that she and Edward Everett Horton were going to do shortly," Astor later recalled. Florence spoke with the director about casting Astor in the play *Among the Married,* which would open at the Majestic Theater in Los Angeles. Astor was cast. "The opening night...I had no first night qualms, nothing but a pleasant glow of anticipation," Astor recalled. "Florence and I made our first entrance together, and she was sort of holding onto me. She told me afterwards that she had no idea what I would do the first time I saw an audience, and I guess she was afraid I'd fall over in a faint or something." After getting into her dialog and achieving her first big laugh of the night, Astor calmed down. According to Astor, it was then Florence who came down with a bit of stage fright. "Florence saw that I was going to be all right, so then she started to think about herself and got jittery…while the action was going on downstage…she whispered to me, 'Oh Mary, I'm so nervous, I'll never get through this thing.' I patted her on the shoulder and said, 'There, there, darling you're doing great.' Imagine me, a mere amateur, 'there, there-ing' Florence Eldridge!"

In her autobiography, Astor would recall that March and Kenneth Hawks, a second unit director at Fox, would meet Florence and Mary for dinner prior to evening performances at the Town House restaurant on Wilshire Boulevard. They all developed a convivial friendship. It was during the production of this play, just after New Year's of 1930, that an accident struck, killing Hawks. Hawks was shooting aviation footage for a film called *Such Men are Dangerous*— the story of Captain Loewenstin who jumped or fell to his death while crossing the English Channel in 1928.

The day of the accident was a matinee day, and Florence and Mary were waiting for March and Hawks to arrive at the theater to take them to lunch. It started to get very late. "We sat and gossiped on the couch… (Under) a lone work light in the dark empty theater," Astor recalled. "The stage doorman called Florence to the phone…she was gone a long time and I was drowsing on the couch when she returned." Eldridge told her that there had been an accident, "We've only just heard—they're not sure of anything yet—we've just got to wait." Astor returned to her dressing room when a Fox publicity man came and told her the tragic news that two camera planes had collided over Santa Monica Bay, killing ten crew members, including Ken. Astor was taken in by the Marches who spent a week caring for the shattered widow. It was only three weeks later that Astor began shooting *Ladies Love Brutes*, with March there at her side to help her get through the filming.

Ladies Love Brutes did okay at the box office but was met with mixed reviews. The *New York Times* critic wrote, "so long as 'Ladies Love Brutes'…concerns itself with the comic actions of a rough diamond intent on giving himself a little polish, all is merry and bright, but when this tale turns to implausible melodramatic incidents, it leaves much to be desired." Astor was lauded for giving an "appealing and easy performance" while March "tackles a minor role with his unfailing skill." The (London) *Independent* didn't like it at all, calling the film "pretty bad…routine and unusually trite."

March was linked with George Bancroft again when Dashiell Hammett joined the Paramount stable of writers (at $400 per week) earlier in 1930. He was promised another $5000 every time he sold an original story to the studio. He convinced the studio to purchase his new detective novel, *The Maltese Falcon*. This was during the period when David O. Selznick was a Paramount executive. He liked Hammett's detective story and thought that its hard-boiled detective, Sam Spade, would make an ideal role for tough guy George Bancroft. Selznick had Hammett begin an adaptation of the novel with the idea of casting Bancroft.

Enter Paramount story editor E. J. Montagne, who worked closely at Paramount with Selznick. He sent an urgent memo to Selznick writing, "I cannot see Bancroft in it at all...This man works mentally, not physically as Bancroft would." He even included his suggestion as to who he believed would make an ideal Spade, "The only man we have who could put Sam (Spade) on the screen is Freddie March." However, it was not to be. Paramount, at this time, still thought of March as a light leading man who specialized in comedy—despite several dramatic films—and the idea fell by the wayside. Then the novel was sold to Warner Brothers, who would produce a 1931 film starring Ricardo Cortez as Spade. (Two other Warner Brother versions would follow this one. In 1936, a loose adaptation titled *Satan Met a Lady* with Warren William as the "Spade" character and then, in 1941, the definitive version starring Humphrey Bogart.)

True to the Navy (released May 25, 1930) reunited March with Clara Bow. It's the (mostly) light-hearted story of a San Diego soda fountain waitress (Bow) who falls hard for a sailor (March). In true life it was on this film that Bow met tall and brawny Rex Bell, cast as another sailor. Bell would soon become her husband and the father of her two children. Eventually they would retire to Nevada where Bell would begin a political career, while the retired Clara would battle mental health issues.

March has little to do in the film but makes an appealing love interest. Still the *New York Times* thought he was miscast, "Frederic (sic) March, who is a competent player, is hardly the type for a sailor."

Clara Bow was supposed to be cast for a third time opposite March in *Manslaughter* (released July 25, 1930), but due to her deteriorating mental health, she was replaced by the up-and-coming Claudette Colbert, in the first of four films that she and March would appear in.

Manslaughter is a remake of a 1922 silent film directed by Cecil B. De Mille. *Manslaughter* cast Colbert as a spoiled woman of wealth and privilege who is attracted by a crusading District Attorney (March). He is attracted to her as well but repulsed by the way she feels she can get away with doing exactly what she wants in her life without any thought of the consequences. She causes the death of a patrolman who is chasing her for speeding. She is charged with manslaughter, the DA prosecutes her, and she winds up serving jail time. Prison renews her and makes her take account of her life and actions. Eventually, through a series of ups and downs—one of the downs is the downward spiral the March character takes with his life once she is convicted and jailed—she and March do eventually find happiness together in the final fade-out.

March didn't mind losing Bow as a leading lady, since he found Colbert to have a "tremendous, smoldering sensuality to her, and that kind of chemistry usually would make the average woman a wanton…but Claudette had dignity and a sense of the fitness of things." He also found her downright sexy with a "wonderful gaiety, a peerless sense of fun, and her chemistry was a marvel." When asked by one of Colbert's biographers (Lawrence Quirk) if he had responded emotionally and physically to her, March replied, "What male costar of hers didn't!" While they got along well and would work together three more times, Colbert also encountered March's "Peck's Bad Boy" complex. On occasion, while waiting for a scene to be lit or while being photographed, she would feel March's hands pinching her voluptuous rear end.

Manslaughter was filmed at Paramount's Astoria Studio in New York, with George Abbott (the famed Broadway producer-director) directing the film. It was not a happy experience for Abbott, who came to dislike film directing. He simply didn't have the autonomy he had on the stage. Despite this, *Manslaughter* turned out to be a success at the box office. It was also, once again, more of a showcase for its leading lady, Colbert, who dominates the film—and does so financially as well. Colbert would make $13,750 on the film while March would take home $4,639.

Laughter (released September 25, 1930) is the early March film that is thought to be among his very best today and the one that gave him his best showcase up to that time—despite the fact that it really didn't do all that well at the box office. Although it was a strong showcase for March, *Laughter* was (again) really a vehicle for its leading lady: top-billed Nancy Carroll.

The film was based on a story by Douglas Doty and Harry d'Abbadie d'Arrast (who also directed the picture), and the screenplay was written by the brilliant Donald Ogden Stewart. Stewart had been a writer and performer on the Broadway stage during much of the 1920s, before trying his hand at screenwriting in 1929. *Laughter* would be the first of several significant film scripts he would write. He would follow-up with *The Barrett's of Wimpole Street, No More Ladies, Holiday* (1938 version), *Marie Antoinette, Love Affair,* and receive a screenwriting Oscar for *The Philadelphia Story.*

Nancy Carroll plays an ex-showgirl—with the Ziegfeld Follies no less—who has married into extreme wealth; the guy makes $80 million per year and lives in a sixty-room Manhattan mansion. (Frank Morgan plays the much older husband, nine years before he is the wonderful Wizard of Oz.) Morgan is likeable but boring and as sexually alluring as a turnip. Carroll has everything she could want in terms of material things, but lacks the gaiety and fun of her earlier life. Enter her former boyfriend, a composer-pianist played by Fredric March. She is still attracted to his spontaneous devil-may-care attitude, but they do not resume their affair—despite what her husband may think. There are also two other secondary characters: a suicidal sculptor (Glenn Anders) who loves the Carroll character, and the millionaire's daughter (Diane Ellis). The daughter sincerely falls for the artist, but the artist only goes after the daughter for her money—she isn't enough of a compensation for not having Nancy Carroll.

Given its title, *Laughter* is not a laugh-a-minute film. It has a dark side epitomized by the suicidal friend—who in the opening sequences is contemplating suicide only to be talked out of it by Carroll. *Laughter* is a mix of romantic, sophisticated comedy and dark melodrama. It is witty and brittle, and most of the comedy is supplied by March, who gives a natural and spontaneous performance.

Until March enters the scene, Carroll pretty much mopes around, grumbling about her rich, yet unhappy, fate. The only joy she seems to get out of life is riding in a taxi around Central Park. March has always gotten a bit of a rap for being stuffy and mannered—and at times he can be—but not in *Laughter*. In fact, in most of his comedy films March is surprisingly loose and spry—and that is certainly the case here.

Soon, March and Carroll are happily looking back on old times, pulling practical jokes, and delivering all kinds of witty one-liners back and forth to each other. At one point, they are caught in a storm and stop at a house where the residents aren't home, so they decide to break in:

MARCH: Do you have a crowbar?

CARROLL: (searching about her) I must have left it at home.

They decide to camp inside the house, and each gets under a bearskin rug, which leads to them crawling around growling at each other—it's sophomoric but at the same time strangely sweet.

Seeing lights on in the house and knowing the owners are away brings the police. March and Carroll claim to know the owners. "He is rather a short gentleman," says Carroll. "But not too short," injects March. "A rather tall-short gentleman," she rejoins as they attempt, very unsuccessfully, to describe the owner. The police cuff them and say "This is the eighth time this house has been broken into this year," to which March retorts, "That must explain why there was no whisky."

It is while they are in the patrol car on their way to jail that March explains to Carroll the film's thesis when tells her that everything they have been doing the last few days has been a charade. That she is dying inside:

MARCH: God didn't mean you to live like this—without nourishment…without laughter.

CARROLL: Laughter?

MARCH: Yes, laughter…You were born for laughter. Nothing in this life of yours now is as important as that. Laughter can take this whole life of yours—that home, those people, those jewels—and blow them to pieces. You're rich. You're dirty rich. *And only Laughter can make you clean…*

March confesses his love to her and declares that he wants to take her away from it all. But she rejects this and instead breaks up the relationship between Morgan's daughter and her artist friend. She miscalculated, and the artist kills himself.

After all of this, Carroll tells Morgan that she is leaving him. He replies that she won't because she needs the "comfort and security," he provides, but she replies that she needs "love." She realizes that the artist really did love Morgan's daughter and that she ruined their chance for happiness, and so she decides she will leave the security that Morgan offers, for the love of Fredric March. The fade-out finds Carroll and March in a café in Paris, promising each other "an early night" out, so they can get to their apartment for what promises to be a long night of love-making. Laughter ensues. Fade-out.

Laughter resembles Philip Barry's *Holiday*, which tells another unconventional love story between a poor but happy young man and a rich woman who longs for more out of life. Like *Holiday*, *Laughter* blends together a combination of witty, sophisticated comedy, screwball comedy, and deep philosophical discussions. Its direction by D'Arrast is assured and free-flowing. D'Arrast had directed such sophisticated fare as *A Gentleman of Paris, Serenade, Service for Ladies* (all starring Adolph Menjou), and *Dry Martini* (with Mary Astor). He certainly had the confidence of Ernst Lubitch, who was overseeing the New York Paramount-Astoria product, and his style imitates (if not equals) Lubitch's famous touch. Strangely, D'Arrast would go on to direct only one more Hollywood film—the superb *Topaze* with John Barrymore and Myrna Loy—before retiring to the Riviera, and enjoying the gambling houses of Monte Carlo.

Laughter opened to good reviews. The *New York Times* wrote that the film combined "clever nonsense, drama and satire." It lauded D'Arrast's "merry" direction and Stewart's "characteristic fun in the dialogue." Carroll's performance is called "delightful," while March is "splendid." *Photoplay* magazine termed *Laughter* "an excellent picture of young people in love," believing that March "does his best work" yet. The *New York Post* called the film "the nearest approach to sophisticated comedy which has yet been made in the talkies."

Despite the good reviews, *Laughter* didn't do well at the box office. Set in the depths of the Great Depression, it seems that moviegoers had a hard time sympathizing with a rich-beyond-words woman who is unsatisfied with her life. Herman J. Mankiewicz, who produced *Laughter* (and is best known as a screenwriter of *Citizen Kane*—with Orson Welles), summed up the box office performance of *Laughter* this way:

> *Laughter was a flop...In our story Nancy was married to a guy who earns eighty-four million dollars every afternoon. She lives in a sixty-room quadruplex on Park Avenue. Her arms are dead tired from carrying so much jewelry... (And) we started off with the assumption that this was no good, because—she didn't have Laughter!*

Despite this, Mankiewicz would later call *Laughter* his favorite film.

Over the years, many film historians and critics have come to see *Laughter* as an important film in the development of early-talkies sophisticated comedy and in providing the geneses for the upcoming vogue for screwball comedy (as exemplified by *Twentieth Century, My Man Godfrey, Nothing Sacred,* and *Bringing Up Baby*). The notoriously hard-to-please Pauline Kael, in her book *5001 Nights at the Movies*, described *Laughter* as a "lovely, sophisticated comedy, an ode to impracticality, it failed commercially but its attitudes and spirit influenced the screwball hits of the thirties." David Shipman in *The Story of Cinema* writes that *Laughter* is "very nearly a masterpiece...watching March and Nancy Carroll in this film is an odd experience, as if the characters of Evelyn Waugh or (Noel) Coward had sprung back into life..." David Thomson writes that "few films are so good at getting the fast, sexy grace of early talkies," than *Laughter*.

Years later, March claimed that *Laughter* was his favorite film. "It was a mad, merry film and I was such a happy idiot all the way through. Anyway I like comedy and clowning better than dramatics."

March next had the opportunity to recreate his stage role as Tony Cavendish (aka John Barrymore) in *The Royal Family of Broadway* (released December 22, 1930). It was the role that brought him his Paramount movie contract and now a much wider motion picture audience would be able to see March as the irrepressible Tony. Joining in the fun are Ina Claire as Tony's sister Julie (read Ethel) and Mary Brian, as Gwen—Julie's daughter whose own stage career is just beginning. The film is March's introduction to George Cukor, who codirects the proceedings with Cyril Gardner. The screenplay was written by Herman Mankiewicz and Gertrude Purcell.

Cukor was just beginning his film career. He had known Florence in Rochester where he was a director with the Lyceum Players, a stock company situated in Upstate New York. He had met March in passing, but with his direction of *The Royal Family of Broadway* they would evolve from casual acquaintances to friends. When sound pictures arrived, Cukor was a beneficiary—like March—in that the studios wanted individuals with a stage background to help Hollywood and its silent actors make the transition. Cukor was often utilized in his early Hollywood years as a dialogue director (which was his duty on the classic *All Quiet on the Western Front*), and in his first few films he was teamed with another director as codirector of such films as *Grumpy* and *The Virtuous Son*.

The French-born Cyril Gardner had worked on several films as an editor, so he understood more about camera angles and how to cut a film than Cukor did. Cukor's specialty was working with the actors on line readings and characterization. This is pretty much how Gardner and Cukor operated on *The Royal Family*, "With *Royal Family* it was Cyril and Cukor," Mary Brian would later recall. "But by this time he (Cukor) was really doing the directing (of actors), and Cyril was doing all the technical things."

Cukor had been approached to direct the Broadway production of *The Royal Family* but had turned it down because the play offended his friend Ethel Barrymore. But, for some reason, he had no problem accepting the direction of the film—unless Paramount forced it on him. He happily recalled, years later, "I was on familiar territory with *The Royal Family*…When I was asked to do the picture I was happy to work with a very distinguished cast. Ina Clair, one of our most accomplished actresses and Fredric March. I thought the material was distinguished and I did the picture."

The Royal Family of Broadway is a fast-paced, witty film but, as with *Laughter*, it also has its moments of pathos. March is a total delight through it all. He all but steals the film as Cavendish, even though his part in the film is small when compared to Clair and Brian. Despite this, March would be billed above the title for the first time in his motion picture career. He is the misfit of the family who has given up the stage to pursue wealth and fame in Hollywood. He spends a good deal of the film trying to avoid harrassed directors, cuckold husbands, and jilted lovers. Just like when he played the role on the stage, March's Barrymore impersonation is unmistakable—the bemused raised eyebrow and theatricality, along with a physical similarity especially when shot in profile, are dead giveaways. Second unit director Arthur Jacobson would later say, "He (March) was the prototype of John Barrymore. He walked like him, talked like him, damn near looked like him."

Like many early sound films adapted from a stage production, *The Royal Family of Broadway* has a stagy feeling, with one glorious exception—a technical tracking shot where the camera follows Tony upstairs to the bathroom as he prepares to take a bath. Arthur Jacobson later recalled this scene:

> *The famous scene in that picture is when the Barrymore character comes home from wherever he's been in the world. He comes in like a wild man with all kinds of crazy things. He goes up a winding staircase, undressing as he goes up. By the time he gets to the top, just as he slips his shorts off, leaving him stark naked, he's into the bathroom. We didn't have such things as camera cranes in 1930, so we had to figure out how to do it.*

According to Jacobson, cameraman George Folsey and George Cukor got together and came up with the idea of going to a flour milling company where they observed a forklift, with a wide pallet on it, which held large quantities of grain. It inspired them to try and use such a device as a camera platform. "We brought it to the studio in Long Island (Paramount-Astoria)," Jacobson later recalled. "Going up and down was fine because it was electric, but it couldn't go forward or back or sideways, except by manpower. We had about twenty men pushing it and we got the shot. That may have been the forerunner of the camera crane."

The film crew got a chance to revel in the March humor during the filming of the staircase scene. "When he (March) was making *The Royal Family*, the Eastern studio (Astoria) crew didn't know him well and weren't used to his kidding," Florence Eldridge later recalled.

> *In one scene he was supposed to start running up the stairs, stop half way up, turn to say something and then continue. They rehearsed the scene a couple of times and prepared to shoot it.*
>
> *The chief electrician approached Freddie."Mr. March," he said, "Which step are you going to stop on?"*
>
> *Freddie surveyed him with a surprised and pained expression. "Which step am I going to stop on?" He ejaculated, "How can I tell? My dear boy, I'm an artiste."*
>
> *"But, Mr. March," the juicer (electrician) protested, "I've got to focus the lights on you."*
>
> *"Ah," said Freddie dramatically, "the lights! That is different. I'll stop anywhere you say."*

The film did well in most large cosmopolitan cities (New York, Philadelphia, Chicago, San Francisco, for example), but didn't do particularly well in smaller towns and rural areas. But, it was met with good reviews by most critics. "Not a second is lost in dealing with the feverish action of *The Royal Family of Broadway*, a thorough and wonderfully effective talking picture version of the play," the *New York Times* reported. "Fredric March, looking as much like John Barrymore as it is possible without any conspicuous make-up plays Tony Cavendish... Mr. March has the greatest opportunity for quick thinking, agility and splendid comedy." *The Outlook* critic wrote, "Fredric March is the whole show. Dressed for the most part in a pair of shorts and a flying bathrobe, he gives a performance that is positively brilliant." For his performance March would be nominated for the first of five times for a Best Actor Oscar. (Coincidentally, he would lose the Oscar to Lionel Barrymore for *A Free Soul*.)

Dorothy Arzner's *Honor among Lovers* (released March 21, 1931) is the third of five Claudette Colbert-Fredric March films. Colbert plays an executive secretary—she must make good money to afford having a maid—to a millionaire industrialist (March) who, in true pre-code glory, is having an affair with her. March is against getting married, but he wants her to join him on a pleasure cruise. Her boyfriend (Monroe Owsley) suspects something is up between the two, so he proposes marriage and Colbert accepts—much to her regret.

Colbert is the typically strong Arzner female protagonist: not just a secretary, at one point in the film she stands in for March at a board meeting and succeeds in persuading the board to adopt March's plans. Colbert and March, as usual, make a good dramatic team with Charlie Ruggles and an up-and-coming Ginger Rogers providing comic relief. Of Arzner, March would recall that as a director she "could raise as much hell as Wyler or any of them. I never felt I was dealing with a woman—she was one of the guys."

Creighton Peet, in *The Outlook*, wrote of *Honor Among Lovers*, "If the story is too involved to be good, you have the lovely Claudette Colbert to make you forget, and Fredric March's performance to keep you interested." David Shipman in *The Story of Cinema* considers *Honor Among Lovers*: "One of the wittiest films of this period." Despite good reviews, the box office take was only on the mild side.

The less said about *The Night Angel* (released July 18, 1931) the better. It rates as one of the weakest films of March's career, despite the presence of Nancy Carroll and director Edmund Goulding, who had just directed Carroll in one of her best films, *The Devil's Holiday*. (Goulding would go on to direct such top 1930s features as *Grand Hotel*, *Blondie of the Follies*, *Dark Victory* and *The Old Maid*.) Set in Prague, March is a prosecutor who sends brothel madam (Alison Skipworth) to jail. Carroll is the madam's daughter who has to keep fending off the attentions of the bordello's bouncer (beefy

Alan Hale). Along the way, Carroll falls in love with the man who put her mother behind bars and March kills the bouncer—only to be acquitted thanks to Carroll's testimony.

Carroll had just come off of two lackluster previous films, *Personal Maid* and *Wayward*, and the box-office failure of *The Night Angel* cemented her fate. She began talkies by becoming one of its brightest stars, but by the end of 1933, Paramount would refuse to renew her contract. She thought of herself as a perfectionist, while Paramount came to feel she was just uncooperative. By 1938 she was billed fifth, under the title, in a film starring Fredric March: *There Goes My Heart*.

Among its many poor reviews was this from the *New York Times*:

> *It seems as though Edmund Goulding aspired to be an Eisenstein in his direction of* The Night Angel, *which was offered last night at the Rivoli, and that the stellar player, Nancy Carroll, had hopes of being a Bernhardt or a Duse. Neither is successful and therefore this screen offering results merely in being an affected study in direction and acting, which hardly makes for entertainment.*

March didn't come off unscathed, with *Liberty* magazine writing, "The usually able Mr. March is as bad as I have ever observed."

My Sin (released October 3, 1931) was the second of six lackluster films that Tallulah Bankhead would make for Paramount over a two-year period. Filmed at the Paramount-Astoria Studio, the film is set in Panama and tells the story of a "nightclub hostess" who kills a man in self-defense. March plays yet another lawyer—this one has hit hard times due to alcohol addiction. He takes on her case, wins vindication, and turns his life around. Rejuvenated morally and spiritually, he attempts to turn hers around too.

In her autobiography, Bankhead lumps *My Sin* with several of her other films of this period and calls it "a mess." Critics tend to agree. "Considering the talented portrayals contributed by Tallulah Bankhead and Fredric March, it is rather disappointing to find them in such a suspenseless production as *My Sin*," wrote the critic for The *New York Times*. Not only that but, according to Bankhead, her portrayal of a "notorious hussy loose in the canal zone," led to the film being banned in Panama.

This was the first encounter between March and Bankhead, but it would hardly be the last. If they didn't make too much of an impression on each other during the five weeks they shot this film, they certainly would a decade later when they teamed up—along with Florence—in the Thornton Wilder Broadway production of *The Skin of Their Teeth*.

Two years and seventeen films completed, March had emerged from his Paramount apprenticeship as a solid leading man who could be depended on to look good and give a fine account of himself without overshadowing his leading ladies—for whom most of these films were built around to begin with. But his next film, *Dr. Jekyll and Mr. Hyde*, would provide March with a stellar star-making vehicle, which would put him among the top rank of motion picture stars.

CHAPTER FIVE
INTERLUDE: DR. JEKYLL AND MR. HYDE

In the late summer of 1931, March began work on the most important film of his career up to that time, an adaptation of Robert Louis Stevenson's novel "The Strange Case of Dr. Jekyll and Mr. Hyde." The novel had been filmed several times in the past, most notably the celebrated 1920 silent version starring John Barrymore. The timing couldn't have been better. Universal was making a mint in 1931 in the horror genre (*Frankenstein* and *Dracula*), and Paramount saw an opportunity to cash in.

Originally, Irving Pichel, another Paramount contract player, was assigned to do the film, but when director Rouben Mamoulian took one look at Pichel's dark hooded eyes, he decided he wouldn't work out in the dual role. "I wanted someone who could play Jekyll, and Pichel could only play Hyde!" Mamoulian later said.

Who Mamoulian did want was March. "He's a natural Jekyll," Mamoulian told Paramount head of production B.P. Schulberg, "He's young, he's handsome, his speech is fine, and I'm sure he can play Hyde." Schulberg was unmoved telling Mamoulian that he couldn't fathom March in such a dramatic film because the thinking at the time was that March was mainly a comedy leading man thanks to his broad antics in *The Royal Family of Broadway* and his recent film *Laughter*. Mamoulian urged Shulberg to give it some thought. After a few days, he got a call from the studio chief telling him, resignedly, "All right, if you're so obstinate, you can have your head, you can have Freddie March."

Despite this, March was somewhat apprehensive about Mamoulian. March confided to his makeup artist, the prestigious Wally Westmore, that he was leery of Mamoulian because of his back ground as a disciple of the Stanislavsky "method" of acting. But, luckily, he and March saw eye to eye on this film, and March turned out to be very happy with Mamoulian's direction. For his part, Mamoulian considered March a ". . . marvelous actor who also is a very intelligent one. With Freddie you can reason. With some of them you can't reason at all, because they don't get it…With Freddie you can discuss it."

Mamoulian certainly could be obstinate, but he was also considered a very fine director and evaluator of talent. Rouben Mamoulian (1897-1987) was born in the Russian province of Georgia, to Armenian parents. He had attended the Moscow Art Theater, and later toured England with the Russian Repertory Theater. After studying drama at the University of London, he began to direct plays. In 1923, he came to the United States to accept an offer from the George Eastman theater of Rochester, New York. In 1926, he went to New York where he began directing plays for the Theater Guild, including a landmark 1927 production of *Porgy and Bess*. With the coming of sound, Hollywood beckoned; it wanted not only actors with trained voices but also directors who were accustomed to directing for the spoken stage, and so Mamoulian was signed by Paramount Pictures. He then made two very well received films: *Applause* (1929) with Helen Morgan, and *City Streets* (1931) an underworld story starring Sylvia Sidney and Gary Cooper. Mamoulian developed a reputation for brilliance in the use of sound and cinematography in his films—and *Dr. Jekyll and Mr. Hyde* would be no exception.

Rose Hobart, the daughter of a cellist with the New York Symphony, was cast as Jekyll's fiancée, Muriel. Hobart had also come from the New York stage. She played the leading lady role in the Broadway production of *Death Takes a Holiday*, later to be one of March's all-time best motion pictures. In films, she had costarred in the 1930 version of *Liliom* (opposite Charles Farrell) directed by Frank Borzage, and *East of Borneo* at Universal, where Hobart was under contract. Paramount soon worked out a loan-out for her services with Universal.

But the pivotal female role in *Dr. Jekyll and Mr. Hyde* was that of Ivy, the prostitute who bewitches Dr. Jekyll and is later brutalized by Hyde. The role called out for a powerhouse actress, and Mamoulian sought out the services of Miriam Hopkins. There was a problem: Hopkins was interested in the film, but not in playing Ivy—she wanted to be 'the good girl', Muriel. According to Mamoulian, Hopkins found Ivy too "unsympathetic." Mamoulian was astonished and told her, "What's wrong with you? Ivy is going to steal the picture." Hopkins told him it was no use—she simply would not play that part. Mamoulian went for the jugular. "All right, that makes it easy," he told her. "I'll have no trouble finding someone to play Ivy. Half the actresses in Hollywood would give their eye teeth for the part." He began walking out when Hopkins called him back and told him she would do it.

Miriam Hopkins (1902-1972) was born and bred in Georgia, and she had—as previously noted—worked with March on the stage in the 1920s. She had signed with Paramount Pictures in 1930. Hopkins was a versatile and intelligent screen actress, one of the finest of the 1930s, but she had also acquired a reputation for being difficult and a camera hog. Rose Hobart would later say of Hopkins, "Difficult is an understatement. I had no scenes with her, but I used to go on the set and hear about her endlessly from Freddie March. She was always upstaging everyone—all the time." Mamoulian would later dispute this. "All of the stories I hear about Miriam Hopkins, her temper tantrums, and her demonic ego were not in play at the time we were filming *Dr. Jekyll and Mr. Hyde*," he told writer David Del Valle. "For me, as a director, Miriam was a very gifted and talented actress who could play comedy (as she did for [Ernst] Lubitsch) or a tragic figure such as Ivy."

Along with this fine cast (which would also include in key roles Holmes Herbert, Halliwell Hobbes, and Edgar Norton) the cinematography was done by Karl Struss, who had begun as a professional photographer before entering the world of film. Among the films he photographed were: *Ben Hur: A Tale of the Christ; Sparrows; Sunrise;* and *Coquette*. Struss was an innovator of soft-focus photography, which rendered a three dimensional image highlighting some planes while deemphasizing others. Rose Hobart would recall Struss as a ". . . very typical European. He concentrated only on what he was doing; he was always absolutely absorbed." Mamoulian would recall that Struss was ". . . up to every challenge I threw his way."

When filming began in August of 1931, March received an encouraging telegram from studio head B.P. Schulberg:

MY DEAR FREDDIE

BEST WISHES TO YOU UPON THE INCEPTION OF THE GREATEST OPPORTUNITY AS WELL AS THE MOST ARDUOUS ROLE AND THE MOST EXACTING TASK OF YOUR SPLENDID CAREER—STOP—MAY IT GIVE YOU YOUR PLACE IN THE SUN FOR ALL TIME—STOP—WE APPRECIATE THE EARNEST EFFORT YOU HAVE MADE TO PREPARE YOURSELF FOR THIS TRYING PART AND HOPE IT S REWARDED BY THE PLAUDITS OF THE WORLD.

March later gave insight, to *Screen Book* magazine, on how he played Jekyll and Hyde:

> *I conceived Mr. Hyde as more than just Dr. Jekyll's inhibited evil nature, I saw the beast as a separate entity—one who could, and almost did, little by little, overpower, and annihilate Dr. Jekyll. And I tried to show the devastating results in Dr. Jekyll as well. To me, those repeated appearances of the beast within him were more than just a mental stain on Jekyll—they crushed him physically as well. I tried to bring this out by increasing lines and shadows of Jekyll's makeup as the picture progressed, until in the last scenes, he looked as though he already had one foot in the grave. Hyde was killing Jekyll physically as well as mentally.*

Dr. Jekyll and Mr. Hyde opens with an objective camera view that shows only what Dr. Jekyll is seeing. The first time that March is shown on camera is when he looks into the mirror as he is getting his coat and hat, and he then immediately switches back to the subjective view as Jekyll gets into his carriage for a ride to the lecture hall. It's an auspicious and stylized beginning to the film and would be utilized throughout the picture.

There is a very funny story told in the DVD of the film, by movie historian Greg Mank. At production meetings, Mamoulian keeps talking about a subjective camera. March had no idea what that was, so he asks Paramount executive Jesse Lasky, "What is subjective photography?" To which Lasky in exasperation replies, "My God, if you don't know what subjective photography is what are you doing in this business?" Well, March didn't know and again asks Lasky what it means to which Lasky replied, "How the hell do I know?"

March's Dr. Jekyll is presented as almost a saint. The pivotal scene that establishes this, is where the little blonde girl throws her crutches aside and slowly but surely—with outstretched arms—makes her way to the good doctor. She is walking towards him with an evangelical glow—he (Jekyll) is her savior. He has given her back the use of her legs just as Christ made the lame walk. Jekyll the good is soon seen coming to the aid of Ivy, the prostitute who is being beaten by one of her customers. He takes her back to her room to give her a medical examination. What follows is one of the most erotically charged scenes of pre-code American cinema.

In the scene, Hopkins provides an infamous striptease slowly removing her garter on both legs and throwing them across to an open-eyed March. She then slowly, and with much seductive glee, removes her stockings. It's clear she is trying to seduce Dr. Jekyll—and he certainly appears tempted. The camera then pans back to March, as Hopkins removes the rest of her clothes and then hides under her blanket. But when Jekyll comes over to examine her, she grabs him and they share a passionate kiss and—in a shot cut in the later 1935 reissue, after the code went into effect—you can clearly see a side shot of Hopkins's breast. The scene ends with Ivy seductively swinging her leg as she is sitting naked on the bed. Ivy would become a definite part of his subconscious and that of Mr. Hyde. "Our version is filled with sexy images," Mamoulian later told writer Jim Bawden. "Hyde is doing everything Jekyll has always dreamed about—and we see a lot of that."

The film had problems with individual censor boards, but miraculously this scene survives, as does a painting of a naked woman seen throughout the film in Ivy's bedroom. In fact, the censors had more problems with the characterization of Hyde than that of Ivy. The feeling was that Hyde was overly suggestive and brutal—which he certainly is.

Yet, Mamoulian didn't think he was presenting Mr. Hyde as a monster, and didn't want to in any case. "I didn't want Hyde to be a monster," Mamoulian later said. "Hyde is not evil; he is the primitive, the animal in us." The makeup used on March as Hyde has often been described as "ape-like." What Mamoulian wanted was to create an earlier image of man—Neanderthal man, to be exact—and the makeup certainly succeeds in this regard.

March would arrive at the studio for a very early call—6 a.m.— to begin the rigorous routine of getting into the Hyde makeup. The process could take up to four hours. A single makeup artist (Wally Westmore) was admitted to the star's dressing room to begin the arduous work. Westmore made many sketches in consultation with March. He then made a plaster mold of March's face to save March from having to undergo grueling hours in a makeup chair. As Westmore's brother Frank later wrote, "the device had to be comfortable enough for March to wear for prolonged periods of time, during which he had to be able to speak his lines clearly despite a mouth full of dental work not his own."

The most difficult aspect of the Hyde makeup turned out to be the fangs. Again, per Frank Westmore:

> *Although they (the fangs) fit the face mold perfectly, they didn't fit correctly into March's own mouth. This time the actor himself had to sit in a chair for hours as the dentist altered this fang and changed that tooth. But when the final full horror make-up (a four hour job) was placed on Fredric March, it was perfect; it combined the Neanderthal with the Satanic without seeming ludicrous.*

The transformation scenes are superbly photographed. In the book *The Celluloid Muse* Mamoulian spoke of this process:

> *The secret of the transformation of Dr. Jekyll into Mr. Hyde is one continuous shot—without cuts and without rewinding the film backwards in the camera to permit the application of additional make-up—lay in the use of colour transparencies which gradually revealed more and more of the actor's makeup. As you know, a red filter will absorb red and reveal all the other colours,*

and a green filter will do the reverse. Working on that principle, we held graduating colour filters one by one before the camera thus allowing successive portions of March's coloured makeup to register on film. It was all rather primitive—the filters were hand-made—but it worked.

According to Rose Hobart, the makeup was a difficult process physically on March. "He was very unhappy about it because that make-up was so rough for him to work in," she later recalled to author Tom Weaver. "He could only stay in that make up for about twenty minutes, or so, and then he'd have to relax—it hurt, frankly. It was ruining his face—wearing that make-up." She would recall that following the film, March would spend some three weeks in hospital due to the wear and tear on his face caused by the makeup.

When March first emerges as the hideous Hyde, we see things, again through a subjective camera, until Hyde, like Jekyll, is first glimpsed in all his horror in the mirror. What are we to make of this Mr. Hyde? He seems so giddy and almost childlike in his wonder at what he—the now subconscious Jekyll—has created. He is not yet showing the brute he would soon become.

As Hyde, he has had enough of good, virtuous Muriel. He wants action and he knows where to get it: Ivy. In a terrific scene, March's Hyde enters the tavern where Ivy hangs out. It's where she meets the men she will bed for their money. Ivy's first look at Hyde is one of shock and disbelief, but he soon overpowers her and with threatening menace he takes over her life and her boarding house rooms. Here, he alternately has sex with and brutalizes her—including whipping her on the back, no doubt to browbeat her into submission.

After Hyde tells her he won't be seeing her for a while—Jekyll needs to pay some attention to Muriel—Ivy wants to make sure that Hyde is out of her life for good. She goes to see Dr. Jekyll—a monumental mistake as it would turn out. Jekyll, seeing and hearing about Hyde's abuse, promises the pleading Ivy—a superb scene by Hopkins—that she will not see Hyde ever again. Hopkins was especially pleased with her work in this scene. "I went through the whole thing…and they all (the crew) applauded. And Rouben too. And I was just sobbing like this and a wreck on the floor, holding on to his shoes at the end, and that was the scene printed. And it was done in one take."

On the night of his engagement party to Muriel, Jekyll happily stops in the park and, observing a bird in a tree, begins to quote Keats. Then the camera cuts to a cat climbing up the tree and it captures and kills the bird—though the audience doesn't see it. It's a metaphoric scene. Immediately Jekyll, automatically and without drinking any of his potion, turns into the sinister Hyde. A split screen shows Hyde running through the park—on his way to the unsuspecting Ivy—while the other half shows a disappointed Muriel wondering what has become of Jekyll at their engagement party.

Ivy's death scene in her bedroom is masterfully shot and is the most horrifying scene in the film. Hyde quotes what Ivy had said to Jekyll, and in terror she tries to escape from him but he catches her and strangles her to death, while saying as she is in her death throes, "Isn't Hyde a lover after your own heart?"

Jekyll tries to emerge from inside Hyde, and he seeks help from his colleague, Dr. Lanyon, for the drugs needed to turn back into Jekyll. After mixing up the formula, Lanyon watches Hyde turn back into Jekyll, who swears him to secrecy. Jekyll believes that to pay for the harm and death he did as Hyde, he needs to break off the engagement with Muriel, and so he goes to see her. However, once again, without any formula needed, he turns back into Hyde and attacks Muriel, but he is thwarted. The police are called in, and they chase Hyde back to Jekyll's lab where Hyde is shot dead— turning back to Jekyll in death.

When *Dr. Jekyll and Mr. Hyde* was released, it became a huge hit for Paramount, one of the studios top box office successes of 1932. The reviews were stellar. Mordaunt Hall, in the *New York Times*, wrote that the film ". . . emerges as a far more tense and shuddering affair than it was as John Barrymore's silent picture." Of March, Hall wrote, "Fredric March is the stellar performer in this blood-curdling shadow venture." The *New York Herald Tribune* critic wrote that March's performance is "In every way, a fine and brilliant portrayal, which adds immeasurably to his stature as an actor." The distinguished playwright Robert E. Sherwood would write in the New York Evening Post shortly after the film's opening:

His [March's] performance of Hyde is inexpressibly good and, what is more remarkable, he even makes a living, understandable being of the usually un-interesting Dr. Jekyll. At all times, he suggests the turbulence that exists beneath the well-controlled exterior of Stevenson's hero. There can be no further doubt that Mr. March is an actor of high intelligence and of hitherto unsuspected power.

Fredric March had arrived.

CHAPTER SIX
1932-1936

*D*r. *Jekyll and Mr. Hyde* played to packed—and at times terrified—
movie houses throughout the late winter and into the spring
of 1932, bringing a huge windfall for Paramount—and for March.
This was (finally) his breakthrough role, and he emerged as a star.
True, Paramount had been building him up for the last three years,
and they had teamed him prominently with several of its leading
ladies, but there really was no film built around him. *The Royal
Family of Broadway* came close, with his dominating portrayal of
Barrymore—and the recognition of an Oscar nomination—but in
truth he had less screen time even in that than did Ina Claire and
Mary Brian.

For the second time in two years, March was nominated for an
Academy Award as Best Actor of the year. His two fellow nominees
were Wallace Beery, for his punch-drunk boxer in *The Champ*, and
Alfred Lunt, recreating his Broadway role in the comedy *The Guardsman*.
It must have been a great thrill for March to be nominated in the
same category as Lunt. He was a great admirer of this prestigious
stage star. A few years earlier, March was quoted as saying, "I should
like to bring to the screen the sort of thing Alfred Lunt has brought
to the stage. I think that is the best—and most ambitious—
comparison I can make. The best illustration of what I hope to do
and be."

Surprisingly, *Dr. Jekyll and Mr. Hyde* failed to become one of the
eight films nominated as Best Picture. Oddly, the winner of the
Best Picture Academy Award would be *Grand Hotel*. It's not that it
won that is odd, but that "Best Picture" was the only category that
Grand Hotel was even nominated in.

Mamoulian was denied a nomination for his splendid direction, and Miriam Hopkins was overlooked for her tour-de-force as Ivy. Along with March, other nominations were in the categories of writing (Best Adaptation) and cinematography—a well deserved nomination for Karl Struss.

The Fifth Annual Academy Awards ceremony was held on November 18, 1932, at the Ambassador Hotel Grand Ballroom in Los Angeles, and it was broadcast live over nationwide radio. The affair was hosted by Conrad Nagel, and the event was completed in less than two hours. Helen Hayes had just been awarded the Best Actress award for her work in *The Sin of Madelon Claudet* when Norma Shearer stepped up to the rostrum to present the Oscar for Best Actor.

Shearer had a surprise in store. There were two winners that year. March had won the balloting by one vote over Beery, and under Academy rules, anything less than a three vote victory was considered a tie. March and Beery had both recently adopted a child, and March in a witty acceptance speech won laughter and applause when he said, "I've never met Mr. Beery although I believe we have something in common. Both Mr. Beery and I have adopted baby girls this year, which makes it seem to me the height of incongruity of awarding us prizes for best male performance of the year."

Following the ceremony, March received a telegram, which he treasured, from his beloved brother Jack and his wife Mary:

NEVER HAVE WE BEEN PROUDER OF YOU—STOP— YOUR RECOGNITION WAS DESERVED AND YOUR ACCEPTANCE SPEECH A MASTERPIECE—STOP— NOT ONLY WILL IT NOT DO ANY HARM BUT THE PACE YOU HAVE SET WILL BE TOUGHT TO FOLLOW— STOP—ONLY HOPE FATHER WAS LISTING IN— STOP—LOVE FROM BOTH OF US.

Indeed, in the summer of 1932, the Marches had adopted a little girl. Florence was unable to conceive and both were desirous of having children. An additional point worth considering is that Florence had a lot more time on her hands in Hollywood than March did. His career was flourishing while hers was fairly stagnant, with only a few minor films here and there and an occasional play with Edward Everett Horton's stock company. A child would be an ideal way for Florence to satisfy not only her maternal needs but also give value to her creative and artistic outlooks. Here was a little child she could help mold and develop.

The Marches approached a prominent orphanage and adoption agency called The Cradle, located in Evansville, Illinois, to find a baby—preferably a boy. Along with the Marches, such Hollywood luminaries as George Burns and Gracie Allen, Bob Hope, Al Jolson, Donna Reed, and Fred MacMurray had adopted children through The Cradle. At the orphanage, Florence told the nurse that selecting a baby is ". . . the hardest thing I've ever done in my life. How do you ever know what to do?" The nurse calmly replied, "Don't worry, Mrs. March. You'll know your baby when you see it." They were taken with a little blonde-haired boy and saw him two or three times, and they were about to make a decision on whether to adopt him when suddenly, out of a corner of the room, they heard a soft coo. They both turned and walked towards a crib. They discovered a golden-haired little girl ". . . trying to stuff her toes into her mouth." The child looked up and reached out her arms to the Marches. They couldn't resist her. They named her Penelope but called her Penny. March later said he called her "Penny-wise-and-pound foolish," and described her as "quite adorable." March would always say that he and Florence didn't adopt Penny, she adopted them.

II

Despite *Dr. Jekyll and Mr. Hyde*, March was put back into a film built more around the leading lady than himself. This time, the leading lady was Sylvia Sidney and the film was *Merrily We Go To Hell*, the final film he would make under Dorothy Arzner's direction. The cast also includes a young Cary Grant in a secondary role. Once again, March plays an alcoholic, with Sidney as his long-suffering wife who truly loves him and makes continual excuses for him.

Sidney enjoyed working with March, and even though this film— as well as a second one they would make two years later titled *Good*

Dame—is far from their best, the two have a fine chemistry together. Like many of March's leading ladies, she came to the set having heard rumors of March's womanizing ways, but, at least for her, she found the rumors to be unfounded. "Fredric March had the reputation of being a ladies' man," Sidney recalled years later. "We made two pictures together...But he never laid a finger on me, never made a pass at me! Freddie was happily married. He'd tease me by saying, 'Look at those boobs!' or 'Look at that toosh!' But it was all in fun." Rose Hobart backed this assessment up in an interview with Tom Weaver years after working with March in *Dr. Jekyll and Mr. Hyde*, "He had the worst reputation, but was probably the most faithful of all the husbands in Hollywood. He put on such an act! Oh, he'd kiss people behind the set, but that's as far as it went. Because he and Florence had this incredible relationship. She knew what was happening, but her attitude was, 'Oh, go ahead and have your fun.'"

When *Merrily We Go to Hell* was released in June of 1932, the *New York Times* praised the "excellent acting" of Sidney and March, while damning the story itself as not being "particularly interesting or edifying."

Next, Cecil B. De Mille requested, and got, March for his spectacular *The Sign of the Cross*. It was also the film that would serve as an introduction for March to the so-called "costume picture." The costume picture is usually set in an earlier period than the current and, as the title suggests, the actors are decked out in the fashions of that day.

The Sign of the Cross is one of those mammoth pre-code DeMille films that today is best known for Claudette Colbert's milk (ass's milk) bath. The oft-told tale is that Miss Colbert had to spend hours slinking about in the asses milk under intensely hot lights until the milk began to curdle and let off an especially pungent smell. "Two men with cardboard stirred up the milk at the other end of the bathtub so it would make waves," Colbert later told Rex Reed, "and the milk went below my nipples. DeMille would yell 'Cut!' till they got more milk above the censorship level. I was sweating like hell in all that hot milk!"

March was cast as Roman prefect Marcus Superbus, a military leader under Nero (Charles Laughton in his American film debut), who falls in love with a Christian girl (Elissa Landi). While Nero's wife, the lascivious Poppaea (Colbert), makes repeated attempts to seduce him.

Unlike Rose Hobart and Sylvia Sidney, Claudette Colbert had a different story to tell of her encounters with a very frisky Fredric March.

> *Freddie March was the worst womanizer I ever knew. His hands had twenty fingers, I swear, and they were always on my ass. I finally said, "If you don't stop I'll walk right out of the scene and tell Mr. DeMille what you're doing". . . So the camera rolled again. I'm on top of my throne surrounded by four blacks—they called them Nubians then, honey—and all the eunuchs. The blacks and the eunuchs were always shooting craps. Anyway, Mr. DeMille yelled "Action" and all of a sudden I felt this hand around my left cheek and I stopped and walked down to camera and demanded to see Mr. DeMille!*

Apparently, even this didn't stop March—who was in one of his Peck Bad Boy moods. The Colbert derriere was so appealing to him, he couldn't resist a pat or pinch even when the famed Hollywood photographer John Engstead was shooting publicity photographs for the film. One photo ". . . with Freddie's hand wrapped around my rear end," Colbert recalled, found its way into the *Police Gazette*. "And the caption read, 'Even if the Marines haven't landed, Freddie March seems to have the situation well in hand.'" Colbert was so appalled by this that she went to the Paramount front office and demanded that she be given approval of any photographs taken of her—the first Paramount star granted such approval—and all because of Freddie March and his "twenty" fingers!

Despite his distracting Claudette Colbert, March got on well with DeMille. Halfway through shooting, DeMille sent March a telegram that read:

WHAT A THOUGHTFUL HUMAN BEING YOU ARE AND YOU'VE MADE ME THE BEST PRESENT A DIRECTOR CAN HAVE NAMELY A REALLY GREAT ACTOR.

March later described DeMille as meticulous. "He worked everything out on paper, how many pages you would shoot per day—and by golly, you shot them. He was a tough son-of-a-gun, firing one assistant director after another. And he always jumped on the little people. He used to carry five $20 gold pieces in his pockets and jingled them like Captain Queeg."

Production on *The Sign of the Cross* ended on September 29, 1932. The film had cost $694,064—a huge sum for those days— and would go on to gross over $2.7 million—a blockbuster—giving Paramount a profit of better than $600,000. When the film was released in November, Mordaunt Hall wrote in the *New York Times*, "There is an abundance of imagination throughout...One feels, however, that the players must have been relieved when the production was finished, for all work hard and thoroughly, even those who merely figure for an instant or so in a death scene in the arena or the fortunate who are patting about their seats."

It was a telling sign that he certainly had arrived when MGM requested March's services for its prestigious production of *Smilin' Through* starring Norma Shearer. Norma was often called "The First Lady of MGM" and was the wife of its hard-working and hard-driving young production head, Irving Thalberg.

Smilin' Through is an old chestnut that had been a stage play and then a silent film that had starred Norma Talmadge. It tells the sentimental story of an embittered man whose bride died on her wedding day when she takes a bullet meant for him. Years later, his orphaned niece comes to live with him and he finds a new lease on life, until he realizes that his niece is falling in love with the son of the man who shot his bride. Shearer and March play the lovers with Leslie Howard as the uncle.

While Shearer was considered the Queen of the Lot, due primarily to her status as Thalberg's wife, she was also a talented and popular screen actress in her own right. She was at her best playing sexually aware women in such pre-code films as *The Divorcee* (which won her an Oscar as Best Actress) and *A Free Soul*, where she suggestively tells sexy tough guy Clark Gable—while she is seductively slinking back on a couch—to "C'mon and put 'em around me." However, Thalberg liked to present his wife in noble roles, and the majority of her films from here on out would portray her as the noble woman who sacrifices all for love. Of course, part of this was inevitable with the change in the production code, which made it harder for the studios to present sexually charged characters without having them pay the consequences in some way by the final reel. To direct the proceedings, Thalberg selected Sidney Franklin, who had also directed the 1922 Talmadge silent version.

Shearer had a clause in her contract that allowed only one male star to share top billing with her. She allowed a concession, which would allow both March and Howard to share billing above the title, but ". . . in type no larger than 75% of her name." Interestingly, the first time that March and Shearer had been seen together was in the early 1920s, when both were struggling actors who helped make ends meet by modeling. One magazine cover featured Norma as a wife who admires her husband's brand new socks—the young husband pictured being March. Yet, while they are pictured on the cover together they didn't pose together, and so they had their first official meeting on the *Smilin' Through* set.

The Marches eventually became social friends with both Thalberg and Shearer. There were tensions, however, due to politics. The Marches were die hard liberal democrats while the Thalberg's— especially Irving—were rock solid conservative republicans. At one of the Thalberg's Sunday brunches, the Marches were shocked and outraged when Thalberg confided that he had been one of the principal people behind a series of propaganda news reels aimed against the progressive writer Upton Sinclair, who was running for Governor of California in 1934. (One of the newsreels used by Thalberg, depicted train loads of Mexicans arriving in California with the message that Sinclair would take away American jobs and give them to the Mexicans if he was elected. Incidentally, the Mexicans depicted in the news reel came from an outtake from the MGM film *Viva Villa!*.)

March told Thalberg that he found those newsreels to be "unfair." Thalberg replied that "Nothing is unfair in politics." This went against the grain of March's progressive beliefs, in which he believed the debate between the parties should be uplifting and informative with the voter given solid choices and then making their decision based on ideas rather than personalities. After this admission by Thalberg, there was a pall cast on their relationship, which gradually thawed because of March's tremendous admiration for Thalberg's talent as a producer of high quality entertainment.

March had conflicting feelings about Shearer. At one point, he spoke of her "wonderful sincerity and poise" onscreen as well as her perfectionism, "She expected everyone else around her to give theirs along with her, and I have always tried to set the highest standards for myself, I could hardly fault her for that." He also found her demanding and on occasion difficult. He thought she was "good, really good" as an actress, but also "behaved like a primadonna."

When *Smilin' Through* was released in the fall of 1932, it turned out to be a tremendous box office success—bringing in a net profit of more than $500,000. When the film opened at the Astor Theater in New York City, the *New York Times* praised it as "infinitely more satisfying" than its silent predecessor. *Variety* thought the picture was "a bit overdone" but overall "a fine presentation." The *Chicago Daily Tribune* critic praised March: "clever, dependable, handsome, was a splendid choice for Wayne," and wrote that in some scenes with March, Shearer "appears shallow and unconvincing."

March's next role got him out of period costume and into a modern Noel Coward comedy, *Design for Living*, which teamed him with Gary Cooper and Miriam Hopkins. Ernst Lubitsch, the acknowledged master of directing romantic comedy, was known for his light "Lubitsch touch." The Lubitsch Touch was something that many filmmakers aspired to but most failed to equal. Billy Wilder was perhaps the most successful in his comedies such as *A Foreign Affair, Sabrina,* and *Love in the Afternoon.* Yet, Wilder told an American Film Institute seminar, "If I knew the formula I would tap into it." Director and film historian Peter Bogdanovich was probably the most successful in defining the Lubitsch Touch when he said:

> *It was as famous a moniker in its day as Hitchcock's "Master of Suspense," although perhaps not as superficial. The phrase does connote something light, strangely indefinable, yet nonetheless tangible, and seeing Lubitsch's films—more than in almost any other director's work - one can feel this certain spirit; not only in the tactful and impeccably appropriate placement of the camera, the subtle economy of his plotting, the oblique dialogue which*

*had a way of saying everything through indirection, but also—
and particularly—in the performance of every single player, no
matter how small the role.*

Lubitsch brought his famous touch to adapting Noel Coward's
successful play *Design for Living*, which Paramount bought for the
princely sum (of its day) of $50,000. But Lubitsch wasn't interested
in simply transferring the play to the screen. He would make
substantial changes. For one thing, the play's ménage a trois between
two men and the beautiful woman needed to be toned down for the
screen. The infamous Hay's office had taken notice of the material
as early as when the play opened on Broadway in January of 1933,
with a censor writing:

> *Despite the author's excuse for the unconventionality of the
> character's actions on the ground that they are artists and responsible,
> according, to their own code of morals, it is somewhat doubtful
> whether a motion picture audience would take that viewpoint,
> and a motion picture treatment would be faced with that basic
> difficulty.*

To adapt the play for the screen, Lubitsch hired the noted screen
writer Ben Hecht at the same $50,000 price tag that was paid to
Coward.

Lubitsch and Hecht were like oil and water. Hecht was a highly
paid and independent script writer, and Lubitsch was the kind
of director who liked to collaborate on the screenplay with the
writer. When Lubitsch suggested to Hecht that they meet every
morning to hash out the script, Hecht told him in no uncertain
terms, "I go home and write the stuff and bring it to you.
Then, if you don't like it, we fight it out." This didn't go over big
with Lubitsch, naturally, and eventually, after one too many
times of "fighting it out" with Lubitsch, Hecht threw in the towel
and began meeting every morning with the director. Lubitsch, a
former actor, liked to act out the scenes, and at one point Hecht
complained, "If he grabs me once more to show how Freddie
March is supposed to embrace (Miriam Hopkins)…I'll turn
pansy."

The Coward play was perhaps considered too avante garde for wide audience appeal outside of the major cities, or at least that is what Lubitsch thought, even though the 1931 MGM adaptation of *Private Lives* with Norma Shearer and Robert Montgomery had been fairly faithfully adapted and was a big box office hit.

The basic premise of the Coward story is kept intact. Two best friends—an artist and a writer—both fall in love with the same girl. Onstage, the two friends were played by Coward and Alfred Lunt while Lunt's wife and stage partner, Lynn Fontanne, played the object of their desire. However, in Coward the protagonists are well-to-do fun-loving snobs who are disdainful of pretty much everybody, and especially those they perceive as bores. In the Lubitsch-Hecht version, the men are not rich and they are American, trying to make a go of things in Paris. Where Coward's play is basically drawing room comedy, with the characters already well acquainted with one another, Lubitsch opens it up to show how they met, by using a superb five-minute introduction, set on a train, with the girl sketching the men as they are asleep. It is also five minutes that are dialogue free.

Miriam Hopkins was an actress that Lubitsch admired greatly and had already used to great advantage in *The Smiling Lieutenant* and especially *Trouble in Paradise*, so she was always his first choice to play the girl. However, for the men, he originally wanted Ronald Coleman and Leslie Howard—neither of whom wanted to be compared to Coward or Lunt. Fredric March was soon signed up to play the writer, with Douglas Fairbanks, Jr. as the artist, but then Fairbanks got sick with pneumonia and had to drop out of the picture. Gary Cooper, who had never played sophisticated comedy before, was a major box office star at Paramount and stepped in to play the artist.

At the beginning of production, Lubitsch called the company together and told them, "The critics will not like our picture. They will say we have ruined Noel Coward's play, and it's true our picture will be quite different. But the people who do not read reviews or care about them will love it, and Noel Coward means nothing to most of them." It was prophetic, except for the bit about audiences loving it.

The film had a relatively moderate budget of $563,000, and

filming proceeded quickly and efficiently in about six weeks. March liked Lubitsch, but found his methods a "little too meticulous in his direction of actors, but I liked the way his movies turned out." Unlike the more open *Trouble in Paradise*, the sanitized *Design for Living* doesn't quite work. It was not in the outrageously provocative form that Coward's play was and yet it wasn't considered sanitized enough for the production code—which still had problems with the story, even though Hecht's script took out most of Coward's double entendres and replaced them with some bland lines such as "Let's talk it over quietly like a disarmament conference."

Mordaunt Hall wrote in the *New York Times*, upon the film's release that:

> *The Ernst Lubitsch-Ben Hecht picture which was inspired by Noel Coward's comedy. . . may be only a skeleton of the parents work, but it has the same familiar rattle. In attacking the problem of translating the play to the screen Mr. Lubitsch was aware of the probability of censorial scowls and the chance that the English author's brilliant dialogue might be a little too lofty for some cinema audiences. . . Mr. Lubitsch, who knows his motion picture as few others do. . . wherein his own sly humor is constantly in evidence.*

The *Herald Tribune* was most critical, in saying ". . . it is, however, neither particularly witty nor properly dramatic, and so I cannot help setting it down as just a little bit of a disappointment." The film also became a box office disappointment for Paramount.

Yet, despite all of this, Lubitsch remained happy about the film and the adaptation of the play. "Motion Pictures should not talk about events in the past," he told Alistair Cooke years later in an interview in the London *Times*. "That's why I've completely changed the beginning of the play. Even on the stage this was dull. One was told where they met, what they had done for many years, how they had loved. I have to show these things, in their right order. Things on the screen should happen in the present. Pictures should have nothing to do with the past tense. The dialogue should deal with what is, not with what was."

After March played a double role as brothers in the dramatic *Strangers in Love* opposite Kay Francis, he made his next costume picture—set during *The Great War—The Eagle and the Hawk*.

Today, *The Eagle and the Hawk* probably holds the most interest as an early film of Cary Grant. But the Cary Grant of this film is a far cry from the Cary Grant most moviegoers would get to know and love in such films as *The Awful Truth, Bringing Up Baby, To Catch a Thief,* and *North by Northwest.* This is the mannered and somewhat awkward and thick-necked Grant of his early Paramount years, the one Mae West tells to "come up and see me sometime" and two years from his breakthrough role as a cockney con-man in George Cukor's superb *Sylvia Scarlett.*

The film's leading lady is Carole Lombard, but this too is not the Lombard most fans would recall as the effervescent 1930s screwball comedy queen—she would come into her own the following year with her delightful performance opposite John Barrymore in *Twentieth Century.*

March is at his best in *The Eagle and the Hawk.* Set during World War I, it's actually an anti-war film. When war breaks out, March's character is typically gung-ho as he becomes a World War I flying ace. But the death toll begins to take a toll on his psyche. The more he is lauded for his daring-do as a pilot the more he sinks into despair. It is accentuated each time members of his team die, but he keeps returning home to face more acclaim. Grant and March have an ongoing rivalry. Grant wants to pilot his own plane—rather than navigate—so that he can win some of the acclaim that comes to March.

Lombard enters the film when March seeks relaxation at a party, and she recognizes that he is a deeply troubled man. She has one great Lombard-like line. In a cab he asks her if he can drop her off somewhere. Lombard replies, "I don't want to be dropped. I want a cigarette. I think you need a glass of champagne." She becomes a safety valve for March and a sympathetic ear for him to tell his woes to. Later, when on a raid, he shoots down a plane only to reveal that the dead pilot was no older than a boy.

Later that night, a depressed March commits suicide. Grant, who finds the body, decides to hide the suicide, so he takes March up in a plane and riddles the plane and March's body with bullets and then parachutes to safety while the plane crashes—making it seem that March went down a hero rather than his death being a suicide.

The Eagle and the Hawk is a dark and biting look at heroism, the bleakness of war, and its toll on men.

William Wellman, who directed the aviation classic *Wings*, was offered first shot at directing *The Eagle and the Hawk*, but turned it down. Stuart Walker is credited as the film's director with a codirecting credit to Mitchell Leisen, but it appears that Leisen directed most of the film himself and Walker forced his sole director credit due to his contract specification. March later backed up Leisen's assertion that he directed the picture, telling Leisen's biographer, "Mitch is 100% correct in stating he directed... *The Eagle and the Hawk*...I know he certainly did the major job of directing..." Leisen loved the script, and he particularly liked the sympathetic scene between March and Lombard. He was understandably distressed when censors cut a key line. March tells Lombard that she has been "awfully kind" to him, to which Lombard replies, "I want to be kind—your place or mine?"

Filming went smoothly except for one incident, which took place on March 15, 1933, when a premature explosion of a bomb on the set brought planks, wiring, and dirt tumbling onto March, Grant, Sir Guy Standing, and Jack Oakie. None were seriously injured, although a plank did strike Grant on the head and bruised and cut the right side of his face from his temple down to his neck. March sustained several bruises. An investigation revealed that the accident occurred when a bomb—intended to blow up a dugout—exploded ahead of schedule.

The *New York Times* praised the film for its sense of realism, *Variety* felt the film was "a formula story" that was "adroitly told in dialog and action."

March re-teamed for the final time with Claudette Colbert in a film—though they would work together over twenty years later in a TV adaptation of *The Royal Family of Broadway*—which was an adaptation of Noel Coward's play "The Queen Was in the Parlor," titled *Tonight Is Ours*. It too is a costume picture but not a period piece. Colbert plays a princess on vacation in Paris who meets an American at a masquerade ball and, of course, they fall in love. If you are thinking this will be a light trifle like *Roman Holiday* you are wrong. The princess is soon called back from Paris to some mythical movie kingdom where she must assume the throne. Naturally, she is then expected to marry a member of royalty, leaving March out in the cold.

The director of record is Stuart Walker (again). Walker had a successful career as a director on the stage, but his work in films had been less than stellar, so Paramount assigned him a codirector, Mitchell Leisen—who had been in the art department and had done second unit work for Cecil B. DeMille on *The Sign of the Cross.* DeMille was happy to recommend Leisen to Paramount executives as somebody who could be of assistance to other directors when he wasn't working for DeMille.

As the Assistant Director (AD), Leisen was responsible for blocking and camera movements, while Walker was responsible for working with the actors on their performances. However, both March and Colbert found little rapport with Walker, and they ended up seeking help from Leisen, who became a friend of theirs on *The Sign of the Cross.* As time went by, Leisen pretty much took over full direction of the film as he had on *The Eagle and the Hawk*, while Walker functioned mostly as a dialogue director—though once again Walker would insist on being credited as director of the film as indicated in his contract. Leisen would later tell his biographer, "Stuart Walker had no idea what a camera was for, or about, or anything else." It was a learning process too for Leisen, who observed the great Karl Struss photographing the film. "I'd tell. . . Struss 'Let's go in, I want to get closer' and he'd say, 'Let's just change the lens.' Instead of a 30mm, he'd put a 2 inch (lens) on, and I could see the difference."

The film was modestly budgeted and utilized the sets that Ernst Lubitch had just recently shot *The Smiling Lieutenant* on, which helped Paramount save thousands of dollars. Leisen would recall Colbert and March as:

> . . . *wonderful together. They both had extensive stage training, and you had to keep them from projecting too much at times, especially in their close-ups. . . One of my shots of Freddy was so close I cut off his forehead and chin. He said, 'you can't get that close to me,' and I said, 'Yes, I can. Remember your face is going to be thirty times normal size, so whisper your dialogue, don't project at all. He did it.*

While they worked well together, it appears that Colbert had to still be wary of March's passes and wandering fingers. Leisen later told Colbert biographer Lawrence Quirk:

> *He (March) was so taken with her that it was hard to tell when he was acting his role and when he was being himself. On the set between scenes he walked around in a kind of daze—one could never figure out whether he was working himself into the mood for his role or just walking off the effects of closeness to Claudette in front of the camera. And everybody hoped and prayed his wife wouldn't come on the set.*

When released in January of 1933, The *New York Times* proclaimed *Tonight is Ours* ". . . quite a pleasant entertainment." The review focused more on the appearances of the lead actors than their actual performance, with the reviewer writing that Colbert is "almost too good looking for a Queen" while March is "handsome and efficient." But the film hardly merits more. It is pleasant, frivolous entertainment—more enlightening for the eyes than the brain.

Meanwhile, March and Paramount were at a crossroads. In five short years, March had emerged as a relatively unknown stage actor to Oscar-winning leading man. But March wasn't happy with some of the films he was being assigned and wanted more autonomy over his career. He also wanted more time off. Paramount had used him in film after film (over 30 films) in these five years, and March wanted more time between pictures so he could travel and spend time with his family. Paramount wasn't willing to let him go without a fight, and they offered a two-year renewal worth $200,000. In the end, he decided that he would complete the final three pictures of his contract. This included two lesser films—the aforementioned *Good Dame* with Sylvia Sidney, and *All of Me* with Miriam Hopkins and George Raft—and one of his best films, *Death Takes a Holiday.*

Instead, he decided he would sign a two-picture deal with 20th Century Fox where head of production Darryl F. Zanuck offered a great deal of money and script approval. Furthermore, he promised March that his first two films for the studio would be truly prestigious: *The Affairs of Cellini* and especially *Les Miserables.* The deal would allow for March to make two pictures a year for Twentieth and allow him to do outside work as well. "I have two reasons," he stated for why he decided to leave Paramount for Twentieth. "I want more money than Paramount apparently thinks I am worth, and which Mr. Darryl Zanuck is ready to pay me and I want a contract that stipulates for not more than forty weeks worth annually."

Death Takes a Holiday, the final film of March's existing Paramount contract, is just that—Death taking a three day holiday so that he can discover why men fear him. He explains that he is "weary of being misunderstood." He also wants to experience what mortal men feel. For the three days that "Death" is on holiday nothing and nobody will die, whether it be person, animal, or plant life. The main setting of the film is the Italian villa of nobleman Duke Lambert, whose son Corrado, is engaged to the beautiful and ethereal Grazia. Early in the film, it's Grazia who feels Death's presence in the form of a shadow hovering above her, as the Duke, Corrado, and a group of friends are in a speeding car on a winding hillside road, and there is almost a fatal accident. Later, alone in the garden of the villa, she feels his presence again as a shadow that passes over her "as if an icy wind seemed to touch me, only it wasn't a wind."

March makes his first appearance some twenty minutes into the picture in the form of the shadow, where he confronts Duke Lambert, who at first takes him for a prowler and attempts to shoot him, only to find his gun won't fire. Death explains to the Duke that he is a "vagabond of space—a point of contact between eternity and time." When the Duke doesn't appear to get his point, he announces he is, indeed, Death, but not to be alarmed as he has no fatal intensions. He explains his intent for taking a holiday and asks the Duke if he can be his house guest—in human form.

He takes the guise of Prince Sirki, an acquaintance of the Duke's who had recently died, but his death is unknown to the rest of the guests. For three days, he will experience the emotions of mortal man. Death/Prince Sirki is immediately taken with Grazia, and the feeling is mutual. There are also two other female guests who are attracted to him, but when they become too close to him and look into his eyes, he exposes his true nature and they recoil in fear. Grazia, however, doesn't. When, at the climax of the film, Prince Sirki tries to tell Grazia that she meant nothing to him, she knows otherwise. Finally, he reverts back to the shadowy form of Death, and he tells Grazia that she must "see me for who I really am." Grazia replies that she has "always seen him that way" and she loves him. Death realizes that the most important emotion of man is love, and Grazia willingly goes off with him, but not before he tells the others that later, "When I call, come bravely through that shadow." In other words they have nothing to fear from Death.

March gives a powerfully seductive and, at times, over-the-top performance, which is almost theatrical in nature, but it fits with the larger-than-life characters he plays in the film—Death and the Prince. He is equaled by a strong cast, many of whom Leisen had used in *Cradle Song*, including Evelyn Venable (as Grazia), Sir Guy Standing (as Lord Lambert), Kent Taylor (as Corrado) and Gail Patrick (as Rhonda Fenton, one of the other women who is attracted by Death/Prince Sirki). Other roles are filled out by Katharine Alexander, Helen Westley, Kathleen Howard, and Henry Travers. Taylor was selected for his role due to a close resemblance to March. "I wanted to get the effect over that March represented Death, and Taylor was life," Leisen later said. "She loved them both, but she loved Death more."

Venable, with her dark-haired delicate beauty was perfectly cast as Grazia. She had a stage background, and her films for Leisen— *Cradle Song* and *Death Takes a Holiday*—gave her film career a strong start. Leisen found Grazia a more complex character than that of Death. "Maxwell Anderson (who wrote the screenplay) and I had quite an argument over this," Leisen later stated. "He said Grazia had no motivation. I said that Grazia had every motivation...Her motivation is simply that she does not want to live. She wants peace and quiet, which is symbolized by death." Venable's performance is warm and less flamboyant than March's—her underplaying is a perfect counterbalance to March. They make a terrific romantic team.

While March and Venable are wonderful in their scenes together, I think the best scene in the film features March and Katharine Alexander (playing Alda—another woman who falls under Prince Sirki's spell). Alda offers herself to Prince Sirki as his bride and lover. The Prince explains to her that she would turn away from him in terror if she knew his who he really was. He tells her that she will take one step towards him, know his secret, and "lose courage."

"Try me," Alda seductively tells him.

Death tells her to look deeply into his eyes. Alda does as he commands, and the Prince's face suddenly becomes a blur of darkness and almost skull-like, causing hysteria on the part of Alda. "No! No! I want to live," she screams, as she runs away from the Prince/Death.

Death Takes a Holiday was filmed for under $400,000 in about twenty-eight days, and is a beautifully photographed film by Charles Lang—who would be nominated eighteen times for an Oscar during his career, and win once for *A Farewell to Arms*. The appearance of Death as a transparent shadow at the beginning and end of the film is superbly shot. Leisen later explained:

> *The effect of Death being transparent was very difficult to do because we wanted to do it right in the camera instead of having the lab put it in. ...We duplicated certain pieces of the set in black velvet. Then we put a mirror in front of Freddy that was only 30% silvered so that you could shoot through it. In order to make him transparent, we simply lit up certain portions of the black set which reflected in the mirror superimposed over Freddy, giving the appearance that he was transparent. Shooting through the mirror had a tendency to make a slightly soft focus, but soft focus was considered very artistic at the time.*

In the middle of filming *Death Takes a Holiday*, March came down with the flu, and he seemed to be recovering nicely when he suffered a serious relapse. Unable to do anything except lay in bed at home, with only a doctor and nurse allowed to see him, it took him more than a week to recover.

When *Death Takes a Holiday* was released in early 1934, it became an immediate smash hit with audiences—it would be Paramount's second highest money-maker for the year—and it was a critical success as well. The *New York Times* called it a "beautiful and thought-provoking film," and it would be on the *Times* list of the best of 1934. *Death Takes a Holiday* is a beautifully made film with its shadows and glorious black-and-white photography. Yes, there are long philosophical speeches, but they are delivered with such conviction that one is not bored. It was the type of picture that only Paramount, that most European of studios, could have made.

Leisen, who would go on to be one of Paramount's top directors of the '30s and into the early '40s, later asserted that, "The effect this film had on people was quite amazing." He stated that Paramount received thousands of letters saying that they no longer feared death, after seeing *Death Takes a Holiday*. "It had been explained to them in such a way that they could understand the beauty of it." By the time *Death Takes a Holiday* was completed, March had left Paramount and was working at Fox.

III

March was cast as Benvenuto Cellini, the celebrated sixteenth-century Florentine sculptor and rogue, in the first film of his Fox pact, *The Affairs of Cellini*. Constance Bennett was cast as the Duchess of Florence, and Frank Morgan was her cuckold husband. March worked hard on his role, which included a great deal of reading about Cellini and that period in history. The film also allowed him to wear a pointed beard in the film—as Cellini had done in life—and perform some acrobatic tricks on a par with Douglas Fairbanks. In the end, however, Frank Morgan's comic performance steals the show, as is evidenced by most reviews. (Morgan was also the only actor in the film nominated for an Oscar, and in the Best Actor category.) The film was made for $549,000 and earned nearly a million dollars when released, which after assorted fees and advertising costs amounted to a very modest profit. Hardly an auspicious beginning with Fox, and later on, March would concede that it was a mistake to make the film.

He then was asked to come back to MGM to work with Norma Shearer in *The Barrett's of Wimpole Street*. When Norma Shearer returned to the screen after nearly two years away—during which time she had a baby—her husband, Irving Thalberg, wanted to make sure it was in as showy and prestigious a production as any. Metro had acquired the screen rights to the 1931 Broadway play *The Barrett's of Wimpole Street*, which had been a big hit for Katharine Cornell and Brian Aherne, as they played out the love story between poets Elizabeth Barrett and Robert Browning. Thalberg believed that presenting Shearer as the invalid Barrett would be a perfect way of bringing Norma back to the screen. Shearer was dubious. She didn't want to spend almost an entire movie suffering while reclining on a sofa.

Shearer suggested that they hire Cornell to repeat her stage role on the screen, but Thalbeg didn't believe she would have the box office clout the film warranted. William Randolph Hearst had his own suggestion: cast his mistress, Marion Davies. Hearst seemed to prefer Davies in heavy, costumed, period films, which surely this one was, but Davies was at her very best in light comedy roles like *Not So Dumb* and *Blondie of the Follies.* She herself knew that she wasn't right for the part, but her beloved "W.R." insisted she would do the film. Hearst had a great deal of clout at MGM, not only because of his newspaper empire but also because a film company he created solely for Marion—Cosmopolitan Pictures—was housed at MGM. But even L. B. Mayer, who cherished his relationship with Hearst, could not imagine Marion playing Elizabeth Barrett. Reluctantly, Mayer explained to Hearst that as much as they loved Marion, the role of Barrett wasn't right for her, and Mayer suggested they build a nice comedy around her instead. Hearst, infuriated, moved Cosmopolitan from the Metro lot over to Warner Brothers.

Finally, with Davies out of the picture, Thalberg talked the reluctant Norma into making the film—and a good thing too, since *The Barretts of Wimpole Street* ended up being one of her all-time favorite films. Now it was down to the business of selecting the right leading man to play opposite Shearer. While Thalberg wasn't excited about the prospect of bringing 'Kit' Cornell to the screen to repeat her performance, he was high on bringing the young and handsome Brian Aherne (as Browning) to play opposite Norma. He had made a few films, none too distinguished, but the opportunity to play Browning on film in a classy MGM production would be a huge boost to his career, and Aherne was perfectly willing to do so until MGM insisted that in return he sign a seven-year contract with the studio. Aherne, made of stronger stuff than MGM thought, turned them down, walked away from MGM, and was soon back on Broadway—playing Mercutio in *Romeo and Juliet* with Cornell (age forty) and Basil Rathbone (age forty-one) as the love struck teenagers.

With Aherne out, Thalberg thought of March as his fallback candidate, after all, he and Norma had worked very well two years earlier in the very popular *Smilin' Through*. March was soon signed, as was Charles Laughton playing the key role of Barrett's domineering father. Domineering is just part of it. The play had suggested that Mr. Barrett may have had incestuous thoughts towards his homebound daughter, and, of course, the censors demanded that this element of the play be downplayed. Of the elimination of the incestuous thoughts, Laughton said, ". . .but they can't censor the gleam in my eye."

March wasn't too excited about playing Browning, as he later told Lawrence Quirk.

> *Let's face it, Robert Browning was a rather flighty, artificial-bonhomie type of guy. Bouncing in and out of Elizabeth's room, applying to moral adrenaline; bouncing up and down and sashaying around with Victorian style flourishes that, to me, bordered on the fey and effeminate. I realized that the character was frantically trying to get Elizabeth off that couch, and I tried to get into his psyche, but he brought out the worst ham elements in me, and I feel I failed in the role.*

Despite this, *The Barrett's of Wimpole Street* was reviewed well and helped add allure to March's box office performance by becoming one of the biggest hits of the year.

At around this time, the Marches thought it was high time that Penny had a sibling to play with, and they again made arrangements through The Cradle to adopt a little boy. A baby boy was born on January 19, 1934, and when he was six months old, the Marches took him home. The boy, whose name was Gerald Frank Perkins, was formally adopted on August 29, 1935, after a year of living with the Marches. (In California law, a year must elapse before final adoption papers are issued.) From the beginning, they decided to call him and formally name him Anthony (or Tony for short) after March's character in *The Royal Family*.

With their expanding family, the Marches built a $100,000 French provincial mansion in Holmby Hills—an affluent area bordered by Beverly Hills on the east, Westwood on the west, Bel Air on the

north, and exclusive Wilshire Boulevard on the South. The heart of
the house, where family and friends would congregate, was the
playroom. The room was a replica of a Dutch Kitchen and was
dominated at one end by a huge stone fireplace. The other end led
to a movie projection room, with a screen that rose electronically
from the floor. A door off of the living room led to a huge stone
terrace, where the family would enjoy eating their meals when the
weather obliged. Beyond the terrace, the lawn sloped towards a
swimming pool, complete with equipment that illuminated the
pool for night swimming. Beyond the pool were the gardens.

Both Marches had their own bedrooms; March's bedroom was
furnished in masculine brown tones and paneling. There was a
separate dressing/exercise room and bathroom. Each morning,
March had a trainer come in who put him through his paces—to
maintain that movie star physique—followed by a rubdown. There
was a separate wing built especially for the children. Each child had
his/her own room, divided by a nurse's room, a bathroom, and a
kitchen. For added protection, the windows in the children's wing
were covered with steel bars and securely padlocked. The Lindbergh
baby kidnapping and murder were still fresh in the minds of many
people, especially celebrities, and the Marches were not alone in
trying to make sure that their home was protected against possible
intruders. "I'll have to work a good many years yet to reach
complete security for myself and my family," March admitted.
"If I'm fortunate as I hope and trust I will be, our family will be
well taken care of as long as necessary."

Both Florence and March loved Christmas, and they would later
specify in their theater contracts that they have Christmas off to
enjoy with their family, rather than give a performance. They wanted
Christmas to be special for their children as well. They constructed
what they called "The Christmas Room" above a large garage on
this property and explained to columnist Gladys Hall that, "The
children…must believe in Santa Claus for as long as possible and
we figured that we could manage better if we had an outside room
where we could put the Christmas toys and not have to bring them
into the house until Christmas Eve."

Parenthood suited both March and Florence. For Florence it allowed
her a creative outlet that she simply wasn't getting in Hollywood.

March believed that no family was complete without children. He had grown up with a close and loving family, and even though Penny and Tony were adopted, neither March nor Florence ever treated them as less than their own. "I can't imagine now what the house would be like without children in it," March told columnist Gladys Hall.

> *Without Penny and Tony specifically. I can't imagine what it would be to live without children's toys all around the place, children's parties, even children's problems—and they are plenty...We have no inhibitions about our children. We can rave about their beauty, marvel at their cleverness, boast and brag about them to our heart's content and no one can say, or think, 'Well, they think they did pretty well, don't they?' And it's very gratifying...to watch Penny and Tony taking on some of the better characteristics of their proud parents...Penny, for instance, speaking with the lilt in Florence's voice. Things like that."*

When asked if they will one day tell their children that they were adopted, March replied:

> *Yes...of course. We'll tell them in the way other parents who have adopted children have done. We'll tell them that other children just come to their parents and their parents have to take them as they are. But that their mother and daddy adopted them, chose them from all the little boys and girls there are in the world just because they were Penny and Tony and no one else at all. We'll make them proud of being adopted, able to feel secure about it.*

About two months after Tony came to live with them, March and Florence made plans to take a two-month vacation to Tahiti. "I especially wanted to go to Tahiti because I have been told that a movie actor is less an object of curiosity and attention there than anywhere else we could go," March explained. "I understand that most of their pictures are three years old, at least, and that their interest in screen actors is very naïve and detached." Accompanying them on the trip would be their good friends: the writer J (John) Ainsworth Morgan (whose best known book was *Oxford Observations by an American*, published in 1925) and his wife Phyllis.

The Marches and Morgans left from San Francisco on August 29, 1934, for a ten-day cruise to Tahiti. Penny and Tony were left behind; Penny was now two years old and Tony only eight months. "The fact that we'd be two months away from Tony and Penny sort of took the edge off things," March later told the readers of *Photoplay*. "They're swell kids and it'll be the first time we've ever left them for so long. Florence insists that they won't even remember us when we get home. Of course Tony won't, but Penny's two, now and she should." In the meanwhile, Uncle Jack and his wife would look after them, along with the Marches nurse, Nana.

While in Tahiti, they took in all the sites, which included the leper colony of Papeete, where March and the Morgans journeyed inside, but Florence decided to stay in the car. "We who did go were badly shaken by what we saw," March later recalled. "I was scared pink when the whole French hospital staff insisted on shaking hands! Evidently the disease isn't as contagious as we imagine it to be . . . But the period of incubation of the disease can extend up to six years, so for that long I'll be inspecting myself for spots at least three times daily."

But, for most of the trip, the Marches and the Morgans were content to lie on the beach and soak up the sun, sail, visit market places, and sightsee in general. They returned in late October, and were reunited with the children before both Marches began work on *Les Miserables*.

Les Miserables became March's second film under the Fox contract, and it is one of his best and most remembered films of that period. Based on Victor Hugo's classic 1862 novel, it tells the story of Jean Valjean, who at the beginning is jailed for trying to steal bread to feed to his sister and her many children. In the course of his incarceration, he attempts to escape many times extending his sentence. Finally he is released, but due to being a convict, he is rejected by society. Through the intercession of Bishop Myriel, he finds a compassionate friend and he begins to begin to turn his life around. However, through an accident he is charged with armed robbery and is pursued again. He takes on an assumed name, and for the next several years he leads an honest and productive life— even building a business and a fortune—but all along he is pursued by the fanatical Inspector Javert, who has made it his life's mission to capture Valjean.

In addition to March, the stellar cast includes Charles Laughton as Valjean, Cedric Hardwicke (not yet a 'Sir') as the Bishop, Rochelle Hudson as Cosette, and Florence—in her second screen role opposite March—as Fantine, mother of Cosette. Polish-born Richard Boleslawski, a proponent and teacher of the Stanislavsky method of acting, is the director. Boleslawski had already directed such highly regarded films as *Rasputin and Empress* (with all three Barrymore's: Ethel, John and Lionel), *The Painted Veil* (with Garbo), and *Clive of India*.

While the film gives strong weight to the trials and tribulations— as well as the desperate conditions of early-nineteenth-century Paris— Studio head and producer Darryl F. Zanuck wanted to emphasize the love story between Valjean and Cosette (Hudson). Zanuck's comments were recorded in conference notes when discussing the screenplay with the writers:

> *The romance between Jean Valjean and Cosette is the most important element of the story and should be developed. His feeling for her when he first takes her is one of attachment. This later develops into devotion and culminates in her being his life blood. By treating it this way, the scene where he finally gives her up will absolutely slaughter audiences. This treatment will strike a human note in the picture and make it something much more important than just a finely conceived melodrama.*

On this film, Zanuck provided March with some star perks, including a one-room house/dressing room painted two shades of green outside, with a white interior finished in black and red to give it a masculine look. It contained a lounge, an electric stove, an electric refrigerator, a built-in water stand with running—electrically heated—water, two wardrobe closets, and a radio.

When the film was released at the Rivoli Theater in New York, in late April of 1935, it broke box office records and would go on to post a healthy profit for Fox—despite costing nearly a million dollars to produce, a huge sum for those days—more than making up for the mediocre showing of *The Affairs of Cellini*. Furthermore, the reviews were on the ecstatic side. The *New York Times* critic wrote, "Mr. March's Valjean is a flawless thing, strong and heartbreaking." Kate Cameron in The *New York Daily News* wrote, "March has never been better... than as he brings a famous literary character to life on the screen." The *New York World Telegram* raved, "As Valjean, Fredric March is splendid, giving a performance that is rare for its sincerity and comprehension."

Despite the reviews, March was not nominated for an Oscar. The Best Actor category was dominated by the three leads of MGM's *Mutiny on the Bounty* (Clark Gable, Charles Laughton, and Franchot Tone) and the fourth nominee, Victor McLauglin won for his performance in John Ford's *The Informer*. It's a shame because March's Valjean is certainly the equal of any of those performances. The film, however, was nominated for four Academy Awards: Best Picture, Best Director, Best Cinematography (for Gregg Toland), and Film Editing.

IV

Greta Garbo had already filmed the Leo Tolstoy novel *Anna Karenina* as a silent film titled *Love*, back in 1927, opposite the man who would become her real-life lover, John Gilbert. MGM decided the time was right to do a sound version of the film, and again it wanted Garbo to play the leading role, but Gilbert was in no way considered to repeat his role opposite Garbo. He had left MGM with a mortal enemy of the tyrannical head of the studio, Louis B. Mayer. He and Garbo had reunited a couple of years before, in *Queen Christina*, getting that film only through the insistence of Garbo. Besides, Gilbert was a very sick man. He was a troubled alcoholic who was throwing up blood and being nursed by the sympathetic Marlene Dietrich. He would be dead by January of 1936, at the age of thirty-eight.

The film is produced by David O. Selznick, in his brief period as a producer, toiling away at MGM, and resenting the snickering jokes about "the son-in-law also rises," referring to his relationship as the son-in-law to MGM chief Louis B. Mayer. Of course, Selznick had a good reputation on his own—especially for his work as head of production at RKO prior to coming to MGM. Selznick very much wanted to present a new Greta Garbo, in modern dress, in a modern picture, rather than in some dusty remake of one of her old silent films. Garbo was not enthused and wanted to stick to her tried and true formula.

Selznick wrote to her on January 7, 1935, telling her that: "We have lost our enthusiasm for a production of *Anna Karenina* as your next picture. I, personally, feel that audiences are waiting to see you in a smart, modern picture and that to do a heavy Russian drama on the heels of so many ponderous, similar films, in which they have seen you and other stars recently would prove a mistake."

He had another picture in mind for her, *Dark Victory*, which had been a Broadway play with Miriam Hopkins that hadn't quite lit up the great white way. But it was modern and a tear jerker, with a sympathetic role for Garbo in which she would gracefully face death at the end. He wanted to buy it for her before RKO snatched it up for Katharine Hepburn.

Garbo had very much wanted Fredric March as her leading man in *Anna Karenina*, and Selznick thought that March would be a wonderful leading man opposite Garbo too, but he preferred to have him cast opposite her as the doctor/lover in *Dark Victory*. "Further Fredric March will only do *Anna Karenina* if he is forced by his employers, Twentieth Pictures," Selznick wrote Garbo. "He has told me repeatedly that he is fed up on doing costume pictures; that he thinks it a mistake to do another…Mr. March is most anxious to do a modern picture and I consider his judgment about himself very sound. We are doubly fortunate in finding in *Dark Victory* that the male lead is also strikingly well suited to Mr. March."

As most film buffs know, Garbo didn't make *Dark Victory*—Bette Davis starred opposite George Brent in the 1939 Warner Brothers classic—but she did make *Anna Karenina*, with Fredric March as her leading man. (Though Selznick later wrote to MGM chairman Nick Schenck that "I begged for Gable, but I got March.")

The reason that Garbo wanted to make *Anna Karenina* was because she was dissatisfied with the ending of *Love*, which she thought unrealistically happy. She wanted the new film to be more faithful to the sadder ending of the novel. March plays dashing Count Vronsky opposite Garbo's Anna. The film tells the story of the wife of a Russian government official (an appropriately ruthless Basil Rathbone) who falls in love with a military officer (March). This leads to the ruin of her marriage, the loss of her social position, and accusations of her being an unfit mother, which cause her to be prohibited from seeing her loving son (Freddie Bartholomew). Selznick surrounded Garbo with her usual crew, including cinematographer William Daniels and her favorite director, Clarence Brown.

MGM had often used Garbo's films as a way of building up their roster of leading men. Thus, early in their careers, actors like Clark Gable (in 1931's *Susan Lenox: Her Rise and Fall*), Robert Montgomery (in 1932's *Inspiration*) and Robert Taylor (in 1936's *Camille*) were cast opposite her, and their careers benefitted in the process. With March, they didn't need to build him up. He was already one of the most sought after leading men in the country, and an Oscar-winning actor to boot. Despite his own achievements, Garbo would get top billing, as usual.

March liked Garbo but wasn't intimidated by the idea of working with her, as the young and inexperienced Robert Taylor would be on her next film, *Camille*. "As the saying went at the time, costarring with Garbo hardly constituted an introduction," March later said. He already knew her, not well, but through his friendship with John Gilbert. In the early thirties, March spent a lot of time playing tennis with Gilbert at Gilbert's home, and inevitably there would be Garbo, who March recalled as just "another vital, healthy, strong Swedish girl."

By the time she was making *Anna Karenina* with March, Garbo was more reserved and suspicious. Still, March found her to be warm (at times) and friendly. In between scenes, they would occasionally bounce a medicine ball back and forth, and on other occasions she would strip to the waist and sunbathe at some secluded part of the back lot. The first time she did that in March's presence, she asked him if it embarrassed him, and March assured her it did not. Despite her apparently stripping in front of him, Garbo was warned about March's reputation as a womanizer. One of her biographers reported that she would chew on garlic prior to love scenes as a "deterrent against unwanted advances."

On the set, they were formal with one another. He was "Mister

March" to her, and she was "Miss Garbo" to him. March would recall that Garbo was "always so afraid, shy, everything bothered her." Garbo had an ironclad rule that anybody who wasn't absolutely necessary shouldn't watch her on the set when she was filming a scene. March violated this once, as he watched her film an especially poignant scene, and then went to congratulate her on the performance:

"Really, you were looking at me, Mr. March?" she asked

"But yes, Miss Garbo."

"Please you should not look at me, Mr. March. It is embarrassing."

Perhaps the relationship most beautifully portrayed in the film is that of Karenina and her son Sergei, who was well acted by Freddie Bartholomew. In fact, it seemed as if the warm relationship between the two was being duplicated offscreen. Bartholomew would recall that off camera Garbo would cover his face with kisses and caress him and tell him how she loved him. Then, one day, an uncle asked Bartholomew if he could get him Garbo's autograph. Bartholomew arrived on the set, and Garbo saw him, immediately kissed him, and began caressing him. Then it happened. A somewhat shy Bartholomew asked if he could have an autographed photo. Immediately, he felt her frost over and she told him, "No, I do not give pictures." For the rest of the filming she was reserved to Bartholomew, and while their scenes on camera continued to be loving—offscreen it became merely correct, much to Bartholomew's great disappointment.

So many people had been captivated by Garbo's beauty, including many of her leading men, but March wasn't one of them. "Actually I was not overwhelmed by Garbo's beauty. I think at the time women were more attracted to her than men."

March later contrasted the love scenes between Garbo in this film and in the silent version.

> I have some passionate love scenes with Garbo… When I saw the finished picture, I couldn't help feeling that we might have made those scenes more intense—had we been allowed. We saw the silent version before we started on the talkie, you know. My part is really quite different from John Gilbert's when Love was made; Garbo had not quite reached the heights, while Gilbert was at the

top of his fame as a romantic lover. His role dominated the whole picture. He was billed above Garbo too. In the talkie, my part is comparatively short. I still have a number of love scenes with Garbo, as I admitted just now—but they are nothing so tempestuous as in the silent film.

He could have mentioned that might have been because the relationship between Garbo and Gilbert was much more intense than the relationship between himself and Garbo.

Anna Karenina was marketed as "Garbo's Tenth Anniversary Film" and opened at the Capitol Theater in New York on August 30, 1935, to tremendous box office and excellent reviews. In the *New York Times*, Andre Sennwald wrote, "Miss Garbo, the first lady of the screen, sins, suffers and perishes, illustriously, in the new ably produced and comparatively mature version of the Tolstoy classic." Most of the review focuses on Garbo—it really is her film—but March "performs handsomely," as the count, according to the critic. About the only criticism of the film that Sennwald offers was of young Freddie Bartholomew, whose scenes he finds "phony." *Variety* enjoyed the performances of the lead actors. They thought that Garbo had "grown" as an actress since *Love* and that it showed on screen in *Anna Karenina*, ". . . there is no flaw to be found" in her performance. March was deemed as "firm" in his depiction of Count Vronsky. Overall, *Variety* found *Anna Karenina* to be superior to the silent version and more faithful to the source novel.

The film went on to earn over $2.3 million at the box office. Garbo won the New York Film Critics' Award and the film was selected as the best foreign film at the Venice Film Festival. In addition, *Anna Karenina* was named one of the ten best films of 1935 by *Film Daily.*

Originally intended for Madeleine Carroll, *The Dark Angel* turned out to be Merle Oberon's first film under contract to Samuel Goldwyn. Goldwyn cast Oberon opposite the man she was having a red-hot affair with, Leslie Howard. But when the affair cooled and then ended, Oberon decided she didn't want to work with Howard and reluctantly he was dropped from the film. An SOS went out to March, who signed on for a fee of $125,000.

Goldwyn selected Norma Shearer's favored director, Sidney Franklin, to direct *The Dark Angel,* and when he heard that Howard was out and March was in, he sent an angry telegram to Goldwyn:

...I CAN UNDERSTAND OBERON WITH HOWARD
BUT I CANT VERY WELL UNDERSTAND OBERON
ALONE STOP WITHOUT HOWARD AND WITH
MARCH I WOULD WANT A GIRL THAT COULD GIVE
ME A GREAT PERFORMANCE BY ACTING ABILITY
AND EXPERIENCE STOP THE SOLE REASON I
THOUGHT YOU WERE NEGOTIATING WITH OBERON
WAS IN ORDER TO GET THE OTHER PERSON WITH
HER.

March stayed.

One of the screenwriters on the film was playwright Lillian
Hellman, who was in Hollywood with her lover, Dashiell Hammett,
who was working at MGM on *The Thin Man* pictures. Hellman
had recently had a big hit on Broadway with *The Children's Hour*,
which Goldwyn bought and would produce the following year as
These Three with Oberon, Miriam Hopkins, and Joel McCrea.
Goldwyn brought Hellman out to adapt the script for *These Three*,
and she ended up working on *The Dark Angel*. Hellman found the
job to be "easy money and easy hours", but referred to the film itself
as an "old silly."

The Dark Angel is a remake of a well-regarded 1925 silent film,
which had starred Ronald Coleman and Vilma Bankley—also
produced by Goldwyn. It's a four hanky effort about a woman
pursued by two different childhood friends (March and Herbert
Marshall). She loves both of them, but is more in love with the
March character. The two men go off to fight World War I, and they
both return, but the March character is blind. He makes the decision
that he doesn't want to become a burden to Oberon, and he takes
on an assumed name and leads her and others to believe he died in
the war.

March admitted that, like on *Anna Karenina*, he saw the silent
version of *The Dark Angel*. "Colman was superb in it," March said.
"I don't think I could have played the part in the silent film,
because it was all pantomime, of course. But I did take one tip from
Colman. His acting—and his love-making too—were so beautifully

restrained and so sensitive. I have tried to keep the character restrained as well."

The film turned out to be a winner with both critics and audiences. The *New York Times* gave it a positive review and noted, "Fredric March...continues to be lacking in good common sense in his relations with his screen loves. At the Capitol, you will remember, he is deserting Greta Garbo five times a day in his passion to go to war. Now in 'The Dark Angel' he pretends that he is dead in order to escape marrying the lyric Miss Merle Oberon." The critic for the *New York World Telegram* wrote, "Produced with the same irreproachable taste that characterizes all of Samuel Goldwyn's productions and acted to utter perfection by Fredric March, Merle Oberon, Herbert Marshall. . . ."

In 1936, Fredric March would make three films. The first was *The Road to Glory* for director Howard Hawks. This would be the only time that March and Hawks would collaborate, and it's not especially high in the career canon of either man—though it does have superb moments.

Set during World War I, *The Road to Glory* tells the story of the French Army's Fifth Company under the direction of Captain Larouce (Warner Baxter) whose methods are under scrutiny due to high casualty rates. March plays Lt. Denet, untested on the battle field and yet among those who question Larouce's methods. As usual with Hawks, there is a woman who intensifies the rivalry between the two men: a nurse played by June Lang. Lionel Barrymore is added to the mix as Larouce's father—who is assigned as the oldest private in the unit.

Darryl Zanuck purchased the American rights to a French filmed, *Les Craix de Blois (Wooden Crosses)*, which had been based on a novel of the same name. It was highly popular in Europe due to its unrelenting anti-war message. In fact, it had made its debut at the Geneva Disarmament Conference of 1932.

Zanuck bought the rights to the film mainly for its raw and realistic battle footage. He correctly surmised that this would save the studio thousands of dollars on the budget. Zanuck then approached Hawks to help adapt the script and direct it. Hawks later recalled that the French film had "marvelous footage in it" and was especially thrilled with its depictions of soldiers making their way to the front, through trenches during the night.

Using this footage, Hawks crafted a film that really had no relation to the French film or novel material. He also enlisted William Faulkner and Joel Sayre to write the screenplay. They fashioned a script that was similar to Hawks's earlier *The Dawn Patrol*, which dealt with the similar theme of a commander who sends his men to their deaths.

Hawks needed to inter-splice new night scenes with the footage from the original film. The new scenes were shot outdoors in late February and early March and were especially difficult due to an unexpected Southern California cold spell. "I was covered with mud and dust throughout most of the picture," March later recalled. "My face was streaked with it. My boots and uniform were caked with it. I was happy—for I could forget personal appearances for the camera's sake. I was free to concentrate entirely on the job of acting." The cinematographer was the superb Gregg Toland, who had only recently photographed March in both *Les Misérables* and *The Dark Angel*. Toland had the difficult task of making sure the new night footage matched that of the footage that was going to be used from the French film. Toland succeeded impressively.

Hawks was not at all pleased with his leading lady. He initially auditioned an alluring young actress named Clara Sheridan, and while impressed with her poise and beauty, he couldn't at the time do anything about a thick Texas accent she had. Later on, he would use this same actress, who now called herself Ann Sheridan, in his classic 1948 comedy *I was a Male War Bride*, opposite Cary Grant.

Hawks, stuck with Lang, was hard on her, but Lang had a supporter in Zanuck, so there wasn't anything he could do about it. "We'd have got more if we'd had a more experienced actress," Hawks later said of Lang. (Lang wasn't exactly inexperienced. She had already worked as Laurel and Hardy's leading lady in the film *Bonnie Scotland* and had given Shirley Temple able support in both *Captain January* and *Wee Willie Winkie*, which had been directed by John Ford.) For her part, Lang enjoyed working with both Fredric March and Warner Baxter. "At 19 it was exciting having established stars like...March and...Baxter for leading men...Those two fellows had a grand sense of humor and I was treated kindly by both of them. It was a very happy atmosphere, which came as a welcome relief from the tense war scenes we had to play."

Hawks was no pacifist, and he did not intend this film to be another *All Quiet on the Western Front*. He later said, "I've never made a picture to be anti-anything or pro anything...I used that theme from *The Dawn Patrol*...and the theme is very simple. It's a man who's in command and sends people out to die and then he's killed himself and some other poor bastard has to send them out to die." Yet, at times, the script does allow us to question the futility of war:

NURSE: What sense does it make just to be brave? Why do you all have to die?

DENET: That question has been asked as many times as men have died, but the answer hasn't satisfied anybody or stopped men from killing each other.

When *The Road to Glory* opened that August of 1936, at the Rivoli Theater in New York, it proved to be a big hit, and it broke house records on its opening weekend. It went on to do well in other cities across the country to enjoy a modest box office run. Frank Nugent in the *New York Times* wrote, "Even though it is a stirring, dramatic and vivid picture, that should not defend it; war should not be considered dispassionately; we should not be beguiled into liking a film that regards it as so. And yet, resentfully or not, we must confess that we did." Nugent found the cast to be "faultless."

Mary of Scotland, March's next assignment of 1936, had been a prestigious hit on Broadway during the 1933-1934 season when RKO bought the play intent on casting Katharine Hepburn as Mary and Bette Davis as Elizabeth. Davis was excited about having the opportunity to work opposite Hepburn, but her home studio, Warner Brothers, refused to lend her out. Thus, we missed the one great opportunity of having the two greatest female stars of their era work together in a film.

Set in 1561, *Mary of Scotland* is the story of the recently widowed Mary Stuart (Hepburn) returning to her native Scotland to rule as

Queen, despite the opposition of her cousin, Queen Elizabeth I. Much of the picture also revolves around Mary's love for the Earl of Bothwell, and the tragic turn that ultimately becomes her fate when she chooses love over ambition.

To play Bothwell, the studio engaged March at a fee of $125,000—nearly three times what Hepburn would receive in playing the central role. By the terms of her contract, Hepburn was given top billing in every picture she made at RKO. March had no problem conceding the point, since he realized that her role was much more important than his and because his salary would certainly compensate for it.

With Davis out of the picture, the studio considered Tallulah Bankhead for Elizabeth, but her box office track record was not good, so producer Pandro Berman decided to look elsewhere. He asked March if Florence might be available and if she might be interested. The answer to both questions was an unqualified yes. However, Florence probably had less box office allure than did Bankhead, but she would certainly come cheaper. The studio tested her, and the test convinced them that she would be ideal in the part and signed her on for a flat $20,000 fee.

When it came to who would be director, Hepburn expressed interest in her favorite—George Cukor—who would also have been welcomed by the Marches, but RKO had recently lost a fortune on a Hepburn-Cukor film, *Sylvia Scarlett*, and didn't want any part of Cukor. Instead, Berman employed one of Hollywood most respected directors, John Ford.

Ford was a superb director, but also a mercurial man. He very often found somebody on the film he would torment throughout the shooting—usually a younger, more inexperienced player that he could bully into giving the performance he wanted. At other times, he didn't hesitate to go after the star, but on *Mary of Scotland*, Ford was relatively sedate. He had too much respect for March and he became captivated by Hepburn, who took to calling him by his Irish name, Sean. Ford turned out to be Hepburn's kind of man—strong, domineering, and needy. He was also an alcoholic, and when confronted with this type of man—Spencer Tracy was another example—it brought out a tenderness that Hepburn didn't ordinarily exhibit.

March liked working with Ford, and this was to be their only film together. He recalled approaching Ford to get his suggestions on how to interpret the role of Bothwell, and Ford, sucking on a dirty old handkerchief, would look up at March and say, "He's a comic, just a comic." Ford then asked March to let Florence know that he didn't want any "preconceived ideas about how she was to play Elizabeth." So March, naturally, asked Ford how he saw the character of Elizabeth. "Elizabeth's a comic," the salty Ford replied, "Just a comic." March recalled saying, "Jesus, there sure are a lot of comics in this movie."

Mary of Scotland turned out to be RKO's second most expensive film of the year, costing $860,000—only *Swing Time* with Fred Astaire and Ginger Rogers cost more. When the film opened at Radio City Music Hall in New York City, the reviews were generally good. Nugent, in the *Times*, called the film "a richly produced, dignified and stirring dramatic filming of one of the most colorful periods and personalities." The *New York Sun* lauded the two lead performances, "Mr. March, although a trifle on the sober side (so much for being a comic!) still does well by the loyal and swaggering Bothwell...Hepburn almost makes up for *Sylvia Scarlett*." Despite doing well in major cities *Mary of Scotland* failed to return a profit. It grossed $1.2 million worldwide, leaving a $200,000 loss on the RKO ledger and added to Hepburn's then growing reputation as "box office poison."

Anthony Adverse was a 1,224 page, two-and-three-quarter-pound historical novel that became an instantaneous best seller when published in the summer of 1933. It became a sensation in the publishing world and the most talked about book until *Gone with the Wind* came out three years later. Its tagline was: "The adventures of a soul in quest of the ultimate truth." The story of a young boy who emerges as an adventurous young man, with his exploits set in nineteenth-century Europe, Africa, America, and Cuba, was bound to become highly sought after by Hollywood. The bidding was especially strong by MGM, Samuel Goldwyn, and Warner Brothers, with Warners ultimately winning the rights with its $40,000 bid.

This was to be a sprawling, lavish production, and one of the most prestigious films produced by Warner Brothers up to this time. Indeed, its budget would be in excess of a million dollars—a very high figure for that time. Hal Wallis, head of production of Warner Brothers, assigned Mervyn LeRoy to direct the film. LeRoy made his reputation at Warner Brothers by directing such gritty social dramas as *I Am a Fugitive from a Chain Gang* and *Little Caesar*. This would be one of LeRoy's final films for the studio before he departed for MGM—ironically not as a director but as a producer (and whose first project there would be *The Wizard of Oz*).

The job of adapting a novel of over 1,200 pages was given to Sheridan Gabney (who had written the screenplays for *I Am a Fugitive from a Chain Gang* and *The House on 56th Street*) with assistance by the uncredited Miton Krims and Edward Chodorvov. The finished screenplay came to 195 pages: enough to produce a film of nearly three and one-half hours.

Who to cast as the in the lead role? Warner Brothers had Paul Muni, for prestige. They also had a young newcomer who had shown such promise in *Captain Blood* the previous year, but instead they decided to cast Errol Flynn in a remake of *The Charge of the Light Brigade*. They considered borrowing Clark Gable from MGM, but Gable had just recently made the adventurous *Mutiny on the Bounty* and neither he nor Metro was interested.

Fredric March had considerable experience as a robust hero of several costume pictures and agreed to star in *Anthony Adverse* at a fee of $15,000 per week with a guarantee of twelve weeks. Rounding out the cast are Olivia de Havilland as the heroine, Claude Rains, Louis Hayward, Edmund Gwenn and, in her film debut, Gale Sondergaard. For the key role of Anthony as a boy, it was proposed that Freddie Bartholemew be borrowed from MGM, but that proved impossible, given his popularity at the time and commitments to his home studio, so the role went to newcomer Billy Mauch, who they felt resembled a young Fredric March.

Following his selection to play Adverse, March traveled on an ocean voyage to Europe. He left with a copy of the novel and a 200 page synopsis from Mervyn LeRoy. It was clear that March was going to immerse himself in all things Adverse while on this voyage. When he returned, he was asked how the crossing had been, and with tongue firmly in cheek, he replied, "Very Adverse."

When the script was presented to the Breen Office to get their input on any censorship problems, it came back with forty pages crossed out. "Their notations said that we couldn't film those forty pages, because the hero was naked in one scene, when he was a little boy," LeRoy later related in his memoirs. "I was furious. I had never done a picture that contained anything offensive in it—I never would—and I resented their lack of trust." After several days of meetings between LeRoy and the head censor himself, Joseph Breen, a compromise was arrived at, where LeRoy would film the scene as written, and then if Breen still wasn't satisfied, he could cut as he pleased. When the film was later presented to Breen, "He didn't object to a single frame," even though the little boy was still nude, he was seen from a distance of a block away. (Interestingly the Breen office approved the depiction of Anthony's mother as a scheming and adulteress wife who makes it through without getting any comeuppance.)

The film was shot in seventy-two days without major difficulty, and preview audiences liked most of what they saw, except for its length, which came in at slightly over three hours. The film was soon twiddled down to 141 minutes of adventure and pageantry, but seen today it seems more like a picturesque—and overlong—travel log than anything else. One problem is that despite its length, its structure is rather rushed, since it has its dashing hero running off from one adventure to another in some distant land. By the time the viewer gets involved in one plotline, Anthony is up and off again. Another problem, unfortunately, is March. At thirty-eight, he is twenty years too old to play the eighteen-year-old Anthony—as is his age when he first comes into the film—and it shows. It's also hard to relate or cheer for a character who is, at one point in the film, an African slave trader—even though he does redeem himself. Still, March gives a performance of verve and determination. The rest of the cast does very well, particularly Sondergaard, whose conniving housekeeper is one of the joys of the film, and was a performance that won her the first Oscar for Best Supporting Actress.

When the film was released in late August of 1936, it became a big box-office hit despite some less than enthusiastic reviews. Frank Nugent in the *New York Times* found the film "bulky, rambling and indecisive." Nugent found praise for the cast with the pivotal exclusion of March who he found "thoroughly spiritless." On the other hand,

Variety lauded March, ". . . playing his role to the hilt. . . March is convincing through a varied series of moods and portrayals," though they too find the film "a bit choppy and. . . long winded."

In addition to Sondergaard's Oscar, the film was nominated for five other Oscars, including Best Picture and Best Art Direction, and it won for Best Cinematography (Gaetano Gaudio), Editing (Ralph Dawson) and Score (Erich Wolfgand Korngold).

After completing these latest three costume pictures, March was finally ready to move on. He declared:

> *I want to do light comedy roles—modern things with a puckish humour to them. Three of the best pictures I have made are The Royal Family, Design for Living and Laughter. In these I played this type of role...I never wanted to dress up and act in costume. Yet I have done fifteen costume pictures. Eight of these had me in military uniform...I have no objection to doing a moderate number of costume pictures. Once I get into them, I feel they are just the sort of thing I should be doing. But I am perverse. I still maintain that I want to stick to modern comedy.*

He gave *It Happened One Night* and *The Thin Man* as examples of the type of picture he wanted to start making.

To his rescue came independent producer David Selznick, who indeed did have a comedy for him—and a terrific one it would be—but he also had a dramatic picture too, with a role that gave March one of his all-time best performances.

CHAPTER SEVEN
INTERLUDE: TWO FOR SELZNICK–1937

In the fall of 1936, Fredric March signed a deal to make two films for independent producer David Selznick. Selznick would pay March $125,000 for each film for the tidy sum of $250,000—or the equivalent of over $4,000,000 in 2012. (The fee paid to March by Selznick was in no small part due to the negotiations of March's new agent—Myron Selznick, brother of David.)

Selznick and March had known each other since the early Paramount years, where Selznick had a hand in producing *Sarah and Son, Manslaughter,* and *Laughter.* Later, when Selznick went to MGM briefly as a unit producer under his father-in-law, Louis B. Mayer, Selznick cast March in his production of *Anna Karenina* opposite Greta Garbo. In 1936, Selznick departed MGM and began his own independent studio—Selznick International Pictures (SIP).

Selznick had a fondness for big productions based on famous novels. The first film for SIP was *Little Lord Fauntleroy*, based on the Frances Hodgson Burnett novel and starring Freddie Bartholomew, who Selznick had a particular appreciation for having cast him in both *David Copperfield* and *Anna Karenina* at MGM. *Fauntleroy* was an overly sentimental but beautifully photographed film which returned a profit of nearly $500,000 to SIP. The second SIP feature of 1936, *The Garden of Allah*, was likewise based on a novel and featured two star names: Charles Boyer and Marlene Dietrich. Unlike *Fauntleroy, The Garden of Allah* proved to be a box office dud—and was one of the films which helped to label Dietrich "Box Office poison."

Unlike the major studios, SIP could only afford to make two or three pictures a year. However, this was fine with Selznick. He was very much a hands-on producer and took charge of every aspect of his productions. Selznick had tremendous respect for Irving Thalberg, who at his peak as head of production at MGM was executive producer of nearly every picture that came out of Metro, but Selznick couldn't see how one man, even one as gifted as Thalberg, could truly put his personal imprint on so many films. "It is impossible for 40 or 50 productions to go through one man's hands and emerge with any degree of quality," Selznick once said.

Selznick had three films on his plate for 1937: *The Prisoner of Zenda* starring Ronald Colman and Madeleine Carroll; and the two March pictures, *A Star is Born* and a screwball comedy—a first for SIP—*Nothing Sacred*. What March truly appreciated about his two pictures for SIP is that they got him out of period costume and in modern clothes.

II

A Star is Born had much in common with a film produced by RKO in 1932 when Selznick was head of production there. That film, *What Price Hollywood?*, starring Constance Bennett and Lowell Sherman, was based on an Adela Rogers St. Johns story about a Brown Derby waitress who is "discovered" by an alcoholic director—whose career deteriorates while hers skyrockets. Unlike the later *A Star is Born*, the waitress and the director do not have a love affair—he doesn't want her to become tainted by how Hollywood now views him. (In fact, in *What Price Hollywood?* The female lead marries another man.) Selznick's good friend George Cukor directed *What Price Hollywood?* but turned down Selznick's offer to direct *A Star is Born*—not wanting to repeat himself. (Although he would go on to direct the 1954 musical remake with Judy Garland and James Mason.)

Selznick hired William A. Wellman to direct. Wellman was a sturdy and respected craftsman who had directed such films as *Wings, The Public Enemy, So Big!, Wild Boys of the Road,* and *The Call of the Wild*. Wellman also worked on the story with a week-by-week young writer named Robert Carson. It was to be called *It Happened in Hollywood*. However, Selznick wasn't pleased with the story they came up with. He felt it had too much drama and not enough humor. Even though the earlier *What Price Hollywood?* had a downbeat ending, it also possessed a good deal of humor along the way—Selznick wanted more of this in *A Star is Born*. He also believed that the outline by Wellman and Carson was too hard on Hollywood—Selznick didn't want the picture to denigrate the picture business, and the people in it, too harshly. After all, they had an image to maintain.

That *A Star is Born* is loosely based on *What Price Hollywood?* is clear in one of the infamous memos that Selznick was so fond of sending to his collaborators:

> *Suggest looking at what we did in What Price Hollywood?...We must be awfully careful that the fall of the star won't seem to have started with his marriage. We should plant his faults very early and try getting over the idea that Esther feels she can help him if they are married. More importantly, after the death of her husband, we should keep the idea that she is through, she won't go on, the producer pleads with her to no avail, but then at the very end, we can have some sort of tremendous lift. . . .*

Ultimately, the script came to reflect all of what Selznick wanted. *A Star is Born* tells the story of small town girl, Esther Blodgett, who dreams of stardom and is urged by her understanding grandmother to seek her ambitions in Hollywood. Esther moves there, finds little success, and ends up working as a waitress, where she meets self-destructive alcoholic actor Norman Maine. Maine takes an interest in her and arranges for her to get a studio screen test. From there, Esther's career soars while Maine's deteriorates due to his egotism and fondness for booze. Esther, whose name is changed to the more box office Vickie Lester, falls in love with Maine, as he does with her, and they are married. Vickie is sure that with her love and tender loving care, Maine can straighten his life out and regain his career. Despite attempts to redeem himself, ultimately he fails, and full of self-pity, but believing that what he is going to do is for Vickie's good, Norman walks into the ocean and drowns himself.

While pleased with the basic story outline, Selznick wanted the lines to have more punch and impact, and so he went to his scribe

of choice for such a task, Ben Hecht. For a change, Hecht proved
unavailable, so Selznick tried Rowland Brown, whose work after a
few days left much to be desired. He, in turn, was replaced by
Dorothy Parker and Alan Campbell, who delivered a script by
October, and later that month production began on *A Star is Born*.

For the Esther/Vickie role, Selznick signed Janet Gaynor—whose
penultimate film this would be—for the identical salary that March
received. Selznick surrounded March and Gaynor with a top-notch
supporting cast, including Adolphe Menjou (as the studio head),
Andy Devine, Lionel Stander (as the studio publicity man much
abused by Norman), and May Robson (as Gaynor's understanding
grandma).

Wellman moved the picture along smoothly and briskly—as was
his forte. By the middle of November—after some seventeen days
of shooting—Wellman had already shot forty-nine pages of the 108
pages of the screenplay. Selznick, who was also supervising *The
Prisoner of Zenda* at the time, pretty much kept off the set during
shooting—unusual for such a hands-on producer, and probably a
good reason why *A Star is Born* managed to move along so smoothly.
But Selznick's ownership of the film would soon be reasserted by
the time production ended. On several occasions, he ordered retakes
of key scenes, and he even went so far as to write new dialogue as
well as break down the camera angles!

Two key scenes were ordered to be reshot by Selznick. One was
of the suicide scene, where March walks down to the beach, disrobes,
and walks into the Pacific Ocean never to emerge alive again.
Selznick wanted a montage of Norman's memories to be shown
just as he goes under. This was reshot in December, just before
Christmas.

There was also some question on how to end the film. As originally
shot, the picture ended with Vickie Lester at Grauman's Chinese
Theater, where she collapses after seeing her husband's footprints
immortalized in cement with his signature "Good Luck, Norman
Maine." Selznick didn't think this worked, and he sent a memo on
to Wellman:

> *I believe we can retain Gaynor's entire approach up the aisle
> in front of the Chinese, simply retaking the reaction to the foot-*

prints, more or less as is; with her pulling herself together; the announcer asking her if she will say a few words;...Gaynor... advancing with all the pride in the world, throwing her head back, with tears in her eyes, and saying 'This is Mrs. Norman Maine speaking.

In the end, Selznick had it shot two ways, with Gaynor saying "This is Mrs. Norman Maine speaking," and also, "This is Vickie Lester speaking." He would leave it up to the preview audience to decide which ending would be used; by and large, it was decided the "Mrs. Norman Maine" dialogue was the strongest and most poignant way to end the picture as well as the most upbeat. You know that Vickie will now go on.

The first preview for *A Star is Born* was held at the Fox Theater in Pomona on Saturday, January 23, 1937. The response exceeded Selznick's expectations, but he still felt that there were a few problems. One of which was the montage of recollections as he goes under the water during the suicide scene. It just didn't work, and in fact the entire suicide scene didn't work—Selznick ordered retakes once again. One problem was that the audience wasn't clear whether Norman's death was suicide or accidental. In a memo, dated January 25, 1937, Selznick wrote, "I find that there is a reaction of uncertainty that March has committed suicide; and we particularly lose a very strong point if it is not clear to the audience that he has committed suicide."

The new scene, as shot, opens with a shot of Norman's feet at the water's edge, then a shot showing his robe falling to the ground with the tide slowly taking it out to sea, and then Norman waist-deep in the water. This is all that was now used to show Norman's suicide: no shot of him going under and no montage of recollections. It would become one of the most stirring and poignant scenes in the entire film, along with Gaynor's final shot proclaiming herself as "Mrs. Norman Maine."

To a large degree, the Selznick version of *A Star is Born* has been overshadowed by the spectacular 1954 Judy Garland musical-drama remake. The remake turns the focus of the story to the girl on her way up, rather than the Selznick story, which is really the story of Norman Maine, the alcoholic star on the way down. While James

Mason delivers a splendid performance as Norman in the 1954 remake, he is overshadowed in every scene they share by Garland. Janet Gaynor was a fine actress and does a good job in *A Star is Born*, but she lacks the dominant personality that Garland brought to the role in the remake.

In *A Star is Born*, Fredric March gives one of the finest performances of his career. His Norman begins the film as one of the most popular stars in Hollywood—if not with the people who work with him. He adds a Barrymore-like zest to his scenes—a dashing, devil-may-care quality that ingratiates him with audiences and has you, despite his many flaws, caring about Norman Maine. March's performance, in my opinion, is more sympathetic than the later Mason portrayal. There is realism to the scene of Norman trying to dry out in a sanatorium so that he can recover his career and make Vicki proud of him. March told writer Lawrence Quirk that he based his acting in this scene on a true story involving John Barrymore. "I had been called the best John Barrymore imitator around at the time of the film *The Royal Family of Broadway*," March told Quirk, "But imitating or even recalling him in that sanitarium scene was no laughing matter—his decline was very tragic."

David Thomson in his biography of Selznick, *Showman*, would write that March's performance is "the most compelling thing in the film: he makes Norman Maine quiet, edgy, very smart and alluring as he advances towards doom; the underplaying is gripping more than fifty years later, the drunkenness is very restrained (repressed nearly, as if to suggest that inhibition was one of Maine's chief problems)." This is certainly in contrast with James Mason's performance in Maine, where the alcoholism is portrayed very broadly.

The final cost of *A Star is Born* was about $1.2 million, and it would gross about $2 million—a strong box office performance for those days. Although in the end, the film made a very modest profit for SIP—mainly due to distribution dealings.

The reviews were glowing. The film opened at the Music Hall in New York City, and the *New York Times* critic Frank Nugent wrote, "It is not as dull a spring as we had thought. Selznick International came to April's defense yesterday with one of the year's best shows, *A Star Is Born*, which probably will find the Music Hall's treasurer turning cartwheels in the streets this morning. For here, at least, is good entertainment by any standards . . . ." The *Herald Tribune* critic wrote that March's performance is "a cruel, authoritative, and perfectly modulated portrait."

March was rewarded with his third nomination as Best Actor, and the film was nominated for a further seven Academy Awards; Gaynor was also nominated for her performance, and the film was nominated as Best Picture. It did win two Oscars—Best Original Story and Color Cinematography.

Selznick was particularly pleased by March's performance and wrote to express his pleasure on April 28, 1937:

> *Dear Freddie,*
> *You must have heard from any number of people the most laudatory sort of opinions on your performance in A Star is Born. Yet I fear that many of these statements may have seemed to you automatic flattery of a type you must be used to, and that perhaps you wonder which congratulations are on the level. It is for this reason that I thought I should send you this note to tell you that on all sides I have seldom heard such praise of any actor in any picture. In New York, as here, people are saying that your job is one of the most able and honest that has ever been done for the screen. That it will do a great deal for you, as it has for the picture and therefore for us, is a certainty...At long last I salute you as I have wanted to through these years, with complete enthusiasm and unstinted admiration...*

III

On June 12, 1937, just a couple of months after *A Star is Born* was released to tremendous reviews and solid box office, March returned to Selznick International Pictures to begin the second of his two picture deal for the studio, *Nothing Sacred*. That day, David Selznick wired his New York partner, John Hay Whitney:

NOTHING SACRED STARTED SHOOTING THIS MORNING. YOU WANTED COMEDY—BOY YOU'RE GOING TO GET IT...

Nothing Sacred tells the story of Wally Cook, a reporter who goes to a small New England town to do a story on Hazel Flagg, a woman who is dying of radiation exposure. The reporter senses that this is a great human interest story and a story that could be his ticket back to the good graces of his publisher, Oliver Stone. Wally soon finds out that Hazel's quack doctor has provided an inaccurate diagnosis and that Hazel is in perfect health. Knowing that he has so much riding on this story, Cook convinces Hazel to pretend that the diagnosis is correct, that she is dying, and even has a dying wish to visit New York City, where she soon becomes the toast of the town. But what happens when the public, which is so sympathetic, is also waiting for Hazel to die and she doesn't?

This is the story concocted by Ben Hecht with assistance on the screenplay by Ring Lardner, Jr. and Budd Schulberg. Once again directing the proceedings is William Wellman, a director not really known for his knack at comedy, but who had performed credibly on *A Star is Born* in keeping that picture moving along smoothly and efficiently.

For the part of Hazel Flagg, Selznick hired one of the bright lights of 1930s film comedy: the radiant Carole Lombard. Among the Lombard comedies leading up to *Nothing Sacred* are: *Twentieth Century, Hands Across the Table* and, perhaps the best screwball comedy of the decade, *My Man Godfrey. Nothing Sacred* was a reunion for Lombard and March who had shared a key scene together back in 1933's *The Eagle and the Hawk*. Lombard was granted top billing over March; while he was entering a peak of his career, Lombard was at the zenith of hers. Not only that but her role also demanded that she be top-billed, as she is the catalyst of the fun and dominates the film. For March, it's a sharp departure and a welcome change of pace.

March's introduction to Warsaw, Vermont, the quaint New England town where Hazel Flagg lives, finds a bunch of closed-mouthed natives who are suspicious of him and his motives. Among them are Margaret Hamilton—two years before the Wicked Witch of *The Wizard of Oz*—as a store keeper who, when March asks if she minds if he sits down, says, "yes", and one young boy who runs out of his yard and bites him on the leg! In a classic scene at the film's climax, March tries to get Lombard's goat—and temperature—up and ends up kicking her in the behind and socking her in the jaw. But Lombard gets her revenge with a well-choreographed sock to his jaw—knocking him out. This scene would attract the ire of the Breen Office.

The ending was originally conceived by Hecht to have Hazel commit suicide so that she fulfills her destiny. Selznick wisely decided that this would hurt an otherwise light screwball affair, and Lardner and Schulberg came up with the perfect ending by having Hazel fake her death, but in fact she and Wally have married and are on a steamship to some far off land. Along with everything else, *Nothing Sacred* is an exposé on tabloid journalism and the elusiveness of celebrity, where you are beloved one day and within a year—by the time Wally and Hazel return from their around the world cruise—forgotten.

The physical altercations between March and Lombard where they push, kick, and slug one another—and reportedly both actors ended up being treated for minor cuts and bruises as the scene was completed in a series of takes—brought out the ire of the ever vigilante Breen Office, which thought that it was excessively violent. Breen was especially aghast by a man socking and kicking a woman—even if it was for comedic effect. Breen also had the usual complaints about excessive drinking and sexual innuendo.

Ultimately, the censor board passed the picture—with reluctance—and with Breen delivering a lecture to Selznick in the meantime:

> *As I told you in New York City, we are reluctant to approve your picture, Nothing Sacred, because of details showing Freddie March kicking Carole Lombard in the posterior. While the shot may not be offensive, per se, it nevertheless is in conflict with our practice. . . In view, however, of the fact that to delete this shot from the picture will cause you great difficulty, we are reluctantly approving the picture with this shot in it.*

Yet, six weeks later, Breen is still worried about the violence in Nothing Sacred, and, despite the film being in national release, he implores Will Hays, the head censor in Washington, D.C., to over-rule the approval, "Can't you stop the showing of *Nothing Sacred?*" But it's too late. The film is released and local state censorship offices, including the toughest—New York City and Boston—have passed it—socks, kicks and all.

In the midst of shooting *Nothing Sacred*, the Marches held a dinner party and special screening of the documentary *The Spanish Earth* written and produced by Ernest Hemingway. The documentary was in support of the loyalist cause in the Spanish Civil War—strongly anti-fascist and Anti-General Francisco Franco, the fascist supported leader of the Spanish nationalists. Hemingway was among the most vocal and ardent loyalist supporters on the world stage. The writer came to Hollywood that summer to give the documentary exposure and to raise money for the loyalist cause. The special screening at the Marches home was just one of several events, and the dinner/ screening guests included John Ford, Joan Crawford, Franchot Tone, Myrna Loy, Samuel Goldwyn, and the writers Lillian Hellman and F. Scott Fitzgerald.

The narration of *The Spanish Earth* was done by a young radio actor with a mellifluous voice named Orson Welles. After the screening, both March and Hellman told Hemingway that while the documentary was superb and the words he wrote were excellent, Welles's delivery of them was too casual and melodramatic, ". . . unsuited for the harsh reality of a war film." They urged Hemingway to do the narration himself, which, after some prodding, he agreed to. His flat yet natural voice on the soundtrack made the film more compelling. After the screening, Florence told Hemingway that the audience was expecting that he would say a few words. "Yes, I guess I should say something," Hemingway told her, "but first I've gotta take a leak." When he finally did speak, most of those in attendance felt he gave a forceful and effective talk. The dinner and screening at the Marches home was a huge success: raising $13,000 for the loyalist cause.

Selznick previewed *Nothing Sacred* in various spots in and around New York City to make sure that New Yorkers didn't take undue offense at the fun poked at their expense—they didn't. The film opened to good reviews, including one from *Variety* whose critic wrote that *Nothing Sacred* is a "meaty and well-edited piece of entertainment from start to finish. There are no lagging moments." *Variety*'s local competition, *The Hollywood Reporter*, wrote that March "gives a performance comparable to his drunken actor in *A Star is*

Born. He delivers a dashing and adroitly faced portrayal, matching point for point the rollicking spontaneity of his costar." Yet the film, which cost over $1.2 million—a good percentage of that budget going to March and Lombard's salaries—lost almost $400,000 at the box office.

While *Nothing Sacred* didn't clean up at the box office, it has stood the test of time. It is considered one of the best films of the golden era of screwball comedy and is a top film in both the March and Lombard filmographies. More than thirty years later, Pauline Kael would write, "While Hecht and the director, William Wellman, jab at just about every sacred cow in the national pasture, the audience may begin to wonder what makes the hero, Fredric March, and the girl, Carole Lombard...any better than anybody else. What makes their feelings true? The answer can only be that they, like the author, hate phoniness. Early catchers in the rye perhaps?" Film historian and writer David Thomson would call *Nothing Sacred* a "boisterous and invigorating film, rueful about sincerity yet full of life and enthusiasm."

1937 has to be considered a major year for Fredric March professionally, thanks to the two Selznick pictures, both of which have become classics. March also shot a costume picture that year, *The Buccaneer*, at Paramount for Cecil B. De Mille. He also became one of the highest-paid actors in Hollywood, and, in fact, the highest-paid freelancer in Hollywood. By the end of 1937, March would report earning nearly $500,000 for the year—five times what the president of the United States earned.

CHAPTER EIGHT
1938-1942

In 1937, March returned to Paramount at the invitation of Cecil B. DeMille to star in his lavish production of *The Buccaneer.* DeMille had wanted to film the story of Jean Lafitte for well over a decade. Originally, DeMille had wanted Robert Donat for the part, but his questionable health—severe asthma—eventually eliminated him. And then he thought about the young Laurence Olivier, but at the time, Olivier wasn't much of a name in America, and Paramount was reluctant to cast him in a $1.4 million film. By process of elimination, the part came March's way.

Lafitte is the French pirate who patrolled the Gulf of Mexico and later aided Andrew Jackson in defending New Orleans against the British during the War of 1812. It was a dreaded costume production, but March wasn't about to turn down DeMille, who he had a very good relationship with. And besides, since he was gearing up to return to Broadway, he wanted to leave behind a film he was secure in the believing would be a big hit—as nearly every film DeMille did became.

The film was heavily promoted by Paramount as DeMille's big twenty-fifth anniversary production. DeMille was as big as life with movie audiences as his films were. He was THE director/showman of his time, whose only rival would later be Alfred Hitchcock. Not only did DeMille become a household name through his movies but also for his hosting duties on the very popular radio program *The Lux Radio Theater.* The film went into production at Paramount on August 12, 1937: DeMille's fifty-sixth birthday. But first, there was a huge luncheon of Creole food at the Paramount Commissary to help launch the picture, with dignitaries and press from around the world.

One of Paramount's largest sound stages was utilized to recreate New Orleans and its bayous of the early-nineteenth century. Evelyn Keyes, cast in the small role of Madeleine, recalls "real trees dripped with real Spanish moss; actual streams wended their way through flowering shrubs, while live pelicans, cranes, and assorted exotic feathered creatures splashed about on their surfaces." No expense was spared from a DeMille epic.

This was Miss Keyes's first film and her first day on the set. She was featured in an intricate scene where she had to walk through shrubbery, streams, and extras, while delivering a few lines with March. She was nervous; not only due to working with a star of March's magnitude but also with such a domineering director, who was seated high above, towering like a god, on a boom crane giving his instructions with a microphone. (See him do this on film in Billy Wilder's *Sunset Boulevard*.)

Keyes recalls becoming "addled" with all the movement, then with the bright lights, and trying to make sure she found her marks while delivering a few lines to March, "It was horrendous." She flubbed the first few takes, and DeMille didn't help things by publicly bellowing at her from his high perch to "pay attention to the scene." She said she was humiliated, and she started to cry when March "came to my rescue" and dug his fingers into her arm and told her repeatedly to "say your lines...say your lines," waking her up from her funk until she finally delivered her lines in a satisfactory fashion, and DeMille got an effective take.

Following the scene, March invited the novice young actress to his dressing room, where she believed he was going to provide a pep talk to her. When they entered, he had Keyes sit on a sofa beside him. He told her not to let DeMille get to her. He was looking deeply into Keyes's eyes and offering soothing words of support. Keyes recalled that March was "so handsome in his elegant, tight white trousers, black boots, and short red jacket. His hair was dark and curly. About forty then, March was in his prime. The complete movie star."

March was courtly and soft spoken. He then picked up her hand, not to pat it and offer further comforting words but "in the gentlest way" placed it on "the bulge in the front of those tight white pants." Taken off-guard Keyes recalled she was so stunned she limply left her hand sit there as if she was in some kind of trance. The trance was apparently broken when there was a knock on the dressing room door telling the star that he was needed on the set. March removed her hand and jumped up and told her to "feel free to rest here." Keyes related in her autobiography that she "got out—fast."

The film was completed by December and ready for its premiere in New Orleans by February 1938. Fifteen thousand fans mobbed outside the Saenger Theater. *The Buccaneer* is a visual feast with a glorious scene of an armada of small boats moving forward towards the camera. It is a lively production, full of a colorful gallery of rogue characters and rousing action. Despite this, it really isn't one of DeMille's great epics, and it is among his least recalled sound films today. It's a shame, because smaller is sometimes better, and while *The Buccaneer* isn't a spectacular on the level of *The Sign of the Cross, Cleopatra,* and (especially) the sound version of *The Ten Commandments,* it has some fine characterization and acting by March, Akim Tarmiroff, Spring Byington (as Dolly Madison) and Walter Brennan. And the film has a colorful and lively intensity of its own. DeMille liked March's performance in the film. He told the *Washington Post*, "Never had Fredric March brought to the screen so dynamic a performance as he gives here." Of course, this is typical DeMille hyperbole, but he believed it. As usual for a DeMille film, the reviews were mixed. The critic for the *New York Journal-American* called the film ". . . a grand show, exciting blood and thunder entertainment," while the *Herald Tribune* movie critic wrote, "Mr. March...is disappointing as Lafitte." The film was not the blockbuster that Paramount hoped for either, making only a modest profit.

It was while filming *The Buccaneer* that Florence broached the idea of she and March returning to Broadway. The previous year, Florence did return to the stage to appear in Lillian Hellman's *Day's To Come*, which had been produced and directed by Herman Shumlin. Unfortunately, the play closed after only seven performances—hardly enough for Florence to get the Broadway bug out of her system. Florence enjoyed her children and home, but she also was antsy to work. It is worth remembering that there was a time when she was a bigger star than March. Now, it seemed to be the only parts in films she was getting were in Fredric March films. It wasn't clear whether she could get jobs—particularly in Hollywood—if her husband's name was not attached to the project.

As usual, March indulged this idea. For years, he too had itched to get back on the stage. After all, he had been in Hollywood for nearly a full decade, churning out movie after movie. The thought of essaying a part on stage—and really taking his time with perfecting a characterization—appealed to him. He may have also liked the idea of a Hollywood star showing the Eastern elite that just because somebody was a success in pictures didn't mean that he couldn't be a fine stage actor too. "I've been howling about the idea (of returning to the stage) for several years," he told reporters.

March told Sheila Graham, the Hollywood columnist, that he was "much more afraid" of a return to stage acting than Florence. "Eight years is a long time to be away from the theater and the public will expect so much more from me now than it did then." When asked about Katharine Hepburn, who failed to find a success on Broadway in an adaptation of *The Lake*—which also seemed to affect her movie box office as well—March scoffed, "I think it is true (that) she is not as popular with moviegoers as she was before *The Lake*, but it has nothing to do with the play. She made her best films before, *Bill of Divorcement* and *Little Women*. Recently the stories haven't been as good." I wonder if March was including the recently released *Mary of Scotland* as among those "not as good" films? March went on to say that he believed that the reason more film actors didn't do stage work was because of the money the studios pay as compared to the stage, and also because they have gotten used to being pampered by the Hollywood studio system.

Another reason that March was supportive of a stage teaming between he and Florence was because he felt he owed it to her. She had sat by while his star got bigger and bigger and her name had dwindled in significance. He understood the sacrifices she made. He may have even been persuaded by Florence, due to her knowledge of his womanizing. "Freddie liked ladies—to a very distressing extent as far as Florence was concerned," Bradford Dillman told Deborah C. Peterson. "But she put up with him. Freddie knew she was a dynamite lady so that every time he got caught in the cookie jar he went running back for forgiveness."

The play that Florence had in mind was a comedy of manners set in the early-eighteenth century, titled *Yr. Obedient Husband*—even on Broadway, March couldn't get away from period pieces! The comedy was written by Horace Jackson, a writer of several Hollywood films including *The Animal Kingdom, No More Ladies,* and *Suzy.* The director was to be John Cromwell, a prospect that gave both Marches confidence, given their long association and friendship.

Yr. Obedient Husband tells the story of Sir. Richard Steele, the Irish writer and cofounder of the daily British magazine *The Spectator.* But the real drama (or comedy) of *Yr. Obedient Husband* is the rocky romance and marriage between Steele and his second wife Mary Scurlock (nicknamed Prue), who he meets at the funeral of his first wife. The play is based on more than 400 letters they wrote to one another over the course of their twelve-year marriage. An example of such a letter is this one, dated October 6, 1707:

Dear Creature,

I write to tell you beforehand, that I am not in a very good humour; but all shall vanish at her signt whome Providence has given me for the banishment of care and the improvement of delight to your most obedient husband, and most humble ser'nt.

The supporting cast included Dame May Whitty, the English-born actress who just scored a triumph as the elderly invalid in the film version of *Night Must Fall,* and seventeen-year-old Montgomery Clift, who appears in one broadly played scene, playing the young Lord Finch.

The play a "robust comedy" by its playwright, rehearsed in New York before beginning a month long series of previews in Cincinnati, Columbus, St. Louis, Pittsburgh, and Detroit. While still rehearsing in New York, March allowed himself to be interviewed by Bosley Crowther of the *New York Times.* "Now, let me get this straight," he told Crowther. "I don't have anything against pictures; they've been more than kind to me. But I've reached the point where it isn't wise for me to make more than a couple of pictures a year—which leaves me time on my hands. Well, I have always loved the theater, have never felt I'd given it up; and now I've a chance to come back to it, so here it is."

The previews opened in Cincinnati on November 13, where it was met by good reviews and solid box office. The only problem was that Monty Clift had developed the measles, and on opening night he went by the old adage that "The show must go on," and he appeared with a 103 degree temperature. However, the next day an announcement was made that he would be out of the show for at least a week while he recovered. "Monty Clift was the juvenile lead; he must have been 15 or 16 at the time," March later recalled. "During our tryout … Monty's mother called the theater and said that Monty had the measles. So, Cromwell's wife, Kay Johnson, had to go on in Monty's place, with John hiding in the fireplace and feeding her Monty's lines." Of Clift, who he would later work with again in the much more successful *The Skin of Our Teeth*, March later said, "Monty had a great talent; he was very much like Alfred Lunt."

When *Yr. Obedient Husband* opened at the Hartman Theater in Columbus, March was asked by a reporter what his favorite thing about returning to the stage was and he promptly replied, "rehearsals." He went on to say, "In the studios, I have several times been called to make one of the last or even the last scene of a picture first. It's really amazing how the rest of the picture builds up to that." The point being that the stage has the right idea; you build up to the climax during the course of the play, rather than in the movies where scenes are usually always filmed out of order.

Florence felt liberated by the show. By the time they arrived in Pittsburgh, she was quoted as saying that she felt she could successfully handle both a career and family life. She also gave her views on what she felt was the recipe of a successful marriage, "Of course you've got to be in love… but love isn't as important as friendship." This comment seemed to say a lot about the Marches marriage. Certainly there was love, but more importantly they liked each other as individuals and admired one another as artists.

The show had its final preview in Detroit over Christmas and was expected to open on Broadway at the Belasco Theater on December 29, but had to be postponed when March landed in the hospital the same day due to an infection of the leg. It was bad enough that he had to have an emergency operation to relieve the infection on New Year's Eve of 1937. Following the operation, he made a swift recovery and was discharged on January 6. Four days later, on January 10, *Yr. Obedient Husband* opened.

The box office on opening night was fine, the reviews were not. The *New York Sun* theater critic wrote, "Mr. March and Miss Eldridge are not, possibly, the most light-hearted of actors for this sort of thing." The play itself was proclaimed pleasant but tepid. The *New York American* critic wrote, "Mr. March makes a brave go of it, but what with the weakness of the script, the lack of style in the acting, and the deadened air of fancy dress friskiness, poor Dicky Steele seems further away than Queen Anne does from the Brown Derby." The same review found Florence "somewhat happier in it than Mr. March." The *New York World Telegram* also found more fault with March than with his spouse, with the comment that March was "strangely unhumorous" while Florence was "highly spirited." The play itself was "too leisurely…to be considered even mildly exciting.

The reviews convinced March and Cromwell that the play would have a hard time generating the kind of audiences they needed to recoup their investments—March invested at least $50,000 into the venture. While the reviews and box office had been solid before preview audiences, they understood that more sophisticated New Yorkers were not going to come out in force. Each night, over the course of a week, the box office dwindled, and finally the decision was made to close the play.

In Hollywood, the scuttlebutt was that March decided to abandon, however temporarily, his successful film career, which was at its peak, because he was pressured by Florence. While some of this is undoubtedly true, it is also true that March stuck up for his wife against such rumors, "I wanted to do this play every bit as much as she did. It's been common knowledge among our friends for several years that we were on the lookout for a play in which we would costar…"

March wanted to return to Broadway in a hit and quiet the naysayers who believed that Hollywood stars were out of their element on the legitimate stage. Unfortunately, the audience reaction and reviews only bolstered their arguments. Not wanting to high-tail it out of town as if tarred and feathered, the Marches and director

John Cromwell decided to take a lighthearted approach that they hoped would result in some good will. They took out a newspaper advertisement in the New York papers with a cartoon of two trapeze artists missing one another in midair and as a caption:

OOPS—SORRY
FREDRIC MARCH
FLORENCE ELDRIDGE
JOHN CROMWELL

March now had the Broadway bug too and wasn't going to let the disastrous reception of *Yr. Obedient Husband* keep him down for long. "I want to make pictures in the summer and play Broadway winters," he told reporters.

II

March decided to plunge right back into filmmaking, and the only project that he could find on such short notice was an invitation by producer Hal Roach to make a comedy, titled *There Goes My Heart*, one of March's least memorable films.

Roach was best known for his slapstick comedies starring Harold Lloyd, Charley Chase, Laurel and Hardy, and the Little Rascals, but the previous year he had begun to experiment with more sophisticated comedy with star names like Cary Grant and Constance Bennett in *Topper* and *Merrily We Live* with Bennett and Brian Aherne. It was *There Goes My Heart* that brought March to Roach's "Lot of Fun" in early 1938 to costar with Virginia Bruce. Norman Z. McLeod was brought in to direct—a terrific choice having helmed such previous comedies as *Monkey Business* and *Horse Feathers* (both for the Marx Brothers) as well as *It's a Gift* (W.C. Fields), *Pennies from Heaven* (Bing Crosby), and most recently *Topper*.

Originally, March had been assured that Carole Lombard would be his costar, and he was excited to be reunited with her in a comedy follow-up to *Nothing Sacred*. Somehow, Lombard dropped out of the proceedings and Bruce was brought in. While March would have preferred Lombard he did get along well with Bruce, and they have a fine chemistry together. Bruce was also well-known to him, having been one of John Gilbert's ex-wives. Bruce was a talented actress who had given good performances in several respectable films, including the dramatic love story that is *Jane Eyre* (opposite Colin Clive); the love interest of Chester Morris and Robert Taylor in *Society Doctor*; Leading lady to Wallace Beery's *The Mighty Barnum*; and a columnist in love with Spencer Tracy's *The Murder Man*.

As it turns out, the story line of *There Goes My Heart* came from an unlikely source—especially for a romantic comedy—Ed Sullivan! Yes, that Ed Sullivan, who at the time was best known as a New York sportswriter and Broadway columnist. The story concocted by Sullivan (with screenplay written by Eddie Moran and Jack Jevne) tells the familiar plot device of a runaway heiress (Bruce) and a reporter who is pursuing her. Many reviews of the time noted that the plot had a more than passing resemblance to Frank Capra's *It Happened One Night.* But there is a device different from that film in that the penniless heiress—who can't depend on her grandfather for money—ends up getting a job at the department store that bears the family name. Roach surrounded his leads with a terrific supporting cast, including Alan Mowbray (as the fiancée that Bruce is running away from), Patsy Kelly, Claude Gillingwater, Eugene Pallette (perfect as March's editor), and in small parts Marjorie Main, Arthur Lake (who would go to play 'Dagwood' in the Columbia *Blondie* films later that year) and Nancy Carroll, March's *Laughter* costar, whose film career had fallen on hard times, playing another shop girl in the film. Of most interest, particularly to movie buffs of the silent era, is a cameo by Harry Langdon as a minister.

During the making of the film, March came down with strep throat. "It's all Norman McLeod's fault," he told Hollywood columnist Sheila Graham. "He goes too far with his realism." Originally, a beach scene was going to be shot at Catalina, but consistent fog threw a wrench into those plans, so McLeod had a sandy beach constructed on a sound stage with a projection screen in the background. "They had to use a wind machine to make spray," March recalled, "and I got wet through and through. A nice little persistent draft had a swell time on my back—and put me on my back." It held up filming for about a week.

Though March and Bruce make an engaging romantic comedy team, the film lacks the sparkle that Lombard might have provided. McLeod keeps the proceedings moving along at a brisk pace for its eighty-three screen minutes. This was the first Roach film to be distributed through United Artists (rather than MGM), and when it premiered in October of 1938, it proved to be a modest box office hit. In New York, the film played at the prestigious Radio City Music Hall, and the *New York Times* review noted its resemblance to *It Happened One Night*: "We prefer our revivals straight and with the original casts; imitations so seldom do justice to the source work." As for its leads, the critic wrote, "Fredric March and Virginia Bruce play it rather more soberly than Clark Gable and Claudette Colbert did, and the script—in its few moments of originality—is not half so resourceful as the classic Robert Riskin-S. H. Adams job." Graham Greene wrote in *The Spectator* that "everything is machine-made except for the blonde beauty of Virginia Bruce and Miss Patsy Kelly's vital underdog humor." On the plus ledger, was Kate Cameron's review in the *New York Daily News*, "a hilarious and dexterous game of passing a fast quip and pulling a smart gag."

Next, March went into *Trade Winds* for independent producer Walter Wanger. It turned out that director Tay Garnett (whose films up to that time included *One Way Passage*, *China Seas* and *Joy of Living*—his most famous film would come several years later, *The Postman Always Rings Twice* with Lana Turner and John Garfield) had a script ready. March and Garnett shared Myron Selznick as an agent who, in turn, sold the script, March, Joan Bennett, and Garnett as a package deal to Wanger.

Trade Winds came about due to Garnett having taken an around the world cruise and taking hours of home movies on board ship and at various tropical locales. There was enough good footage that Garnett got the idea that a story could be fashioned that would include some of this home movie footage, which Garnett also sold to Wanger. Garnett's two biggest prior hits had been *One Way Passage* and *China Seas*, both set on ships, and so, he reasoned, he couldn't miss with a sea picture.

In *Trade Winds*, Joan Bennett plays a San Francisco socialite, wrongly accused of the murder of the man who caused her sister to commit suicide. Knowing she is being pursued, she dyes her blonde hair dark, assumes a fake identity, and boards a ship bound for the orient, all the while being pursued by a (comic relief) city detective (Ralph Bellamy) and a private investigator (March), who she falls in love with aboard ship. It's a wisp of a story—a light mystery-suspense-comedy. For Bennett, this would be the first film that she would be a brunette. She would remain so for the rest of her career and in doing so would go on to enjoy a more spectacular career, often as a femme fatale, in a variety of films throughout the forties.

Along with Ralph Bellamy in providing comedy relief, there is a female counterpart, and it was thanks to Florence that Ann Sothern was cast in this part. One day, March went to Garnett and said to him, "Florence has an idea for the comedienne's role. Now, don't laugh. I've learned through the years to take Florence's hunches seriously. Florence said she has seen this girl do comedy and she's magnificent. Her name is Ann Sothern." Garnett knew who she was and correctly identified her to March as "The Queen of the B's." But Garnett too took Florence's hunch seriously, and he sent a script to Sothern, who accepted the part playing the ditzy blonde "to the hilt"—much to Garnett's delight.

The film offers breezy entertainment and is a lot of fun. Part of the fun is seeing Fredric March on a surf board. On his cruise, Garnett shot a background of a group of Hawaiians in the ocean, hanging ten. This was used as a backdrop for a process shot of March surfing. "Today's hot doggers could learn a lot from watching Freddie, hanging ten, in his surf shot in process," Garnett later wrote. "At the end of the scene he stepped off the board, bone dry." Of the film, March would tell reporters that it was "fun to make, different from anything else. I never really got over being fascinated by those process shots. They just didn't seem possible. We'd make a scene up in front of a screen. Then we'd look at the rushes, and swear we must have been in China."

The critics didn't take the film too seriously, correctly identifying it as nothing more than an entertaining way to spend an hour and a half. "There isn't the hilarious slapstick element to (this film) that distinguished *Nothing Sacred*, but March's performance…is on par with his work as the reporter in the earlier comedy…," wrote Kate Cameron in *The New York Daily News*. The film cost $738,000 to produce and grossed $964,000, which represented a net profit for Wanger of only $71,000.

It was while filming *Trade Winds* that the Marches signed on to do the George S. Kaufman and Moss Hart play *The American Way*. The two-act play tells the story of Martin Gunther, a German immigrant whose life in America is portrayed from the time he arrives at Ellis Island until his death more than forty years later in a typical small Ohio town. In between, he and his wife Trina (played by Florence) grow to love their new country and become good, productive citizens who build a business and raise a family. They are proud when their son fights and dies in the First World War. The play moves along through the years with the rise of fascism and ends with Martin losing his life when he tries to stop his grandson from joining a Nazi organization. But his life is celebrated at the end, with the whole town turning out for his funeral.

Kaufman and Hart were two of the greatest playwrights of the era and had just won the Pulitzer Prize for their superb social comedy *You Can't Take it With You*. It was Kaufman's wife, Beatrice, who offered up the idea that the two playwrights write a play that would pit them firmly against the fascist threat that was all too real in 1939. For this piece of Americana, *The American Way*, they knew they wanted the Marches for the leading roles. Kaufman and Hart made an appointment and were soon sitting in the Marches living room with the tall, thin, bespeckled Kaufman reading the script out loud, while his equally tall and thin partner nervously paced the room. "It was just the kind of thing we wanted to do," March later said, "A great, big heart breaking play that would reach every American." Florence added that it "was a revelation." They had no problem signing on for the mammoth $250,000 production, which would have a cast of 250 with some 1,700 costumes.

The play was staged at the new Center Theater, which had a capacity of more than 4,000 seats. To add a little more intimacy, the orchestra pit was covered over and became part of the stage, which permitted the actors to play scenes as close to the audience as possible. The orchestra itself was housed six floors above the auditorium and was conducted by Oscar Levant, who also wrote the music. The music was then piped into the theater through speakers.

Among the cast of *The American Way* was ten-year-old Dickie Van Patten, who played the part of the Gunther's grandson as a boy. Van Patten would grow up in the theater and later achieve success as an adult as the star of TV's *Eight Is Enough*. Van Patten recalls anxiously waiting to make his first entrance on opening night in *The American Way*. He was, in many ways, a typical American boy. He loved listening to the fights, and his hero was the great champion, Joe Louis. The night the play opened, Louis won an important fight, which Van Patten had been listening to in his dressing room. When he reached the wings to prepare for his entrance, Van Patten was joined by March, who was to make the entrance with him. March took his hand and they waited. "At that moment," Van Patten later wrote, "I was only vaguely aware that Fredric March was special. Standing there with him, I wouldn't have known why. I wouldn't have known that he won the Academy Award…, nor that just a year before he was nominated again…None of that mattered to me. I had far more important news to relate."

The news Van Patten had to relate, and could hardly conceal his excitement about, was "Louis won!" The boy expected that March would be equally excited, but that was not the case, as the somber-faced actor looked at the boy and said, "Get your mind on your acting! This is more important than the fight." Chastised, Van Patten was devastated. But as they walked onto the stage and began to perform, all this lifted, and soon he came to understand what March was trying to convey to him. "For the next seventy years in this line of work, I've come to realize that the show is *always* more important. That's a lesson I first learned from Fredric March—and one I'd never forget." This would not be the last time he would work in a play with Fredric March.

The play, produced by Sam Harris and Max Gordon, opened at the Center Theater almost a year to the day after the opening of *Yr. Obedient Husband*. The reviews were largely excellent. The Dean of the New York Theater critics, Brooks Atkinson, wrote, "…the earnest convictions of the authors and the actors endow *The American Way* with patriotic authority that is both solemn and stirring. Lovingly acted by Fredric March and Florence Eldridge, staged throughout with infinite skill, it is a first primer in Americanism worth the storm of bravos it received on the opening night." *The New York*

Sun critic hailed the play as "movingly patriotic…a gigantic spectacle, ordered and directed with extraordinary theatrical skill." John Anderson of the *New York Journal American* may have been the most effusive when he wrote, "No audience that I can remember in my time on the circle has been so shaken with emotion as we all were at the Center Theater on Saturday when in the last few moments of *The American Way* a vast rising rumble began at the back of the enormous theater and swept forward until nearly 4000 playgoers were on their feet."

The American Way became a critical success and ran an impressive 244 performances. Even though the show was generating strong box office, it wasn't enough. The show cost $225,000 and ended up losing $60,000—it was just too big and too expensive to become a financial success.

During a Sunday off from *The American Way*, the Marches flew to Washington to be present on April 9, when the world famous contralto Marian Anderson presented a concert at the Lincoln Memorial. The concert had been controversial in its day. Originally, Miss Anderson was going to present her concert at Constitution Hall, but the Daughters of the American Revolution (DAR) protested because of her skin color. First Lady Eleanor Roosevelt and some other DAR members resigned, and the concert was, instead, given the new venue in front of the monument to "The Great Emancipator" with an audience that was not segregated. The Marches are listed as among the sponsors, along with other notables including Katharine Hepburn and Tallulah Bankhead. Miss Anderson signed March's program, "To Fredric March, Gratefully, Marian Anderson."

At around this time, Florence decided it was high time that the March family had a real home in the east. They had discussed such a possibility in the past, and the idea appealed to March as well. They also believed it would be good for the children to spend summers in the fresh country air. Florence took this project on herself. "I went East, found a farm in New Milford, Connecticut and, by virtue of my savings plus mortgages scattered all over New Milford, bought it," she told writer Gladys Hall. "Upon completion of the purchase, I wrote Freddy. 'It is clearly understood,' I said, 'That the place is to be no obligation to you. You don't even have to look at it if you don't want to.'" He did look and he did like. For the next thirty-five years it would be the place they would retreat to and find comfort in. The 200-year-old farm house was on forty acres of land. The house itself was fairly small, but they would add on and modernize it over the years. They would also add a swimming pool and tennis court and convert the barn into a guest house. The property was named "Firefly Farm" due to the high number of fireflies on the property. "When the children were small they used to put them in jars and they lit their rooms with them on summer nights," Florence later recalled. Since they now had a farm house and property in Connecticut and an apartment in New York, they decided to downsize their living arrangements in California by selling their large French provincial home there and buying a smaller ranch house on Mandeville Canyon Road.

III

1940 began with some embarrassing news for the Marches. They were sued by their former cook, one Mary Bulavaska. Bulavaska sought damages of $15,000 for injuries she sustained when she slipped on paint splattered linoleum and fell against a radiator in the kitchen of the Marches New York apartment. Fortunately for the Marches, Justice Isidor Wassaervogel, of the New York Supreme Court, dismissed the charges.

In between theater engagements, March returned to MGM for the first time since *The Barrett's of Wimpole Street* to accept George Cukor's invitation to be Joan Crawford's leading man in *Susan and God*. For his efforts, MGM paid March a fee of $100,000. Cukor surrounded his stars with an impeccable supporting cast that included Ruth Hussey, John Carroll, Rita Hayworth (borrowed from Columbia, where Harry Cohn was just beginning his big build-up that would within a few short years make her one of the most popular stars in the world), Nigel Bruce, Bruce Cabot, Marjorie Main, and working in a film with March for the first time since *Dr. Jekyll and Mr. Hyde*, Rose Hobart.

Susan and God tells the story of Susan Texel (Crawford), a society lady, who discovers and allows religion to take over her life at the expense of her alcoholic husband (March) and their young daughter

(Rita Quigley). Crawford was thrilled to be playing a part that Gertrude Lawrence had acted on the Broadway stage—and that her archrival at MGM, Norma Shearer, had turned down because she didn't want to play the mother of a teenage daughter on the screen.

March was happy to be working with Cukor—a professional as well as social friend. The prior year, when Cukor was fired from *Gone with the Wind*, several newspapers interpreted his firing due to Cukor's reputation as a "Woman's director"—a term that would dog Cukor for his entire career—who couldn't handle the sweeping action scenes of GWTW. One clipping indicated that Cukor was let go because he favored Vivien Leigh over Clark Gable. March clipped out this item and sent it to Cukor with a tongue-in-cheek note, stating "Hope you've learned your lesson—F". March knew as well as anybody that Cukor was a director who could direct anybody—male or female—and had directed many top male stars superbly including himself, Cary Grant, Spencer Tracy and, later, guiding Ronald Coleman and Rex Harrison to Oscar-winning performances.

Their rapport is highlighted in an exchange of letters between the two in the weeks before filming began on *Susan and God*:

Dear George,

This is belated thanks for all the dope that you so kindly sent me regarding the picture. I must say it sounds like a swell set-up, and I can only hope, as I am sure you do, that we get something pretty swell out of it…I understand…that you would like me to dress 'carelessly' like a Jock Whitney or a George Cukor, rather than a Menjou or Eddie Lowe. I wasn't so terribly concerned about suits actually, as I was to find out what you suggest for shirts. Please tell me what the big shots you have worked with do in the way of shirts when playing straight parts. Must they always be slightly off-white? I usually go through at least a couple a day and, if I do go for having some made up in patterns, it can become rather complicated. What do you think is the best solution? Do let me hear from you on this and any other matters that may come to your mind. Do you see him wearing more than two sports outfits, for instance, or anything other than a double breasted shawl collar dinner jacket?…Believe me, when I tell you that I look forward with great anticipation to your charmingly insulting direction. . ..

Cukor responded, with his tongue also firmly in cheek, within days:

Dear Freddie,

Now that we've got you in the bag, signed, sealed and almost delivered, I don't have to be so god-damned polite to you anymore. Writing that first letter to you was really tough, I had to rack my brains, brush up on my spelling, rewrite and generally put myself to beaucoup trouble. But now all you're going to get is one of those old sloppy letters I write to any stock leading man. It is obvious that you have been off the silver screen for quite a spell—when you ask about shirts being off-white!! We no longer shoot pictures on out-door stages with 'inspirational music', nor do we use off-white shirts. However, on second thought, your white shirts won't be so damned white anyway.

p.s. God help me if the cameraman raises hell about the shirts after all this.

Crawford, who had just made a big hit of playing the "bitch" Crystal in Cukor's *The Women,* was delighted to be cast in a film that one would have thought best suited for one of the regal ladies of MGM like Shearer or Greer Garson. She makes the best of her opportunity and turns in a good performance. March's alcoholic is sympathetically played but seems to belong in another picture. His is a dreary and forlorn character, which seems out of place with the drawing room comedy aspects of the film. The best performances are those done by the supporting actors—especially Ruth Hussey and Marjorie Main. Still, March decided to make his return to the screen in a Joan Crawford picture that really is a Norma Shearer picture.

March would recall Crawford as "a nice person, but a real movie star. She even brought her own music to the set—a whole entourage, a violinist and a pianist, to play her favorite songs, to get her into the proper mood for the scene. Cukor never said much about the music –or anything else—to Joan. She was the star." On the set, though, March was helpful and patient with his costar. "It was a very difficult part," Crawford later said, "...I owe a lot to Fredric March, who played foil to me very generously." Later, when March's brother Jack, whose opinions he respected, saw *Susan and God*, he expressed disappointment in the film, which seemed to surprise March who wrote back, "Sorry you didn't like S& God better. Most critics have indicated it was Crawford's best to date and my best since 'Star is Born.'"

When the film opened in New York in July of 1940, Bosley Crowther of the *New York Times* found it "generally disappointing." He faults Crawford for trying too hard to act like Gertrude Lawrence, but "she lacks her predecessor's rich and abundant vitality." March too didn't come out unscathed as Crowther found him "strangely listless in an aggravating role." Variety in its review was more enthusiastic, calling the film "smartly cast, deftly directed and elaborately mounted." Despite the mixed reviews, *Susan and God* returned a profit for MGM, but wasn't the blockbuster that the studio hoped it would be.

In the summer of 1940, Rep. Martin Dies, the blonde chairman of the Special Committee on Un-American activities—commonly known simply as "The Dies Committee"—came into Hollywood to pursue allegations of communists and communist sympathizers. Dies, a die-hard anti-New-Deal conservative from Texas, once famously included eight-year-old Shirley Temple on a list of communist sympathizers in Hollywood, which led FDR's Secretary of Interior, Harold Ickes, to snort, "They have found dangerous radicals there (Hollywood) led by Shirley Temple."

This time, Dies was tracking down allegations made by an ex-Communist named John L. Leech, who described himself as the one-time chief functionary of the Hollywood chapter of the Communist Party of America. Others, however, described Leech as a "pathological liar." There are those who believe Leech had been a paid police informant who infiltrated the Communist Party of the USA. Leech alleged that Fredric March, Humphrey Bogart, James Cagney, Franchot Tone, Francis Lederer, writer Philip Dunne, and Lionel Stander, among others, supported the Communist Party financially and in terms of doctrine. The inquiry was led by Los Angeles District Attorney Burton Fitts, a hard-nosed conservative, who was up for reelection. Among the tidbits that Leech alleged, was that March, Bogart, Cagney, and the rest, would meet at the beach house of former Paramount Pictures Chairman B.P. Schulberg where they would, "read the doctrine of Karl Marx." Bogart, when confronted with that allegation would later say, "If I were going to read the doctrine of Marx it would be Groucho not Karl."

Dies jumped on this testimony and immediately decided to bring his committee to Los Angeles where it would hold secret hearings. As for those named by Leech, they were unanimous in their denials of the allegations. "Leech is an unmitigated liar," March proclaimed. "I have never knowingly contributed a single penny to the Communists or any other un-American cause." Bogart dared the committee to call him to the stand. "I want to face them myself," and deny the charges. Cagney, through his brother and manager, also denied the charges. What March, Bogart, and Cagney had in common was their support of the New Deal and their general support of liberal causes. "They were all good, liberal-minded citizens who weighed the issues and fought for what they believed," is what Myrna Loy later wrote of them in her autobiography. The Screen Actors Guild jumped to their defense as well issuing a statement, which read, "To smear prominent persons without any reliable evidence is to play into the hands of Hitler and Stalin by confusing the innocent with the guilty." The accused would be questioned by Dies in a special session at the Biltmore that August.

On August 17, March appeared before the committee with Florence at his side. For nearly two hours, March vigorously denied all allegations of communist sympathies and told the committee that he never knowingly donated any money that would support communist causes. He proclaimed his solid support for, and love of, the United States. He also went on record calling his accuser a liar. The bottom line is that Leech provided no solid evidence beyond his own testimony.

Four days later, Dies formally cleared four of those who were named by Leech, "The chair has carefully considered evidence received to date, including the testimony of some of those who have been accused," Leech said in a statement, "and is of the opinion that Mr. Humphrey Bogart, Mr. Fredric March, Mr. James Cagney and Mr. Phil Dunne are not and have never been members of the Communist Party." While March was exonerated, it would not be the last time he would be confronted with allegations of communist sympathies.

III

Officially, in 1940, The United States was a neutral in the European war. Franklin Roosevelt was campaigning for a third term that year under the theme that he kept American boys out of the war. But behind the scenes, the United States quietly supported the Allied cause and publicly they had supported such programs as Lend-Lease, which would supply allied nations with ships necessary to the successful prosecution of the war. Still, Hollywood wasn't overly keen on taking on the Nazi menace. Anti-Nazi films were few and far between, and included *The Mortal Storm* (MGM, 1940), *Confessions of a Nazi Spy* (Warner Brothers, 1939), *The Man I Married* (20th Century Fox, 1940), and the devastating lampooning of Hitler and Mussolini in Charles Chaplin's brilliant *The Great Dictator* (United Artists, 1940). While the Nazi menace was all too real, it was not something that American audiences wanted to be reminded of at the movies, where they often sought out light entertainment to help them forget everyday problems.

March was a dedicated anti-fascist. So when a script titled "Flotsam" came his way—based on a novel by Erich Maria Remarque, the German writer whose brilliant novel of *All Quiet on the Western Front* was made into the classic and compelling 1930 anti-war film—he was very interested in having the opportunity to say something about the world situation. The film was an independent production produced by Albert Lewin and David Loew and would be released through United Artists. Eventually, the title of the film would be changed to what was considered to be the more commercial *So Ends Our Night*. The title change may also have been inspired by the successful Alfred Lunt-Lynn Fontanne anti-fascist Broadway play *There Shall Be No Night*.

The plot was summed up by the foreword of the film, which onscreen reads:

> *When the present rules of Germany came into power, thousands of people, compelled to take refuge in neighboring countries, found themselves in the most fantastic dilemma of our times. For they had no passports…Without passports, these refuges had no legal right to live anywhere. They were forced to keep on the march-an endless march interrupted only by arrest and imprisonment for illegal entry. Then deportation into another country where the same fate awaited them. This is the story of the people without passports. It begins in Vienna in 1937, before the German occupation of Austria.*

March plays a German political dissident, with Frances Dee cast as his wife, who he urges to divorce him so that she will be free of harassment from the Nazis. The luminous Margaret Sullavan is cast as a Jewish refugee studying to be a chemist. Young Glenn Ford, age twenty-four, is cast as another Jewish refugee who shares a room with the March character. March's old friend John Cromwell was chosen to direct.

This was Ford's first really important film, and he had to be borrowed from his home studio of Columbia. But first, he had to audition for the producer, David Loew, and was invited out to Loew's beach house to do so. Ford was surprised when he found March and Sullavan also in attendance (both actors had been given casting approval). Ford later recalled:

> *I managed to read as ably as I could in front of these two legendary actors. March started teasing. He'd say, "Margaret, doesn't he remind you of a young Hank Fonda?" Sullivan, of course, had once been married to Hank Fonda. But it was just in fun. Later, when I was getting ready to leave, March patted me on the back and said, "Congratulations! We all agreed you'll be perfect in this part." I mumbled, "Th-thanksss, Mr. March" and then I drove home in a daze.*

The film opened at Radio City Music Hall in New York City on

February 28, 1941. Bosley Crowther in the *New York Times* wrote a less than sterling review:

> It would indeed be gratifying to be able to say that it is told with great dramatic effectiveness, too. But it isn't. For the story which Talbot Jennings has derived from Erich Maria Remarque's novel, "Flotsam," follows too rigid and monotonous a narrative form; it documents rather than dramatizes the wretched lives of its characters. And although John Cromwell has drawn much pathos and affecting tenderness from individual scenes, his direction of the picture as a whole has been too slow, too solemn and much too tedious. "So Ends Our Night" continues for the seemingly interminable length of two hours.

The *Times* review would pretty much sum up what most reviewers thought of the film: some wonderful individual scenes and performances but too long and too text book. The moviegoing public was also not prepared to spend two hours in a dark theater spending their money on a largely depressing subject. But, seen today, the film has much to recommend. Yes, it is a tad long but the performances are uniformly superb, the sets (filmed at Universal) are realistic and the score by Louis Gruenberg (who the previous year had also scored *Stagecoach*) is beautiful and compelling—and earned Gruenberg an Academy Award nomination for the scoring of a dramatic picture.

John Cromwell had always been a big fan of Joseph Conrad's 1905 novel *Victory: An Island Tale.* As far back as 1920, Cromwell had wanted to direct an American stage version of the play, which he ultimately did. During his early days as a contract director at Paramount, the studio undertook a film version of the Conrad novel titled *Dangerous Paradise* starring Richard Arlen and Nancy Carroll. The film had a light touch and was generally unfaithful to the novel. Cromwell later called the William Wellman directed film "deplorable" and vowed that one day he would make a faithful version of the story. Finally, in 1940, Paramount green lighted such a project with Cromwell as director.

Victory tells the story of Hendrik Heyst who takes his father's advice and decides to live in isolation on an island. Unfortunately for Heyst, he didn't take his father's advice completely. He ends up getting involved with a trader named Morrison, to whom he lends money, knowing it will never be repaid. The business venture goes bankrupt. Heyst travels to another island to attend a concert and meets the beautiful Alma. She asks him why he lives on an island and he replies, "Whenever I return to the outside world, I run into another Morrison. There must be something wrong with me." It turns out that Alma will need his help too. Ultimately, he takes her to live with him on his island sanctuary. More complications arise with the arrival of Mr. Jones, a "business man" who wants to open a casino on Heyst's island, convinced that there are riches buried on the island. Will this lead to an end to Heyst's sanctuary and way of life, or will Heyst and Alma have the final *victory*?

Originally. Charles Boyer was approached to play Heyst, but, in the end, Cromwell requested and got his good friend Fredric March. The other key roles went to Betty Field as Alma, Sigmund Ruman as Schomberg, and Cedric Hardwicke as Jones. The screenplay was by John Balderston, who contributed to several Universal horror films including *Dracula, Frankenstein,* and *The Mummy.* Much of the background process shots were filmed on the island of Surabaya in Java.

Victory is a much more faithful rendition of the Conrad novel than *Dangerous Paradise*, and is an equal to Maurice Tourneur's 1919 silent version, which had starred Jack Holt. Its chief asset may be Fredric March as Heyst. As Gene D. Phillips writes in his essay, *Conrad and Cinema: The Art of the Adaptation*, "On the one hand, Jack Holt makes a competent Heyst in the Tourneur movie, but he does not come across as a strong leading man." Another plus is Cedric Hardwicke's performance as the chief villain. The *New York Herald Tribune* critic wrote that, "The Hardwicke characterization of the evil, woman-hating Mr. Jones…comes through with the impact it had in the book. Terror stalks from the first moment that Mr. Jones appears (wearing dark sunglasses) and builds into an irresistible crescendo." (Ironically, Cromwell disagreed, he thought that Hardwicke's performance was the only weak link of the film.)

One problem with this version is the lack of sexual chemistry between March, who is stalwart, and Field, who is a good actress but is lacking dazzle. According to Phillip's essay, the most common problem with each of the three versions of *Victory* is the ending, "The one flaw…is the contrived upbeat ending which has been grafted onto all three of these versions of Conrad's story, which Conrad would not have sanctioned, wherein the hero and the heroine survive to enjoy a long life together," Phillips writes. "The insistence of the front office at Paramount on attaching a happy ending to all three films was dictated by the fact that many producers still subscribed in those days to the belief that films with upbeat endings usually attracted a larger segment of the mass audience than films which did not." But John Cromwell appeared to be well satisfied with his adaptation. March wrote his brother Jack shortly after the film was completed, "Finished *Victory* on Friday, and John Cromwell says it looks swell."

The film received generally favorable reviews, but failed to excite at the box office.

The Theater Guild appealed to, and got, a commitment from the Marches to star in Sophie Treadwell's new play, *Hope for a Harvest*. Miss Treadwell was a prolific playwright who wrote nearly forty plays during her long career. Today she is probably best known for her 1928 expressionist drama *Mechanical*, which dealt with an infamous Ruth Snyder murder case of the 1920s. (This also inspired author James Cain to write the book that eventually became the movie *Double Indemnity*.) There was one catch to the Marches commitment to *Hope for a Harvest*: The play would have a month-long road tour from April to early May of 1941 and then close so that March could return to Hollywood for some movie obligations. Then—six months later—it would reopen in Philadelphia on November 17, before moving on to Broadway a week later.

Hope for a Harvest tells the story of Carlotta Thatcher's (Florence) return to her family farm in California after living abroad for twenty years. She finds that the farm has fallen into disrepair and, in contrast to the farmers of war-torn Europe, her American family and friends are lethargic, bitter, and gone to seed. She is especially stunned to find that the once robust man she had loved, her distant cousin, Elliot Martin (March) is especially sour, not only about how his once prosperous farm has gone to seed but about life in general. He now runs a gas station and rails against the "Japs and Dagos" who have bought up the land and created prosperous farms.

Carlotta goes to work to get the farm in shape again and to also help Elliot rediscover the vibrant man he once was. By the end of the play, there is hope not only for the future of Carlotta's farm but also for a future between Carlotta and Elliot. The play, a comedy-drama, also tackles racist attitudes among the white farmers towards the successful and diligent minorities.

The play opened at the Shubert Theater in New Haven on April 4. "Everyone in New Haven and Hartford counties turned out last night to see Fredric March and Florence Eldridge in the new play...*Hope for a Harvest*," wrote one critic, "The enthusiasm with which the audience greeted the play indicates a successful career for it. Fredric March's enormous popularity may have had something to do with the volume and fervor of the applause, but the play has much to recommend it." A few days later in Boston, Elliot Norton of the *Boston Post* wrote that *Hope for a Harvest* was "one of the major theatrical events of the season." And so it went on to Washington, D.C., Baltimore, and Pittsburgh, garnering enthusiastic reviews and strong box office. When the play closed, following the Pittsburgh engagement, everybody connected with it was convinced it would be one of the major successes of the upcoming Broadway season. But, in the meanwhile, March returned to Hollywood to begin work on a wonderful piece of Americana, *One Foot in Heaven*.

IV

One Foot in Heaven contains one of Fredric March's finest and most understated screen performances in a film that is not all that well known today, but at the time was much admired. The film is based on a best-selling novel by Hartzell Spence about the life of his father, a Methodist minister, who served small town parishes in Iowa and Colorado from the early part of the twentieth century through the 1920s. The pastor and his family are seen living in one dilapidated parish after another, never getting rich but building community bonds around them. The film captures the flavor and nostalgia of a simpler time extremely well.

The novel was purchased by Warner Brothers, and both Raymond Massey (best known for playing Abraham Lincoln on stage and screen) and Alexander Knox (who would later be acclaimed for his playing of Woodrow Wilson in the prestigious 1944 Fox film *Wilson*) were tested for the lead. Massey was the top choice of the author of the novel to play his father, but producer Hal Wallis passed both Massey and Knox over when March expressed interest in the property. So enthused about this film was March, that he requested and got the approval of the Theater Guild to postpone the Broadway opening of *Hope for The Harvest*, so he could participate in this film.

For the pivotal role of the minister's wife, Wallis originally wanted Olivia de Havilland, who would have excelled at playing the loving and dutiful spouse—but at the last minute she was switched off this picture and put on *They Died with Their Boots On* with Errol Flynn. To replace de Havilland, Wallis signed Martha Scott, the talented and attractive actress who was big hit as Emily in the Broadway production and later film version of *Our Town*. More recently she had won good reviews as a dedicated school teacher in *Cheers for Miss Bishop*. She turned out to be an inspired choice. In addition to March and Scott, the film contained an excellent supporting cast including Beulah Bondi, Gene Lockhart, Harry Davenport, and Laura Hope Crews.

The film was to be a major release for Warner Brothers, and with Europe at war, though not yet the United States, it represented the kind of feel good, nostalgic type of entertainment that audiences would seek and appreciate in times of stress and worry. Anatole Litvak was initially assigned to direct the picture. The Ukrainian director previously helmed such superb Warner fare as *The Sisters, All This and Heaven Too,* and *Castle on the Hudson* but, just as with de Havilland, he was reassigned to another picture that Wallis felt was more up his ally: *Out of the Fog.* He was replaced by a relative novice director, Irving Rapper, who had only one other directorial film under his belt, *Shining Victory.* Rapper would go on to direct several Bette Davis films, including one of her signature films: *Now, Voyager.* March had directorial approval, and after viewing *Shining Victory* he gave him his thumbs up.

The film was an actor's dream for March, who ages twenty years in the film. The pastor he plays is inspired by the ministry and gives up medical school to follow his heart. He begins playing the pastor as a fairly strict fire-and-brimstone type, but as he comes into contact with different people and experiences, he comes to temper that fiery spirit and accept that not everything that gives pleasure is sinful. A case in point is that in several instances the pastor preaches against watching movies, but later finds out his own son has been sneaking off to the local cinema. He takes his son aside and tells him that he need not sneak off to the movies, that he will take him to see one, and he will point out why they are inappropriate. They go and see the western *The Silent Man*, which starred William S. Hart (actual scenes from the Hart western are shown) and, rather than the pastor finding fault with the film, he is uplifted himself by its moral message and begins to change his own tune towards movies—how could it be otherwise in a major motion picture?

Rapper was excited with the project. "Casey Robinson's screenplay was pretty wonderful…," Rapper later told writer James Bawden. "It indeed was episodic rather than dramatic but Fred got to age and act all over the place. A whole wad of money went for the sets and the shoot was very leisurely for me—six weeks." He couldn't believe that in just his second film he was able to direct one of the foremost actors of his time. "He was one of my favorite actors," Rapper later said. "Florence Eldridge, who was a fine actress herself, said to me in front of Freddie, after she'd seen the first week's rushes, 'Irving, you're the first director who has taken the ham out of him.' I said, 'I wasn't conscious of it.' Fredric March was a director's pet."

As usual, when March approached this type of role he studied it. In this instance, he had an actual person to study: the real Rev. Spence. He studied old photographs and sermons, and he made careful notes in copies of both the book and the screenplay. He also had long talks with Mrs. Spence, who was a presence on the set. "When Hartzell Spence saw the picture," March recalled, "he even thought I looked like his father—although, of course, I didn't. I just tried to get his way of speaking and of walking. The director, Irving Rapper, kept me from using my own mannerisms. He tried to keep me natural. He even talked with Florence for a week before we started work so he could find out all my weak points!" March was also influenced by the pastors he met with when researching. "Make him a two-fisted person," he recalled of their advice. "Ministers can be regular people even if they aren't that way very often on the screen." March was most appreciative of Mrs. Spence's advice and opinions. "This is the first time I have ever played a role in which I could talk to the widow of the man I portrayed," March recalled. "My finest compliment occurred when she visited the set and said with gratified surprise, 'Why, you are as handsome as will was, after all. Mr. March, I'd like you to know my husband was a very handsome man. And then she added, a little later…'sometimes you are so much like him that it hurts me.'"

The film was shot in the summer of 1941, and production moved along smoothly. When released in November, it turned out to be a very big box office hit and was acclaimed by clergy around the country. This provided good word of mouth, as clergy on the pulpit or in religious publications endorsed the film, providing Warner Brothers with a windfall! (Nearly twenty years later, many more fundamentalist clergy would turn on another March picture, *Inherit the Wind*, with a vengeance.)

The reviews were excellent as well. The film had its big New York opening at Radio City Music Hall, on November 13, and Bosley Crowther in the *New York Times* called *One Foot in Heaven*, "one of the finest pictures of the year" and compared it to *Life with Father*, except set in a parsonage. Crowther was equally enthusiastic about the performances—particularly the leads:

> And Fredric March and Martha Scott, under the superbly lucid and restrained direction of Irving Rapper, infuse with warm and sentient life the characters of William Spence and his wife. Mr. March is truly excellent as a man of stout conviction and resolute faith—a man who is not above a bit of honest chicane when it is a matter of coaxing a new Tree of Jesse window out of a parishioner or disposing of an unmelodious choir, but who is blessed with a deep humanity and walks in paths of righteousness all his life. Miss Scott abets him magnificently as his loyal and loving mate—a woman of fine sensibilities who endures the humiliations of a poor parson's wife and offers her comprehending self as the patient foil to his willful outbursts.

While March's own impeccable performance was not nominated, the picture itself was, for a Best Picture Oscar.

Before returning to Broadway for *Hope for the Harvest*, March had time to knock off a quick comedy over at Columbia, *Bedtime Story*, which he began scarcely a week after finishing *One Foot in Heaven*. *Bedtime Story* was produced by movie pioneer B.P. Schulberg. Schulberg was an authentic movie pioneer, getting his start in the silent era, and at one time he was the head of production at Paramount pictures—having Ok'd March to star in his Oscar-winning role(s) of *Dr. Jekyll and Mr. Hyde*. He was now an independent producer who worked at whatever studio would finance his films.

The film tells the amusing story of an actress who has just finished her greatest stage triumph and is now ready to retire to a farm in Connecticut with her husband, a producer-playwright. However, he has different plans and a new play that he's anxious for her to star in. She will have nothing doing. When she finds out that he sold the Connecticut farm to finance the play, she packs up and goes to Reno to file for divorce. Naturally, he follows her in a zany attempt to win her back, while still hoping that she will see things his way.

Originally, Columbia wanted either Cary Grant or Henry Fonda for the leading male role, with Rosalind Russell and Carole Lombard under consideration for the female part. In the end, Columbia cast Loretta Young for the wife, since she owed them a film, due to a $150,000 two-picture deal she signed with them after she left 20th Century Fox earlier in the year. March was lured into the role of the conniving husband when both Grant and Fonda proved unavailable—and by a $100,000 salary.

The fast-paced comedy was shot in about five weeks under the guidance of Alexander Hall, a terrific comedy director, who had guided Young in two previous comedies, *The Doctor Takes a Wife* and *He Stayed for Breakfast*. In addition to *Bedtime Story*, 1941 would be the same year that Hall's most famous film, *Here Comes Mr. Jordan*, was released. *Bedtime Story* features a sterling supporting cast including Eve Arden, Allyn Joslyn, Joyce Compton, and Robert Benchley.

Filming went without incident except for a brief flare-up between Young and Columbia chief Harry Cohn, when Young paid $100 for a dress, but the studio was charged $700 mainly for alterations and changes by the famous designer Irene. Cohn fumed that "nobody was going to cheat me," and threatened to put Young below the title in retaliation. He couldn't get away with doing that, and in the end

Columbia ended up making up the difference. Future film director Michael Gordon (*Pillow Talk*) got his start in movies working as a dialogue director at Columbia and recalls that he ran dialogue on *Bedtime Story*, "I'd later use Freddie in films," he later said, "but Loretta always scared me. She was so imperious!"

At one point during the filming, Schulberg visited the set and got reacquainted with March, whose early career at Paramount he had help foster. March pointed out to Schulberg that the title, *Bedtime Story*, sounded familiar. "Wasn't it the name of a picture done years ago at Paramount?" March asked Schulberg. Schulberg acknowledged it was the name of an early Maurice Chevalier film, ". . . and I produced that one, too." It had been a big hit, and he wanted to use the title again for good luck. March was happy with the film and enjoyed making it. He later referred to it as "the lightest of comedy."

Columbia went all out on the picture and booked it into the prestigious Radio City Music Hall. It was to follow the Spencer Tracy/Katharine Hepburn romantic-comedy *Woman of the Year*. However, *Woman of the Year* kept being held over—breaking records at the Music Hall. When *Bedtime Story* finally opened, it was compared unfavorably with the just exited *Woman of the Year*. "They finally got *Woman of the Year* out of the Music Hall yesterday and made way for Columbia's *Bedtime Story*, which is also about a headstrong dame," wrote Bosley Crowther in the *New York Times*. "But this time the lady is neither original nor is she Katharine Hepburn; she is just Loretta Young, flouncing and posing airily in a light-weight and silly marital comedy which runs through a routine rigmarole. So put "Bedtime Story" down as a trifle of small consequence. The ushers and attendants at the Music Hall should be able to catch some well-earned rest." James Francis Crow was downright giddy about March in his review in the *Hollywood Citizen News*, "This department has long been of the opinion that Fredric March is without peer for versatility among motion picture leading men, and the opinion is completely confirmed—as far as this department is concerned, at least—by the performance which March is giving in Columbia's 'Bedtime Story.'"

The film went on to make a modest profit for Columbia but was hardly a blockbuster.

With his picture commitments completed and with the tour of *Hope for the Harvest* to begin again in November, the Marches spent some time visiting family. First and foremost was a trip to Centralia, Washington, where they visited March's sister Bess and his father, who had moved to Washington to live with Bess due to his declining health. March later wrote to his brother Jack that the trip was "worth it" because his father was "slowly declining," though March's sister "would not admit it."

Hope for the Harvest reopened in Philadelphia on November 17, and picked up where it left off by garnering critical raves and strong box office. Henry Murdoch of the *Philadelphia Public Ledger* called it "the first play of the season to lay claim to stature."

Maybe so, but the New York critics didn't seem to think so. Despite the enthusiastic reviews on the road, the Broadway critics were decidedly mixed in their responses when it opened at the Guild Theater on November 26. Brooks Atkinson wrote in the *New York Times* that he came away from *Hope for a Harvest* "un-elated by what it had witnessed." He found Eldridge's performance, in the pivotal role, to be "attractive though slight." But he gave kudos to March who he believed delivered a "superb characterization." The *Herald Tribune* critic wrote, "Because 'Hope for a Harvest' has something of importance to say, and says it with unmistakable sincerity, one has from the start a sympathetic concern with it and a far deeper respect for its heart and mind than for more expert dramas of a lesser integrity." March gives a "splendid performance, which proves once more what a good, straightforward actor he really is." As for Eldridge, the reviewer felt that she "has a part which forces her at times to be too saccharine for comfort, but...plays with admirable directness, simplicity and feeling."

The next day, Walter Winchell wrote in his column, "The Theater Guild presented *Hope for a Harvest*, and kept up its run of bad luck. This drama by Sophie Treadwell is an earnest back to the farm plea. Some of its wordage was persuasive, but it's harvest was more hope than drama." *Time* magazine, a week later, was even more pessimistic, "Hope for the Harvest brought Fredric March from Hollywood to Broadway, but for no good reason."

On the third night of the Broadway run, March received the sad but not unexpected news that his father had died at the age of eighty-two at Bess's home in Washington. The body would be transported back to Racine for the funeral, scheduled for Sunday, December 7, 1941. The date was selected, in part, to accommodate March, who would leave for Racine following the Saturday evening performance of *Hope for a Harvest*, take an overnight flight to Chicago, and then motor up to Racine just in time to attend the 10 a.m. service. John F. Bickel would be buried next to his beloved wife. Afterwards, they spent time with relatives and friends before driving back to Chicago to board an overnight train back to New York. Earlier that day, they heard the shocking news that the Japanese had bombed Pearl Harbor. Within twenty-four hours the United States was at war, not only with the Japanese but the entire axis command—especially Nazi Germany and fascist Italy. With Pearl Harbor, any hope for the success of *Hope for a Harvest* probably died due to its sympathetic treatment of enterprising Japanese and Italian farmers. *Hope for a Harvest* closed on December 27, 1941, after only thirty-eight performances. March later maintained that it was a "fine play" but that it was "the wrong time to show it."

However, March didn't have long to wait before he would begin yet another film. One that would cast him as one of America's best loved writers and humorists.

V

The Adventures of Mark Twain is probably one of March's most famous films and performances. Yet, at the time, Warner Brothers wasn't eager to film it. Producer Jesse L. Lasky, who had brilliantly brought *Sergeant York* to the screen, fought for over a year to get Warner Brothers' executives interested in producing the picture. They weren't sure that a biography of Twain would have much relevance with wartime audiences. But, having produced one of the studios most prestigious pictures (*Sergeant York*), which brought in a huge bounty at the box office, Lasky finally convinced Jack Warner to bankroll the film.

Lasky understood that he needed a star name to play Clemens/Twain (just as he did when he got Gary Cooper to play Alvin York). He immediately thought of Fredric March. As a Twain fan from early on, March was enthusiastic about playing the man (whose real name was Samuel Clemens) who rode Mississippi steam boats, later reported on the California gold rush, and then found literary immortality under his pen name of Mark Twain.

One of the people who read the news reports about the film, and possible casting of March, was Twain's only living child, Clara Clemens Gabrilowitsch. She wrote March. "Rumor has again reached my ears that you have been selected to play the part of my father in the screen production of the new Mark Twain biography," Gabrilowitsch wrote March on February 17, 1942. "I am writing to express my complete satisfaction in this decision. You are, in my opinion, the one artist capable of impersonating the many sides of my father's nature. It will require a special kind of art to faithfully represent the deeply serious, even tragic strains of his disposition that alternated with the light, humorous impulses. I'm thankful the producer has placed you in this difficult role."

After March sent her a "gracious" reply, she wrote again on February 26, this time to let him know that she had telephoned the producer, Jesse Lasky, to present her "strong convictions as to who was capable and who was not capable of representing my father." She wrote March that the producer had inquired if she would be willing to come to the studio and pose for photographs with March and endorse him in print as her candidate to play her father. "Most certainly," was her response. Then she told Lasky she would only do this if they formally selected March, "If you select any other actor, I shall be unable to cooperate with the studio in any way." Lasky indicated to her that he was in favor of March, but that the final decision would be made the following week. She added to March, "If it all turns out according to my wish, I shall, of course be happy to give you any points about my father that I am capable of giving."

Despite this, March wasn't convinced he should play the role. He felt he could never physically impersonate Twain and that would not be helpful to his performance. March wasn't too worried about the earlier years, but he wanted to be sure he captured the elderly Twain that most people knew from photographs. According to a contemporary newspaper account, "Every day for twelve weeks, March secluded himself in the makeup department with a full-length mirror and a couple of Twain photographs. From time to time he watched the real Twain walk across the screen in about a hundred feet of film recorded just before the humorist's death. Then he ran an old phonograph record of Mark Twain's voice." With the help of three fake noses, March was finally convinced he could look like Twain as well as play him.

Lasky wanted Irving Rapper to direct, and the studio agreed, having been impressed at how well Rapper and March had worked together on *One Foot in Heaven*. However, Rapper wasn't at all sure he wanted to do the Twain film, but when he heard that March was set to star, he agreed. "I couldn't think of any other Hollywood actor who could do it and that includes Spencer Tracy," Rapper later said. "It came from the Harold Sherman play and the amount of money spent on décor and sets were truly huge. We had a two-month shoot, which was luxurious. Fred got better with this one as he aged." March later returned the compliment by saying that "Irving's a darling, an extraordinarily sensitive fellow. Perhaps it's that sensitivity that makes him so fine a director. Besides, he's always thinking up cute little things for each scene. I've been delighted to make two pictures with him."

For Mrs. Samuel Clemens, the producer wanted Olivia de Havilland (once again), but she was suspended by the studio for initially turning down the film *Princess O'Rourke*, and so she was replaced by Alexis Smith, an up-and-coming Warners contract player. Other parts were filled by such stellar contract players as Alan Hale, C. Aubrey Smith, John Carradine, and Percy Kilbride.

Most of the film was shot on the Warner Brothers back lot or on sound stages, but some second-unit footage was taken in Twain's hometown of Hannibal, Missouri, his study in Elmira, New York, and his home in Hartford, Connecticut. March would later say that the role of Twain was the "hardest" of his long career up to that time—harder than even Jekyll and Hyde. It was, he said, because he was playing such a larger-than-life character.

During production, March turned forty-five, and Lasky sent him a birthday telegram that praised his work:

DEAR FREDDIE MAY YOU ALWAYS REMEMBER THIS
BIRTHDAY AS THE YEAR OF YOUR GREATEST TRIMPH

PORTRAYING MARK TWAIN. CORDIAL BIRTHDAY GREETINGS. JESSE.

When the picture was completed, the studio had a backlog of films—as did most of the studios during the war years—and it was nearly two years later when *The Adventures of Mark Twain* was finally released. Twain's daughter attended a screening and wrote to March:

> *I have just seen the picture and am fully as delighted with your impersonation of my father as I expected to be. Your treatment of the various sheaths of his disposition was characteristic and convincing. Serious you were when making your jokes, just as he was. A certain pathetic wistfulness of mood also crept into your interpretation. And the bursts of temper lacked no bit of his warmth in quality and degree. There were times indeed, despite slight faults in the make-up, when the illusion was supreme. I lost you and found my dear father.*

When the film went into wide circulation, it proved to be a solid performer at the box office, and it received favorable reviews from most critics. "Fredric March, looking startlingly like all the familiar photographs of Twain, plays the character with respect and understanding...March, in his finest screen performance, captures Clemens's essential eagerness, the gift of seeing the world through youthful eyes," wrote the critic for the *New York Sun*. The *Hollywood Reporter* called Rapper's direction "great" and said March's "sincere performance really triumphs." March, himself, was proud of the film and always included it as one of his favorites. March would later be asked to play Twain again for a television production of Horton Foote's *The Shape of the River*. March turned the part down and instead Franchot Tone played the part.

By the time the film was released, March had already appeared on Broadway in his biggest triumph up to this time, which pitted him and Florence against one of their most formidable foes: Tallulah Bankhead.

PICTURE GALLERY
1915–1942

Fred Bickel at age 18 in 1915

Fred during World War I, circa 1919

An early Paramount publicity photograph of Fredric March, 1929

His big break—and first Oscar—*Dr. Jekyll & Mr. Hyde*, 1931

With Norma Shearer in the very popular *Smilin' Through*, 1932

With Kay Francis and Stuart Erwin in *Strangers in Love*, 1932,
photo courtesy of Scott O'Brien

With Charles Laughton and Claudette Colbert in Cecil B. DeMille's epic *The Sign of the Cross*, 1932

With Elissa Landi in _The Sign of the Cross_

With the lovely Evelyn Venable in one of March's finest films, *Death Takes a Holiday*, 1934

From Les Miserables, 1935

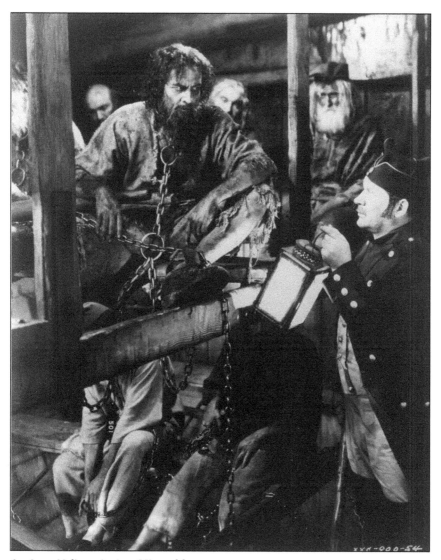

As Jean Valjean in *Les Miserables*

Warner Baxter, June Lang and March in Howard Hawks's *The Real Glory,* **1936**

One of the most popular March films of the 30s *Anthony Adverse*, 1936

Perhaps his finest screen performance as Norman Maine opposite Janet Gaynor in the original *A Star is Born*, 1937

As the pirate Jean Lafitte in DeMille's *The Buccaneer*, 1938

Publicity photograph for _Trade Winds_, 1938

With Joan Crawford in *Susan and God*, 1940

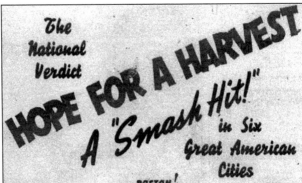

The National Verdict

HOPE FOR A HARVEST

A "Smash Hit!"

in Six Great American Cities

WASHINGTON!

"A beautiful and inspiring play...one of the genuinely exciting events of the year."
Bernie Harrison—Times Herald

"One of the most substantial hits of the season . . . the Marchs' triumph!"
Nelson B. Bell—Washington Post

"Simple, sincere, honest and humane in the light of this dark day."
Jay Carmody—Washington Star

"What you enjoy most is a collection of living, thinking, real people . . . the adjective to emerge is satisfying."
Don Craig—Washington News

BOSTON!

"A beautiful play, wise and sane and stirring . . . one of the major theatrical events of the season."
Elliott Norton—Boston Post

"Very good and exceptionally interesting . . . you will like the Marchs who play their parts as if they were born to them."
E. F. Harbiet—Boston Record

"Pleasant and refreshing . . . Miss Treadwell goes after an important social problem . . . but she takes along her sense of humor."
Boston Daily Globe

"An honest, sympathetic and eloquent picture filled with the heroic spirit which is the heritage of America."
Helen Eager—Boston Traveler

BALTIMORE!

"A thoughtful and most interesting drama done in that superb style for which the Guild has long been famous."
Norman Clark—Baltimore News Post

"A fine and provocative play saluted at the end with a prolonged burst of applause demanding many curtain calls."
Gilbert Kanour—Baltimore Evening Sun

"One of the most solid, thoughtful and stimulating evenings of the season . . . beautifully cast are Fredric March and Florence Eldridge."
Donald Kirkley—Baltimore Sun

The Theatre Guild Presents
AN AMERICAN COMEDY by SOPHIE TREADWELL with

FREDRIC MARCH
FLORENCE ELDRIDGE

ALAN REED

Staged by LESTER VAIL • Settings by WATSON BARRATT

PHILADELPHIA!

"A warm pulsing play . . . a play the actors seem to love and that affection was, inevitably, passed on to the capacity audience at the Walnut last night and held it throughout the evening in a glow of satisfaction."
Robert Sensenderfer—The Evening Bulletin—Philadelphia

"Authentically American, and it has a quality of engaging sincerity. The Theatre Guild has done itself proud."
Linton Martin—Philadelphia Enquirer

"The first play of the season to lay claim to stature."
Henry T. Murdoch—Public Ledger

PITTSBURGH!

"A play certainly superior to a lot of plays Broadway has already stamped with its approval this year and some of the best acting of the season."
Harold V. Cohen—Pittsburgh Post-Gazette

"'HOPE FOR A HARVEST' challenges America . . . March's play doesn't slight humor in attacking serious issues."
Kaspar Monahan—Pittsburgh Press

"A plea for tolerance in a vein of beautifully sustained simplicity."
Karl Krug—Pittsburgh Sun-Telegraph

NEW HAVEN!

"Beauty and wisdom and penetrating criticism of one phase of the American scene make this intensely moving drama an outstanding play."
New Haven Register

"'HOPE FOR A HARVEST' compelling . . . intense enthusiasm shown at the opening."
F. R. Johnson—New Haven Journal-Courier

"A play of striking beauty . . . 'HOPE FOR A HARVEST' has warmth, subtlety and vitality."
Bridgeport Post

"A play not to be overlooked."
Bridgeport Herald

—Enjoyed by over 75,000 theatregoers!
—Praised highly by 24 drama critics!
—Seats Selling Six Weeks in Advance!

GUILD THEA. 52d St., W. of B'way. Eves. 8:30. Mats. Thurs. & Sat. at 2:30. • CO. 5-8229

Hope for a Harvest brought March and Florence
Eldridge back to Broadway with a hit

FREDRIC MAR??
in Paramount Pictures

P1047-394

Publicity photo from the early '40s

CHAPTER NINE
INTERLUDE: SURVIVING TALLULAH
BY THE SKIN OF THEIR TEETH
1942–1943

In late December of 1941, only weeks following the Japanese attack on Pearl Harbor, one of America's most preeminent writers, Thornton Wilder, had just completed one of the most unusual and engrossing plays ever written—let alone produced.

The Skin of Our Teeth tells the story of a family that narrowly escapes one calamity after another that could lead to the end of the world. These calamities include the Ice Age, flood, famine, and war. The title is taken from the King James Bible, Job 19:20: "My bone cleaveth to my skin and to my flesh, and I am escaped with the *skin of my teeth.*"

In 1938, Wilder's play *Our Town* became an immediate critical and popular success. It had been produced and directed by Jed Harris on the Broadway stage and eventually won the Pulitzer Prize. Now, just three years later, with the world engulfed in war, Wilder wanted to express his own personal feeling that, contrary to the beliefs of many people who looked around them and saw nothing but death and sorrow, the world—mankind—would survive.

The play introduces the characters of George and Maggie Antrobus of Excelsior, New Jersey—married 5,000 years with two children. Gladys is perfect and sweet, while Henry (also known as Cain—he murders the Antrobus's other son) is imperfect and temperamental. The other leading character is their maid, Lily Sabina. At times during the play, Sabina will break character and address the audience directly, to explain some of the action—if she can! Even Sabina is confused at times, and at one point tells the audience, "I don't understand a word of this play." That there is confusion on the part of the audience was something that Wilder seemed to anticipate.

The play has esoteric themes and was heavily influenced by Wilder's love for, and appreciation of, James Joyce's *Finnegans Wake*.

Despite Wilder's great reputation, several prominent Broadway producers turned down the play. They simply couldn't understand it and felt that audiences too would have a hard time understanding its themes. Clearly Wilder wanted a producer who would take the play on faith. At this point, Wilder wasn't interested in making a lot of changes. He was rather satisfied with what he had written. Later on, he would concede some changes needed to be made. Wilder was clearly proud of his product and pretty much wanted it produced as-is. Finally he found thirty-five-year-old Michael Myerberg, who had just spent five years managing Leopold Stokowski, whose only previous Broadway show (in 1935), *Symphony*, had lasted only a few performances.

Myerberg was hard working, efficient, and a penny-pincher. He was also a sickly man. Elia Kazan would write of Myerberg as a "tall man, without the grace some tall men have, unnaturally thin, rickety, his complexion a washroom green." He also was a man who could stand up to actors without fear. Tallulah Bankhead would call Myerberg an "erratic, tactless man." But Wilder thought that Myerberg would be good at "dickering, middleman, promotion." Myerberg decided to take on the production because with the world at war he "foresaw war conditions favoring theatrical productions and limiting concert work." Despite not being the first choice to produce the play, Myerberg had ego enough to say, "There was never any doubt that I was the one to do the play." And instead of lining up a long line of big money investors, Myerberg ultimately ended up investing eighty percent of the money himself.

Wilder had initially wanted either Jed Harris or Orson Welles to direct his new play. Harris, however, wanted to make big changes in the script—particularly to the second and third acts. Wilder was opposed to this, and so slowly Harris faded from the picture. (Though later, Wilder would see some of Harris's points and did make some changes.) As for Welles, his movie commitments in Hollywood ruled him out. (Soon Wilder himself would be going to Hollywood to work with Alfred Hitchcock on the script for one of Hitchcock's best films *Shadow of a Doubt*.) In the end, Wilder and Myerberg would choose another young man, Elia Kazan (thirty-three), who had acted professionally on stage and radio, and who had been a member of the Group Theater for a decade. By the mid-thirties he had begun directing some Group productions, alternating between staging and performing. Earlier in 1942, Kazan had directed his first major Broadway production, *The Strings, My Lord, Are False,* which had run for a total of fifteen performances. Now available, Kazan accepted the invitation to direct a major play written by Thornton Wilder.

Myerberg told Kazan that he wanted "stars!—big ones" in the principal roles. Clearly Myerberg wanted to protect his investment as much as possible, and big star names could certainly help build advance ticket sales. At first, Myerberg had the provocative idea of casting Groucho Marx and Margaret Dumont as the Antrobuses, with Fanny Brice as Sabina. Wilder was intrigued, but reminded Myerberg that the play wasn't farce but a comedy-drama. This casting idea was soon abandoned. Then came the idea of casting the Lunt's as the Antrobuses, but they were confused by the script and politely declined.

Soon into the mix came the name of Fredric March to play Mr. Antrobus—an idea that both Myerberg and Wilder were excited about. What they were less than excited about was the idea of Florence playing Mrs. Antrobus, which they assumed that March would suggest. They felt that Florence could certainly handle the delicate dramatic moments but that she lacked a humorous touch in the comedy scenes. Wilder and Myerberg wanted Helen Hayes as Mrs. Antrobus. March later recalled that his agent sent the script of *The Skin of Our Teeth* to him and March said he was "excited and eager, of course…I read it and was enthusiastic about it. Then I passed it on to Mrs. March. We never try to influence each other in these things, so I said nothing."

They were correct that March would only do the play if Florence were cast along with himself. By this time, Helen Hayes had decided she couldn't play the part. For some reason, she had the idea that Wilder and Myerberg wanted her to play Sabina, rather than the wife, and she just couldn't see herself in that part. With some reluctance, they approved Florence for Mrs. Antrobus. Luckily— like March—Florence was enthusiastic about the script and wanted to play Mrs. Antrobus.

Soon, both Myerberg and Kazan were invited to the Marches' New York apartment to discuss the play with them. The Marches contract gave them directorial approval, so the meeting was very much an opportunity for them to scrutinize Kazan. If they decided they didn't want him, he would be out—despite Myerberg's assurances that he was the man who would direct.

Kazan later recalled waiting in the living room of the Marches apartment overlooking the East River with expensive art work on the wall, "I liked our kids' crayon dabbings better." Finally the Marches entered—Florence first, followed by a black servant who was pushing a cocktail cart, and then March. The servant prepared drinks while March attempted to lighten the mood with a few jokes to break what was for Kazan a tense scene. "Florence forced a laugh," Kazan later wrote. "I noticed that Freddie kept looking at Florence, rather like an anxious boy."

Kazan goes on to write:

> I continued "putting it on" for Florence, but Freddie and I understood each other immediately and without a word. He was an overgrown boy in a pin-striped blue suit and a banker's tie, but his smile promised mischief. I believe that this interview, which was an audition, embarrassed him. I'd find, as I came to know him that one of his pleasures was to be naughty and have Florence—his surrogate mother—chide him, "Now Freddie." He made me smile, as I still do when I remember him. He was, I'd find, one person when he was in the general vicinity of his wife and quite another out of her sight and hearing. Freddie seemed anxious to conclude the interview, she to prolong it.

Despite this, in the end Kazan found Florence to be a "decent, honest sincere, reliable woman," but found that these virtues could become "tedious" if they didn't include "doubt, self-deprecation, and openheartedness." He liked her but certainly wouldn't want to be married to her.

In the end, the Marches endorsed the selection of Kazan as director, and March also became an investor in the play. Now that the producer and director had their Mr. and Mrs. Antrobus, they needed to find their Lily Sabina. In the meanwhile, since rehearsals wouldn't begin until September, March had time to shoot a film.

II

I Married a Witch is a witty and amusing fantasy-comedy, which March completed in about six weeks in the spring of 1942, at Paramount, for the French director Rene Clair. Clair was acclaimed for his French comedies of the '20s and '30s, and this would be his second American film after *The Flame of New Orleans* (shot at Universal and starring Marlene Dietrich and Bruce Cabot, which turned out to be unsuccessful). Universal decided not to use Clair on another picture, so he accepted a one-shot deal at Paramount.

Clair later recalled that his agent, Myron Selznick (David Selznick's brother), had sent him a copy of a novel by Thorne Smith (with Norman H. Matson) titled *The Passionate Witch.* Smith was best known for his humorous supernatural novels featuring ghosts— such as his most famous *Topper* and *Topper Takes a Trip.* Both had been made into highly successful films and now, with *The Passionate Witch,* Paramount hoped gold would strike again. "I read it and thought I could do something with it," Clair later recalled in an interview for *Film Quarterly.* "I met Preston (Sturges), who eventually became a good friend of mine—he spoke French as well as I do—and who was then the leading director at Paramount. We talked over the project and he agreed to produce it for me." Friend or not, Sturges eventually left the project—finding Clair too fussy and authorative. Clair wound up producing the film himself.

The title of the film was changed to *I Married a Witch,* and it followed the novel fairly closely. It begins some 300 years in the past when Jennifer, a beautiful woman accused of being a witch by Jonathan Wooley, is burned at the stake, along with her father—a ripe beginning for a romantic comedy, huh? At the stake before being consumed by flames, she puts a curse on Wooley and all of his descendants so that they all would be unlucky in love. To keep the (supposedly) evil spirits from rising, an oak tree is planted over their grave. From there, we get quick comic vignettes showing the Wooley men and their unhappy unions—revolutionary times, civil war era, and in the early-twentieth century.

Next, the story is updated to current times and opens at a country club dance where budding politician Wallace Wooley and his fiancée, a social climber named Estelle, are celebrating their engagement. Suddenly, a storm causes a lightning strike, which topples the oak tree, freeing the spirits of Jennifer and her father. Jennifer takes human form, and has great fun in trying to break up Wallace and Estelle—eventually falling in love with the mortal Wallace. They eventually marry, and she confesses to be a witch. After some further complications by her father, Daniel, the two live happily ever after. Sound familiar? This film, along with the later *Bell, Book & Candle* (Columbia, 1958), were inspirations for the long-running classic television comedy *Bewitched*.

Paramount wanted to do something fresh with one of its most potent leading ladies, Veronica Lake. They decided that she needed a change of pace from films like *This Gun for Hire* and *The Glass Key*, and so cast her as the beautiful witch. For Wooley, Paramount initially wanted to cast Joel McCrea, who had worked well opposite Lake in Preston Sturges's terrific *Sullivan's Travels*. Apparently, McCrea wasn't hip on working with her again and begged out—though they would later reunite for the Andre de Toth western *Ramrod*. With McCrea out of the picture, Paramount offered the role to March, who liked the script and the fantasy element, and he accepted enthusiastically. It was also a quick way for him to make an easy $100,000 before returning to Broadway that fall for *The Skin of Their Teeth*. For the spoiled Estelle, Paramount cast another of its contract players, Susan Hayward. Cecil Kellaway is cast as Daniel, Jennifer's father, and Robert Benchley, Elizabeth Patterson, and Robert Warwick fill out other key roles.

Veronica Lake was enthused about playing the role of Jennifer and was happy to be cast in a comedy. At first, Clair wasn't sure he wanted her. He thought she was at her best playing bad girls and might not have the necessary light touch for a project such as this. Lake appealed to Sturges who agreed to talk to Clair and convinced him that she could handle the job. Later, after viewing the first week's rushes, Clair apologized to Lake for initially having doubts about her.

While Lake and Clair ended up working harmoniously together, the same couldn't be said of March and Lake. March viewed the film as a profitable vacation and a bit of a trifle to work on before heading to Broadway in the fall. He was in full-fledged "mischievous Freddie" mode when he came on the set. He came to regard Lake as a "brainless little blonde sexpot, void of any acting ability." However, he did pull his usual "twenty fingers" routine of fanny pinching, much to Lake's annoyance. Paramount publicist Teet Carle later recalled, "Fredric March had worked with many beautiful actresses, and found Veronica every bit as breathtaking. Well, she used to rail into him about being a horny old guy, since he tried making advances on her and the other women working in the film." When March's advances towards Lake were thwarted, he turned openly antagonistic towards her. Lake responded in kind.

Lake didn't try to make it easy when March had to pick her up and carry her in one scene. She had a forty-pound weight sewn into her gown. March, nonplussed, asked Lake how such a small girl could weigh so much. She slyly replied, "big boned."

Lake was more forward in her next prank on March. In a scene where she is knocked out by a falling picture frame while sitting on a chair, March enters the room and approaches her, believing that she is awake, and speaks dialogue to her. As he stood over her, and out of camera range, Lake shoved her foot into March's groin, ". . . and I moved my foot up and down, each upward movement pushing it ever so slightly into his groin," Lake later wrote. "Pro that he is, he never showed his predicament during the scene. But it wasn't easy for him, and I delighted in knowing what was going through his mind. Naturally, when the scene was over, he laced into me. I just smiled."

While March was his usual dependable self, Lake had a reputation for not showing up for her calls on time and keeping cast and crew waiting. This didn't endear her to the Paramount front office or the crews of the pictures she worked on. She later told a story on herself, which was repeated in the book *Peekaboo*:

> *I had been called in for a portrait sitting with Freddie March for a certain day—and, well, time got away from me. Freddie, however, was on time. So was the photographer. There they sat and waited for me. Finally, they notified the front office and the front office called me. I tore down to the studio and found*

Freddie ready to slit my throat, for which I couldn't blame him, but at the moment it made me mad too. The crazy part of the whole affair was that we had to take love scenes, and, when I saw the finished results, I roared with laughter. Such pure loathing you've never seen on any two faces, particularly when they were lying so alluringly cheek-to-jowl. So I went to Freddie and apologized. He agreed to make the sitting over, and that time the results were slick.

Susan Hayward was also unhappy on the film. She was back playing third fiddle after having been top billed in her last picture. She also didn't particularly like playing the shrew. She could be withdrawn and difficult with her fellow players, but March later forgave her. "She was touchy on the set, and it was a rare day (when) she mingled with the cast," March later said of Hayward. "But somewhere along the line she learned to act. Every inch of that woman is an actress. . .."

Despite the troubles between the two leads and a sulking supporting leading lady, the film comes off well. Pros that they are, you can't tell that March and Lake were antagonistic towards each other for the entire shoot. March was twenty-five years older than Lake but their love scenes have passion and sex appeal. The film is fun, droll, and romantic. Robert Pirosh, Marc Connelly, and Dalton Trumbo did a superb job of adapting the novel into screenplay form, and Clair directed with a light and sophisticated touch—almost Lubitch-esque. The black-and-white cinematography (by long time Paramount pro Ted Tezlaff) is beautiful. In fact, of the films made out of Thorne Smith novels, I think this is the best adaptation—including *Topper*.

During the war years, the studios had a backlog of films, and Paramount decided to sell *I Married a Witch* to United Artists who then released it under their banner. When the film was released in October of 1942, it proved to be a big financial success for UA—perhaps making Paramount have second thoughts about selling it. Most of the reviews were favorable. Bosley Crowther in the *New York Times* wrote:

Mr. Clair has devised... quaint and agreeable nonsense...

Mr. Clair, in his old pre-Hollywood fashion, has a lot of fun with spooks and camera tricks—a bit stiffly, perhaps, in comparison with the sport of his better French films, but till a high bounce above the usual run of cinematic whimsies. Miss Lake, with her mocking eyes and soft drawl, exorcises herself most fetchingly, and Mr. March is amusingly sozzled by her baffling bedevilments.

III

Meanwhile, as March was filming in Hollywood, Myerberg and Wilder were thick in the hunt for an actress to play Lily Sabina in *The Skin of Their Teeth*. Lily Sabina appears in several guises throughout the play: chambermaid, bathing beauty, and camp follower, as well as stepping out of character and addressing the audience directly. It could be argued that with the Marches they had star names—at least with March—but Myerberg was certain that they also needed a major name for Sabina too. Wilder had considered his good friend Ruth Gordon, but her lack of sex appeal worked against her. Myerberg didn't think Ruth Gordon could seduce Mr. Antrobus while wearing a swimsuit. Enter Tallulah Bankhead.

Bankhead had actually been suggested by Helen Hayes, when Hayes was under the misguided thought that she was being considered for Sabina rather than Mrs. Antrobus. She had written Wilder that she could only see Tallulah in the part. The more they thought of it, the more Wilder and Myerberg liked the idea of Bankhead as Sabina.

Bankhead was a fine actress with a flamboyant personality. For a long time she was considered a personality actress—who carried whatever plays she did through the force of her own distinct personality. Then came *The Little Foxes* and her ruthlessly unbendable performance as Regina Giddens. It silenced her detractors and won her the New York Drama Critics Circle Award for best performance by an actress.

As with the Marches, Kazan also had to "audition" for Bankhead. This proved to be a much more unpleasant experience. Years later Kazan would write, "I've hated only two people in my life. One was Tallulah Bankhead." The meeting with Bankhead took place in

Bankhead's sitting room at the Elysee Hotel. After keeping Kazan and Myerberg waiting for fifteen minutes, the great lady finally made her entrance, looking, as Kazan recalled it, "as though she'd had a bad night." Kazan recalled smiling at her but only to receive an icy stare back. Bankhead ignored Kazan and spent all her time speaking quietly in one corner with Myerberg. When they left, Myerberg told Kazan "not to worry," but worry he did. He was certain that Bankhead would try to get rid of him. He would begin rehearsals but not without continued difficulty from Bankhead.

With three stars—or four if you count Broadway character actress Florence Reed, cast as the fortune teller—there was a question of billing. Bankhead's contracts always specified solo top billing, but finally she was convinced to relinquish this and agreed to share star billing above the title with both Marches—provided that she receive the more prominent leftward position. The Marches agreed.

By mid-September of 1942, rehearsals began at the Plymouth Theater in New York, in preparation for a four-week series of previews that would begin in New Haven in Mid-October. Kazan later recalled that first day of rehearsals:

> *Four stars and Monty Clift (cast as the Antrobuses' son Henry), were lined up before me. I introduced them to each other. The traditional show business embraces were not forthcoming; they nodded, smiled, waved hands, kept their distance. Monty was visibly impressed with the select company he was part of. Florence Reed…was visibly impressed with no one. Florence Eldridge March chattered, straining to be believed the cordial one—for the record, I suppose; I can't imagine she had any liking for Bankhead. Tallulah responded with her horse's laugh and nicotine cough. I'd anticipated that Mrs. March, with her rather artificial manners, 'society' laugh, and inflated big-star posture, would be an irresistible target for Tallulah, and I could see from the glint in the bitch's eye that she smelled blood. As for Freddie March, he was on guard, anticipating that Miss Bankhead's purpose would be to make rehearsals so tense that she, not the play, would become the problem and everyone would be spending his best energies satisfying her wishes. With these observations in mind, I'd seated Freddie between his wife and Miss Bankhead.*

By this time, Thornton Wilder was serving in the Air Force at Hamilton Field in California. He put his starstruck sister Isabel in the rehearsal hall to be his eyes and ears. Isabel would later state that Bankhead "tried to have everybody fired. She tried to run everything. It wasn't nastiness; it was just the way she lived." As for Myerberg, Isabel believed him to be only concerned about "the bottom line." She felt that Kazan "did a very good job for such a young man, but he was too new to have such a big show." She also found him to be "crude and cocky, a young man who didn't know how to conduct himself." It was also her observation that Kazan was "horrid to Tallulah."

The Marches had insisted that there only be four weeks of previews before opening the play in New York. Myerberg wrote to their agent at the Myron Selznick agency on September 28, 1942:

> *...our present plans call for four and one-half weeks. The extra half weeks is New Haven which will enable us four days of dress rehearsals with sets. I am sure that Mr. and Mrs. March will understand the wisdom of this and I hope you will be able to get their immediate consent to this additional half week.*

They did.

Myerberg, to keep his stars happy, had "two star dressing rooms on the stage of the (Plymouth) theater" built for occupancy by the time the play made its Broadway opening. There would be one dressing room shared by the Marches, and another for Bankhead.

Meanwhile, things were not going well during rehearsals. "The tensions between the Marches and Bankhead, which I'd anticipated, were really there," Kazan recalled, "and it was my job daily to prevent fights between them." Kazan contends that the prospect of playing opposite Bankhead "terrified" Florence. He said that daily Florence warned him to be "on guard" against "the bitch." Meanwhile, Bankhead despised Florence as a "goody-goody" and somebody who pretended to be above it all. Kazan says that Florence, as an actress, wanted his "protection and endless explanations" while Bankhead wanted "unwavering attention and admiration"—a prospect that Kazan found odious. Dick Van Patten, signed for the role of a delivery boy, later said that there was "real jealousy" between Tallulah and

Florence, but that it was more so on Florence's part. Florence Heflin (sister of Van Heflin) cast as the daughter, Gladys, later recalled Florence and Tallulah having words, which ended with Bankhead telling Florence, "Oh, why don't you stop being such a tight, neurotic bitch."

As for March, Kazan found him to be a dream and really his only real buddy in the cast. March's only request of his director was "don't let me ham it up." He, as well as anybody, knew that he had a tendency to over play things unless a director took a firm hand. Kazan found this request "the simplest to satisfy."

One morning, at the end of the first week of rehearsals, Bankhead didn't show up. Kazan knew this was it; Bankhead was going to demand that in return for coming back, Myerberg get rid of him. Kazan called Myerberg, and found that the producer would back him up. "Put the understudy in" he told Kazan. Kazan protested that the understudy had had no time to prepare, and Myerberg told him to do it anyway. March knew that something was up, with no Bankhead and the understudy suddenly taking the stage for rehearsals, and came up to Kazan to reassure him that he was behind him. "That meant a lot to me."

Bankhead's gripe was that Kazan "didn't know how to direct a star." He told her that there were three other stars also in the company who were not complaining, and Bankhead replied, "Of course not, you're throwing it all to them." Finally, Myerberg made it clear that the understudy was being prepared, so if it was an either Kazan or Bankhead proposal, the producer was going to side with his director. Grudgingly, Bankhead returned.

Cast tensions seemed to cool prior to the first preview in Hartford on October 14. Florence Heflin later said, "everybody was getting along quite splendidly. Tallulah was a terrible hypochondriac, as were all the actors in the show. Tallulah, Freddie and Florence would get together and decided who would find the various doctors in every town for the various ailments they might have: throat doctor, internist, chiropractor, and masseuse."

The era of good feeling didn't last. Tallulah was especially nervous regarding the Hartford opening, and was, per Kazan, "looking for something to rant about…Even when she was off stage, she could be heard cursing the set, its designer, the management and me. She demanded that 'wings' be set up to shield her entrances. Myerberg refused to alter the sets." In this, Tallulah had an ally in Florence March and Florence Reed, enough for Myerberg to send out a memo to the three actresses stating, "The fundamental basis of our plan is the free use of the stage. We believe that the open stage adds immeasurably to the atmosphere and effectiveness of the play and the players. In this style of production consistency is the challenge and while the changes you have individually requested, may appear trivial, the lightest variation destroys our plans."

Kazan later wrote of the first dress rehearsal before the Hartford opening:

> *The first dress rehearsal was a nightmare of hysteria. Bankhead was never quiet off stage, never on time for her entrances, never anything but hateful to the other actors. Florence March was wretched and, it seemed to me, frightened. Freddie furious; Florence Reed haughty and scornful of all; and Monty Clift awed by the minefields of temperament exploding all around him.*

The opening in Hartford went well. There was a full house, and the audience reaction was good. Myerberg later said, "I tell you, if we hadn't had a full house when the play opened in New Haven, we might never have gotten out of town." On this Bankhead concurred, writing in her autobiography that if Hartford hadn't gone well they would all have had to hitchhike to their next stop in Baltimore.

The play moved on to Baltimore, Washington, D.C., and Philadelphia, where the *Philadelphia Record* critic wrote, "As strange and as brilliant, as cockeyed as a profound, as farcical and as moving as anything the stage has seen in many a season." *The Philadelphia Inquirer* critic was equally pleased calling *The Skin of Our Teeth*, "An outstanding event and an arresting experience in any season." Yet, despite good box office and strong notices, there was an element that didn't understand the play. It was above their heads—it didn't make sense. At each of the preview cities, there were patrons who left the theater at intermission and demanded their money back, despite the star cast.

Bankhead continued to be difficult—enough so that Myerberg ended up writing about her behavior while Wilder was at officer training camp at Hamilton Field in California. On October 27, the playwright responded:

Naturally I am astonished at the degree of Tallulah's difficulty; but I am convinced by your description. So conceding what are lion-tamers technique is necessary still hope for the day when such provocation of her hatred can be gradually transferred to something more paternalistic, that would be the real triumph...The Marches have each written good 'manly' letters and I have more and more admiration for them as persons. I hope you can find occasions to express your admiration for their work and to do them some kind of 'favors' of regard. . . .

IV

The Skin of Their Teeth opened on November 18, 1942, at the Plymouth Theater, but just prior to the curtain rising, the Marches sent a telegram to Myerberg:

MAY THIS LAUNCH YOU ON A TOP FLIGHT PRODUCING CAREER.

BEST WISHES
FREDDIE AND FLORENCE

The advance ticket sales had been excellent, and the play opened to strong box office as well as strong reviews. Brooks Atkinson wrote in the *New York Times*, "An original, gay-hearted play...one of the wisest and friskiest comedies written in a long time." His counterpart at the *Herald*, Howard Barnes wrote, "Theater-going became a rare and electrifying experience last evening. A vital and wonderful piece of theater, brilliantly staged and decorated. A major event of this or any season." The *New Yorker* theater critic Wolcott Gibbs wrote:

Fredric March and Florence Eldridge, as Mr. and Mrs. Antrobus, achieve just the proper combination of the normal and the supernatural; they speak with the unmistakable accents of suburban America, but it is also easy to believe that they have been married for five thousand years. This is an impressive accomplishment, surpassed only by that of Miss Bankhead, who gives what may be the most brilliant and is certainly the most versatile performance of her career.

By December 5, 1942, *The Nation* was writing:

The Skin of Our Teeth is an interesting experiment by any definition. A few nights after it opened in New York the S.R.O. sign was out, and patrons were hanging over the rail at the rear of the auditorium. Something that looked to the best judges like a perfect example of what closes Saturday night, something that provoked audiences in the try-out towns to demand their money back, was, in Broadway's own language, a smash hit.

Yet the walkouts still continued—even in New York. "The show opened…and Thornton had what he deserved, an enormous hit," Elia Kazan later wrote. "*Skin* became the only thing to see, and we were set for a long run. Many of the audience were mystified—what did the play mean?—and there were walkouts. But those reactions were part of the talk that made the play immediately famous."

But, behind the scenes, things were still tense. You would think that being in one of the biggest and most talked about hits on Broadway would bring some cessation of the backstabbing, but that wasn't the case. With Myerberg in Florida, recuperating from an illness, and Kazan moving on to other projects, Tallulah began upstaging Florence to draw attention away from her during a key speech that she delivers in the second act. Florence had a special affinity for this dialogue, and one has to think that she was not only thinking of Mr. and Mrs. Antrobus as she was delivering these lines, but also Mr. and Mrs. March:

I didn't marry you because you were perfect. I didn't even marry you because I loved you. I married you because you gave me a promise. That promise made up for your faults. And the promise I gave you made up for mine. Two imperfect people got married and it was the promise that made the marriage. And when our children were growing up, it wasn't a house that protected them; and it wasn't our love that protected them—it was that promise.

Florence called Kazan, and tearfully asked him to come to a performance to observe what was happening. Kazan sneaked into a matinee and saw for himself that during Florence's big scene Tallulah was "throwing her head back over a railing downstage, letting her blond hair fall free, then combing it out slowly and proudly, Florence was right, of course—this byplay distracted from the effect of her big moment, and Bankhead knew what she was doing and was doing it on purpose." Afterwards, Kazan approached Bankhead in her dressing room, and told her in no uncertain terms that he knew what she was doing and she should stop it. She angrily told him to leave.

Kazan told March that his mission had been unsuccessful and apologized. March, suffering from a bad sore throat, told Kazan that he would handle it. Kazan recorded what March proceeded to do during that night's performance:

I watched the show from the wings. Bankhead did it again. Then, in the next act, she had her own big moment, one that was her favorite because it was both serious and sentimental. It followed an exit by Freddie. I saw him walk into the wings, where his dresser was waiting with a small enamel bowl in which there stood a glass containing a medical solution. Freddie lifted the glass to his lips, tilted his head back—he was standing just off-stage, where some of the audience could see him—and he gargled. Then he emptied his mouth into the enamel bowl and, as Bankhead spoke, gargled again—I could hear it clear across stage—and again emptied his mouth. As he went on, his gargles were timed to coincide with the lady's lines. I saw her look in Freddie's direction and get the message.

Bankhead relented and let Florence have her big scene without upstaging her. But she did attempt revenge on March. During a scene where Bankhead plays a beauty queen trying to seduce Mr. Antrobus, they share a kiss. The uninhibited Bankhead thrust her tongue deep into March's mouth. March's solution? He bit it. Bankhead never tried that again.

With Myerberg off in Florida recuperating, his eyes and ears became the company production manager, a man named Benny Stein. He kept his boss up to date on how things were going financially and with the personalities involved—and their assorted ups and downs:

> **DECEMBER 12, 1942:** *The Company is getting along fine. Everybody seems to be quite happy backstage, and I feel it best, as long as they are happy, to leave them alone.*

> **DECEMBER 16, 1942:** *Business in New York is the worst we have had in many years, and for what reason, I do not know. It is of course a well-known fact that during the Christmas weeks business in general slides about 15%, and hits about 5.*

By the eighteenth, the show lost March, who got an infected eye from a cut—his doctors told him that under no condition should he work with this injury or he could be blinded.

> **DECEMBER 18, 1942:** *I'm terribly sorry that Freddie March, if he is really in such great pain as Miss Eldridge tells me he is, is suffering so much. It seems that the cornea was torn, or cut into, and that, I understand, is a very painful thing.*

> *Tallulah had made the remark to Eldridge that Freddie had better hurry back because the understudy (an actor named Blair Davies) was giving a brilliant performance, and apparently that upset her.*

> *Took it upon myself in spite of everything to call March up and find out how he felt...he admitted to me on the phone that he was terribly surprised that we only had to refund $41.00.*

> **DECEMBER 21, 1942:** *Spoke with March today, and am afraid he will not appear at least until Saturday. He was, however, much more cheerful on the telephone and told me that the doctor*

definitely told him to stay out or he might be laid up for quite a while.

December 23, 1942: *Freddie March's understudy does an excellent job—I caught about an act and a half of his performance last Saturday afternoon. I thought he was quite effective in the latter potions of the first act which is when I arrived, and at the beginning of the second act you couldn't tell him from Freddie…I understand Florence felt that the show should have closed during Freddie's absence and he is probably a little miffed that the refunds have not been staggering.*

Yet, it doesn't appear that the Marches had any problems with Blair Davies, the understudy, who sent March a Christmas greeting:

Dear Mr. March,

Thank you for your encouragement and consideration. Your faith in me has been the well from which I gathered courage to carry on. I can only hope that all those things you want most will be yours. Merry Christmas and Happy New Year.

Sincerely,
Blair Davies.

On Christmas Eve, in a telegram to Myerberg, the Marches thanked the producer for "the lovely poinsettia" plant he sent them, and let him know that "the eye is mending rapidly and plans to brave the footlight Saturday matinee."

March returned the day after Christmas and by December 30, the next crisis rose, as recorded by Stein to Myerberg:

December 30, 1942: *Understand that Montgomery Clift is being inducted about the 18th of January. However, from his own doctor's report, he doesn't think he will be accepted, but as you know, they are taking anybody his age whose blood is warm, so Kazan is busy looking around for somebody to step in, just in case. He had a few readings yesterday, for protection. Have suggested to*

001

Clift that he go to his Draft Board and request an immediate examination, because I believe that in cases where a draftee might be turned down on his physical and then find his job gone, they are willing to co-operate, so that he may discover his exact status before the date on which he is called. In any event, will see that we are covered.

JANUARY 4, 1943: *Monty Clift is having his examination tomorrow and we will know definitely by tomorrow night whether he will be in or out. Kazan was very happy about the boy getting the examination so soon so that we will know where we stand.*

JANUARY 6, 1943: *Monty Clift, as I wired you, has been deferred for the time being, but am sure that on Tuesday when he goes for his final examination, he will be rejected as I have had some big people work on this with me.*

JANUARY 27, 1943: *Tallulah, who has been ailing for quite a while, has been having a check up at the hospital since Monday, cardiograms, etc. Last night she sent for me and told me that she has been diagnosed as having ulcers of the stomach. She told me that although other people pretend to have so much sympathy for her, she is quite sure they don't believe she really has ulcers (meaning the March's.) She is now on a strict diet of milk, and she will carry on with the play regardless.*

Meanwhile, by the end of January, it was Myerberg who was in hot water with Florence over the firing of Morton Da Costa, who played the announcer in the play. Da Costa—later to become well known as the director of such stage hits as *No Time for Sergeants, Auntie Mame,* and *The Music Man*—was felt by Myerberg to be disposable, as were other minor actors, and his nightly announcement was to be assumed by March's understudy, Blair Davies. Florence wrote a "Dear Mike" letter, which in part read:

You're not very popular around here at the moment…I want to present what goes on here, in terms of human values. Da Costa was good in his job and his performance…He was a pleasant person in the company, cheerful, well-meaning and not given to intrigue. I personally found him to be an oasis back stage...Now people have said to me—don't mention the fact that Blair Davies is bad as the announcer. It will cost him his job...Please get De Costa back and keep Davies for his month as understudy—you owe it to them and to your own future reputation as a square producer. We are all working under pressure with Reed out, Tallulah with a bad ulcer...and Monty Clift is not a well person...Never has a play seen so many catastrophes and never have I been so conscious of an inharmonious experience...Freddie and I have really struggled to keep some kind of happy, healthy spirit afloat and in this you can throw your weight on our side I've asked very little of you, Mike, and I've worked very hard sometimes against odds, and now I ask you to be just and decent. I hope you won't fail me.

Sincerely,
Florence Eldridge

Myerberg was not at all pleased by the letter and quickly wrote a reply to "Dear Florence":

Your letter is a strange mixture of a stone hatchet with feathers—the edge still cuts. At any rate it is nice to hear from you, even with my scalp the object of your affection. . . .

He went on to defend the cuts he made, and pointed out that after a gross of some $350,000, she had received $10,000 while March and Bankhead had received $35,000, and while he had put up eighty percent of the money for the show, he had so far received no salary. He ended the letter giving Florence the victory by telling her to tell Stein to "reengage Da Costa."

As it turned out, the Marches and Bankhead were united in their disdain for the producer. They all felt that Myerberg tried to cut too many corners and had insufficient understanding of how to treat and run a theatrical company.

By March, all three stars informed Myerberg that they wouldn't return to the play when their standard six month contracts expired. It was a united and almost unprecedented move for a play that was still performing well at the box office. Myerberg attempted to keep the play going. He enlisted Mariam Hopkins to replace Bankhead. He put out a feeler to Spencer Tracy to replace March, but Tracy declined due to movie commitments. Eventually, Conrad Nagel took on the part. With new stars, a new tour began, but the show didn't perform well at the box office, so Myerberg made the decision to close the production, despite it winning the Pulitzer Prize as the Best play of 1942.

Late in March's life, he and Florence were interviewed by the *New York Times* and asked what it was like to work with Tallulah Bankhead. Here is the response:

"What was it like to work with Tallulah?" gasped March, his eyes popping, and then narrowing. "It was…"

"Freddie!" Miss Eldridge interrupts, in the nick of time. At seventy-one, she was still a handsome woman—a pleasing mixture of delicacy and strength. "Tallulah is dead, and I don't think we should go into all that ancient history. Let's just say that we used to stop by the doctor's before each performance for our B-1 shots and so we managed to make it through all right."

CHAPTER TEN
1943–1945

March was exhausted by the end of the production of *The Skin of Our Teeth* and wasn't eager to get back into another play or filmmaking. He thought that, maybe by the fall, he and Florence might find another play to go into so, for the summer, the family spent much of their time at their farm in New Milford, Connecticut. He and Florence worked their Victory Garden, getting bronzed by the sunshine in the meanwhile. The garden produced tomatoes, potatoes, corn, beans, asparagus, and strawberries. The chicken coop was also busy with egg-producing hens. There was also a little brook that Penny, now age eleven, and Tony, nine, would fish. "Yes," Florence told a reporter, "it is really our idea of a complete home."

March did take time off from the farm to put in a few days recording narration for a wartime documentary about our wartime ally, Russia, titled *Black Sea Fighters*. Like American war documentaries of the same time, it contains actually war footage and tells the story of the 250-day battle for the naval base of Sevastopol, which the Nazis had expected would be a relatively easy battle for them to win. The script was written by the noted playwright Clifford Odets. March's role in the production of this documentary would be one of the issues that would later dog him with accusations of being a Communist sympathizer.

After recording the documentary, March returned to the farm to while away a tranquil summer, but as the long summer days drew to a close, no film or stage offers came about that interested him. Instead, he decided to embark on a USO tour. Fredric March on a USO tour? Sure, he was one of the great actors of his time, but what could he do to entertain GIs? He wasn't a singer, a dancer, or a comic. Of course, that didn't matter, and the USO was enthusiastic about having him. March later said he had ". . . war jitters very badly and was anxious to get in where I could be of most service."

In the fall of 1943, March embarked on a 33,000 mile tour that took him to military camps and hospitals on five continents (North and South America, Africa, Asia, and Europe) and along the way delivered some 160 performances. Joining him were comedian Sammy Walsh, singer Jeanne Darrell, and accordionist Evelyn Hamilton.

The first two weeks of the tour were spent in South America, and from there they would fly to the Ascension Islands, in the South Atlantic, and then on to Africa. They then proceeded to tour across Central Africa to the Indian Ocean and then fly up to Iran, where they would travel the entire country by railroad and automobile. From there, they would fly on to Cairo and head up to North Africa, playing in Tunis and Algiers, before flying into Italy for a visit that was only a few miles from the front.

Beginning in Brazil, March quickly realized that the act he originally planned for himself would need tweaking, due to the expectations of his audience who knew him primarily as a dramatic actor. "I had a lot of humorous stuff, kidding news commentators and radio in general. Something light to make them laugh," March later recalled. "But it wasn't what they wanted from me. I found out from letters the men wrote home after our performance. The censor gave me a line on this. The men wrote that we'd 'given a swell show and all that, but they'd hoped for something more serious from Mr. March.'" One particular performance in Brazil stuck in March's mind, and he later spoke about it on radio:

> We had done three shows that day, at two separate Navy Camps and one hospital. We were told that the USO had invited us to join them at their very attractive diggings in town after our last show. We arrived tired, but happy to be able to let sown a bit and enjoy some Brazilian lemon-squash, or whatever, and doughnuts. Imagine our surprise when we discovered some one hundred and fifty chairs all set up neatly out under the stars facing the stage. I'm afraid we gave a synopsized version of our one-hour and twenty-minute show, but they were most appreciative and their subsequent

hospitality was infinitely better than our performance had been.

March telephoned Florence and requested that she send some scenes from plays he had done. The March troop, known as Unit #109, came and went from one locale to another so quickly that the material never caught up with him, so instead he decided to perform a passage from Thomas Paine's Pamphlet ("There are times that try men's souls") and an excerpt from President Franklin Roosevelt's "No Compromise Speech." This turned out to be a high point of the show, as March would face his audience at the climax of the show and say:

> *Gentlemen, I would like to read to you a message from your commander-in-chief—your commander-in-chief and mine, from his radio address to the nation in January, 1942, when we had been in the war less than a month, which many of you may recall having herd before you left I quote the last two paragraphs:*

> *"We are fighting, as our fathers have fought, to uphold the doctrine that all men are equal in the sight of God. Those on the other side are striving to destroy this deep belief and create a world in their own image, a world of tyranny and cruelty and serfdom. That is the conflict that day and night now pervades our lives. No compromise can end that conflict—there never has been—there can never be successful compromise between good and evil. Only total victory can reward the champions of tolerance and decency and freedom and faith. . . ."*

March was a political supporter and great admirer of the president, and he had once met with President Roosevelt at the White House. "I came into one of the downstairs rooms and saw him before a battery of cameras—those were the days of theater news reels," March later recalled.

> *He was making a speech and behind him was Jimmy, Elliot, Franklin, John and Betsy and some of the other wives who have since gone. FDR read a few paragraphs, then said, "Cut!" Change*

lenses!" Afterwards I met him and he asked, "How do you like the way I direct my own scenes, Mr. March?" I told him, "I like the way you direct everything, Mr. President," I wanted to add, "Except my income tax," Later I told Jimmy (FDR's son) who said if I had told it to his father, he would have gotten a big laugh.

The March show usually opened with the comedy of Sammy Walsh—not well known today, Walsh was at that time a highly regarded night club comedian and spent a good deal of the war entertaining the troops. Then, Jeanne Darrell would come on to sing a few songs, of which the highlight would be her performance of "All of Me," while in the arms of some lucky serviceman. Darrell was doing her bit for the boys, while her husband was serving in the Marine corp. Then Evelyn Hamilton would appear and play a few songs on her accordion. Finally, March would begin his perform-ance in a humorous vein before launching into the Thomas Paine and FDR excerpts. He also amazed the troops by performing the transformation scene from *Dr. Jekyll and Mr. Hyde.* "It was quite a contrast to do that, just standing there on a platform," he later recalled. Finally, the entire cast would come out and take a bow together and then meet and shake hands with audience members—many of whom would give them messages for family members back home.

They were in Cairo on Thanksgiving Day, 1943, where they dined, with American troops, on turkey with all the trimmings, and then enjoyed an impromptu football game between different divisions. In Iran, they performed a special command performance for the Shah—with whom March also played tennis with. At one point, he had the opportunity to meet General Eisenhower in North Africa. "What a man he is!" March recalled, "He really believes we're fighting to make things better for people, and he has such wonderful enthusiasm. 'When you talk to the men,' he told me, 'they'll listen to you because they don't have to. Won't you say something about how we Allies must all stick together?'"

Noted wartime journalist Ernie Pyle covered the March show from Algiers, where he wrote, "Usually these camp shows are very light. Fredric March brings the first serious note to soldiers' entertainment that I've run onto. It's pretty touchy business, but he gets it over…Since he has played mostly to non-combat troops in isolated areas, he does some morale building by telling them their jobs are as necessary and contributory as anybody else's."

Towards the end, they spent six days in Italy—where one performance was staged only twenty miles from enemy lines. March's pilot, Lt. Norton Goodwin, later recalled a close call they had when flying to Italy when one of the "prop governors" (engines) went out. "… I was worried. I passed the word back that we might encounter trouble, but everybody took pretty lightly… we managed to get to our destination on one motor."

Lt. Goodwin had happy memories of March, who, like everybody, called him "Freddie." "Freddie was a lot of fun to travel with," Goodwin recalled. "It always used to make me laugh when I saw (him) trying to make himself comfortable in the 'bucket seats' we had on the bomber. The seats resembled an ice cream freezer and were as uncomfortable. Freddy told me he felt he understood crabs perfectly now since he had traveled about 10,000 miles sidewise like a crab in these bucket seats."

The excellence of the March show was reflected by several letters found in the March archives at the State Historical Society of Wisconsin, including one from Lt. Commander Dunn of the US Naval Reserve who wrote to the head of the Camp Shows, "The performance by the Fredric March troupe were especially good. March's fine attitude toward the many demands made upon him in addition to his stage appearances is most commendable. Your organization is to be congratulated for sending out big name stars who are top performers and regular people."

The men certainly seemed to enjoy his efforts on their behalf. "Seeing Fredric March and the reception the boys gave him, when I was over in Persia, gave me a kick…March is as natural and as regular as they come. Nothing theatrical about him. He is sincere. That's what the boys like," said Sgt. Sam Conn of Air Evacuation.

March returned from his tour in January of 1944, fatigued but grateful for the opportunity to be of service to the men. "On that trip I came to have the greatest admiration for the average run of our G.I.s," he later recalled. "They were so gentle, and not very talkative… Most of all they had a feeling of comradeship. They were a real brotherhood." March's homecoming to Florence and the family almost seems like a scene out of *The Best Years of Our Lives*, which he would film in 1946. He returned to the New Milford farm earlier than expected, finding Florence busy in the kitchen—their cook being ill—and surprised her. "Every time he'd start to tell me about some place he'd been," she recalled, "I'd interrupt him. I'd say, 'Wait. The potatoes are boiling dry' and I'd rush to the kitchen. Many a returning soldier will find home like that."

He also came back home with a message from the boys to the women they left behind: write to them! It was a needed morale booster. Not only write him, March asserted, but let him know how much you feel about him. He gave an example:

> *This soldier in Persia showed me a letter from his wife,"* he told reporters. *"The men always pass their letters around, you know. She told him where she'd been that day, what the Joneses said, how the baby was growing. Then she added at the end of that paragraph, "I love you." She went on to mention things about the house and some financial matters. At the end of that paragraph "I love you." It was like that all the way through. At first I thought the woman was psychopathic or something. Then I began to feel what that letter was putting across. The soldier was smiling all over. He'd got the news from home—some cheerful, some just necessary. But the main thing was he knew she loved him.*

In the summer of 1944, Warner Brothers was finally going to release *The Adventures of Mark Twain*, which March had filmed back in 1942, but had been held up due to a war time surplus of films. Knowing that the men needed entertainment, March urged Jack Warner to release the film early—for soldiers. Warner responded by telegram on February 3, 1944:

> DEAR FRED CHARLIE EINFELD GAVE ME YOUR MESSAGE. AM IN ABSOLUTE AGREEMENT WITH YOU ABOUT RUSHING PRINTS TO BOYS AT THE FRONTS. HAVE ISSUED ORDERS TO PUT OUT MARK TWAIN AS FAST AS HUMANLY POSSIBLE...

II

March let it be known in his communication with Warner that he was available for a film project that summer, and Warner was eager to have him work at the studio again. Warner let March know that the studio was working on a film about the famous American humorist and performer Will Rogers, and he felt that March would be wonderful in the role. However, perhaps correctly, March was dubious about this, as he didn't quite think he would be able to capture Rogers's folksy charm. March politely turned Warner down. (The film was later made in 1952 starring Will Rogers, Jr.) A project that March was much more interested in was rumored to be in the works at Paramount: a film version of the popular Gene Fowler biography of John Barrymore titled *Good Night, Sweet Prince*. It appealed to March because he had been a friend and admirer of Barrymore's, and also because he had come to the notice of Hollywood thanks to his impersonation of Barrymore in *The Royal Family*. However, nothing came of this project.

What did come March's way was *Tomorrow the World*, based on a popular 1943 Broadway play that ran some 500 performances. The play was about a German boy who is sent by his anti-Nazi father— who eventually dies in a concentration camp—to live with his college-professor uncle in a small American town. The boy is welcomed with open arms, but we soon discover that he has been indoctrinated by Nazi propaganda from his time as a Hitler Youth. The boy is particularly unpleasant to the professor's Jewish fiancée. On Broadway, the uncle was played by Ralph Bellamy with Shirley Booth as the Jewish fiancée. Thirteen-year-old Skip Homeier was the boy, Emil.

Independent producer Lester Cowan bought the film rights to the play for $75,000 and considered March a better box office choice to play the professor than March's friend Ralph Bellamy. March was signed for a flat $100,000. Shirley Booth was a name to be reckoned with on Broadway but had not yet made a motion picture—instead Betty Field was cast as the Jewish fiancée. Agnes Moorehead was signed on to play the maiden aunt and, though they considered other young actors, Skip Homeier was cast as the boy. Cowan considered either Elliott Nugent and, particularly, Leo

McCarey as director, but instead decided to go with the craftsman-like Leslie Fenton, a former actor-turned-director whose biggest film this would be. If the director was rather pedestrian, Cowan went all-out in engaging screenwriters to adapt the play, by hiring Ring Lardner, Jr. and Leopold Atlas. Lardner was fresh from winning an Academy Award (with Michael Kanin) for his script of the Spencer Tracy-Katharine Hepburn hit comedy *Woman of the Year.* By 1949, Lardner was blacklisted in Hollywood as a Communist and would not have a screen credit under his own name until 1965. In 1970, he would win another Oscar for his screenplay for the film *MASH.* Atlas would go on the next year to write the screenplay to one of the finest World War II films ever produced: *The Story of G.I. Joe.*

March told a visiting reporter to the set of the film in the summer of 1944:

> *When Lester Cowan announced he was going to make Tomorrow the World I was eager for a chance to make it, and was grateful when he offered me the role. This picture has something of supreme importance to every American in fact to everyone in the world. The problem not what to do with the adult German people, but what to do about 12,000,000 young Nazi-trained youngsters who have been shaped in hate, bitterness and a fanatical love for Hitler. The play and the picture offer one solution; whether it is the right one I do not profess to know, but at least it brings the problem to the public.*

Originally, Cowan wanted to change the name to "The Intruder" but theater owners revolted. The reputation of the play was under the title *Tomorrow the World,* so Cowan threw in the towel and retained that title for the film. Not that it seemed to matter all that much, since the film of *Tomorrow the World* turned out to be only mildly successful at the box office despite generous reviews. *Variety* wrote, "Reformation of Nazi youth, a problem forcefully projected in *Tomorrow the World* on Broadway [in the play by James Gow and Arnaud D'Usseau], is dealt with no less assiduously in Lester Cowan's screen presentation of the same story...Fredric March and Betty Field both give dignity to the parts of the professor and his bride-to-be. But the main accolade must go to Skippy Homeier, as the young Nazi." The *New York Telegram* critic maintained that March delivered one of his "most sincere and ingratiating performances." Of *Tomorrow the World* March later said, "I passed up several other pictures to do *Tomorrow the World*. My part...isn't outstanding—the picture really goes to the boy—but I wanted to be in it for what it has to say. You like to have your heart in your work."

John Hersey's book "A Bell for Adano" tells the story of Major Victor Joppolo, an Italian-American from the Bronx, New York, who becomes the military mayor of the allied captured town of Adano, Italy, during World War II. The people of Adano are suspicious of authority, having lived under the doctrines of the fascists—who during the war had taken their beloved 700-year-old town bell and melted it down for rifle barrels. Joppolo wins the respect and loyalty of the citizens when he finds them a replacement bell. Hersey, who had served as a war correspondent in Italy during the war, won the Pulitzer Prize for his book, which became a runaway best-seller.

March's agent, Leland Hayward, who at the time was the husband of actress Margaret Sullavan, branched out into producing, and he bought the rights to the novel with the intensions to produce a play on Broadway. He hired playwright Paul Osborn to write a dramatization of the book. By chance, Hayward ran into director H.C. Potter, who had spent much of the war as Superintendent of Operations at Falcon Field in Arizona, where he trained Royal Air Force pilots. Hayward told Potter about the play and asked if he would like to "come around sometime and we'll talk about whether you want to direct it." Potter replied, "Talk? Hell, I'm going to do it." His enthusiasm was enough for Hayward, who signed Potter on as director of *A Bell for Adano*.

To play the leading role of Major Joppolo, Hayward had nobody else in mind than March, who he approached about playing the role of Joppolo while attending a party at the home of film producer William Goetz. Hayward sent March the script. "It was then too long, but I knew the minute I read it that it was what I wanted to do." The script was still being fine-tuned by Osborn, and by August of 1944, March was at the farm in New Milford studying it before beginning rehearsals in September. "Mrs. March and the two children were with me," March later explained. "How could I study in the midst of a family? Well, there was always the barn." The second floor of the barn had been converted into an area where March could get away and have some quiet time. "Upstairs in the barn, away from everybody, I broke the back of this part," March continued. "I kept reading the script and comparing it with the book. Then I marked the book for character. My copy is full of those marks, in every place where some little thing sheds light on the kind of man Victor Joppolo is. Before rehearsals started I knew him well. That's what I call breaking the back of a part." The part was also a long one, "This Major Joppolo is a long part—nearly one hundred sides, as we say in the theater. It's the longest I ever had for New York, but I might have had more lines in something in stock."

March later spoke of his feelings for the character of Major Joppolo and the principals he represented:

> *I have played dozens of characters over the years, many of them outstanding historical figures, but never have I had the opportunity to create so humble and human a man as Joppolo. Above all else, he typifies hope, the hope of mankind that through right teaching wars will end and peace with dignity will come for all. It is for this that our boys are wallowing in the mud of battle, sweating in steaming jungles, dying in treacherous mountain passes, living in fox-holes like hunted animals. Bullets can settle the war, but only ideas can prevent another.*

The show previewed in Boston to box office that was "simply wonderful." The play ran over the Thanksgiving holiday, allowing Florence and the children the opportunity to join him. "Tony and Penny have been here for their Thanksgiving holiday," March said at the time. "We've managed to have fun in between rehearsals, performances and interviews. This morning we all took sightseeing bus drawn by a span of horses, and went around Boston. I was through in time for the matinee."

The reviews were good, with the critic for the *Boston Herald* writing:

> *A Bell for Adano has many virtues, among the largest being the honesty, sincerity and complete reality of the central character,*

the AMG officer Maj. Victor Joppolo. As Mr. Hersey wrote him, Mr. Osborn transferred him to the theater and Fredric March plays him, Joppolo is not an intellectual giant or a professional hero: he is an ordinary man, what we like to think of as an average American, throughst by circumstances into war and reconstruction, and trying to do the best he can...

A Bell for Adano opened at the Cort Theater in New York on December 6, 1944, and the show was met by overwhelmingly positive reviews. The notices for March were among the best of his career. "Fredric March, who makes Joppolo a living man, desperately tired, fallible, but always passionately devoted to the interests of the people he has been sent to serve. It is the best performance he has given and as such rather obscures the work of the rest of the cast," wrote the critic for the *New Yorker*. Ward Morehouse wrote in the *New York Sun*, "The role of the major is played with tremendous force and variety by Fredric March. His is a beautiful job." *Newsweek* called March's performance, "one of the finest of his career." The public was equally enthusiastic and the play settled in for a run of nearly 300 performances.

One of the things that most impressed March was the effect the character of Major Joppolo had on men who were in the same kind of leadership position as Joppolo, or training to be. "Many come back stage to tell me not only how much they like the play, but also that they intend using Joppolo as a stencil in their jobs. The play gives them this exalted feeling and it is one of the most gratifying experiences of my life to know we are setting a pattern which in actual practice will do so much for the advancement of democracy."

It was while the play was running that the movie rights to *A Bell for Adano* were sold to 20th Century Fox. The film went into production while the play was still running, and so March couldn't play the leading role. Instead, John Hodiak was cast as Joppolo, and he gives a fine performance in a superb film adaptation directed by Henry King. Still, it is a shame that March couldn't have played the film of what, by most accounts, was one of his best performances. Still, when he did return to films in 1946, it would be in one of the most talked-about, revered, and successful films of its time—and would win him a second Academy Award as Best Actor.

CHAPTER ELEVEN
1946–1949

Frances Goldwyn, the astute wife of producer Sam Goldwyn, read with interest an article about returning veterans and the challenges they faced in an August 7, 1944, issue of *Time* magazine. The article made such an impression on her that she approached her husband about the idea of making a film about the readjustments on the home front that will await returning vets. At first, the irascible producer wasn't much interested, but the more he thought about it the more he came to believe that Frances was right. Goldwyn approached the writer Mackinlay Kantor about the idea, and with typical enthusiasm gushed, "Returning soldiers! Every family in America is part of the story." Kantor was offered the opportunity to write a screenplay based on this idea, but instead he decided to develop it into a novel, which was titled *Glory to Me*, and it was centered around three returning servicemen of different backgrounds who live in the same fictional Midwestern city. Naturally, Goldwyn bought the rights to the novel with the express purpose of turning it into a motion picture.

Enter William Wyler, one of the most distinguished of all motion picture directors. He had a long, often rocky, relationship with Goldwyn. For Goldwyn, Wyler had directed such classic films as *Dodsworth, These Three, Wuthering Heights,* and *The Little Foxes.* Wyler was approached to direct another Goldwyn film of his choice. Wyler was browsing through Goldwyn's un-produced properties, when he came across Kantor's *Glory for Me.* It was the only property that excited Wyler, who had only recently returned from serving three years in the U.S. Air Force. He, like Goldwyn, was drawn to the returning GI theme. Goldwyn signed him up to direct the movie adaptation of Kantor's novel.

Goldwyn and Wyler agreed that the perfect man to adapt Kantor's work for the screen would be the Pulitzer Prize winning playwright and screenwriter Robert E. Sherwood. Sherwood had written such distinguished plays as *The Road to Rome, The Petrified Forest, Abe Lincoln in Illinois,* and *There Shall Be No Night.* Sherwood was busily preparing for the Broadway production of his latest play, *The Rugged Path*, which would present Spencer Tracy in his return to the Broadway stage. He wasn't sure he would have the time, let alone the inclination to work on Goldwyn's project. At one point, he told Goldwyn, "In all fairness, I should recommend to you that we drop it…By next Spring or next Fall this subject will be terribly out of date."

Goldwyn wasn't inclined to drop it, and he immediately replied to Sherwood that, "I have more faith in it now than I had six months ago because I feel the subject matter will be even more timely a year from now than it is today." Finally, Sherwood acquiesced and settled down in a guest cottage on Goldwyn's estate, and began the process of hammering out the screenplay, which became one of the most acclaimed films of its time—and retains its power even today: *The Best Years of Our Lives.* Sherwood submitted the final draft of his 220 page screenplay on April 9, 1946, and by April 15, the picture was ready to begin rolling.

The Best Years of Our Lives tells the story of three returning servicemen. Each has his own individual story to tell, but the key story is that of Fred Derry, an air force bombardier, who returns home to his less-than-adoring wife with hopes that he will be able to make a better living than the one he provided prior to the war, when he worked as a clerk in the local drugstore. Despite his attempts, he ends up back at the drug store and then discovers his wife with another man. Eventually, he finds a soul mate with the daughter of one of the other returning veterans—though he continues to try and salvage his marriage for a time. The other two vets returning are Homer and Al, the established family man.

Homer originally was going to be portrayed as a borderline spastic, drooling from the mouth and psychologically tormented. But then Goldwyn saw a wartime documentary titled *Diary of a Sergeant*, featuring Sgt. Harold Russell, who lost his hands in an accident involving TNT. He had been fitted with hooks replacing his hands and impressed Goldwyn by the way he was able to maneuver the hooks and the positive attitude he processed despite such a wrenching injury. Goldwyn then decided that he wanted the character of Homer to be a man overcoming this type of injury, and, more to the point, he wanted the non-professional Harold Russell to play the part. In the film, Homer returns home with his "claws" and is afraid that the girl next door, who he had promised himself to prior to the war, will reject him.

Then there is Al Stephenson—the oldest man returning, in his early forties—a married man with two children and an important job at a bank. His family is happy and excited to have him back, and yet he finds that after four years away, his children have grown and his wife is self-sufficient. His bank gives him an important promotion administering the new GI loan program, and yet they make it clear that they want him to approve loans only to those who are deemed credit worthy, not on the value of the caliber of men applying. His frustration is such that he eventually turns to drink. It is with Al's daughter, Peggy, that Fred becomes attached—much to the consternation of Al and his wife Millie.

The film turned out to be a boom for Goldwyn's gallery of contract players. Dana Andrews, who found stardom as the obsessed cop in *Laura*, was perfectly cast as Fred. Virginia Mayo, who up to this time had been an admirable (and beautiful) foil in Danny Kaye and Bob Hope comedies, was cast as Fred's floozy of a wife. (Mayo later joked that she was responsible for Wyler receiving his Oscar, "Because people say, 'If he could do that with Virginia Mayo! . . ..'") Farley Granger, who had a rocky relationship with Goldwyn, was originally cast to play Homer, but that was before Goldwyn had seen Harold Russell, and so now Granger was out. Teresa Wright, who had been a Goldwyn contract player for several years, and appeared in such films as *The Little Foxes* and *Pride of the Yankees* and won an Oscar playing Greer Garson's daughter in *Mrs. Miniver*—though her best film may be as Young Charlie in Hitchcock's *Shadow of a Doubt*—was cast as the Stephenson's daughter Peggy, who wants to break up Fred's marriage. Cathy O'Donnell, a newcomer to the Goldwyn stable, would be making her film debut (like Russell) with *The Best Years of Our Lives*, playing Wilma—Homer's girl next door. A small but colorful role is also played by

Hoagy Carmichael as Butch, the proprietor of the bar where the veterans often meet up. He also teaches Homer how to play chopsticks on the piano using his hooks.

For the key, but secondary, roles of Al and Millie Stephenson, Goldwyn originally offered those parts to Fred MacMurray and Olivia de Havilland. In the end, both actors turned him down for the same reason; they thought that the parts were too subsidiary, or as MacMurray later said, "Third banana." It was not the most astute decision either star had ever made. Instead, without any such hesitation, March and Myrna Loy agreed to play the parts.

March, who had spent much of the war years working on stage and for the USO, believed this to be the perfect big picture to come back to the screen with and was as enthusiastic about the screenplay as he had been about Kantor's novel. Loy, due primarily to her work as Nora Charles in *The Thin Man* films, was considered the screen's "perfect wife," and this film is the ultimate "perfect wife" role for the actress—even though she hated the term. Teresa Wright later wrote that she felt that the March-Loy scenes in *The Best Years of Our Lives* "stand as the epitome of married love on the screen."

Ironically, March only played the role of Al due to Loy's frequent acting partner, William Powell, besting him for the part of Clarence Day in the screen version of *Life with Father*, which was going before the cameras at around the same time. March didn't cry in his coffee for long after this, and later said that he "liked the book (*Glory to Me*) from the beginning and I had the feeling it would make a good picture." While it can be stated that the focal character in *The Best Years of Our Lives* is Fred (Andrews), it is Myrna Loy who gets top billing, followed by March. The old pros may have smaller (yet pivotal) roles, but they certainly had earned their billing due to years in the trenches.

Shortly after he had gotten the part of Al Stephenson, Wyler wrote to March to remind the actor, who was prone to weight gain, that Al had just returned from the war, and "it's very important that your figure suggest a K-ration diet rather than the 21 Club…you should make every effort to be as trim and wiry as possible…I know it's not easy for fellows our age…the entire approach to this picture will be along realistic lines…I would hate to have something like the proverbial little 'pouch' spoil the illusion." March followed orders, watched his diet, and reported to the set having shed ten pounds. Wyler had great admiration for March. "He adored Freddie," according to Teresa Wright.

The film was in production for more than 100 days (from April 15-August 9, 1946). William Wyler was an exacting director who often asked for twenty or more takes until he was satisfied with a scene, and then would just as often print one of the earliest takes. He rarely could put into words what he was looking for but knew it when he saw it. "He didn't give you anything particularly himself," Teresa Wright (who worked in three Wyler directed films) once said, "... He required a certain something from you that he seemed to be unable to put into words. I sometimes wonder if he really was unable to, or whether his method is that he does not want to impose himself or any other ideas on you, because he's waiting to see if the right thing comes out of you."

Case in point is the first scene featuring March and Loy. It required nearly a dozen takes, but what appears on the screen is fresh, alive, and deeply poignant. Al has returned home, and his children excitedly greet him at the door. He hushes them and moves on toward the kitchen where Millie is. She inquires who it was at the door. Then suddenly it hits her, and she realizes it is Al. The look in her eyes of love reborn and in full bloom stands as one of the finest scenes of Wyler's career—and memorable ones in the careers of Myrna Loy and Fredric March.

The Best Years of Our Lives is a superb ensemble picture and March has more than a few opportunities to shine in a richly modulated performance. As usual, March told Wyler to keep him from "hamming it up," and Wyler succeeds, as March gives a natural and moving performance every step of the way—and also what little humor there is in *The Best Years of Our Lives* comes primarily from March's character. Perhaps his best scene in the film is at the banquet, which the bank is giving in his honor. With Loy at his side, and with her face registering concern as he takes one drink too many, he gets up to deliver a speech. At first, the audience believes this will be a fiasco and Al will embarrass himself, but he recovers and proclaims that he loves the bank and it can do good for the community, "I say that our bank is alive, it's generous, it's human, and we're going to have such a line of customers seeking and

GETTING small loans that people will think we're gambling with the depositors' money. And we will be. We will be gambling on the future of this country." He is putting the bank hierarchy on notice that these men, regardless of assets, will be getting loans—or else.

It was this type of scene that Wyler later recalled that they had the most problem with the censors about. "The only trouble with censorship on this picture was in explaining why we did things," Wyler recalled. "Take the matter of March's drinking. One of the best scenes is making a speech at a banquet after he has had a few. He really has something important to say—but to do that you have to be entertaining to keep from sounding soapbox. Played as it is, the scene is amusing but it has a lot of vital truth in it...His (March) isn't the biggest part, but he is magnificent in it."

When it came to working with a novice actor like Harold Russell, March was helpful and tolerant. "This classically, tall, dark-haired and handsome actor made it a point to help me with my role whenever he could, usually by observing my performance in a scene and offering tips of technique that would improve my acting," Russell later wrote in his autobiography. Yet March was an actor who, when the scene called for it, wanted the attention squarely on himself. For a scene set in Butch's bar, Russell recalled March telling him, "When I say my lines, keep those goddamned hooks down! Don't lift that bottle of beer, because I want people listening to what I'm saying, not watching you drink beer!" March recalled that Russell kept a sense of humor about the loss of his hands. He recalled that once while making the film, Russell told him that he was so nervous, "I was biting my nails."

Despite having a script that Sherwood was guaranteed wouldn't be tampered with and a director of exacting discipline, there was a sense of fun on the set of the picture that allowed the actors to add little bits of business, as Wyler later described. "Take that hangover sequence. In rehearsal, Fred was mixing a bromo in two glasses and suddenly lifted the empty one to his mouth, by mistake. He stopped the scene to do it over again. But it was Myrna who suggested that we keep the business in. And it brightened up a sequence that had more talk than action to start with."

The Best Years of Our Lives is expertly photographed by Gregg Toland in naturalistic deep focus, which is reminiscent of his equally superb work on *Citizen Kane*. (Toland had photographed three previous March films, including *Les Miserables* and *The Road to Glory*.) In 1975, at a film festival in Iran, Wyler was asked about his use of deep focus in this film, and he paid lavish praise to Toland:

> *I had, Mr. Gregg Toland. He was the Director of Photography on several of my pictures and it was he who permitted me to use this technique, which was very, very helpful to my style of direction. It allowed me to compose scenes in a way that eliminated a lot of focusing back and forth. I could arrange a group of people with someone in the foreground, someone in the middle ground and someone in the background, with all of them being seen sharply and clearly. This eliminated the necessity to cut from one to the other. I could get them all together in one big shot and, in this way; the scene was often heightened in effect, because you could see action and reaction together. In effect, the audience could do their own cutting by looking from one person to another, as they would do in real life. This was made possible by Gregg Toland.*

When principal photography was completed on August 9, 1946, the film was nearly three hours long. Both Wyler and Goldwyn wondered if the length would be detrimental, since it was nearly twice as long as the average motion picture. Yet, when Goldwyn watched the rough cut, he didn't find it too long. Despite its length it flowed, and the story never got bogged down. Instead, they would leave it up to preview audiences to tell them where the film should be cut. On October 17, a sneak preview was held in Long Beach, and its length was never called into question. At the end of the preview, the audience rose as one and gave the picture a sustained standing ovation.

Goldwyn was going to wait until early 1947 to release the picture, but was convinced by Wyler, among others, that they should premiere the film in 1946, at least in New York and Los Angeles so that it could qualify for the 1946 Academy Awards. The film was booked into the Astor Theater in New York City, for a November 21, 1946, release.

The reviewers were enthusiastic when the film opened in New York. Bosley Crowther in the *New York Times* wrote, "It is seldom that there comes a motion picture which can be wholly and enthusiastically endorsed not only as superlative entertainment but as food for quiet and humanizing thought. Yet such a one opened at the Astor last evening. It is *The Best Years of Our Lives*." Crowther praised the entire cast and was particularly astute regarding March's performance, "Fredric March is magnificent as the sergeant who breaks the ice with his family by taking his wife and daughter on a titanic binge. His humor is sweeping yet subtle, his irony is as keen as a knife and he is altogether genuine. This is the best acting job he has ever done." On the other coast, the trade paper the *Hollywood Reporter* wrote that March played his part "magnificently."

The film became a huge box office bonanza. It became the most successful film since *Gone with the Wind*. The film cost $2.3 million to produce—considerably less than GWTW—and went on to gross over $10 million in its first year of release. Of course, the Academy of Motion Picture Arts and Sciences took notice, and the film was nominated for eight Oscars in the categories of: **BEST PICTURE**, **BEST SUPPORTING ACTOR** (Harold Russell), **BEST DIRECTOR**, **FILM EDITING**, **MUSIC**, **WRITING**, **SOUND RECORDING**, and **BEST ACTOR** for Fredric March. It is a mystery that Gregg Tolland's superb cinematography was overlooked. Of the eight nominations, the film won seven—losing only in the Sound Recording category. For March, winning a second Oscar put him in a special league among actors—only four other actors had won the Oscar twice up to that time: Spencer Tracy, Luise Rainer, Bette Davis and Walter Brennan— three times in the Supporting Actor category. In addition to winning Best Supporting Actor, Harold Russell also won an Honorary Academy Award "for bringing hope and courage to his fellow veterans through his appearance in *The Best Years of Our Lives*."

March hadn't expected to win his second Oscar. He told columnist Gladys Hall that he thought Laurence Olivier would be triumphant for *Henry V*. He felt that fellow nominee "Jimmy (Stewart) was simply wonderful in *It's a Wonderful Life*" but hadn't seen "Greg" (Peck) in *The Yearling* or Larry Parks in *The Jolson Story*.

The Best Years of Our Lives resonates to this day. Roger Ebert wrote in 2007, "The film makes no effort to paint these men as extraordinary. Their lives, their characters, their prospects are all more or less average, and Wyler doesn't pump in superfluous drama. That's why the movie is so effective, and maybe why it doesn't seem as dated as some 1946 dramas." Film historian and author David Thomson wrote in 2002 that, "Fredric March is quite brilliant (his reunion scene with Myrna Loy remains one of the most touching moments in American film.)" In 2007, the American Film Institute (AFI) listed *The Best Years of Our Lives* thirty-seventh in its list of the 100 greatest film ever made. March later said of *The Best Years of Our Lives*, "It was a picture worth doing, done right in every way, and one of the most satisfying experiences I've ever had."

II

March wasn't present to accept his second Academy Award—which Teresa Wright accepted on his behalf—because he and Florence were in New York starring on Broadway in Ruth Gordon's autobiographical play *Years Ago*. Set in 1912, it tells the story of sixteen-year-old Ruth Gordon Jones and her life-defining decision to become an actress over the initial objections of her stern but loving ex-sea-captain father, Clinton. March was cast as Gordon's father, with Florence once again joining him on stage playing the understanding mother role. (Patricia Kirkland, the daughter of March's *Laughter* costar Nancy Carroll was cast in the Ruth Gordon role.)

Ruth Gordon was one of the leading lights of the Broadway stage, on which she had been performing since 1916. She would not be playing any part in *Years Ago*, originally titled "Miss Jones," beyond the writing of it. But her husband, Garson Kanin, would direct.

It's probably a good thing that the play was retitled from "Miss Jones" to *Years Ago*, because the focal point of the story is the father figure. As theater critic Howard Barnes put it:

> *The character of the father dominates "Years Ago" so completely that the main theme becomes a bit blurred and repetitive. With a shaggy mustache and a Yankee accent March builds it unerringly until Clinton Jones is a figure of stature, curious subtlety and sympathy. In merely recounting his awful youth as an orphan until he shipped as a cabin boy at age eight, he suggests a drama that would have more amply deserved the pains which have been*

lavished on this Max Gordon production. His sudden acceptance of his daughter's desire to act… constitutes the heart of Years Ago.

As mentioned, March did grow an enormous handlebar mustache for the part, much to Florence's consternation. "That mustache," she told a visiting reporter, "I don't mind it so much now, but when Freddie first grew it he looked like a badly singed chicken. I told him I would go out with him, but not with those pin feathers." March adds, "Just to please my wife, I keep nicking off the loose hairs, and that keeps it neat. I refuse to wear a fake mustache with spirit gum!"

During rehearsals, Ruth Gordon was often in attendance but said little, leaving things up to her husband, the director. However, on one point she did approach March. "Just once, she gave me a suggestion," March recalled. "It was about chilblains, a subject I talk of in the play. She said, 'Father always took chilblains seriously.' After that I took them seriously too." March added that Gordon had been "extremely patient with our version of the Joneses."

As they rehearsed, Florence described the differences in how they prepared for their roles, "Freddie's method is what he calls twenty-four-hours-a-day-and-worry-every-minute. He mulls it over at home. But I get my ideas at the theater, working with people around me." March adds to this, "I might point this out, Florence and I never try to influence or criticize each other in our work beyond making a few suggestions. It's a rule with us. She wants to be down in the theater rehearsing her lines, and I might be pacing the floor right here (at home), learning mine. That part of our lives is separate."

The first preview was much ballyhooed because it was held in Gordon's home state of Massachusetts (in Boston). Kanin—who Florence described as "understanding of actors"—decided to take the company to Boston a week early so that they could get familiar with the theater and also with the props and sets. "He had everybody handling 'props'…, and we women were walking around in long skirts to get used to them," Florence later recalled. "Let me tell you, a dress rehearsal when the chairs and doors and clothes are all new to you is a dreadful affair."

The Boston opening proved successful both at the box office and with critics. The theater critic for the *Boston Herald* wrote, "Miss Gordon was more than fortunate in securing Fredric March and Florence Eldridge to play the Jones parents, for this admirable pair of actors catch the basic honesty, loving kindness and simple loyalty of the characters, portray them with humor, skill and, I suspect, attention, and you leave the theater the better for having spent the evening in their company."

When the play opened on Broadway at the Mansfield Theater on December 3, 1946, the reviews were equally kind. "And since Fredric March is playing the part, Miss Gordon's father will now have to be added to the gallery of stage worthies to be remembered and respected. For Mr. March, acting in very high fettle indeed has created a vigorous, colorful character out of many simple details...," wrote Brooks Atkinson in the *New York Times*. The *New York Herald Tribune* called the play a "rich fund of amusement...particularly when March is exploding as an irascible factory foreman who likes to remember his early sea-faring days." The reviewer added that Florence, "aided and abetted March at every turn in giving color and meaning" as the mother.

The play settled in for a successful 206-performance run, ending on May 31, 1947, when the March's had to return to Hollywood to fulfill some movie commitments. In the end, March tied with Dudley Digges of *The Iceman Cometh* as the best actor in a poll of New York critics, and he won the first Tony Award given for Best Actor in a Broadway play. In 1952, MGM made the film version of *Years Ago*—retitled *The Actress*—but neither March nor Eldridge were invited to recreate their Broadway roles as Mr. and Mrs. Jones. Instead, Spencer Tracy and Teresa Wright were cast with the beautiful Jean Simmons cast as Ruth. Perhaps it's just as well for the Marches, since the film bombed at the box office.

Universal Pictures had a long history in Hollywood dating back to the silent era, with such prestigious films as *The Hunchback of Notre Dame, Stella Maris,* and *The Phantom of the Opera*. Its sound films included the Oscar-winning *All Quiet on the Western Front, Back Street, Magnificent Obsession, Show Boat, My Man Godfrey, Destry Rides Again, My Little Chickadee, Shadow of a Doubt, The Egg and I,* and *The Naked City*. But its mainstay surefire box office films were Deanna Durbin musicals; Abbott and Costello comedies;

horror films (like the classic *Dracula, Frankenstein* and *The Bride of Frankenstein*) featuring monsters that were used and reused in sequel after sequel; and the Sherlock Holmes series featuring Basil Rathbone and Nigel Bruce. Universal could boast having the finest back lot in Hollywood and soundstages that were more than adequate. Its makeup and special effects departments were considered among the best. Despite these advantages, Universal was not considered one of the top Hollywood studios. Unlike the "majors" of MGM, Paramount, Warner Brothers, and 20th Century Fox, Universal didn't own its own theater chains, and so much of their product was produced to be on the bottom half of a double bill. Columbia, also considered a "major-minor" had moved ahead of Universal by the late-'30s thanks to its brilliant series of films directed by Frank Capra. Universal was certainly in a stronger position both financially and commercially than RKO—which at one time during its 1930s heyday was also considered a major—Republic, and lowly Monogram. But where MGM had Clark Gable and Judy Garland, Universal had Donald O'Connor and Yvonne de Carlo—talented, yes, but hardly in the same league.

Still, Universal did aspire to make a certain number of quality "A" pictures each year. They could make a bundle with their low-budgeted but high-grossing *Francis the Talking Mule* and *Ma and Pa Kettle* films, but most studios (even Republic and Monogram) also aspired to produce a few high-quality critically acclaimed films as well. Two of Universal's efforts for the year 1948 would be based on popular stage productions: Arthur Miller's *All My Sons* and Lillian Hellman's *Another Part of the Forest*—a prequel to the stunning Samuel Goldwyn 1941 film *The Little Foxes*, which had starred Bette Davis in one of her greatest performances and directed by William Wyler.

On Broadway, *Another Part of the Forest* had run 182 performances and had made Patricia Neal a star with her interpretation of Regina Hubbard. Samuel Goldwyn wanted to buy the rights to this play since he had also produced *The Little Foxes*. But in a sudden dash of opulence, Universal out-bid Goldwyn and other studios and won the rights. The only condition is that they had to wait to produce the film until after the New York production had closed.

Set twenty years before *The Little Foxes, Another Side of the Forest* focuses on the patriarch of the Hubbard family, Marcus Hubbard, who profited by selling smuggled Union salt during the Civil War for eight dollars per pound. It had made him rich and despised by his neighbors in the small Alabama southern town where he lives. Add to the mix an obedient wife (Lavinia) and three conniving children, and you have pure southern melodrama.

Universal cast the Marches as Marcus Hubbard and his wife Lavinia. This would be the first of three consecutive films that March and Florence would appear in together—not to mention three major Broadway productions they would undertake together in the next few years.

But, in other ways, Universal decided to cut corners. They paid a huge amount for the play, and the Marches together set them back another $150,000. For the key role of Regina, the studio was unable to sign Patricia Neal, who had played the part to acclaim on Broadway. Instead, the studio cast its own contract player Ann Blyth, in a role that called out for a young Bette Davis or Susan Hayward. Other casting choices were more appropriate with Edmond O'Brien and Dan Duryea cast as the Hubbard sons. Duryea had played in the stage and film versions of *The Little Foxes* and here he plays the father of the character he played in the earlier version. John Dall, Betsy Blair, and Whit Bissel are also featured. As director, it was rumored that William Wyler was interested, but in the end the studio went with its own contract director, Michael Gordon. Gordon had just directed a nifty film noir with Edmond O'Brien, Ella Raines, and Vincent Price, called *The Web*. His most famous film would come more than a decade later, *Pillow Talk*. Gordon, himself, would later say he got the job in *The Other Side of the Forest* because of his stage background and "because I was cheap."

Gordon recalled to columnist Jim Bawden that "casting (on *Another Part of the Forest*) was tough." He thought that March was "marvelous" as the father, "he was a true villain here." He found Florence to be "sturdy" and was enthusiastic about both O'Brien and Duryea, but less enthusiastic about Blyth, "She was a good little Catholic girl. But she had been such a magnificent baddie as the daughter in *Mildred Pierce*, we thought she could get away with it and we were almost right."

Florence approached the preparation for her role as if she were rehearsing a stage play rather than making a motion picture. "About 10 days into filming, Florence, who initially struggled with the part, comes to me and says, 'don't worry, Michael, in another week I'll have this character down pat,'" Gordon later recalled. "You see, in the theater there's a long period of rehearsal, which is unknown in movies. And I had to remind Florence that in another week we'd be halfway through filming. She thought about that for some time and then disappeared to memorize her lines far in advance. Shooting out of order discombobulated her, but in the end she gives a magnificent take on the only nice member of the family."

The film also features a hard-eyed look at the Ku Klux Klan, when Duryea's Oscar Hubbard gets involved with them and at one point even arranges for the Klan to beat-up a northern carpetbagger—on orders from Marcus. This caused some distress with Universal executives who were afraid of angering white southern audiences. "The suits really pressed me to delete the KKK scene," Gordon later stated, "but I refused. It was true. Lillian Hellman swore it had happened that way (part of this is autobiographical) and it stayed put."

The film opened on May 18, 1948, at the Rivoli Theater in New York City. Most of the reviews compared it less favorably than its illustrious predecessor—though not without interest for its own virtues. The *New York Times* critic wrote, "While the new picture definitely doesn't have the stature of *The Little Foxes*, it is an entity in its own right and a compelling entertainment." The *Times* review went on to laud March, who "brings this tyrannical, soulless man to full life." The review felt that Florence gave a "sensitive performance," and the other actors, except for Blyth, were also commended. The *Times* felt that Blyth "is too wholesome-looking a girl to be completely convincing."

Despite generally good, if not rave, reviews, the film was a box-office bomb. Gordon felt that the film itself was "one of the scariest I'll ever see, a true horror tale. Only the monsters are inside us all...for that reason it failed at the box office. This time there was no great (box office) star like Bette Davis to bring in the crowds. Theater owners complained about all the empty seats." By this time, however, the Marches and director Gordon were hard at work on the second of the two-picture deal, *An Act of Murder*.

Another Side of the Forest was not yet in release when the Marches began work *An Act of Murder*. *An Act of Murder* was a story that interested the Marches a great deal. It dealt with euthanasia, which at that time was very rarely discussed in films. March was cast as a strict law-and-order judge who has a moral dilemma when his wife (played by Florence) is diagnosed with a fatal brain tumor. As her pain grows more acute, he contemplates killing her to put her out of her misery.

"We started production before 'Forest' came out and became this big bomb...," Director Michael Gordon later related. "The original title was 'Live Today for Tomorrow.' I think it's the finest movie I've ever seen about euthanasia. It's also the only one. How we got the front office to make it I simply do not know. Everything was done on the Colonial Street on the Universal back lot." The film was made for a budget of below a million dollars because U-I understood they were dealing with a very un-cinematic subject.

The censors had their problem with the theme and especially with the resolution where the judge purposely crashes his car over an embankment, killing his wife. After he has recovered from his injuries, his conscience gets to him and he turns himself in. Later, it is revealed that the wife had discovered she had an inoperable tumor and took an overdose prior to the crash and that, in fact, she was dead at the time of the crash—so the judge is found to be innocent. It's a cop-out of an ending because, in those days, if the judge had actually killed his wife he, in some way, would have to suffer the consequences for doing it. "Remember the code forbade any suggestion that assisted suicide could be an acceptable option," Gordon recalled. "Old Joe Breen (the censor) really hollered when he first read the script, but I got him on Christian principles." Still, the film is well acted by the Marches, compact, and, for its time, very up front about a controversial issue.

When it was released, *An Act of Murder* generated good reviews. "The controversial subject of murder for mercy is dealt with in convincing and adult fashion in 'An Act of Murder,'" wrote the critic for the LA *Herald-Express*. *Variety* called the film a "hard-hitting, uncompromising melodrama." Edwin Schallert, the critic for the *Los Angeles Times* wrote, "*An Act of Murder* is not a production to be scoffed at. It is far better than the general Hollywood output in its attempt to say something, and be interesting while doing this." Bosley Crowther in the *New York Times* wrote, "In scenes of uncommon revelation of a married couple's mutual tenderness—an attachment which all too often appears synthetic on the screen—Mr. March and Miss Eldridge manage, with Michael Gordon directing them, to build a plausible situation into a personal drama that is genuine, moving and profound."

Despite the excellent reviews, the subject was enough to keep moviegoers away in droves. The film was another big box office flop for the Marches and U-I. "Would people race to theaters to see her suffer?" Michael Gordon later asked. "Nope! And I think we proved that. I went to a matinee in Westwood and there were three people watching... so what if we were daring? It lost a bundle and hastened the end of UI's management team."

Despite the box office drubbing, March was proud of his participation in the film. "I've talked to Freddie about this one in later years," Gordon recalled, "and he thinks it's better than *The Best Years of Our Lives*, which garnered him a second Oscar."

III

In April of 1948, the Marches set sail on the Cunard White Star line ship "Queen Elizabeth" for England, where they would film the J. Arthur Rank production of *Christopher Columbus*. Rank was a prestigious studio, whose quality films include *In Which We Serve, Henry V, Brief Encounter, Great Expectations, Black Narcissus, Odd Man Out, The Red Shoes,* and *Hamlet*. Rank would produce and distribute the film in Europe, while Universal, which produced the two previous March films, would distribute in the United States. Unfortunately, *Christopher Columbus* would not be in the same league as the films listed above—despite a sincere belief in its subject matter and big budget.

March was terribly fatigued as they set sail. To Jack and Mary Bickel, Florence would write on the second day of their crossing, "We were in bed before lunch—slept all afternoon—had dinner in bed and then went back to sleep. So today we are full of vim and vigor." She went on to describe the Queen Elizabeth as a "floating

hotel—the days of the wind swept decks seem to have passed."
Florence closes the letter by stating that Universal "as a little treat"
booked *Another Part of the Forest* to play in the ship's movie theater,
"We're going to suggest they run it the last night so we won't have
so far to swim should it fail to please." (Who said Florence didn't
have a sense of humor?)

March was excited to play the explorer from Genoa, Italy, who
discovers the new world while trying to find a route to Asia. "I'd
wanted to do 'Columbus' for a long time when this chance came
along...the story to me, of course, ranks among the most dramatic
in history." Continuing their acting partnership of recent years on
both stage and screen, Florence plays the plum role of Queen
Isabella, whose help Columbus seeks in financing his voyages.

Once in London, they took a suite at their favorite hotel, Claridge's,
in the heart of London—within easy walking distance of both Hyde
Park and Hanover Square. But the fatigue that March had been
under didn't seem to pass, as he was still recovering from a previous
illness. While in London, and prior to starting the picture, he
suffered a relapse and was put in hospital. After a few days, he was
released and Florence was able to relate to relatives, "At last we're on
a normal keel. Freddie had a setback, I think, due to too much
traveling and rushing too soon after his operation." She goes on to
describe the hospital, which was situated in a secluded spot about
thirty miles outside of London as "small, sunny, well-staffed." In
addition, so that she didn't have to commute every morning and
then return to London each night, the doctor and his wife opened
their home to Florence. When he was released, the hospital refused
to accept payment for their services, ". . . as the American boys
quartered there during the war had left a reserve of friendship and
affection whom which we drew." In return, the Marches made a
donation to fund a scholarship for nurses.

All in all, March felt physically and psychologically stronger
following this hospital stay, as he and Florence began preparations
for the picture. "We're beginning preliminaries," Florence wrote.
"Today, Box (Screenwriter Sydney Box) and MacDonald (director
David MacDonald) came for lunch to go over script changes—we're
fitting boots and costumes—an experience in itself." In addition,
Florence began daily diction lessons, "Isabella must in Castile

speak as the other Castilians do—so I am in quest of an English accent."

But it wasn't all work and no play. In between fittings and diction lessons, the Marches did a great deal of sightseeing. They took in the Royal Silver Wedding procession of King George V and Queen Elizabeth. Florence wrote:

> *It was like stepping back into all the fairy tales of childhood. The household Cavalry mounted on shiny black horses with whitebear skin saddles and silver bridles... The King and Queen (with) Princess Margaret Rose in a carriage drawn by eight splendid grays—and old Queen Mary in a limousine of almost solid glass. (Princess) Elizabeth and the Duke of Edinburgh in another open carriage and all of them at eleven in the morning in spangled pale colors. It's no wonder people here are happy to support this bit of childhood dream—especially in the grey drabness of their post war cares.*

Britain was still operating under severe food shortages, but the Marches were well fed by the Claridge's staff. "Here at the hotel we fare perfectly well for food," Florence wrote. Yet she was aware that the average British food budget was quite stringent. "They get, per-person—a shilling's worth of meat a week—2 eggs—and while fish and chicken are un-rationed—chicken is scarce and terribly expensive. They lack fats of all kinds and rice, etc., but seem very healthy. We are convinced that we eat too much in America."

A few days later, in another letter to Jack and Mary Bickel, Florence wrote, "I'm in my dressing room having finished... waiting to fit court robes and crowns. We just finished a concentrated week of work and now have four or five days off until we move into the court sequences. This week I've been getting Columbus off to America and when next we meet he'll be coming home from his triumphs."

In the meanwhile, Penny was preparing to join her parents. (March wrote his brother Jack, "We're counting the days 'til she arrives...I'm sure she'll have a grand time.") Tony stayed back in United States, where, according to Florence he was "apparently thriving at Springdale (CT). He is happy & busy—up in his work—singing in the church and on the radio—writes 2 & 3 times a week." Penny, now in London, was "having a whirl," per Florence. "The boat was filled with congenial young people apparently and there were games and dancing and even a glass of champagne as, 'all European children love wine.'"

March, with two days off, took his daughter off for a visit to Ascot, and with Florence they attended the London premiere of the Rank Company's *Oliver Twist*, "we have seats…directly behind Old Queen Mary so Penny can crane her neck at the rest of the family. The others, of course, all turned out for Ascot."

All in all, as Florence reported to Jack and Mary, *Christopher Columbus* was "coming along and will be beautiful to look at…the color of the costumes and sets is heavenly. Freddie is doing a splendid job of making a historical character come to life."

In the meanwhile, even though March was busy with the making of his new picture, he was curious about how *Another Part of the Forest* was faring in its US release, writing to his brother Jack, "Bless you and thank you for sending the (NY) Tribune notice. I've lugged it around over here, because it's so good for Florence, particularly." He asked Jack to try and send more reviews. As for *Christopher Columbus*, March wrote, "We are happy about this whole thing. It's really wonderful fun. Everyone is charming and helpful and most cooperative." He reported that he is working in much of the picture without makeup. "This is quite revolutionary in Technicolor," March wrote. "The bags under my eyes bother *me*, but everyone else things they are fine…Over here, the so-called star is very top-dog (different from home) and helps much with directing. So I'm having fun on this, too (say a prayer.)"

And so it went. The Marches worked hard on the picture—particularly Fredric due to his appearing in nearly every scene—and yet found time to enjoy sightseeing in London and the surrounding countryside together. At one point, they decided to leave behind the Rolls Royce and driver (provided by Rank) and take a walking tour of London. Florence wrote about it to Tony, back home in school:

>…*Dad and I set out to wander, one can't learn a city by car—one must go by foot. So we wandered over through Berkeley*

Square to a little section called Shepherd's Market—narrow winding street that used to be the place that the shepherds brought their flocks to market. Then on through Green Park. The city is filled with parks and all the grass is meant to be walked on and sat on and picnicked on. Londoners have a great sense of privacy and they bring their own folding chairs and make little groups of friends or family, like islands. Through Green Park to Buckingham Palace where the guards no longer wear red coats and busbys, but where they still walk their sentry beat like wooden toy soldiers and stand in their little boxes between walks... Then on to Westminster Abbey—such a beautiful Gothic church crowded with the tombs of England's great—and tablets to their memory—some great because of inherited title and some because of what they gave to England in service, in politics, army or the arts. Passing the Houses of Parliament—Lords and Commons—with the same Big Ben on the tower that we hear striking at home on New Year's Eve over the radio...Sunday again we went walking...We walked through Hyde Park, stopping at the Marble Arch to hear the street speakers. The English people were the first to love the tradition of free speech and they cling to it fervently—so any man can pay his few shillings for a soap box and start spouting and collect a crowd. The crowd is the most fun as they have side arguments and heckle the speaker and each other. . ..

They loved England. They loved the sightseeing and they enjoyed making the picture. March felt that they really "did a big job" on *Christopher Columbus*. At one point, the company was sent to do location filming in Barbados using ships built to scale representing the Nina, Pinta, and Santa Maria. "The only mishap was that one of the ships caught fire, but fortunately for us it was near the end of shooting," March related.

The film, released on Columbus Day of 1949, didn't please either moviegoers or critics. March gives a strong, earnest performance and Florence matches him, and the film is beautifully photographed (by Stephen Dade) in glorious Technicolor, but the film itself is slow and tedious—even at only ninety-nine minutes of screen time. The *New York World-Telegram* said that March played Columbus "with a gallant dash and vigor, a fine figure of Technicolor swashbuckle," yet, "the most revealing portrayal in the picture is Florence Eldridge as Queen Isabella, an earnest effort at insight into the emotions and struggle of a wavering woman." Still, "the picture is too sprawling and static to rank high as entertainment." The *New York Sun* called the film "highly loquacious…using words and speeches where a look or a gesture might have been more eloquent. The picture talks away its chances at excitement." The film failed at the box office—both at home and abroad.

While they enjoyed the making of the film and sightseeing in London, it was a busy late spring and summer of work, and the Marches returned to the United States thoroughly exhausted. Soon after coming home, writer Arthur Miller and director Elia Kazan approached March to play the similarly exhausted Willy Loman in their upcoming Broadway production of *Death of a Salesman*. March, much to his later chagrin, wouldn't even read the play—he was too pooped out—and one of the great roles of the American theater fell from his grasp.

Given the busy last few years, the Marches decided that they would take it relatively easy in 1949. March had *Christopher Columbus* completed and ready for release later in the year. The one big event would be making his television debut on *The Ford Theater Hour* on October 7, in a production of *Twentieth Century* opposite the lovely Lili Palmer. The Ben Hecht-Charles MacArthur play had been a big hit on Broadway. It also became one of the best early screwball comedy films of its time with the movie version in 1934, which had starred John Barrymore and Carole Lombard set on the Twentieth Century Limited train making its way from Chicago to New York. March would play the egotistical Broadway producer Oscar Jaffe, with Palmer as his temperamental ex-lover, Lily Garland, whose career he had once guided, and who now wants nothing to do with him. Now, Jaffe is in need of a hit and is desperate to have her to star in his new play. She is just as determined not to. The telecast was presented live and went almost without a hitch. "You don't dare to blow a line," he later recalled. "I missed one in a production with Lilli Palmer. Subconsciously I was waiting for the 'Cut!' of movies or for a stage manager's assist. I didn't get it. Lilli finally pulled me out of it but it was an uncomfortable moment"

For much of the year, the Marches would be content to stay on their farm in Connecticut and enjoy the country and get reinvigorated. The summer of 1949 would find the entire family together at the farm for the first time in two years. The children were growing up. Penny was now seventeen, had an avid interest in art, and hoped to begin school at Vassar that fall. Tony, now fifteen, was less academically inclined. He attended a boarding school, which specialized in farming in North Carolina. He had a passion for horses and enjoyed strumming on his guitar.

The summer in New Milford found Florence sewing a blue and white print dress for Penny. Whenever possible they would escape and go to art galleries together and broaden Penny's knowledge in preparation for school. Tony pitched for Buck Rock camp, and March—who had a passion for baseball and seldom missed listening to the Brooklyn Dodgers on the radio—was often present to cheer his son and the team on.

While March was a baseball nut, Florence was not; she enjoyed the ballet or symphony concerts. Neither of them enjoyed going out to nightclubs, as they were, according to Florence, "too crowded and noisy." They used to enjoy playing charades and card games with friends, but now they were content to just get together with a few friends and talk—conversation about current affairs, books, art, or whatever came into their minds. Neither could cook very well and rarely tried. "No Lunt's we," Florence remarked. (At least one Lunt—Alfred—was the cook in that family. He enjoyed cooking for those who worked on his Wisconsin farm and even wrote a cookbook.) When it came to food, the Marches didn't like to have too many courses. They were content with no more than three courses, "Otherwise its agony," March explained. "One thing we learned from our USO tour during the war was to eat like peasants." They did enjoy a few drinks from time to time. Rye on the rocks was a particular favorite. "Freddie likes huge glasses, on the theory that you don't have to get up and down so much," Florence offered. The "farm" was scaled back. "We started with big ideas, chickens, pigs and a steer," March explained. "We soon discovered that each egg cost us a dollar, no economy at all! So we did less and less. This year we had only asparagus and strawberries, which we deep freeze."

The idyllic summer on the farm was rudely interrupted on the morning of June 8, 1949, when the *Los Angeles Mirror* screamed out the headline:

FREDRIC MARCH COMMUNIST, SAYS SECRET FBI REPORT.

It was the kind of headline, in those terrible days of the crusade by Washington against real or alleged communism in Hollywood, which an actor would dread. Many careers had already been disrupted or destroyed and, though Hollywood denied it, a blacklist was initiated by the studios against those accused of being a Communist.

According to the article, March's name was among several read from a secret FBI report, and by the defense counsel, to the jury in the Judith Coplon espionage trial. Coplon was a twenty-eight-year-old Justice Department employee who was accused of being a Soviet spy. She maintained that she was meeting a Russian agent on the streets of Manhattan because she was in love with him. The FBI maintained that she was handing over sensitive documents. "She had a job right there in the Justice Department, so it became a high priority for the FBI because this was someone in their own shop," Cold War historian John Earl Haynes later said. "This was a time when there was something of a drought in terms of KGB sources, and it turned out she was one of their most productive agents." She was convicted, but later the convictions were later overturned and eventually, in 1967, the case against her was dropped.

The report was read over "vigorous opposition from the government," by Coplon's attorney, though it isn't clear why. The report included the names from several "informants" of alleged communist and communist sympathizers in Hollywood, including March and Eldridge, Edward G. Robinson, Sylvia Sidney, Danny Kaye, Frank Sinatra, Gregory Peck, Paul Muni, John Garfield, Melvyn Douglas and his wife Congresswoman Helen Gahagan Douglas, and radio writer Norman Corwin. Of course, this wasn't the first time the Marches had been accused of being communists due to their left-leaning progressive politics, but it was one of the most devastating accusations yet.

The report was particularly hard on March, and pointed out that he had supported a group that was critical of the growing United States nuclear arsenal. (In fact, he had supported Progressive Party candidate and former Vice-President Henry Wallace on this very issue in the 1948 presidential campaign.). But March was by no means alone on this issue: Danny Kaye and Helen Keller also supported this group. The report also made clear that March had also supported efforts to provide relief to the postwar devastation in Russia.

Another tidbit in the sensitive report: The informer stated that on one occasion, a few years ago, March was criticized in the communist newspaper *Daily Worker* for his acting. "March was upset about this and thorough someone...sent word to the *Daily Worker* that he did not mind criticism generally, but he did not like criticism when it came from the world in which he believed." The report went on to state that March had tears in his eyes when he conveyed this message!

March's response was immediate. "It's an unmitigated lie. My record and conscience as an American and as a man are clear." Others who had been accused of communist sympathies also responded. Danny Kaye cabled from Scotland, where he was on vacation, "It's a lot of hooey." Frank Sinatra said, "If they don't cut it out, I'll show them how much an American can fight back, even against the state if the American happens to be right." Gregory Peck added "I have been denying these allegations for several years and will do so once more." March was in good company.

Three weeks later, while appearing with former Postmaster General James A. Farley—who had run Franklin D. Roosevelt's campaigns for president in 1932 and 1936—at a dinner to raise money for a hospital in the Crotchet Mountains in New Hampshire, March addressed the issue and offered a vigorous denunciation. He began by stating, "Mrs. March and I are not Communists; we never have been Communists; we never intend to become Communists." He went on to tell the crowd of 350 people:

> *Let me also make clear that false accusations and opprobrious labels do not deter either of us (he was also including Florence) from doing those things which we consider our prerogative and duty as*

good citizens. Today our country is required to assume unprecedented responsibility and leadership in a troubled world. We can only lead if Americans are free to live by the principles which our ancestors shed blood to secure for us and by the Jewish-Christian code of ethics that lights the lamp of man's spirit. What threatens this freedom today? First, I believe it is threatened by the spreading of poison of the non-democratic theory of 'guilt by association.' Each American citizen has the right to be judged by his words and deeds and by the issues for which he stood up to be counted. The second threat to American citizens today is the acceptance and encouragement of the testimony of secret information...As for Mrs. March and myself, we don't intend to stand for such libel, loose accusations and intimidation.

In his speech, he also mentioned that "another informer reports that I received an acting award from the magazine *New Masses* for my acting in the play *Bell for Adano*—but the informer omits the fact that I happened to receive seven or eight other awards that year, including the Eisenhower medal for—now don't laugh—the actor who contributed most to democracy in 1945." The crowd leapt to their feet and gave March a vigorous ovation.

Eventually this died down, and unlike some, such as Edward G. Robinson and John Garfield, neither March nor Eldridge were summoned to testify before any committees that might have asked of them to "name names." The gossipy nature of the "secret report" didn't give it a lot of credibility. Also, the Marches won a moral victory in their suit against *Counterattack*. On December 22, 1949, *The Hollywood Reporter* reported that the next day's edition of *Counterattack* would state that it "withdraws and retracts its previously published statements that Fredric March and Florence Eldridge are Communists." In commenting, March said that the retraction gave he and Florence great satisfaction but more importantly, "we have been able to demonstrate that ours is a country where a man can still exercise his democratic right to put his accuser to the proof, and that an innocent person cannot be destroyed by the application of the un-American theory of 'guilt by association.'" Florence's comment was even more personal, "We are glad, that we, and our children, can again walk in honor."

Despite this, it seems pretty clear that while the Marches were vindicated, the momentum of March's film career, particularly considering he was a two-time Oscar winner, had suffered from the allegations. Despite winning this retraction, it would be several more years before he would be reestablished in motion pictures—mostly in leading character roles—and it could be argued that he never really reclaimed the position he held in pictures prior to the war. The stage, however, would continue to claim Freddie and Florence, and despite no big success for several years, they would continue to seek its refuge and support.

CHAPTER TWELVE
1950–1955

Despite the Marches having won their suit against *Counterattack*, they still had to face innuendo from some in Hollywood who felt it would be dangerous to hire them due to the communist accusations and their general left-wing political stands. While it has been generally assumed that March was on a "pink list" as opposed to a "black list," one other possibility as to why movie offers had nearly dried up was the general softness at the box office of his most recent films: *The Other Side of the Forest, A Matter of Life and Death* and *Christopher Columbus*—all of which had performed poorly. However, there was always New York and the Broadway stage, where, from early 1950 through the first six months of 1951, March and Florence appeared in three ambitious productions.

First up, there was an invitation to act in *Now I Lay Me Down to Sleep*, based on a novel by Ludwig Bemelmans. March is cast as Leonidas Erosa, a fifty-ish Ecuadorian General, who is incredibly wealthy and never travels without a huge entourage to indulge his every whim. He also happens to be epileptic. Florence is cast as a prim spinster, Leonora Graves, the English Governess to his children, who the General had once saved from drowning and to whom he would like to marry. Leonora is not only prim but eccentrically dark as well—for instance—she takes a coffin with her wherever she goes. This black comedy was adapted to the stage by Elaine Ryan, best known for writing such light musical films as *Listen Darling, Second Chorus* and *Babes on Broadway*.

Chosen to direct the play was actor Hume Cronyn. This wasn't Cronyn's first fling at directing *Now I Lay Me Down To Sleep*; he had previously directed a stage version of it at Stanford University with Akim Tamiroff as the General, and his wife Jessica Tandy as Miss Graves. When the opportunity to perform the play in New York came, Tamiroff was by-passed while Tandy proved unavailable, "and was I suspect, relieved," Cronyn later wrote. Cronyn enjoyed working with the Marches. "Freddy was not only a superb actor but he had great panache: a charisma that overshadowed Florence and was absolutely right for the general," Cronyn later said. "Florence, on the other hand, was, I think, an even better actor. Less Flamboyant than Freddy, she was at least as talented and extremely intelligent. She was the balance wheel in their relationship."

March and Eldridge were both enthusiastic about their roles. "General Leonidas Erosa gives me a chance to play a really flamboyant character on the stage for the first time since *The Royal Family*, many years ago," March recalled. "I even wear a dressing gown with chinchilla collar." Florence found her character to be "so wonderfully queer."

While the play was on the road in Philadelphia, they gave a visiting reporter the lowdown on how they interact and prepare for their roles. They said they never try to "upstage" the other, "That's one of the wonderful things that comes from acting together for many years," Florence said. "We get to know which scenes are important for each of us. It's like conducting an orchestra. You know when the woodwinds should come up, and when the strings should be stressed." Florence chuckled as she recounted how March prepares for a role, "Freddie's preparations are much more fun for the children at home. He strides all over the house, reciting his lines. I just sit in a corner and worry. I like to act, but not before an audience."

Twenty-six-year-old Rick Jason (who would go on to several years of success on the television series *Combat*) played the part of March's faithful servant, Anselmo. Jason recalls that March seemed insecure during the rehearsal period. "March was doing this play as a way to get back in the business," Jason later said. "He'd been falsely branded a communist sympathizer by the McCarthy Committee. Film work dried up for him, as it did for many in his predicament. He probably grabbed at the first vehicle that looked good on paper—anything to get back to his pre-eminence in films." Jason also contends that March was having a "devil of a time trying to get a handle" on his part. "I could see him experimenting during rehearsals, which continued every day on the road as the play was rewritten, scenes cut, some deleted." Jason, however, played most of his scenes not to March but with Florence. "I worked very slowly into the part, my voice hardly audible during rehearsals, and I must say she must have known how I was approaching the performance and showed me infinite patience. Eldridge, ever the pro, never complained, at least to me," he later recalled.

Now I Lay Me Down to Sleep opened at the Broadhurst Theater in New York on March 2, 1950. Prior to the performance, the Marches seventeen year old daughter Penny, then attending the Shipley School in Bryn Mawr, Pennsylvania, sent a telegram:

IM ROOTING FOR YOU HERES TO A GREAT
SUCCESS LOVE PEN

Howard Barnes wrote favorably in the *New York Herald Tribune*, "March and Miss Eldridge were perfect choices for the starring roles in an animated fresco. *Now I Lay Me Down to Sleep* is showy and it captures most of the drollery and profundity which Bemelmans had in his original." Brooks Atkinson in the *New York Times* liked both lead performances ("Mr. March and Miss Eldridge are giving... especially winning performances") but had a problem with the play itself, claiming that Cronyn and playwright Elaine Ryan have not solved the difficult task of translating Bemelman's novel to the stage. Most of the reviews were in this vein—applause for the Marches and reservations regarding the play overall.

The Marches friend, the playwright Clifford Odets, attended a performance and wrote a fan letter calling it "one of the best entertainments I've seen in years, interesting (but sometimes crude), everywhere, touching—with some heartbreaking scenes." He went on to add: "Freddy—the epileptic scene I will never forget in my life—I found myself weeping Row F. And then, how you died, my brilliant dear. But everything was exciting and theatrical and entertaining to me. I liked Hume's direction, too, and can't wait to come again to cry in Row F. Then I'll come back and shake your hands...Florence, the best performance I've ever seen you give."

Another prominent attendee was Former First Lady Eleanor Roosevelt, who attended the April 5, 1950, performance and wrote in her *My Day* column the next day:

> *The play was fantastic and amusing in spots and serious in others. Leonora Graves was a curious character, typically English, bedeviled by standards that never seem to leave anyone whose roots are in that little island, really loving and yet never able quite to give herself. Ultimately she does give the general's baby all that she has in her heart but never can really give herself to the fabulous, amusing and lovable old rascal.*

Mrs. Roosevelt saw one of the final performances of *Now I Lay Me Down to Sleep*, for the play closed only three days later, on April 8, 1950, after just forty-four performances.

For much of the remainder of 1950, they were biding their time until a new play came up. In the meanwhile, the Marches didn't try and appease their critics by being less active politically or in matters of social welfare. For instance, March narrated a documentary that was presented at a testimonial dinner for one of his political heroes, six-time socialist nominee for President, Norman Thomas. Thomas acknowledged March's contribution in a thank you note, in which he wrote, "I know how deep is the debt I owe busy people like you for giving their time to the undertaking. What you achieved was really something better than a testimony to me. It was a story in praise of civil liberty. I hope you have heart part, at least, of the chorus of praise of your work which I have heard from all side."

He donated his time on a radio program to raise funds for the Salvation Army, and then introduced Former First Lady Eleanor Roosevelt on another radio program. That summer, when he wasn't relaxing at the farm in Connecticut, he attended his thirty-year college reunion. It was a good opportunity for him to meet up with his old college gang and catch up on their lives. The wife of one of his college buddies, Larry Hall, was recruited to pick March up at his hotel and take him to the reunion. Florence was not around, as she didn't particularly care to attend these college reunions. Mrs. Virginia Hall picked March up and during the drive, as she recalled years later to Deborah C. Peterson, found him to be "quite a rascal," adding that it "was all in fun." She also maintains that the March who showed up in Wisconsin with Florence—when she did travel with him—was not the same fun-loving, charming rascal that he was when he turned up without her, "he was under wraps—he was not the fun Freddie March."

By the fall of 1950, the Marches were busy rehearsing their next stage endeavor—Arthur Miller's adaptation of Ibsen's *An Enemy of the People.* Set in a small Norwegian village that has gained wide spread notoriety from its medicinal spring waters, it features March as Dr. Stockmann, who discovers that the springs are being contaminated from industrial pollution. By the third act, Dr. Stockmann is on the verge of losing everything, and while he is offered some compromises, he turns them down because he won't allow his integrity to be trampled with. When he tries to make the town aware of this, they turn on him because the springs are the economic life blood of the community. Florence is cast as Stockmann's understanding wife. (If the plot seems somewhat familiar, think of the popular novel and film *Jaws*, which also features a man of integrity wanting to alert the community to the dangers of a man-killing shark in the economically profitable waters of Martha's Vineyard and the political and business interests who oppose—this was inspired by Ibsen.) In making his adaptation, Miller cut the play down from five acts into three as well as deleting many long monologues in the process.

Miller believed that he could say something through this adaptation about the current political discourse in the country. How people were being persecuted for standing up for their beliefs. In a letter to Elia Kazan Miller wrote, "My main interest in it is that through the guise of Ibsen—sssssh!—I have managed to say things that I would-n't dare say alone." As for the Marches, they were not about to turn down the chance to work with Arthur Miller again, after the lost opportunity of doing *Death of a Salesman* on Broadway. March too was interested in a production that had something relevant to say. According to Miller, March was "interested in some response to the crucifying of left wingers." Florence later contended that it was she and March who brought the idea of doing such a project together to Miller, "We took the idea to Arthur Miller in the first place. It seemed to us that a lot of people were being tarred and feathered, when the only crime they were guilty of was trying to clean up the sewers. . .."

While the author and the stars were simpatico in the political content of *An Enemy of the People*, Miller, who was in attendance for some rehearsals, had problems with Florence's performance. According to the director, Robert (Bobby) Lewis, it came to a head one day:

> *Arthur sensed this wish of Florence's to be loved by the audience. Blowing his top in the middle of a scene one day at a run-through, Arthur yelled up to Mrs. March, 'Why must you be so fucking noble?'...Florence flew off the stage and into her dressing room, followed by her equally anguished husband. The Marches insisted neither of them would return to the production until Arthur apologized in front of the company. The playwright compromised by offering a private apology, and the Marches finally accepted that.*

An Enemy of the People fared well with critics when it opened at the Broadhurst Theater on December 28, 1950. In the *New York Times*, Brooks Atkinson lauded the production as a whole, "You can hardly escape the power and excitement of a bold drama audaciously set loose in the theater by actors and stage people who are not afraid of their strength. . . ." Atkinson went on to laud March for "an incredibly rousing performance." But positive reviews were not enough and, due to weak ticket sales, *An Enemy of the People* closed on January 27, 1951, after only thirty-six performances.

It didn't take the Marches long to find their next project; an offer to star in Lillian Hellman's new play *The Autumn Garden* came their way almost immediately after the closing of *An Enemy of the People*. Set at a guest mansion in the Gulf of Mexico, *The Autumn Garden* tells the story of an artist who returns to his native home with his wealthy spouse whose love for her husband isn't reciprocated. His return is the catalyst in a drama of self-appraisal and revelation to those he comes in contact with, in a community of individuals in the autumn of their lives—including a retired general and his shallow wife.

March plays the key role of the returned native son—for $1,500 per week or ten percent of the weekly box office. For a change, Florence wasn't cast as March's wife, but rather as the flighty and shallow wife of the General, for which she was compensated at a rate of $750 per week. Jane Wyatt was cast in the unsympathetic role of March's wife, receiving the same $750 per week that Florence drew. Kermit Bloomgarden produced, and originally Hellman herself planned to direct the play but, ultimately, Harold Clurman, one of the founders of The Group Theater, took on the directorial reins.

Hellman and her lover, novelist Dashiell Hammett, both thought that *The Autumn Garden* was her best play—even better than her ground breaking *The Little Foxes*. Hammett usually edited many of Hellman's plays, but he did even more than that with *The Autumn Garden*. He actually did some rewrites and wrote an entire scene. In return, Hellman gave him fifteen percent of her royalty for the remainder of his life. The Marches also believed in the play, with March calling it, "(a) mature, sincere chunk of life."

Hellman, as was always the case, was on hand during rehearsals and was full of suggestions. "She began to give me notes on the second or third day," Clurman later recalled. "She'd take notes and whisper most audibly at rehearsals. I said, 'Don't do that. It's disturbing to me and it's disturbing to the actors. They hear whispering going on when they've hardly begun working.'" In her critiques of actors, Clurman recalls that Hellman was "relentless." Eventually, feeling his authority was being undermined, Clurman began refusing to review Hellman's notes until she finally gave up. Florence recalled that Clurman was "rather overshadowed by Lillian. She had a small desk in front of a center seat in the fourth or fifth row of the theater with a light behind it at which she made notes. Poor Harold would give a piece of direction and then almost jerk his head off looking over his shoulder to see if it was approved." Jane Wyatt would later recall that she didn't like her character at all but "it was an important play and Fredric March was extremely good in it." Wyatt also thought that director Harold Clurman, "spent the entire time directing Florence Eldridge and Colin Keith Johnson (who played Eldridge's husband in the play). We'd all sit around there, hour after hour, while he'd work on scenes between Eldridge and Keith Johnson."

The Autumn Garden opened on March 7, 1951, at the Coronet Theater to mixed reviews. The *New York Times* found the play "scrupulous" and yet "boneless and torpid." At the same time, the reviewer applauded the cast as, "brilliantly drawn, vivid, fascinating and admirably played by Fredric March, Florence Eldridge, Jane Wyatt..." In fact, it was the cast that got the lion share of the accolades from the critics:

> "A flawless, extraordinarily interesting cast"
> —*New York Daily News*

> "No other play in town has so many excellent performances. . . ."
> —*Brooklyn Eagle*

> "I cannot recall Fredric March or Florence Eldridge in better form"
> —*New York World-Telegram*

> "A brilliant cast"
> —*Newsweek*

As it turned out, *The Autumn Garden* became the most successful of the three plays that the Marches performed in over a year and a half from 1950-1951—achieving 101 performances. The play closed on June 2, 1951, and ended up losing money. Though the play closed on Broadway, the Marches made a commitment for a road tour to begin in the fall of 1951. In the meanwhile, with the summer off, March finally was able to take on the role of Willy Loman in the film adaptation of *Death of a Salesman*.

II

When the opportunity to play in the film version of *Death of a Salesman* came to March, he wasn't about to let that opportunity pass him by again. Over the years, he had kicked himself for not accepting the offer to play Willy Loman in the original Broadway production. But then he watched, as one actor after another left the part due to illness or fatigue. Lee J. Cobb, perhaps the definitive Loman, only played the part for three months out of the play's 700-plus-performance Broadway run—before nerves and a shattered voice forced him to quit. When Sheila Graham, the film columnist, asked him if he was glad or sorry he didn't play Loman on the stage, March replied, "Both. It's good to be in a hit, but that's such an exhausting hit." But, in making the film version, March would be able to play Loman before a wider audience without having to perform an exhausting part night after night for several months.

Stanley Kramer produced the film version for Columbia Studios. It was the type of project that Kramer loved and Columbia Pictures chief Harry Cohn deplored. Cohn was certain that the film was a certain loser at the box office. Cohn believed the story of a down on his luck salesman who reviews his life in one twenty-four hour period, and finds it lacking so much that he commits suicide, was too depressing for movie audiences. He especially didn't want Lee J. Cobb for the part, so Kramer countered with March—explaining that March had been the original choice for Loman to begin with. This didn't particularly enthuse Cohn either—it had been years since March had been in a bona fide box office film. Kramer somehow got the agreement to do the picture with March and most of the stage cast—Mildred Dunnock, Cameron Mitchell, Don Keefer, Royal Beal, and Howard Smith. Kevin McCarthy portrayed "Biff" in the London production of the play and would play it again in the film. Cohn finally reasoned that the picture would eventually be made by some studio and it may as well be Columbia if for no other reasons than prestige and Oscar possibilities.

Stanley Roberts was chosen to adapt Arthur Miller's play to the screen. After selling the rights to Kramer, Miller had little to nothing to do with the film adaptation. Roberts was a screen writer with a lot of "B" westerns under his belt with titles such as *Red River Range, Colorado Sunset,* and *Under Western Skies.* He had also written an amusing Abbott & Costello picture *Who Done It?,* and the final *Thin Man* film at MGM, *Song of the Thin Man.* At Columbia, he became a favorite of Kramer's and would go on to adapt *The Caine Mutiny* for him. On the whole, Roberts script is faithful to the stage play in form and dialog. However, Miller wasn't impressed. "My sole participation was to complain that the screenplay had managed to chop off almost every climax of the play as though with a lawnmower, leaving a flatness that was baffling in view of the play's demonstrated capacity for stirring its audiences in the theater," Miller later complained.

In his autobiography, Miller demonstrated his point. Roberts met with him and tried to get an understanding as to why Miller wasn't happy with what he felt was a near flawless straight adaptation from the play. Miller pointed out that there was a scene where the mother, Linda, pleads with her sons to have more compassion for their father. Biff will do so as long as he can stay out of Willy's way. The mother felt that this wasn't good enough and Biff ends up yelling at her, "I hate this city and I'll stay here! Now what do you want?" The mother finally lets the son know that the father is dying after that tirade. This was skipped over and Miller asked Roberts for an explanation. "How can he shout at his mother like that?" was Roberts's response.

Unable to get the play's director, Elia Kazan, Kramer selected Laslo Benedek, a Hungarian-born second unit director and editor whose most famous film prior to *Death of a Salesman* was a Frank Sinatra misfire called *The Kissing Bandit* (though Benedek did make a gritty little noir called *Port of New York* as well). Prior to filming, Benedek did put the cast through the paces with two weeks of intensive rehearsals—as if for a stage play. "By the time the sets were built and dressed," Benedek later recalled, "I could rehearse the script in continuity with the whole cast and the key members of the technical crew. As the picture began to take more concrete shape I had the wonderful—and in pictures, most unusual—experience of getting the first glimpse of an audience reaction from the crew, as they followed the unfolding of the story with growing interest." *Death of a Salesman* was shot in only twenty-six days.

March ended up playing Loman with a slight limp. Some critics thought it was a little something that he added to his interpretation, but, in actuality, on the second day of filming, March had fallen and twisted his knee, "So I had to superimpose a limp on Willy all the way through the picture."

March's acting of Loman has been a subject of debate over the years. Many feel his performance is brilliant while others believed it was over the top. March later said that "Willy is on the verge of insanity throughout the play. It's just a day out of his life, but the insanity is always there. I worked hard to find some normal moments and to make the most of them." Florence too would look at March's performance as a more human Willy Loman than that of other actors who had played the part on stage. "In the flash-backs to Willy's youth," she later said, "I think he brings out some of the charm, the warmth, some of the glad hander that made Willy a good salesman in his early days."

When the film was released in New York on December 20, 1951—where critics and audiences were most acquainted with the stage production—the film got a rave review by Bosley Crowther in the *New York Times*.

> *Mr. Kramer's production is so faithfully transcribed and well-designed that it stands as a nigh exact translation of Mr. Miller's play, both in its psychological candor and its exhibit of a bleak bourgeois milieu. Except for a few small omissions of dialogue lines and words, the drama is offered in Toto, right down to its torturing graveyard scene.*

Crowther also felt that March brought out a more sympathetic dimension in his Willy Loman.

> *Mr. March's performance does a lot to illuminate this broader implication of the drama, for it fills out considerably the lack of humanity in the main character that Mr. Miller somehow overlooked and thus makes the character more symbolic of the frustrated "little man." The weakness of Mr. Miller's "salesman," in this corner's opinion, is a petty and selfish disposition, unredeemed by any outgoing love. Mr. March, by his personable nature, gives occasional fleeting glints of tenderness. Otherwise, he is the shabby, cheap, dishonest, insufferable big-talker of the play.*

Other reviews were favorable as well. The *Boston Globe* called the film "magnificent cinema." The *Christian Science Monitor* called the film "vividly powerful" and "Fredric March's Willy is the unsparing portrait of a confused, wretched man."

However, not all the reviews were favorable. *Time* magazine called it "a disappointing picture." Some critics thought that March's interpretation was over-the-top. One critic (for the *Sunday Herald*) said that March was "several shades below that of Lee J. Cobb" and that he acts Loman as a "crackpot." It is with this assessment that playwright Miller agreed. "Fredric March was directed to play Willy as a psycho, all but out of control, with next to no grip on reality," Miller wrote in his memoirs. "He could certainly have been a wonder in the film, but as a psychotic, he was predictable in the extreme." The producer Stanley Kramer liked to have it both ways about March's performance. "Fred was Willy Loman. I felt very deeply about him. He rarely made a wrong move," Kramer told Deborah C. Peterson in 1990. Yet he also told author Donald Spoto, "I made a mistake in wanting March for the role. He was a wonderful actor, but there's something emotionally wrong here...I was rushed and frustrated (at the time), and I chose March because I loved and respected him." March himself later sounded less than thrilled by his performance, "No, I was not that good in 'Death of a Salesman.'"

In terms of the box office, Harry Cohn was right. *Death of a Salesman* turned out to be a resounding failure.

March was nominated for the fifth (and final) time for an Academy Award for his performance. If he won, and there were some columnists who predicted he would, he would be the first to win Best Actor three times. His competition, however, was stiff: Humphrey Bogart for *The African Queen*, Marlon Brando in *A Streetcar Named Desire*, Montgomery Clift—how he must have felt being up against the actor he supported in two Broadway plays—in *A Place in the Sun*, and Arthur Kennedy in *Bright Victory*. Bogart, who had never won before, prevailed. The only other acting nomination was for Kevin McCarthy as Best Supporting Actor. (Other nominations for *Death of a Salesman* included Black and White Cinematography and Scoring of a Dramatic or Comedy picture.) His performance was also nominated for a BAFTA (the British equivalent of an Oscar) as Best Foreign Actor, and he won the Best Actor Award at the Venice Film Festival, and a Golden Globe.

The Autumn Garden tour began in the fall of 1951 at the Nixon Theater in Pittsburgh. This would be the Marches first cross-country tour with a play since the 1927-1928 Theater Guild tour. The tour would last into February of 1952 and close in Toronto. It was while on tour that the Marches took time out to emphasize that they were now concentrating only on things that interested them when it came to acting opportunities. "When we reach the middle years there's not enough time for just make-believe," March told reporters in Detroit. "Both Florence and I want to appear in plays or movies which are important to people and which contribute something to understanding life as it is in our time." Florence added, "If Freddie weren't an actor, I'd be content not to act at all. But as it is, it's so companionable—traveling about from city to city always together just as we began." In Boston, Florence let it be known what it was like to be married to a man who was—or at least had been—the idol of millions of women. "Whenever we were in public together," she related, "I had the feeling people would look at me and look at old glamour puss over there, and say: 'I wonder what he sees in her.'"

During the tour, the whole family would be reunited for the holidays, with Penny—age nineteen and a student at Vassar—and Tony—now seventeen and attending a prep school in Philadelphia—joining their parents over the Thanksgiving holiday in Chicago and then again in Indianapolis and Milwaukee over the Christmas holiday. The Marches let it be known that they were pleased that neither of their children had shown an interest in acting—Penny's goal at the time was to be a writer, while Tony wanted to take up ranching. The Marches wanted their children "to have work that will allow them to live full, well-rounded lives."

The Marches opened on Christmas Eve in *The Autumn Garden* in Milwaukee. The Marches stayed at the home of Mr. and Mrs. Edwin P. Davis—Mrs. Davis being one of March's cousins—and had Christmas dinner with them. "We haven't planned anything special," Mrs. Davis told inquisitive reporters. "Our ordinary schedule takes a bit of readjusting to fit into the theater's, but the rest of our plans are very much family stuff. It's been about two years since I've seen Fredric." She did note that she served the Marches "an early and light" supper before the play, and then they would eat a regular meal after the show. Mrs. Davis was asked if there was any sign of temperament with their famous guests, "My heavens, no," she replied, "Not when you've been in the business as long as they have."

It was while in Milwaukee that March got together with an old college friend, Jack Ramsey, after the play, and the two old friends ended up drinking a great deal. The impression that March made at the time on Ramsey's daughter Jackie was not a positive one. "Fred embarrassed me. Father and Fred drank a lot—Fred was loud-voiced and made fun of me, which I did not appreciate," Jackie Ramsey Macaulay related to Deborah C. Peterson, nearly forty years later, "It seemed he was too much like the character in the play. Too obnoxious, as he was in the play."

When the road tour of *The Autumn Garden* ended in Toronto in February, the Marches spent much of the spring and summer of 1952 at the Farm in Connecticut resting up. It was during that summer that March got an offer from 20th Century Fox to make a film on location in Bavaria: *Man on a Tightrope.*

March was reunited with director Elia Kazan, for the first time since *The Skin of Our Teeth*, in the anti-communist film *Man on a Tightrope. Man on a Tightrope* tells the story of a small, broken down Czechoslovakian circus run by Karel Cernik (March), who also doubles as a clown. The circus is considered government property and is to be used for propaganda purposes more than for entertainment, which vexes the independent-minded Cernik. Along the way, Cernik finds out that one of the circus performers is a communist informant who reports to the secret police. Cernik is determined to transport his circus over the border, seeking asylum in Austria.

Actually, Kazan wasn't the original choice to make *Man on a Tightrope.* Henry Hathaway, who was a Fox contract director, had been working on the screenplay with Robert E. Sherwood and felt that they had "a good script" when Studio Chief Darryl Zanuck called Hathaway to his office and told him, "I want to take this picture and I want to give it to Kazan, because there's been all this talk in Hollywood that he's a Communist and it's not true, and we want him to do an anti-Communist picture to prove that he wasn't a Communist." Actually Kazan was indeed a former Communist, who renounced and testified before the House Un-American Activities Committee (HUAC) naming names. It was why he actually was working in films when others who didn't cooperate with the committee were blacklisted. The taciturn Hathaway told Zanuck, "What the hell, give it to him."

Kazan found the screenplay "mediocre" and full of one dimensional characters—a poor later effort by Robert E. Sherwood, who had written the screenplay to *The Best Years of Our Lives*. He also was resistant to doing the film because, as a former Communist himself, he felt to do so would only "satisfy a pack of red-baiters who wanted my ass." Kazan was ready to turn the picture down for all of these reasons, but was persuaded by Zanuck that the film was based on a true story, and he could film it on location in Bavaria. In the end, Kazan thought he might be able to make it into a presentable tense action-drama.

Kazan knew he wanted March as the lead. He believed the film and his own contribution to it had many shortcomings, but he did believe that what does ring through is "genuine affection for the circus and for Freddy March, whom I really loved." In an interview years later, Kazan called March "a marvelous, marvelous man" and said that he was one of the rare people that he actually stood up and made a speech for (at the Players Club in New York), "that's how much I liked him." He also wanted March because of the accusations against him that he was a Communist or at the least a Communist sympathizer. "Freddie was no more a Communist than my cat," Kazan later wrote in his memoirs. What else Kazan looked forward to when working with March was his humor, including "his latest dirty jokes—an endless supply." March also felt that his presence in a propaganda picture such as *Man on a Tightrope* would dispel some of the lingering effects of the accusations that had been made against him. Besides, there weren't many other pictures being offered to him, and this one at least offered the central role in a major studio production with one of the most acclaimed directors of the day.

Gloria Grahame was cast as March's unfaithful wife. Kazan thought Grahame seemed "slightly over-the-hill." Terry Moore, a Fox contract player, was cast as March's daughter. Kazan liked Terry Moore—even though she came on the set and announced in no uncertain terms that she was Howard Hughes's girlfriend. He admired her guts in a river scene. Cameron Mitchell, from the stage version of *Death of a Salesman*, was cast as Moore's boyfriend and Richard Boone was cast as March's confidant, who turns out to be the spy. In true against-type casting is Adolphe Menjou, who was cast as the head of the communist secret-police. In life, Menjou was a rabid reactionary, anti-communist, and supporter of HUAC. Menjou was a professional who "behaved marvelously," according to Kazan. He and March work well together.

Location filming went well, and when the time came to shoot interiors, the cast and crew traveled to Munich where March stayed with Kazan in a suite at the Vier Jahreszeiten Hotel. Kazan later related in his memoirs that March got into trouble with a married chambermaid that he was seeing. He was threatened by the husband, and at some point Kazan even had to "rush to the police station and intercede for him… this unreasonable man was out to become famous for killing a movie star." Naturally, Florence wasn't around which, according to Kazan, meant "Freddie was a child who couldn't keep his fingers out of the cookie jar." When Florence did come over for a visit, March, as usual, became "another person." A woman in the company also appraised Florence of what had been going on but, as Kazan relates, "Mrs. March was used to Mr. March being 'naughty.' She didn't like it, but she wasn't unaccustomed to it."

When the film was released in the early summer of 1953, March received excellent reviews, overall, while the picture in general got mixed notices. "His portrayal of the clown-manager who loves his calling and his colleagues no less than freedom is sensitive and moving," wrote the critic for the *New York Times*. "He is truly a steadfast rock to which his frightened flock can cling." The film is considered one of Kazan's weaker efforts (along with *Sea of Grass*), but of the films that March had made since *The Best Years of Our Lives*—his last hit film— it may actually be among his best. However, the film was unsuccessful with audiences and became March's fifth straight film to tank at the box office.

III

While March's most recent pictures had been box office failures, he did have one hit when Samuel Goldwyn re-released *The Best Years of Our Lives* in December of 1953. "Most theaters allow re-issues to sneak out," Goldwyn told columnist Bob Thomas, "as if they were something to be ashamed of. I'm bringing back *Best*

Years of Our Lives proudly—as if it were a new picture." Goldwyn backed up that statement by promising to put up a $250,000 advertising campaign. The campaign worked, as the reissue brought in an additional $2 million on top of what the picture had made over its original release—doing better at the box office than most of March's most recent films.

March had just celebrated his fifty-sixth birthday when he began work on the all-star MGM film *Executive Suite* produced by John Houseman. Houseman and director Robert Wise put together an extraordinarily talented cast (in addition to March) including William Holden, June Allyson, Barbara Stanwyck, Walter Pidgeon, Paul Douglas, Nina Foch, Dean Jagger and Shelly Winters. The film—about boardroom maneuverings over a twenty-four-hour period at a top furniture company when its president suddenly dies—managed to sign all these star names and still stay within a budget of $1.25 million. (Holden and Allyson were the most expensive, given their current box office potency.) In his memoirs, Houseman wrote of how they managed to make the film on such a miniscule budget—most of which went to the actors—explaining that the sets were reused from other MGM films, altered slightly, and that "they looked fine in black and white—with a used look that gave them unusual authenticity." Furthermore, there is no background music. Instead, Houseman, an old radio hand, incorporates the sounds of the city: church bells, horns, cars braking, traffic, crowds, etc. March was cast as a devious efficiency expert, Loren Shaw, but he doesn't play him simply with a black hat—throughout the performance we see shades of gray. He is superb. In fact, all the stars shine, and the climax of the picture set in the board room is full of dramatic tension and suspense.

It may seem strange but this was the first time that March and Barbara Stanwyck had ever properly met. Nina Foch, who would win an Academy Award as best supporting actress for her performance as the executive secretary, recalls that these two pros were not above trying to outdo each other in attention-getting. "Barbara Stanwyck screamed her head off (and) Freddie March used every trick in the book. He'd take his hankie out and furiously wipe his brow every time Paul Douglas tried to speak." As usual, March made his director aware of his tendency to overact at times, and according to

Wise, "I devised a motion just to signal to him if he was overdoing it."

On the whole, the cast got along fine, except for June Allyson who, Houseman says, walked into rehearsals "with all the insouciance of an old ex-Metro star." She had a tendency to come to the set late, and was unsure of her lines. Once this happened one time too often, the pros gave her the cold shoulder, which caused Allyson to tearfully call producer Houseman complaining about the treatment she was getting. Houseman explained to her why, and from that time forward Allyson made sure she was on time and line perfect. Wise recalls that the cast "were very professional, very good. And maybe when we were relighting a shot or maybe between takes or reloading the camera, they would sit there and kid each other …just swapping yarns or whatever." Sadly, it was during the shoot of *Executive Suite* that March's oldest brother, Harold, died of cancer at the age of sixty-six. March took time off and, with Florence, attended the funeral in Pasadena.

When the film was released it was met by mostly favorable reviews—especially for March. *Variety* wrote, "Eight scene-stealers vie for the star billing and each is fine, with some standing out over what amounts to standout performances by all concerned in the drama. Certainly Fredric March's characterization of the controller will be remembered among the really sock delineations. So will William Holden's portrayal of the idealistic, but practical, young executive." The film also went on to make a solid profit for MGM. (Houseman recalls that when the film opened at Radio City Music Hall in New York it had "the biggest Saturday and biggest Sunday and then the biggest week in the history of the nation's biggest theater.) And the film was nominated for four Oscars: the afore-mentioned nomination of Nina Foch for Supporting Actress, Best Cinematography, Art Direction and Costume Design—winning for Supporting Actress and Costume Design. Even though he wasn't the leading actor in the film, Executive Suite broke March's run of box office failures.

Political causes continued to occupy their time still. In May of 1954, the Marches attended a meeting of the liberal leaning Americans for Democratic Action (ADA), meeting at "21" in New York City. They were seated with their old friend, playwright Moss Hart, and his vivacious wife, Kitty Carlisle, at the event. Also prominent in attendance were former First Lady Eleanor Roosevelt and U.S. Supreme Court Justice William O. Douglas. Hart recorded in his diary, "There was entertainment that went on until half-past two in the morning...We sat with the Fredric Marches and very pleasant they are. I have no idea why we do not see them but somehow we don't."

The summer of 1954 was spent relaxing once again at the New Milford Farm, but there was urgency that summer—a happy one. For on August 14, Penny, who had only recently graduated from Vassar, married twenty-three-year-old Italian, Umberto Fantacci— called Bert for short. The ceremony was performed in the garden of the farm by a minister of the First Congregational Church. The groom was a Yale class of 1951 graduate. Sadly for the Marches, the young couple would be living in Italy where Bert was embarking on a business career. This meant that they would see much less of their beloved daughter. A decision was made that on alternating summers, March and Florence would go to Italy for visits and the Fantacci's would reciprocate by coming to the New Milford Farm for two-month visits.

March was pleased to be cast once again in a William Holden picture when he accepted the role of the kindly navy admiral who takes a paternal interest in Holden, in an adaptation of James Michener's best-selling novel *The Bridges at Toko-Ri*. Holden was a big admirer of March's and once said that his two favorite actors and inspirations were March and Spencer Tracy. Originally, March was to be second-billed to Holden but, by the time the film was released, leading lady Grace Kelly was a top Oscar contender for her performance in *The Country Girl*—and would, in an upset, win over Judy Garland for *A Star is Born*. March was relegated to third billing, but still above the title. Rounding out leading actors is Mickey Rooney, in a delicious turn as a bowler-hat-wearing Irish helicopter pilot. The story deals with Navy fliers during the Korean War and the lives they left behind. Holden, then probably the biggest name in films, would consent to do the film only if it didn't try to put on a happy ending—he wanted the ending from the novel retained, with his character dying. The producers, George Seaton and William Pearlman, and director Mark Robson agreed.

March was realistic about his days as a romantic leading man being over, and with it, assuming more character orientated roles—though in a few years he would have the opportunity to enact a May-December love story with Kim Novak. "The size of the role does not interest me much—I'm the admiral commanding a task force of carrier-based jets," March told a reporter. "The admiral knows no war is a good war to be in and that it nearly always must be fought in the worst possible place at the worst possible time. He has seen two of his own sons killed in action. This affects the admiral's relationship with the young pilots he must send off into battle."

At about this time, March was asked who he thought was the best actor working on stage or screen, and he immediately answered Marlon Brando. "I've seen everything he's ever done," March replied, "He's the best since John Barrymore." Maybe so, but a poll conducted of more than thirty top stars, directors, and producers, that was made public in newspapers in January of 1955, named March as their choice as the screen's best actor. March was the top choice by a 2:1 margin over the runner-up—Marlon Brando.

When *The Bridges at Toko-Ri* was released in January of 1955, it became yet another big box-office hit for William Holden and Grace Kelly—who had begun a brief, discreet affair during the making of the film, and would resume with their next picture *The Country Girl*. It offered March a sympathetic role in a big film, and in that way enhanced his screen career too. He also received some excellent reviews. "Fredric March shows great acting skill, but not acting tricks," wrote the *New York Times*. *Variety* wrote, "March delivers a sock portrayal of the admiral, who is drawn to Holden because he reminds him of his two sons lost in war."

IV

Television was gaining a supremacy over motion pictures as a form of popular entertainment during the 1950s, and the Marches, unlike some of their contemporaries, decided to embrace rather than run from it. "TV may develop a crop of actors similar to the old stock companies," Florence maintained. "TV also provides more rehearsal time than in the movies. Of course, in the theater we devote more time to rehearsing, but here is a case of some being better than none, I think."

In March of 1954, March cohosted the Oscar telecast with Donald O'Connor. March handled the MC duties from New York, while O'Connor did the same from Hollywood—telecast live over NBC. The two hosts had a bit of split-screen repartee, with O'Connor introducing March and then greeting him with a "Hi, Dad." On the telecast, March had the opportunity, from his position in New York, to guide Audrey Hepburn to the podium when she was declared the Best Actress winner for her work in *Roman Holiday*. Prior to his hosting duties, March appeared on TV's *What's My Line?* as the mystery guest—spending over six minutes stumping the panel (Arlene Frances, Margaret Truman, Steve Allen and Bennet Cerf) with a bravura supply of dialects and eliciting many laughs from the studio audience.

On September 15, 1954, March did a live telecast on the first episode of the new *Best of Broadway* adaptation of "The Royal Family," allowing him to reprise Tony Cavendish some twenty-five years after last playing the role. The telecast would also reunite him with Claudette Colbert for the first time since the early '30s. Also joining the production were Helen Hayes, Charles Coburn, and Nancy Olson. The cast was compensated well for their efforts. Both March and Colbert received $7,000, Hayes $6,000, and Coburn and Olson each about $2,000. Telecast over CBS, the telecast failed to win strong ratings.

On December 23, March donned the makeup wizardry of Perc Westmore to play Ebenezer Scrooge in a musical version of Charles Dickens's *A Christmas Carol* on CBS's *Shower of Stars*. Broadcast in color with a sizable budget, the show also starred Basil Rathbone as Marley's Ghost, Bob Sweeney as Bob Cratchit, Ray Middleton as Fred (and the Ghost of Christmas Present), and featured carols by the Roger Wagner Chorale. The behind the scenes talent was equally impressive, with the adaptation of the novel done by Maxwell Anderson, the writer of such plays as *Winterset, Knickerbocker's Holiday* and *Key Largo*. The distinguished composer Bernard Herrmann (who did the music for such films as *Citizen Kane, North by Northwest* and *Psycho*) conducted the orchestra. Ralph Levy, a TV veteran, directed.

March called Dickens's novel "a literary rock of ages" and went on to say, "Naturally, I am thrilled that I've been chosen to play Scrooge on TV this coming week. In preparing for the role, I have pondered the qualities that have made this tale immortal. Whence comes its appeal, its unerring instinct for striking the keynote of Christmas?"

The TV production was shot over a five-day period at the Desilu Studios in Hollywood, with March giving a superb turn as Scrooge—matched every step of the way by Rathbone as Marley's Ghost. The production is now available on DVD, and in watching it, I can't help but wish that it had been presented as a straight dramatic production rather than a musical—as the rather ordinary songs get in the way of the story. Still, it is worthy production of that Christmas chestnut.

Humphrey Bogart very much wanted to make the film version of the 1955 Broadway hit *The Desperate Hours* with his good friend Spencer Tracy. Tracy put off a decision for six weeks before declining the role. Tracy didn't like the script, and that is the real reason for his declining to act in the film, though Hollywood legend has it that Bogart and Tracy couldn't agree on who would get top billing—obviously if Tracy had been in the film his prestige would have warranted top billing. After Tracy was out of the equation, the film's director, William Wyler, gave some thought to casting Henry Fonda or Gary Cooper, but ultimately he turned to March, thanks to the suggestion of Don Hartman, Paramount's head of production. He had recently attended a sneak preview in Santa Barbara of *The Bridges at Toko-Ri*, "the audience loved him," Hartman told Wyler. Wyler didn't need much convincing, since he also greatly admired March. Unlike Tracy, billing was not an issue with March, who was soon offered the part. March knew that at this point in his career it was Bogart who had the bigger movie marquee name and was more than willing to accept that he would be second billed—but still with star billing.

Filming began in October of 1954 on the $2.4 million Paramount production. It was a smooth shoot except for the fact that Bogart was already beginning to suffer from the cancer that would eventually kill him within slightly more than two years. Many scenes were interrupted due to his coughing fits and had to be reshot. While March was available to work any and all hours, Bogart's contract had a six o'clock quitting time—and he was not shy about insisting on this prerogative. It seems that Wyler may have gotten a bit of revenge when he did twenty takes of Bogart running up and down a staircase. (Of course had Wyler known about Bogart's precarious health it's likely he wouldn't have insisted on so many takes or even had used a double, but at this point not even Bogie knew he was a dying man.) But Wyler was like that, and did shoot many takes without really expressing what he wanted. On the first day of shooting, he had March and Martha Scott, cast as his wife, shoot a supposedly simple scene that called for March to kiss Scott as he exited the front door on his way to work—a scene the director took fifty takes on, until finally Scott asked what he was looking for. Apparently, Wyler wanted March to have a harried look because his character was running late for work. March later said, "He (Wyler) doesn't articulate his criticism. But you sense his dissatisfaction. He seems to know when there's more to be gotten than you're giving. And he's relentless until he has it."

The film wrapped in late-January of 1955, and was released in October in New York. Bosley Crowther in the *New York Times* called it a "crafty and crackling screen thriller." While Crowther had some problem with some characters behaviors and motivation, he did find that March performed with "extraordinary spirit and versatility." *Variety* called the film "expert," declaring Bogart "at his best," with March giving a "powerful" performance. The best review that March got may have been from the writer of the novel and screenplay, Joseph Hayes, who saw a rough cut of the film in September and immediately wrote March with his reaction:

Dear Freddie:

I have just seen THE DESPERATE HOURS picture. The whole thing was overwhelming! And a large part of that effect is due to your fantastically right performance. It is a great thrill for a writer to conceive something in his mind and to have a character portrayed so precisely as imagined. You captured in your face, not only the terrible struggle within Dan, but you were able to suggest so many conflicting emotions at the same instant. I have seen your performances over the years—including DR. JEKYL AND MR HYDE and, of course, THE BEST YEARS—but I think this tops them all. I don't know whether you have been told or not, but I am a hard guy to please, especially with characters I have written, so I am not writing this for any unusual reasons. I am really grateful to you for the dignity and depth that you gave the characterization...

    Sincerely Yours,
    Joe

Despite mostly good reviews, *The Desperate Hours* failed at the box office.

March was now the busiest he had been in films in several years. Within a couple of weeks of completing *The Desperate Hours*, he and Florence left for Spain, where March would spend several months shooting Robert Rossen's ambitious historic spectacular *Alexander the Great*. March was cast as Alexander's father, King Phillip of Macedonia and Captain General of Greece—the man who conquered the Greek states by force and built the army that his son Alexander would one day use to conquer the Persian Empire.

The first half of the film explores the relationship between Alexander and his father—a relationship driven by hate and jealousy. Sporting a beard, March once again is cast in a costume picture—his first since *Christopher Columbus*—and as Phillip he gives a lusty performance. To play the leading role, writer-producer-director Rossen initially considered John Cassavettes, who would have been a daring, if unusual, choice. But in the end, he went with Richard Burton. The cast is rounded out by Claire Bloom, Danielle Darrieux, Harry Andrews, Stanley Baker, Peter Cushing, and Barry Jones. Not to mention 6,000 extras playing soldiers and cavalry men.

The film was in production for eight months, but March filmed most of his scenes between mid-February and June of 1955. When March wasn't working, he and Florence made their way to Italy to visit their daughter, who was pregnant with their first grandchild. On October 15, they were on hand when Penny gave birth to a boy, who was named Gianni.

Initially, the film was budgeted at $2 million but ended up costing twice as much. It was a labor of love for Rossen who had spent years on research, and it does have some scenes of majestic beauty, impressive action sequences, and good interplay between Burton and March. But at the same time, weighing in at two hours and twenty minutes, there are also long moments of tedium and endless speeches. Yet, Rossen was of the opinion that the film was better at its original three-hour length, "Actually it's a much better picture in three hours than it is in two hours and twenty minutes, precisely for one reason. It unveils the various guilt's Alexander felt towards his father much more deeply." Richard Burton also lamented the cuts when he said, "I know all 'epics' are awful, but I thought *Alexander the Great* might be the first good one. I was wrong. They cut it about—played down to the audience. I say if the audience doesn't understand, let 'em stay ignorant." Burton kept trying, though. Five years later, he would be in Rome, filming another epic that would change his life: *Cleopatra.*

When the film was released in early 1956, most reviews came down on the negative side. *Variety* wrote that "Rossen is not always able to hold interest in his story and action, resulting in some long, dull stretches." However, the critic for the *New York Times* wrote that "although this spectacle runs lengthy two-and-a-half hours, its moments of boredom are rare." Of March's performance, the *Times* wrote, "Mr. March is a tough, bearded, designing warrior consumed by lusts, preoccupied by wars and harried by suspicions. And he is hindered by jealousy of his son and hatred of his estranged wife, who, he feels, is pitting his brilliant son against him. Mr. March gives him natural attributes and imperfections." The box office was hardly great—audiences stayed away in droves.

Returning from Italy, elated by the birth of his first grandchild, March accepted the role of a broadcast TV executive whose life has been consumed by work duties and his family neglected, in Nunnally Johnson's adaptation of Sloan Wilson's novel *The Man in the Gray Flannel Suit.* (For which Wilson was paid $200,000 for the screen rights.) March was third-billed after Gregory Peck and Jennifer Jones. The film offers a reunion between March and Ann Harding, twenty-seven years after they starred together in *Paris*

Bound. In *The Man in the Gray Flannel Suit*, Harding plays March's neglected wife.

In the film, Peck is a young advertiser on his way up, and March cautions him to slow down and not be too eager, because being top man can be a lonely position. Jones was cast as Peck's typically 1950s stay-at-home wife, who is seemingly more ambitious about her husband's career than he is. The film is an effective look at the conflicts of the business world and suburbia circa the mid-1950s. Its exteriors were shot on location in both New York City (Madison Avenue) and Westport, Connecticut—representing the home life in suburbia. Johnson and Peck thought that the film could represent *The Best Years of Our Lives* ten years later, since the Peck character was in World War II, had spent the last ten years getting an education, and then worked his way up in the business world.

In the film, March plays a wealthy, but increasingly disillusioned, man. He is so wealthy that in his New York penthouse apartment he has a large bar on one end of the room and a smaller bar on the other. March asked Nunnally Johnson why this was the case, and Johnson replied, "You're playing a rich man. The tiny bar is there so that in case you get thirsty on your way to the big bar, you can stop and have a drink."

The Man in the Gray Flannel Suit opened in New York's Roxy Theater on April 12, 1956— the eleventh anniversary of the death of President Franklin Roosevelt and, not coincidentally, the premier benefited one of FDR's favorite charities, The March of Dimes. On the whole, the film received favorable reviews. Kate Cameron in the *New York Daily News* called it a "deeply moving domestic drama." Bosley Crowther in the *New York Times* called it "a mature, fascinating and often quite tender and touching film." Many critics thought that March's performance as the world weary executive was the stand out. William Zinsser of the *New York Herald Tribune* felt that March "steals the show," and Harrison Carroll in the *LA Herald & Examiner* wrote, "March's portrait of the tycoon, who has given all his energies to the building of a big business, to the ruin of his marriage and the neglect of his children, is a masterly study of an older man." *The Man in the Gray Flannel Suit* went on to a profitable run grossing over $4.3 million, which made it the twelfth biggest box office film of 1956.

The Man in the Gray Flannel Suit would be March's last film for three years. In the meanwhile, he and Florence would return to the New York stage to begin the greatest triumph of their career.

PICTURE GALLERY
1943–1973

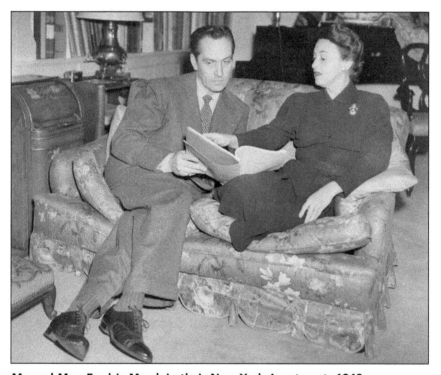

Mr. and Mrs. Fredric March in their New York Apartment, 1943

A brilliant hit with backstage rivalries, *The Skin of Our Teeth*, From L to R, Tallulah Bankhead, Florence Eldridge, March, Frances Heflin and Montgomery Clift

The Skin of Our Teeth won a Pulitzer Prize for playwright Thornton Wilder

Playing Mark Twain opposite Alexis Smith in *The Adventures of Mark Twain*, 1944

One of the screens finest examples of mature love with Myrna Loy in *The Best Years of Our Lives*, 1946, brought March his second Academy Award

The Best Years of Our Lives was one of the
most acclaimed films of its time

Florence Eldridge and Fredric March, publicity photo, 1948

Publicity photo, late '40s

With Kathleen Ryan in *Christopher Columbus*, 1949

As the elderly Christopher Columbus

Now I Lay Me Down to Sleep was the first of three plays that March and Eldridge did from 1950-1951

March and Eldridge in Lillian Hellman's *The Autumn Garden*, 1951

As Willy Loman in the film version of *Death of a Salesman*, March received his fifth Oscar nomination. With him is Mildred Dunnock, 1951

March towers over an all-star cast including (L to R) Louis Calhern, Paul Douglas, Barbara Stanwyck, William Holden and Nina Foch in *Executive Suite*, 1954

With Martha Scott in William Wyler's *The Desperate Hours*, 1955

His greatest stage role as James Tyrone in *Long Day's Journey Into Night*, 1956

© C.P.C. 8536-R1493

His last romantic lead, opposite Kim Novak in *Middle of the Night*, 1959

His last Broadway play, as the Angel of God in *Gideon*, 1961

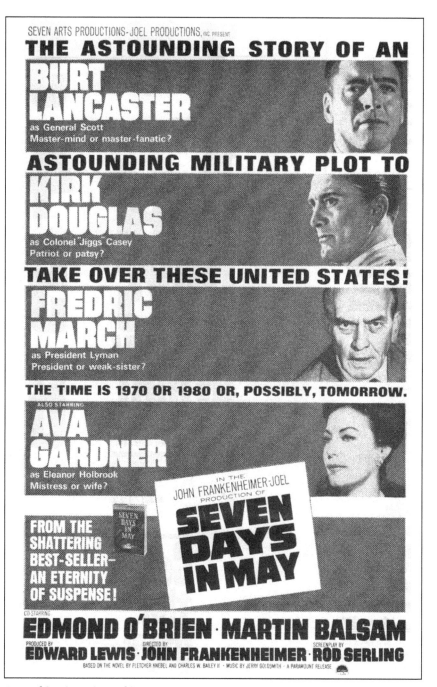

One of his best later films, *Seven Days* in May, 1964

As the President of the US in *Seven Days* in May, with Edmund O'Brien

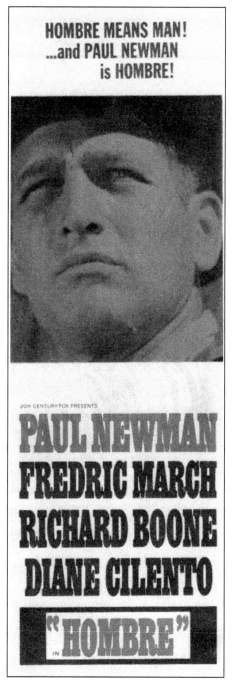

'Hombre means man' was the slogan for
March's only western, Hombre, 1967

The racial drama *Tick...Tick...Tick* cast March as a small-town southern mayor, 1969

Two dying actors giving majestic performances in their final film—March and Robert Ryan in *The Iceman Cometh*, 1973

March as Harry Hope in *The Iceman Cometh* opposite Lee Marvin

CHAPTER THIRTEEN
1956–1960

In early May of 1956, March confided to Hollywood columnist Bob Thomas that he was done with the stage and would from this time forward concentrate only on films and an occasional TV production. "I'm 58," March told Thomas. "When you get as old as I am, you want to enjoy life. Mostly that means traveling to me. I couldn't face another long run in a Broadway show...That's for the kids—the ones with stardust in their eyes." Yet, within five months of making this statement, the Marches would be opening on Broadway in their longest run yet, in one of the most exhausting plays ever presented: Eugene O'Neill's autobiographical play *A Long Day's Journey into Night*.

At the time that March was talking with Thomas, he was preparing to star in a TV production of Sinclair Lewis's play *Dodsworth*. Telecast as part of the *Producer's Showcase* program over at NBC, Dodsworth tells the story of a Midwestern automobile manufacturer whose vain wife needles him into retiring so that they could embark on a tour of Europe, and in doing so they discover truths—not so pleasant—about one another. *Dodsworth* had been a hit play in the thirties for Walter Huston and Fay Bainter as well as a well-regarded film. Taking on the role of Mrs. Dodsworth was Claire Trevor, with Geraldine Fitzgerald who becomes the other woman in Dodsworth's life.

John Crosby, the television critic for the *New York Herald-Tribune* gave a positive review to the production and wrote, "Fredric March has long proved that he is one of the most competent actors we have, but I was astonished by Miss Trevor's fine performance as his selfish wife. It's a thankless and difficult part and she managed to make it believable and even, within limits, sympathetic." For their fine performances, both March and Trevor were each nominated for Emmy Awards—with Trevor winning the award.

March had planned to spend another contented summer at the farm in Connecticut and then hopefully work on a picture in the fall, when out of the blue he received the offer to do *Long Day's Journey into Night* produced by Theodore Mann and to be directed by Jose Quintero. Mann and Quintero were the team that had helped revive interest in Eugene O'Neill when they presented a prestigious off-Broadway production of *The Iceman Cometh*. It was that successful production and the care in which the team of Mann and Quintero gave it that convinced O'Neill's widow, Carlotta, to allow them to produce *Long Day's Journey into Night*—even though O'Neill's will had asked that the play not be produced until twenty-five years after his death. "Carlotta was very much conscious of wanting to resurrect [O'Neill's] reputation," recalled Mann. "She thought he was a great playwright, and her whole life was dedicated to that— to bringing her husband back to prominence. She was very angry about the Broadway producers who had ignored him for so many years."

Long Day's Journey is biographical in nature and revolves around James Tyrone, Sr., a sixty-five-year-old former stage star who's full of stories of past glories, when he isn't indulging in alcohol. He is parsimonious and spends money on useless real estate rather than the needs of his family, which include his sad, drug addicted wife Mary and their two sons, James (Jamie) Tyrone, Jr.—an aspiring actor—and youngest son, Edmund—who suffers from Tuberculosis, but what everybody tries to downplay as simply a "summer cold." These four people will spend a "long day" coming to terms with their fears, dreams, and lost hopes. The play offers four perfectly drawn out parts and required four superb actors—actors with stamina to boot.

Mann had March in mind for James Tyrone from the very beginning, but he told Mann that he would only accept the part "with the proviso" that Florence be cast as Mary Tyrone. "We knew Freddie was perfect for James Tyrone and that Florence was a gamble," Mann later said, "but it paid off because Freddie was so fantastic as the father." Mann agreed and signed both Marches to a contract. Jason Robards, Jr., a favorite of Mann and Quintero since his ground breaking performance in the stage version of *The Iceman Cometh*, was cast as Jamie, and Bradford Dillman was signed to play the tubercular Edmund.

Dillman recalls March as "an impressive man—a great actor—which was enough of a shock to intimidate a relative newcomer like myself. He had the guts of a bandit—he never hesitated to go out on the limb. He was totally secure as an actor." He recalls March as being "very protective of Florence," who he recalls as "not being fully comfortable with her role."

The first rehearsal took place at the Marches farm in Connecticut.

> *I had the guts to call him 'Freddie' from the start because he insisted on it*, Dillman recalled years later.

> *Jose (Quintero) and I stayed overnight as his guests. Freddie and Florence excused themselves and went to bed but Freddie let us know that we could have the run of the place which included the bar—and we certainly made ourselves welcome there. We drank too much and became a bit drunk. We began to explore the place and I opened a closet and in the closet was an Oscar. I said, 'Take a look at this, Jose.' We took it out and each of us took turns reciting acceptance speeches in our drunken state. I'm happy neither Freddie nor Florence showed up to see us!*

As for their director, Dillman found the Panamanian-born Quintero to be ". . . very intense. He came in having very definite ideas...how he would indicate how he wanted you to play a scene is that he would almost act it out for you—and expect you to copy him. I began to imitate him in my performance which is not what I really wanted. Eventually I would get away from that. He couldn't do that with Freddie, of course."

In his autobiography, Quintero gave some examples of how he communicated what he wanted from his actors and how he involved them in the decision making:

> *Now, Florence and Freddy, you're coming from the dining*

room. That's the upstage entrance. Freddy asks, "Do you want us to enter together, or one a little behind the other?" I'll let you answer that yourself. What is it that you are trying desperately to do in this scene, the total scene? Freddy (replies), "I want to keep her happy and give her all the love I have so she won't go back to taking those terrible drugs that made us send her to a sanitarium. She has just got home and we don't want her to worry." Well, how then should you enter? Freddy says,"With my arms around her of course." You're right, Freddy. Now, do you mind starting the first line off-stage, for you have been talking to each other since you left the dining room? All right let's try that. Just hold it for a minute until I get down into the house.

Despite the difficult role, March had an affinity with James Tyrone. "Another thing about the old boy, James Tyrone, it wasn't too far away from my natural bent, because he was an old-time ham actor, too, you know," he later said. Mann said that March would excitedly tell him about his early days as an actor and how it helped him relate to James Tyrone. "Freddie and James had similarities in their careers, particularly in that they both achieved great fame," Mann later recalled. "James just explained to us his downfall. Freddie's movie roles had thinned out, because of his alleged left-wing friends, which got him in hot water during the Hollywood black-list days."

The play had its first preview in New Haven, in October, at the Shubert Theater. Mann recalls that, "Opening night did not go well. The press was mixed, some of them commenting on the play's length, which didn't help ticket sales. Our confidence was shaken by the indifferent reception. Each day we continued to rehearse even more intensely. We were determined to achieve O'Neill's intentions."

At one point, Mann felt it might help cast morale and give a needed shot in the arm if the cast took a side trip to the O'Neill house in New London, a short car ride from New Haven. "As we drove along… I was dismayed to see the commercial development: souvenir shops, fast-food joints, and cheap five-and-dime markets. They were all one-or-two story buildings, garishly painted, sprawling out onto the avenue and taking away from the beauty of this water-front town." When they got to the house, they were met by the agent who would show them the property who told them about young people who gather in the back yard at night, build a fire, and then read one of O'Neill's plays aloud. It gave the cast hope that if young people were still into O'Neill then maybe they can reach a mainstream audience. They then toured the house—breathing in the same dining room, stairway, and bedrooms that scenes of the play take place in. "That visit had a profound effect on us," Mann later stated, "...we were at the very origins of *Journey*. It was like finding a rare treasure at an archeologist dig—it sent reverberations through all of us."

When the play reached Boston, Florence lost her voice, which threw the production into chaos; a sore throat so severe she wasn't able to speak. Mann recalled going to the Marches suite at the Ritz Carlton. It was a Monday, and the first preview for Boston would be Thursday, and so all they could do was hope and see. By Tuesday morning she was no better, and the efforts of a local doctor proved unsuccessful. March called his doctor in Connecticut, but due to a severe snow storm he couldn't make the trip. "I kept seeing Mrs. O'Neill in my mind the day she entrusted us with rights of the play," Mann recalled, "and after our mild reception in New Haven, here we were in Boston with a disaster about to happen." At this point, Mann thought of Dr. Max Jacobson from New York, who had proved successful in helping many people with various ailments. Somehow, and Mann doesn't know how, Jacobson chartered a plane and successfully arrived in Boston.

Jacobson treated Florence and told her she had to keep absolute silence if his remedy was to work. Meanwhile, the cast rehearsed with Ruth Nelson, John Cromwell's wife, and Florence's under-study, just in case this latest remedy didn't work. As it turned out, Nelson did have to go on for Florence at the first preview on Thursday night—script in hand. But, by Friday morning after sleeping away most of Wednesday and Thursday, Florence's voice was totally normal and she was ready to take the stage for the Friday night performance.

In Boston, Dillman recalls big climactic scene "where Freddie as James gets up on a chair while wearing his tattered robe and begins to recollect glories of his past." It's a long exhaustive scene coming towards the end of a long and exhaustive play.

He dried up—he couldn't recall his lines, Dillman recalled over fifty-five years later.

> *This is his big speech and I had done a lot of live TV pervious to Long Journey so my first instinct was to feed him some kind of line to help him recall what he was supposed to say. Anyway he has a five minute monologue. I had been positioned to stand off to the side as it was his big scene. So he gives me this wounded sound. I know he's gone dry. So I considered helping him but then another thought raced into my mind, "He's the star of the show— maybe I better not open my yap." Remember I was pretty inexperienced of working with a star of his magnitude. So seeing that he wasn't getting any help from me, Freddie looked for another anchor. He went over by where the stage manager was supposed to be positioned off stage, and again gave this wounded cry. The stage manager was away from his post so he didn't get any help there. Finally the line came to him and he performed the rest of the scene beautifully. Afterward, after the play was completed and we had our bows, I was backstage and suddenly I felt a tug of my collar and was being lifted up and slammed against a wall and it's Freddie! He says to me, "Why the FUCK didn't you help me? You knew I had gone dry. Don't ever do that to an actor again!" And I never did!*

The Boston run turned out to be a triumph and gave the company some needed confidence coming into New York. "We did not expect a success in New York for the major reason being the length of the play," Dillman later recalled. "It was just too damn long and there was a provision that we couldn't delete or eliminate any lines or scenes."

One day, while rehearsing for the New York opening, Carlotta O'Neill asked Jose Quintero to take her to the Helen Hayes Theater so she could watch, unobserved, the cast rehearsing. Dressed all in black, she sat in the darkened theater. Afterward, she went backstage to speak with the actors. "I don't know what to say," Mrs. O'Neill said, "How to express it." So she said nothing, except to go and "very solemnly" shake March's hand, tenderly kiss Florence on the cheek—and so on—until she looked for Dillman, "Where's my baby?' she asked. She found him over by the stage door and "embraced him with great tenderness."

Long Day's Journey into Night opened at the Helen Hayes Theater on November 8, 1956. The reviews were everything that any play could wish or hope for. "With the production of 'Long Day's Journey into Night' at the Helen Hayes last evening, the American theater acquires size and stature," wrote Brooks Atkinson in the *New York Times*. Atkinson praised all the actors—none more so than March. "As the aging actor who stands at the head of the family, Fredric March gives a masterly performance that will stand as a milestone in the acting of an O'Neill play. Petty, mean, bullying, impulsive and sharp tongue, he also has magnificence—a man of strong passions, deep loyalties and basic humanity. This is a character portrait of grandeur." Atkinson felt that Florence played the mother "with tenderness and compassion." Walter Kerr in the *New York Herald Tribune* wrote that March "cracks down on the skinflint monarch that O'Neill remembered as his father with majestic authority from the outset… he is in every way superb."

Those who saw the performances came out of it almost as emotionally drained as the actors, and, rather than go backstage to congratulate the Marches, they sent notes:

JOSEPH L. MANKIEWICZ: "Rosa and I wanted to come back, and meant to come back—but we couldn't. It was too shattering an experience…It would be just using words to say you were both 'superb' or 'unforgettable' or you name it. You were both—you were *all*—that something which goes beyond acting and beyond a performance. This is an experience very few audiences are ever privileged to share, and very few actors are ever permitted the opportunity to fulfill."

MARTHA SCOTT: "Realizing how much energy these roles take from you, I felt you should be spared a backstage visit and let me tell you this way how moved and thrilled I was. The play and your beautiful performances devastated me…"

CHARLTON HESTON: "I don't have to tell you it's a wonderful play, and I can't believe you don't know yours is a great…really great, not in the Hollywood flip-talk sense…performance. If you don't know it, Atkinson, Kerr and company will say it better than I can anyway, I'm sure…"

HELEN KELLER: "You two must have been weary indeed after the toll of energy the play had imposed on you. Yet you were darlings in the way you understood our fewness of words as we struggled to compose our shattered emotions and disturbed minds, and it was you who helped us to regain our equilibrium. With what power and perceptiveness you interpreted the doomed family passing a dreadful, sordid day in despairing wretchedness!"

There was no traditional opening night party at Sardi's. "It was so emotionally draining that we all went home and collapsed," recalls Dillman.

The actors got along well. Dillman and Jason Robards both looked up to and admired March. Robards too, by this time, had a strong reputation in the theater. "The great thing about Jason was that he always surprised me," Dillman recalled. "We had a 40-minute scene together in the second act and Jason was such a great actor that I never knew how he would enter the scene. I never dared take my eyes off of the guy which made the scene even better." Dillman and Robards became good friends and "backstage would joke and imitate Fredric March's vocalizing—'high me, low me,'" recalled Mann. "Freddie's vocal coach would often be in the audience and advise him after the show of his vocal enunciation and projection." Despite this lighthearted ribbing, Robards greatly respected and admired March.

Jason loved his father and also loved Fredric March as a father figure, author Yvonne Shafer, who interviewed Robards for her book *Performing O'Neill,* would recall.

He felt he (March) was a superb actor and that the great success of Long Day's Journey into Night lay in part in March's modest approach to acting and his eagerness to take direction and learn. Jason said that even when he (later) played the role of the father, he could hear Freddie's voice. One of the actors at Jason's memorial service said that he had asked Jason how he learned how to act and he said by sitting in the wings and watching Fredric March.

March was fifty-eight and performing a demanding role in a play that lasted four hours—eight performances per week. "Freddie had the physical stamina but it was tiring, certainly," Dillman recalled. "Some nights by the fourth act he didn't have the same strength when performing his big scene. Freddie and Florence came from the school of acting that Jason (Robards) called GBI—Great Big Indicators—never bothered to create the genuine emotion but yet acting it—indicating it."

During the run, March was very protective of Florence and wanted to make sure she got as much attention as he did—if not more. Theodore Mann recalls congratulating March following a performance. March asked Mann, "How do you think Florence did tonight?" and Mann replied, "very good, wonderful." March took him by the arm and told him to go and tell her, adding, "Isn't she the greatest thing since sliced bread?" Dillman recalls March as "very protective of Florence. He always wanted to make sure she was comfortable and confident." He also offered up a reason for why (perhaps) March was so protective of Florence. "Part of this was because Freddie was a womanizer. He definitely liked the ladies and I think out of guilt he was very solicitous of her." Dillman recalled an incident once after a performance:

> *Everybody was talking and suddenly there was a lull in the conversation and out of nowhere we could hear Freddie talking to my nineteen year old wife—'do you know I dreamt about you again last night?', practically propositioning her in front of the entire company—except for Florence who was in her dressing room. He could be very naughty when Florence wasn't around, but she certainly knew about his wandering ways.*

Another reason for his protectiveness, according to Dillman, is that Florence may not have been equal to her role, despite giving a very good performance. "The play is really about the wife. That was apparent, but for some reason Florence never really got fully comfortable with the role," Dillman says.

> *She was good, of course, but she didn't dominate the play the way she should have, so Freddie, Jason and myself had to over compensate and in doing so our roles began to overshadow hers—*

which is not how it should have been. The mother was supposed to be the towering figure of the play. It threw the play somewhat out of kilter which is why we had to compensate for Florence.

The accolades and awards continued. The New York Drama Critics poll for the 1956-1957 season awarded March as "The Best Male Lead in a Straight Play," while Florence won the award for female lead. In addition, March won his second Tony Award as Best Actor, beating out such distinguished stage actors as Maurice Evans, Wilfred Hyde-White, Eric Portman, Ralph Richardson, and Cyril Ritchard. However, Margaret Leighton beat out Florence for the Best Actress Tony. *Long Day's Journey into Night* also won for Outstanding Dramatic Play.

The play closed in the spring of 1957 so that the cast could take it to Paris where it would represent the United States at the Paris Festival of Plays. By this time, both Robards and Dillman had indicated they were ready to move on once their contracts were up. Dillman was convinced to stay through the Paris Festival.

I needed to leave the show, Dillman later recalled. I was getting too freaked out. It was affecting me. I'd drink myself under the table every night. I finally told them I needed to be released. Well, Florence was very upset by this. Freddie was of the live and let live school so he kind of accepted it but he wanted me to stay with the show long enough to go to Paris. I'm glad I did as it was an interesting experience. Everybody in the audience had a head phone and because it was an international event each line was being interpreted.

After returning from Paris, the Marches reopened on Broadway with *Long Day's* but sans Robards and Dillman, who were replaced by their understudies—and who March would later call "two weak actors." The run continued until March 29, 1958, for a total of 390 exhausting performances. The Marches had planned to take the play to London but ended up not doing so for two reasons:

1) The producers refused to allow them to have the say in who would play in the supporting cast as the sons.

2) They were just plain tired.

Late in the run of *Long Day's Journey*, Broadway columnist Walter Kerr and his playwright wife Joan attended a performance again, to see how the performances were holding up after nearly two years. "I think both of us were even more taken with the play than in the first instance, which was plenty then," Kerr wrote to March. "I think Florence has increased enormously in stature and force, your own work continues to impress me as the best there is around, anywhere. . . ."

The 1956-1958 production of *Long Day's Journey into Night* is considered one of the milestones of dramatic Broadway Theater, and March's performance is considered the definitive one as James Tyrone. Sr. Jose Quintero would later say, "I have seen other great, great actors perform James Tyrone in other productions of *Long Day's Journey into Night*. And with all due respect, I will have to tap them on the shoulder and say, 'Excuse me, your lordship, let's step aside and let the one and only James Tyrone pass by.'"

II

After taking the summer off to recuperate at the Connecticut farm, the Marches were offered the opportunity to star in a TV production of Terrence Rattigan's play *The Winslow Boy* on CBS Television's *Dupont Show of the Month*. The story of a father who fights to prove the innocence of his teenage son who is accused of the theft of a five-shilling money order from his boarding school. The case goes all the way to Parliament! Florence is cast as March's wife with a supporting cast including Denholm Elliott, Rex Thompson (as the Winslow Boy), and Noel Willman.

Based on a true story that occurred in Edwardian England, March pondered that, "It makes a parent wonder how he can be sue when he is doing the right thing...the father's dedicated efforts to bring the truth to light won such a victory for the rights of the individual that any ultimate sacrifice might have been justified." It was telecast over ninety minutes on November 13, 1958. William Ewald, the UPI TV critic, thought, as a whole, the show was "thumping good theater" with a couple of thuds, which he pointed out as being "a terribly clumsy speech" that Florence delivers to March in the climax of the play, and some sketchy relationship between some of the supporting actors.

Within two months of doing *The Winslow Boy* for television, March began his first film in three years and his first leading role since *The Desperate Hours*. Paddy Chayefsky's play *Middle of the Night* is the story of a widowed middle-aged clothing manufacturer (named Jerry Kingsley) who falls in love over an afternoon with a pretty, much younger (age twenty-four) divorcee who happens to work as the secretary at his garment factory. The role of the widowed older man was played on Broadway by Edward G. Robinson, providing the one-time movie tough guy with a big late career boost as well as a Tony nomination. It had been expected that Robinson would recreate his Broadway triumph in the movie version that Columbia Pictures was producing, but when Chayefsky sold the screen rights to Columbia, he insisted on having the leading man be played by the actor he originally had in mind in the first place: Fredric March.

For the part of the younger woman, the studio was interested in Elizabeth Taylor, then the biggest female box-office draw in films. Taylor was interested too, having seen the play on Broadway with her then husband Mike Todd. When Todd died, Taylor was in the middle of shooting *Cat on a Hot Tin Roof* and it took all her strength just to get through that production. By the time they were casting *Middle of the Night*, Taylor was embroiled in an affair with Eddie Fisher, Todd's best friend—and a married man (to Debbie Reynolds) with children, to boot. Taylor eventually decided she had too much going on in her personal life to do the film, and so she withdrew.

Columbia then thought of the talented young actress Hope Lange. Lange had impressed critics and movie audiences alike with her work in *Peyton Place* and *The Young Lions*, but ultimately the studio thought that she was not a big enough box-office name, and it was decided that with March past his box-office prime that they needed a bigger box office name as the female lead. At this point, Columbia's beautiful young contract player Kim Novak entered the picture. Novak had decorated such films as *Picnic, Pal Joey, Bell Book & Candle*, and had shown her acting chops under Hitchcock's direction in *Vertigo*. Novak had recently renegotiated her contract with Columbia, which had given her the right to choose her future film roles. When she became aware that *Middle of the Night* was available, she was eager to make the film.

A top-notch supporting cast was assembled including Martin Balsam and Lee Philips, who were both in the Broadway production. Other cast members included Glenda Farrell, cast as Novak's mother, and Lee Grant took on the role of her best friend. Delbert Mann, who had directed the 1954 TV version of *Middle of the Night* was also hired to direct the film. Mann was the Oscar-winning director of the film version of Chayefsky's *Marty* and had just directed an all-star cast in the prestigious *Separate Tables*. Filming began on location in early January of 1959, with interiors shot at the Gold Medal Studios in the Bronx and exteriors in the Garment district of New York City. Mann decided to help bolster a nervous Novak by holding two weeks of rehearsals prior to filming.

Novak was notoriously high-strung and insecure—performing such a pivotal role in a prestigious film opposite an actor of March's stature brought her nerves to a breaking point. Mann recalled that she arrived at rehearsals "shaking. This was a new experience for Kim. Here she was faced with a very high-powered, theatrically experienced company. She was very frightened." Casting director Everett Chambers would recall that Novak "didn't know how to break the role down, or what a subtext was either."

By the end of the two-week rehearsal period, Novak showed no real improvement. Hope Lange entered the picture again as a possible replacement. However, Chambers decided he would work night and day with Novak, coaching her on a pivotal monologue, in which her character would pour out her heart to March—four pages long—in preparation for a post-Christmas rehearsal, which would seal her fate. It was tough going, but at the rehearsal and before a tough audience consisting of Mann, Chayefsky, and March she performed the speech superbly. "She was extraordinary," Mann would recall. It saved her job too.

Middle of the Night is a superb May-December romance, which contains the last of Fredric March's romantic leads. As Kingsley, March gives an assured and touching performance. His is a portrait of a lonely man seeking to fill the void in his heart after two years of loneliness, and finding (to his surprise) that this much younger and beautiful woman is falling in love with him as much as he is with her. His life has become a humdrum of mere existence; "I'm 56 years old, I come home, I'm tired, and I want to go to bed." Certainly this relationship is an ego boost for him too—proving that he is still a vital man. The affection that the Novak character feels for Paul Kingsley, as a reflection of the virtue of his character, is contained in one of the key lines in the monologue that Novak worked so hard to master:

> *If you weren't such a decent man, you'd probably make out a lot better with me. I mean if you were just on the make I'd probably be saying to myself, "Well, I'm pretty lonely and he's a gentleman." The way I've been feeling lately, who cares anyway? I think what really scares me to death about you is that you might really fall in love with me.*

These two lonely people do find love but it's not without bumps in the road. Chayefsky changed the script of the movie from the TV and stage versions to allow the girl a moment of doubt, which culminates with her having sex with her ex-husband. She is ashamed of what she has done and decides to admit her indiscretion to March, in a scene that takes place as they are sitting on a bench in Central Park. Upset, he reacts with anger and breaks it off with her. Later, however, he has an epiphany of understanding and forgives her with these lines, "It is better to be unhappily in love, to be sickly in love, to be neurotic, diseased, gruesome, sordid, as long as it involves the passions of life. It is better to be all that than to be careful."

The film wrapped after six weeks, and when a rough cut was shown at Columbia in early March, Chayefsky responded with elation. He believed that the film was "going to be an enormous hit, and Freddie and Kim will both win Oscars."

When the film opened in New York in June, Bosley Crowther in the *New York Times* thought that "Fredric March…looks a little too old and doddering to be taking a 24 year old bride. And the young lady, played by Kim Novak, seems too much of a badly mixed-up kid to be settling down quietly with grandpa on West End Avenue."

Crowther compared the performance of March with that of Robinson in the Broadway play, and March came out wanting. "Mr. March is an excellent actor when it comes to showing joy and distress but isn't' successful in pretending to be a Jewish papa and business man... he isn't the garment manufacture that Edward G. Robinson played." (In fact, the Jewishness of the character was considerably toned down in the film.) Novak's performance was called "shifty" by Crowther. But *Time* magazine thought the film better than the play, "Middle of the Night transforms an honest but clumsy play by Paddy Chayefsky into a cruelly beautiful and moving film, a story of life and love as a man grows older." The magazine praised both March and Novak and thought that it had a "deeper maturity than *Marty.*" The *Los Angeles Times* called *Middle of the Night* "intimate and rueful" and "while Edward G. Robinson was cast closer to type in the part of Jerry Kingsley, March's achievement is perhaps even greater in that he succeeds in spite of being cast away from it."

The film did good business. In San Francisco, at the Paramount, the film had the biggest first week that the theater had experienced in two years. In Philadelphia, the Trans-Lux Theater had the best business in more than a year. The New York Fifty-Second Street Theater its stay was extended to six weeks. The Krim theater in Detroit reported "smash business." While the Washington D.C. Playhouse reported *Middle of the Night* as its "biggest grosser in four years."

Despite creating a beautiful film with touching performances, neither March nor Novak were nominated for Oscars as Chayefsky had predicted. But the film was the official United States entry at the Cannes Film Festival and was on the National Board of Reviews list of best films of the year, and March was nominated for a Golden Globe for his performance. This was not the last time that March and Chayesfsky would work together either. In two years, March would be back on Broadway playing God in a production of Chayesfsky's play *Gideon*.

III

While March was filming *Middle of the Night* in New York, he took a day off to fly to Washington, where he had the honor of addressing a joint session of the U.S. Congress, reading Abraham Lincoln's Gettysburg Address on the 150th anniversary of Lincoln's birth. The main speaker of the day was the poet and Lincoln biographer Carl Sandburg. Both March and Sandburg were escorted into the house chamber by a committee of senators and representatives. An orchestra played softly in the background as March spoke, and following the 270-word speech he received thunderous applause and a standing ovation. March called it "the greatest thrill an actor's life to address a joint session of congress." What a turnaround for March. At the beginning of the fifties he was accused of being a Communist, or at least soft on communism, and here, just nine years later, he is the one actor selected to deliver the best-loved speech of the greatest president in US history before the congress of the United States.

The Marches spent much of the summer of 1959 at the farm in Connecticut, where their daughter Penny, son-in-law, and their now two grandchildren, Gianni and Michael, spent the summer with them. They converted a large room in the bathhouse into private quarters for the family. "There is one consolation about having your daughter live in another country," Florence related to a reporter. "At least, when she comes home to visit, she'll be under our roof for two or three months." March chimed in, not mincing any words, "She's too far away. She should be living closer!" By this time, March related that Florence had completely redecorated the house and, all out of projects to work on, she suggested to March that they sell the house and build a new, one-story house on the top of the hill on their property. "I decline to even consider it," March said. "I love this house. It's perfect. I don't want to leave it, so I threatened her. I said if she went through with this plan, we would call the new house F.F.F., for Florence's Final Fling.'" Florence countered by stating that March went further than that, "He threatened to divorce me if I ever mentioned the idea again."

In March of 1958, as March was finishing up with *Long Day's Journey into Night*, producer Richard Zanuck was casting about for

20th Century Fox's film version of the Broadway hit *Compulsion*, about the Leopold-Loeb murders and subsequent trial. Their attorney had been the great defense attorney Clarence Darrow. Zanuck told Hollywood columnist Louella Parsons, "I would like to have Fredric March for the Clarence Darrow role." When the film was eventually made, it was with Orson Welles in the Darrow role. But less than two years later, March would be asked to play opposite Spencer Tracy, who was playing the Darrow role, in the movie version of the Broadway play *Inherit the Wind* for producer Stanley Kramer.

Kramer was a producer and director known for making movies with a message. He produced *High Noon*, which he saw as an allegory about the then-present-day McCarthy Communist witch hunts, and how the town's people who ran away from helping the Marshal (played by Gary Cooper) represented those "friends" and acquaintances who refused to stand by those who were alleged to be Communists. His two most recent pictures as a producer-director were *The Defiant Ones* (two escaped prisoners, one black and one a bigoted white man, who must learn to cooperate to survive) and *On the Beach* (the story of a group of people who await certain death from Nuclear fall-out following World War III).

For his next picture, Kramer wanted to explore anti-intellectualism, and would do so by producing and directing a film based on the hit Broadway play *Inherit the Wind*. *Inherit the Wind* had been written for the stage by playwrights Jerome Lawrence and Robert E. Lee. Lawrence and Lee based their play on the 1925 Scopes "monkey" trial, in which John T. Scopes was convicted of teaching Charles Darwin's theory of evolution to a high school science class, breaking a Tennessee state law. A rather routine trial became a major media event of the day, when the famed defense attorney Clarence Darrow— the so-called people's lawyer—volunteered his services to Scopes. In response, three-time democratic presidential candidate William Jennings Bryan, known to his millions of supporters as "the commoner" for willingness to stand up for farmers and wage earners against the big money interests, joined the prosecution team. Bryan was a strong opponent of Darwinism and a religious fundamentalist. Darrow was an atheist who believed that by banning the teaching of evolution you were closing your mind to science. Lawrence and Lee used the Scopes Trial partly in response to the communist hysteria of the late forties and early fifties, when political and intellectual freedom seemed to be under assault. This type of project was catnip to Kramer.

Kramer went to United Artists to put up the money for the film and found great resistance to the subject matter in terms of how it would perform at the box office. "Was I out of my mind? Did I think they were a charitable or an educational institution?" was how Kramer later recalled their response. Kramer was proud of his skills at persuasion, and spoke about the prestige of the production based on a well-known historical event and a well-regarded and *profitable* Broadway play. He also promised that he would cast the picture with stars. UA grudgingly agreed to finance the film.

The 1955 Broadway show had starred Paul Muni and Ed Begley as the Darrow and Bryan figures. The play changed their names and added characters for dramatic impact, but Lawrence and Lee did draw heavily from the Scopes trial transcript. For the film, Kramer wanted two stars to play the leads. He immediately thought of Spencer Tracy and Fredric March. "At first glance, March didn't quite look the part," Kramer later wrote. "Bryan was a rough-hewn, portly man, less urbane than March, but March was an actor of such skill and range that he could adjust." He also felt that March was one of the few actors of stature who could stand up to Tracy's steely-eyed determination. As an additional incentive for March, Kramer offered Florence the part of Brady's loving and concerned wife.

In the fall of 1958, while still working on post-production of *On the Beach*, Kramer wrote the Marches, "Herewith a draft of INHERIT THE WIND, which I would appreciate both you and Florence reading. Naturally, I want you both very badly for the parts and I will look forward to hearing from you." Kramer realized that the part of Mrs. Brady was under developed and told the Marches that the script can "stand plenty of work and I've made no attempt to develop Mrs. Bryan (Brady) further—but indications are there." March and Florence both liked Kramer and believed in the project and its message. So, with the promise that Florence's part would be enhanced, they agreed to do the picture.

Production, however, didn't start until the following fall. Kramer kept in touch. In September of 1959, he sent two updated copies of the script to the Marches and wrote, "God knows, we are still trying to improve and sharpen." Florence was still somewhat disappointed in her part. Kramer would add a scene between her and Spencer Tracy, which would demonstrate that, at one time, the Brady's and Drummond had been friends and political allies. However, Kramer told them that "the key scenes are pretty well lined out for both of you—let me remind you that we will be having a rehearsal period for ironing out and most of the lengthier scenes will probably stay put beyond any rehearsal deletions for pace and effect." Kramer also reminded March that his role would require more time for preparation in the makeup department than Tracy's—who famously rarely used makeup. "It may be that you won't need a hair piece if you hair is long enough and seems thin enough on top. At any rate, we can determine that when you get here and set up everything so that we can make photographic tests and recheck on our decisions." (In the end, March would require a skull cap, and when production began March had a call time of 7 a.m. to get made up, while Tracy wasn't expected on the set until 9 a.m.)

Besides Tracy and the Marches, the film is full of familiar faces. For the third major role in the film, that of the cynical newspaper man based on H. L. Menken, Kramer cast Gene Kelly (in a role played by Tony Randall in the Broadway production). Kramer rather enjoyed off-beat casting—having the previous year cast Fred Astaire in a key role in *On the Beach*. Also in the film were: Dick York, later the original Darrin on TV's *Bewitched*, as the teacher put on trial (York won the role over such contenders as Anthony Perkins and Roddy McDowell); Claude Akins as the fundamentalist preacher; Donna Anderson as the preacher's daughter and love interest of York; Elliott Reid as the prosecuting attorney; and Harry Morgan as the trial judge. Rehearsals began on October 12, 1959, at the Revue Studios on the Universal lot.

March and Tracy liked and admired each other and took to ribbing each other on a daily basis. For instance, a reporter visited the set, and Tracy pointed out that March had two doctorates and was thus a "doctor-doctor." March retorted that Tracy too had a doctorate: one he had received after making *Captain's Courageous*, but that the school threatened to take it away from him after Tracy made *Dr. Jekyll and Mr. Hyde*—a joking reference to Tracy's 1942 remake of one of March's most famous films. Yet, when filming, they went at each other ferociously. There was one particular take, which was full of tense moments between the Drummond and Brady characters, and Kramer thought that his actors would carry over the antagonism when the scene was completed. But, when it was over, March said, "You played the scene magnificently," and Tracy replied, "That's because you fed me my lines magnificently."

Yet the two were also powerhouse actors and competitive. "We had Tracy and Fredric March nose to nose for long courtroom confrontations and assorted histrionics," Kramer later told writer Bill Davidson.

> *The sound stage was filled with celebrities and executives from every studio in town. And how Tracy and March luxuriated in the applause of this audience. Every take brought down the house, and their escapades were something to see. They teased and goaded each other with every trick they had learned over the years. It all showed up on the screen. For example, everyone who saw the picture will remember how Freddie would fan himself vigorously with a large undertaker's fan each time Spence would launch into an oration. And then how Spence would cause a distraction by pulling at his nose, especially during March's three and a half minute summation to the jury.*

Among those on the set almost every day, and not in the picture, was Katharine Hepburn, who was looking after Tracy. "She was spending all her time looking after Spence," recalled Kramer, "Arriving with him in the morning, making sure he took his medicines and drank his milk, leaving with him when he was through in the afternoon. She was like a nurse-companion to him—or a wife." In an unpublished interview found in the March papers at the State Historical Society of Wisconsin, March spoke about Tracy and Hepburn in rather candid terms. "I like both of them very much and I think that they are excellent actors," he began. "But I do not understand or approve of their romance. There is a missus Tracy, and it is not exactly nice to her." Given his own reputation as an offscreen lothario, there is a bit of hypocrisy in those words—even if there was never a long-term March mistress.

Others on the set recalled the delight they had working with these two acting icons. "I came to the set each day full of excitement and anticipation," Elliott Reid later recalled. "To be working with two of the best actors in the world was a dream come true—and oh! They didn't disappoint." Gene Kelly was awed to be working in the company of Tracy and March. Because both he and March came from a stage background, he could see how March creative flow worked. "He was like Olivier," Kelly later said of March. "A wonderful technician. You could see the characterization taking shape—the cogs and wheels beginning to turn. If you studied his methods closely, it was all there, like an open book." With Tracy, who tended to underplay, it was harder to see the characterization. Kelly would perform with him and wonder where the magic was, but then, when he watched the rushes, "it was all there." While Kelly had done serious, non-musical/dance films in the past, he was insecure about his ability as a straight actor. He studied both actors in hopes that some of that magic would rub off. "All you could do was watch the magic and be amazed," Kelly later said, "and I really learned from them that no matter what I did, I would never be as good as they were." Filming went along smoothly and principal photography was completed in mid-December.

While filming *Inherit the Wind* in Hollywood, the Marches twenty-five-year-old son Anthony was injured when his car crashed into a stone wall in Briarcliff, New York. According to Anthony, he fell asleep at the wheel of his car as he was traveling to visit friends. It was a close brush for Anthony, who police estimated was driving at sixty miles-per-hour. The motor of the car was pushed back to the floorboards, but luckily Anthony only suffered facial and tongue cuts. The Marches had been increasingly frustrated about Anthony over the years—his lack of academic achievement, brushes with the law, and inability to keep a job. In 1961 he was sentenced to thirty-days in jail for stealing an automobile battery, tire, and a riding saddle. He told the judge he could give no "tangible" reason as to why he committed these thefts.

Shortly after filming was completed on *Inherit the Wind*, and just after New Year's 1960, the Marches left on a four-month trip that would take them to Israel, Iran, India, Ceylon, Singapore, Thailand, Hong Kong, Japan, and then wind them up in Honolulu. The trip was not without incident. On February 22, 1960, newspaper headlines around the world blared out:

Fredric March Arrested in India

And so he was, along with Florence and a couple from New Milford who were traveling with the Marches—a Dr. Crohn and his wife. Up to that point, they all had been enjoying a very pleasant month-long visit to India. They were returning to Madura by car from Kerala, where they had been visiting a game sanctuary. On crossing the frontier into the Madras state, their car was stopped by police who believed that it was operating as a taxi without a permit. During a search of the car, the police found "unauthorized liquor." This violated an Indian liquor prohibition law.

The group tried to explain that the several ounces of liquor found in a medicine case belonging to Dr. Crohn was "normal practice for physicians." As for the car, which the Indian police believed was operating as an unauthorized taxi, the group pleaded ignorance. They had rented the car from a travel agency. Apparently the police had been given orders to be on the lookout for taxis smuggling liquor. The Marches and Crohns were bailed out of jail by a representative of the travel company. March was incensed and said that he and his group had been "treated like criminals," and "it is ironical that Prime Minister Nehru should urge that every tourist be treated as an honored guest, but that his officials should harass visitors in the manner in which we have been. I feel humiliated."

Florence was so upset by the incident that she wrote a letter of complaint to the Prime Minister. Eventually, the charges were dropped, and Prime Minister Nehru wrote Florence a letter dated February 25, 1960:

> *Dear Mrs. March,*
>
> *...I had read in the newspapers about the unfortunate incident to which you refer. I received information about it also from other sources. I was deeply distressed that you and your husband and those who were with you were harassed by some of our petty officials. In fact, the moment I heard of it, I asked for an immediate*

inquiry to be made, and we have addressed the Madras Government on the subject.

Please accept my apologies for the trouble and harassment caused to you and Mr. March. There is nothing in our rules or instructions to warrant such an intrusion, but sometimes our petty officials exceed the limits of their authority. One possible good result from this unfortunate episode is that we can pull up our tourist officers and others so that they might behave better in the future.

With all good wishes to you,

Yours Sincerely,
Jawaharlal Nehru

Once that unpleasantness was out of the way, the rest of the year went along relatively smoothly. *Inherit the Wind* was first screened at the Berlin Film Festival on June 25, 1960, where it represented the official United States entry, and won awards for Best Foreign Actor (March) and Best Feature Film Suitable for Young People. The film then opened in London before having its official American premier in Dayton, Tennessee—the sight of the actual trial—on July 21—the thirty-fifth anniversary of the trials conclusion. John Scopes was still alive and attended the premiere as an honored guest.

Today, *Inherit the Wind* is probably one of March's most remembered films, thanks to its availability on DVD and repeated showings on cable channels such as TCM. When the film was released, however, it was a financial disaster—just as the United Artist executives who Kramer had persuaded to finance the film had initially predicted. The film also came under attack from certain religious publications such as *Limelight*, which accused Kramer of "trying to burlesque religion." The film did generate good reviews. Bosley Crowther in the *New York Times* wrote, "Kramer has wonderfully accomplished not only a graphic fleshing of his theme, but he also has got one of the most brilliant and engrossing displays of acting ever witnessed on the screen... When the two men come down to their final showdown and the barrier of dogma is breached, it is a triumphant moment for human dignity—and for Mr. Tracy and Mr. March." *Variety* was equally enthusiastic, "A rousing and fascinating motion picture. Virtually all the elements that make for the broadest range of entertainment satisfaction—drama, comedy, romance, social significance, even suspense—are amply present.... Pairing of Tracy and March was a masterstroke of casting."

Variety predicted Oscar nominations for both Tracy and March, but, when the nominations were announced, only Tracy was nominated. March graciously sent a congratulatory letter to Tracy, which Tracy responded to on March 3, 1961:

> *Dear Freddy,*
>
> *I have to admit to you—Freddy—that I am wondering a bit if maybe the votes were tabulated in Cook County...but I thank you—a good Democrat—for giving me the benefit of the doubt— and how I miss you in the daily entanglements of Stanley Kramer's camera moves. Love to you and Florence.*
>
> *Spence*

The mention of vote tabulations in Cook County is in reference to the 1960 election where Republicans alleged that John F. Kennedy won Illinois through fraudulent votes in Chicago—it was Tracy's way of telling March that he was astounded that the academy had not nominated March as well.

CHAPTER FOURTEEN
1961–1965

March returned to films with *The Young Doctors* distributed by United Artists and directed by Phil Karlson. Karlson was once a gag-man for Buster Keaton, but had made a name for himself as the director of such gritty and modestly budgeted crime films as *Scandal Street, 99 River Street,* and especially *The Phenix City Story.*

At sixty-three years of age, March obviously wasn't cast as one of the young doctors (they would be Ben Gazzara, Dick Clark, among others). March plays a veteran Chief Pathologist of a large New York City hospital who is less than thrilled about the arrival of a new doctor (Gazzara) assigned to the pathology department, and takes his presence as a commentary on his competence and the way he has run the department.

The Young Doctors was based on a novel (*No Deadly Medicine*) by Arthur Hailey, who would go on to write the mega blockbuster books, *Hotel* and *Airport,* both of which would be made into major motion pictures. Adapting the novel was Joseph Hayes, who had last worked with March on *The Desperate Hours,* who had written the role of the veteran doctor with March in mind. When *Newsweek* asked if March had ever played a doctor before, the actor answered, "No. Wait a minute. One. Dr. Jekyll!"

Filming began in January of 1961, on location at several hospitals in New York. The younger actors in the cast were excited to be working with a veteran of March's reputation. Ben Gazzara, who had made a big impression just a couple of years earlier in his first film, *Anatomy of a Murder,* thought of March as one of his acting gods. "Here was an actor in command of his craft," Gazzara later said. "I felt like a boxer in the ring with the champion. I had to go the distance and show what I had while doing so." Gazzara went on to say:

When I played my first scene with him, I couldn't help watching his performance so intensely I almost forgot what I was doing. He had all the moves. The way he threw a line away was often more interesting than when he framed one. He knew how to use the camera; it was his friend. I on the other hand was still having trouble with it...March seemed to have blinkers on when he played a scene. His eyes zeroed in on me as though they would never look away. Everything else around him was shut out.

Dick Clark, the *American Bandstand* host, was cast in a rare movie role, as an intern, also had strong memories of working with March, as he related to Deborah C. Peterson:

The one thing that impressed me most about working with Fredric on The Young Doctors was his consistency of performance. If he scratched his nose in the master shot, he scratched his nose in the close-up in the exact same way. Things that appeared to be so natural and unstudied were obviously meticulously planned by him. His tone of voice, his physical movements, his bits of business were all crafted to perfection. In addition to his professionalism, I appreciated how kindly he dealt with me, knowing I was scared to death.

One scene may have caught March off guard, but he kept his cool when the cameras were rolling. The scene in question has March addressing a group of medical students at an autopsy, and at one point he picks up a brain and begins to discuss and dissect it. In rehearsals he used a fake brain, but just before the cameras rolled, director Karlson let March know that he would be holding a real brain. (Karlson is the director who on *The Phenix City Story* had one of the actors wear the actual clothing that a real murder victim wore—when he was murdered!) March handled the scene like the pro he was—if he was disturbed by holding the brain he didn't show it—and as usual, was letter perfect.

March enjoyed making *The Young Doctors*, even if he initially had some qualms about doing the film. "I was a little leery about *The Young Doctors* at first," March told *Newsweek*. "I got concerned that it wasn't such a good idea to throw out to the public that doctors disagree among themselves. Then I said the hell with it, they probably do. I was astounded when the AMA gave it their recommendation."

When the film was released in the fall of 1961, it received excellent reviews—especially for March. *Variety* wrote that March "proves he's one of the finest actors to be found on the contemporary screen. It is a tribute to this man that one is barely aware or conscious of the fact he is acting." The *New York Herald Tribune* critic wrote, "Fredric March gives a memorable performance as Dr. Pearson, the super annulated man at the head of a metropolitan hospital's pathology department." Arthur Knight in *The Saturday Review* was particularly enthusiastic about the film writing, "From New York comes *The Young Doctors*, and not only New York's earnest film-makers, but the entire industry might well be proud of it." The film went on to be a solid box office performer and was voted one of the year's Ten Best Films by the National Board of Review.

Writer Paddy Chayefsky grew up worshiping Fredric March. He saw all of his movies and was a committed fan. Chayefsky's first legitimate play, "The Man Who Made the Mountains Shake," in the late forties, was written with March in mind. He wanted to give March the script, but being a newcomer, he had neither connections nor an agent. One day, Chayefsky read that March would be presenting an award at Sardi's. He thought that maybe he could catch up with him there and present him with his script. Chayefsky waited outside of the famous New York restaurant for up to two hours until March emerged, and without a word he thrust the script into the actor's hands. To Chayefsky's delight, March took the bundle of pages with him. March liked the play, but his agent of that time didn't think the play was "worthy enough" for March, and March passed on it. The play was eventually produced on TV and then on stage as *Fifth from Garibaldi*. March still liked the play and liked Chayefsky. "Freddie was very fond of Paddy," producer Robert Anderson later stated. "He would sit there and read his speeches."

Years later, Chayefsky wrote the play *Middle of the Night* and wanted March for that venture, but ended up with Edward G. Robinson—though March would later play the leading role in the movie version. But Chayefsky still wanted to work with March on an original play, and in 1961 he got his wish when March signed on as the Angel of the Lord in Chayefsky's play *Gideon*. Based on three chapters of the Book of Judges, *Gideon* explores the relationship between man and God. The Angel of the Lord appears before Gideon, a semi-doltish farmer, whose mission is to save mankind from idols other than God. It's an ambitious play. March later recalled:

> *I was in the country...when Paddy told me about the play "Then he sent me a script and Florence read it and I read it. Florence said to me, 'you've got to do this play,' She recognizes a good script and she has always been wonderful at casting. So here I am. My friends have kidded me a bit. They say things like, 'well, where do you go from here?' or, 'so you finally made it, Freddie, you're playing God at last.*

Originally, director Tyrone Guthrie was to play the role of the Angel himself, as well as direct, but ultimately he was prodded by Chayefsky to sign March. To play Gideon, several actors were considered, including Anthony Franciosa, Robert Morse and Peter Sellers, but in the end a relative newcomer, Scottish actor Douglas Campbell, was signed after giving an especially powerful reading at his audition.

March's makeup and costume in *Gideon* was based on Michelangelo's painting of God in the Sistine Chapel—long white hair and beard and a flowing robe with sandals. March later related that one of the robes weighed at least eleven pounds "and it gets awfully hot under those lights." During rehearsals, March had a hard time keeping his balance wearing this heavy robe with sandals. The stage was "sharply tilted" to try and give the impression of a "hilly landscape...and also to provide a place above man for the Angel of God." It was Guthrie's idea for the sloping stage, "I want actors to really work, to scramble hard to get up to the top of the hill," he was later quoted as saying. To better maneuver this tilted stage, March decided to lose the slippers and instead wear ballet slippers, which gave him better balance.

Gideon enjoyed an unusually long preview of three weeks at the New Locust Theater in Philadelphia, where it received solid box office and strong reviews. As usual in a preview, some changes were made, "Some of Paddy's big words and a few of the deeper but irrelevant musings."

The play then moved on to New York where it opened at the Plymouth Theater on November 9, 1961. The first night didn't go without incident. When March was to make his first speech, he was supposed to have a single spotlight shone upon him as if from directly above. However, no light appeared. He was in total darkness. It seems that during the afternoon, publicity photos had been shot, which led to some lighting plugs being pulled and then forgotten to be replugged, which led to no spotlight on March in his first big scene. Luckily, an electrician rushed backstage and plugged in the correct lighting and, dramatically, as March was in his fourth or fifth line of this monologue, the light shone upon him—it actually may have enhanced the scene. Nevertheless, Chayefsky rushed backstage and demanded that the electrician responsible for the mishap be fired; however, Guthrie downplayed it with humor by replying that, "happily I'm here too late to do any real damage."

The reviews were mixed. John McClain called the show an "unqualified hit" in the *New York Journal-American*. He went on to add that March and Campbell gave "two towering performances." Walter Kerr in the *New York Herald Tribune* felt that there was too much repetition, which "made the evening stand still." *The Daily News* thought that play "distinguished" while the *Post* praised the first Act but felt that "in the second half, Mr. Chayefsky courageously plunges in beyond his depth." *The Christian Science Monitor* called *Gideon* Chayefsky's "most mature and penetrating work." *Time* declared *Gideon* "a lustrous and compelling experience…to watch March and Campbell in the light and shadows of their relationship is to see something like acting genius at work." Despite the mixed notices, the play proved to be a solid hit for the 1961-1962 season.

March and Douglas Campbell got on well. As a matter of fact, March was so impressed with his costars performance that he went to the producers and requested that they put his name on the marquee above the title along with his. March's contract called for single star billing, so this was quite a compliment for the young actor who deeply appreciated what the veteran did. Campbell did think, however, that March quickly grew tired of his part. Playing

God may be distinguished and awe-inspiring but it is Gideon who actually has the bigger and stronger part.

There may be some truth in this, because by April, March received an offer to make a undistinguished film *The Condemned of Altona* with Sophia Loren. To make the movie, March requested that he be permitted to leave the play before his contract expired on May 5, 1962. This was denied. Instead, March had to pay $10,000 to buy out the remaining weeks of his contract, and he apparently felt that the movie was economically worth his while since he would be paid $200,000. *The Condemned of Altona* would be shot over six weeks in Germany and Italy, produced by Loren's husband, Carlo Ponti, and directed by Vittorio De Sica. When Chayefsky found out about March's intentions to leave the play, he scoffed, "Can you believe this? I give him the best role of his life, to play God, an actor's dream. And he wants to quit to do a movie with a Spaghetti actress!" March did get the consolation of being nominated for a Tony Award for his performance but lost to Paul Scofield for his magnificent performance in *A Man for All Seasons*.

Shortly after winning his release from *Gideon*, and just prior to leaving for Germany to begin the film with Sophia Loren, the Marches were invited to Washington where, on April 29, 1962, they were guests at one of the most distinguished and glittering White House dinners in memory. It was the occasion when President Kennedy honored forty-nine Nobel Prize laureates from the Western Hemisphere. That dinner elicited one of the most famous quotes of the Kennedy Administration, when JFK said in his prepared remarks, "I think this is the most extraordinary collection of talent, of human knowledge, that has ever been gathered together at the White House, with the possible exception of when Thomas Jefferson dined alone."

After a meal of beef Wellington, March began a program of reading excerpts from the works of deceased Nobel Prize winners, including, most notably, a portion of Ernest Hemingway's *Islands in the Stream*—a manuscript that would not even be published for another eight years—in fact, this event was to be the first public reading of *Islands in the Stream*. The reading was done at the suggestion of Hemingway's widow, Mary. The other selections that March read were from Sinclair Lewis's introduction to *Main Street* and Secretary of State George C. Marshall's June 5, 1947, address at Harvard, outlining "The Marshall Plan," certainly one of the most far-reaching humanitarian relief acts in American history. But it was to be the first reading from *Islands in the Stream* that was the most anticipated. Originally, according to Mary Hemingway, the White House had suggested a reading from Hemingway's short story *The Killers*, but she then suggested a "better idea" with the excerpt from *Islands in the Stream*.

March would read from the "At Sea" portions of the manuscript—which in book form would be chapters fifteen and sixteen. These selections were later described as "a shrewd and provocative selection, (it) captures an extended scene of anticipation in Chapter 15 before the release of action in Chapter 16. These two moments—Hudson engaging in profound thought and then sensational action—highlight a theme of *Islands in the Stream* that generally gets lost in consideration of the entire novel." The selections were made by Mrs. Hemingway herself, and she cut some of the more salty language from the excerpts as far as possible. For instance, instead of March reading "give a shit" he would say "give a flip," and "that fucking forward hatch" became "that fogging forward hatch." Mrs. Hemingway also wrote to March seeking his advice, "Do you think the profanity is sufficiently cleaned up or disguised? If not, please let me help with any further expurgations." March offered no further suggestions.

Since March would not have access to the complete manuscript, Mrs. Hemingway also sent him sketches of the major characters so that March could incorporate some of this into his reading. For instance, she describes the hero of *Islands in the Streams*, Thomas Hudson, as "(A) man in his middle forties, is a man of art, education, many sports, wide travels and large experience in war and on the sea. Sometimes, for emphasis, he says things very softly, if coldly. Much of the time his voice is warm and heartening."

There was an audience of 177 distinguished guests, and March was nervous. The First Lady's social director, Letitia Baldrige, later recalled that she escorted March to the Lincoln Bedroom prior to his presentation so he could compose himself. "There was moisture in his eyes," she recalled. "He told me how he had played before many distinguished audiences in his life and in palaces before many kings and queens. But never had anything touched him so much or meant so much as this night to him. . . ."

March was composed as he rose to begin his portion of the program. He began by reading the 223-word introduction to *Main Street*, which begins, "This is America—a town of a few thousand, in a region of wheat and corn and dairies and little groves. . ..." He then moved into his two-and-a-half-minute reading of four paragraphs from General Marshall's speech regarding the Marshall Plan, adding, "I wish I had time to read it all." The longest reading was from *Islands in the Stream*. While the reception March got for his presentation was good, not all were impressed. Writer William Styron, one of the honorees, wrote in a letter to a friend, "After dinner there was a boring reading by Fredric March of a garbled and wretched piece of an unpublished Hemingway manuscript, it was done in semi-darkness, and most of the Nobel Prize winners—most of whom are over 70— nodded off to sleep."

March took away one very special gift from this dinner. Since he was going to Italy to make a movie, he certainly would be seeing his grandson Gianni. He had President and Mrs. Kennedy, and astronaut John Glenn—a national hero thanks to his being the first American to orbit the earth—sign a place card, inscribed to Gianni. A big thrill for the boy.

March then flew to Munich to begin shooting *The Condemned of Altona*, in which he plays a dying German war profiteer who has two sons—one a playboy (Robert Wagner), married to the Loren character, and the other an ex-Gestapo agent (Maximilian Schell) who is kept hidden in his father's attic.

Wagner was nervous about being directed by the great De Sica, "I became physically sick with nerves," Wagner later recalled. "Then in the morning I saw Freddie March's hands shaking too, and I thought: 'God if he's nervous with all his experience, what am I worried about?' I felt better after that." In his autobiography, *Pieces of My Heart*, Wagner writes that De Sica had a hard time keeping March's performance from becoming too maudlin. March was playing a man who is dying and, according to Wagner, "Every day Vittorio would tell him, 'Freddy, do not play self-pity. Do not fall into that trap' and every day Freddie would play self-pity and Vittorio would have to pull him out of it."

Wagner maintains that March's reputation as a womanizer was "completely deserved." In his book, he tells of March pretending to admire a piece of jewelry that his then wife, Marion Marshall, was wearing, and he "very obviously copped a feel of her left breast" as he pretended to look at the jewelry. "The man was sixty-five years old, but he would have fucked mud if someone had held it for him," concludes Wagner.

When the film was released in the US in late October of 1963, Bosley Crowthers in the *New York Times* summed the film up best when he wrote, "I am afraid *The Condemned of Altona* must be condemned to the fate of a disappointing film."

After his work on *The Condemned of Altona* finished in September, March joined Florence and the entire Fantacci family in Greece, to enjoy the reviving water and sun at Montacantini, before setting sail for home.

Once back home, he and Florence participated in a program that kicked off a campaign to raise funds for a National Cultural Center that would rise up on the east bank of the Potomac River in Washington, D.C. (Later Kennedy Center). A two-hour closed circuited program was produced and presented in five cities— Washington, New York, Chicago, Los Angeles, and Augusta, Georgia. President Kennedy made brief remarks, but a highlight of the presentation was of the Marches reunited with Jason Robards, Jr. and Bradford Dillman (as well as Colleen Dewhurst), to present scenes from the works of Eugene O'Neill, including—obviously— *Long Day's Journey Into Night*.

As 1962 turned to 1963, March received an offer to play in a significant film opposite a powerful cast, in a story that would cast him as the President of the United States.

II

Seven Days in May, based on a best-selling novel (at the time the film was being made, it was in its seventh printing), tells the story of a military plot to overthrow the liberal-minded president of the United States, who the Joint Chiefs of Staff think is too accommodating towards the red menace. The fictional president,

Jordan Lyman, just recently signed a nuclear disarmament treaty that right-wing General James Scott believes constitutes an act of treason, and as a loyal upholder of the Constitution of the United States General Scott will lead the coup.

The film was produced by Kirk Douglas's production company and he hired John Frankenheimer, who had directed such films as *The Birdman from Alcatraz* and *The Manchurian Candidate*, to direct. Frankenheimer was an inspired choice and would be the best director that March would work with in the final decade of his career—creating two memorable performances. Rod Serling, who had written many classic scripts during TV's golden age but was best known as the on-camera host of the anthology series (many of the episodes written by Serling) *The Twilight Zone*, was chosen to adapt the novel into a screenplay. He did so in two weeks, writing what he described as "a battle of two philosophies."

Originally, Douglas was going to play the renegade General, but the more he thought of it, the more he envisioned his friend Burt Lancaster in the role. When Douglas informed Frankenheimer that he wanted Lancaster, the director almost quit on the spot—having worked twice previously with Lancaster—he didn't want to do another film with him. Douglas somehow calmed Frankenheimer's nerves and said he would take responsibility for Lancaster. But Frankenheimer did tell Douglas that giving up the part of the General to play the subordinate role of the military aide, Col. 'Jiggs' Casey, who discovers the coup, was a mistake that he would later regret.

Paramount eventually was brought in as a partner to finance and distribute the film, but first they insisted that the original budget estimate of $2.75 million be reduced to $2.3 million. To accomplish this, Douglas took a fifty percent pay cut, bringing his salary down to $250,000, and Lancaster took a similar percentage cut, bringing his salary to $200,000. March was signed for a flat $100,000 for four weeks of filming, to be paid at $1000 per week over a period of time to reduce his tax burden. Rounding out a stellar cast are: Ava Gardner, as a Washington hostess (at $75,000); Martin Balsam, as the president's press secretary ($1,250 per day for approximately 12-days of work); and in a colorful role as a drunken Southern senator, Edmund O'Brien (also at $1,250 per day for up to 20 days).

If March's services were required beyond that four-week period, he would receive nothing for an additional two weeks of filming, however, if filming went beyond that point, he would receive an additional $25,000 per week. March was also guaranteed above the title star billing in third position on its own card—of equal size and significance as that of Lancaster and Douglas. March would also be provided with first-class roundtrip transportation from New York to Los Angeles, but he would be required to stay in Los Angeles during the course of making the film so that the studio would not have to pay additional transportation fees. In addition, he was to be granted $700 per week for expenses. It was a sweet deal that got even sweeter; he was to be given a portable "star dressing room" to be located on the sound stage, and his working hours were not to exceed eight hours per day, and he would have at least twelve hour rest periods between calls and "at least 36 consecutive hours off in any given period of seven-days."

Frankenheimer was nervous about directing March, "I didn't know what it was going to be like to direct a man of his stature and experience." March soon put Frankenheimer to ease.

> *On meeting Freddie, I was amazed at how open and how natural he was. It was almost as if he were an actor doing his first movie. We sat around the table and began to read the script. I noticed that Freddie didn't have a script in front of him. He already knew every one of his lines perfectly. The reaction of the other actors was, in retrospect, very funny. Most of them just could not believe it. But after two days of the ten day rehearsal, not one actor had a script in his hands.*

Filming began on May 29, 1963, with the full cooperation of the Kennedy White House. For example, while the President and his family relaxed at Hyannis Port on the weekend of July 27-29, 1963, the filmmakers were given access to use the front exterior of the White House to stage the opening shot from the film of a riot between pro-disarmament demonstrators and anti-disarmament demonstrators. In addition, the President had given them permission to sketch and make photographs of the interior of the White House so they could duplicate it on soundstages in Hollywood.

Lancaster arrived on the set a couple of weeks into the filming, as he was recovering from an arduous shoot of *The Leopard* in Italy as well as hepatitis. According to one of Lancaster's biographers, Lancaster was in "careful awe" of March, who was one of his acting heroes. In filming a pivotal confrontation scene between the General and the President, Lancaster proceeded to flub lines in take after take until finally he said, "God Dammit! I knew these lines in my office!" To which the unflappable March attempted to ease his tension by saying, "Why didn't you take your office with you?" The next day, Lancaster arrived back on the set ready to go and line perfect, and they did the eight page scene in one take. "I've never seen two actors," Frankenheimer later said, "more concentrated. Burt had to show March he could do it; March had to show he was king." Frankenheimer would later call this scene "one of the best I ever directed."

Richard Anderson, who later scored big on TV as Oscar Goldman in the *Six Million Dollar Man* and *Bionic Woman* series, appeared in *Seven Days in May* as a military aide to Lancaster's character. "On the set, people are always trying to do their best," he recalled of the atmosphere on Seven Days in May, "...but when people are trying to do their best, tempers run high," even with old friends like Douglas and Lancaster. Douglas may indeed have been sorry he gave up the role of the General. "It's a highly volatile game," Anderson says, "and when you get two highly visceral guys (Douglas and Lancaster) like that together, there could be fireworks." A calming influence was old-pro March. "He was wonderful," Anderson recalled.

> *As a kid, I watched him in those Fox movie houses in the thirties, I grew up on him. I told him, "It's such a pleasure to meet you." He said, "Thank you, Mr. Anderson." One day, I watched him work. Right after filming, he turned to the wardrobe man and said, "Bill, don't take the coat and fix it up for tomorrow. Leave it like it is. We're continuing the scene." He wanted the coat to look the same way. How'd you like that for an actor?*

Towards the end of filming, March had to perform a difficult six-and-a-half-page monologue and demonstrated to his director that he was a pro bar none. "We had to film it from many various angles, sometimes using live television cameras simultaneously with film cameras," Frankenheimer recalled years later. "Freddie must have done the speech ten different times for ten different multiple camera angles. He never missed a word and the performance was just as good the tenth time as the first time."

The film was previewed in New York, Washington, Philadelphia, Pittsburgh, and Cleveland, in early December of 1963. According to a report prepared for Douglas, "The New York screening was an over sell-out. Nearly three hundred people were turned away, and only after hundreds sat on the floor in the aisles to watch the movie. If ever there was a salute to the 'importance' of the movie, it was this." In Philadelphia: "Applause came several times during the film. Once when you answer Burt Lancaster about Judas…again during Fredric March's speech about 'The enemy is an age…not a man'… several times during the confrontation scene; and long, sustained applause at the end of the picture. Not one scene with anything but the intended audience reaction."

While the previews were held only two weeks after the assassination of President Kennedy, Paramount decided not to formally release the film until February of 1964, out of consideration of the national tragedy. When the picture opened in New York on February 19, Bosley Crowther in the *New York Times* wrote, "… there is a great deal about this 'Seven Days in May' that is rousing and encouraging to a feeling of confidence and pride—and this is in addition to the feelings of tension and excitement it stirs…There is, in its slick dramatic frame, a solid base of respect for democracy and the capacities of freedom-loving men." Of the performances, Crowther writes, "Fredric March's performance as the President is the firmest and the best. In it is reflected an awareness of the immensity of the anguish of this man. Kirk Douglas is sturdy and valiant…and Burt Lancaster is impressively forceful."

By the end of the year, *Seven Days in May* had grossed a little more than $2.9 million in the US and Canada, and almost an equal sum outside of the US, where it proved especially popular in France and Germany. The film provided March with one of his best screen performances as the supposedly milquetoast president who out maneuvers the coup and saves the constitution. At a tribute dinner to March, years after his passing, John Frankenheimer would say,

"He was an inspiration for everyone in that film. He held the picture together. He came beautifully prepared. He set a tone for that movie that everybody felt they had to follow. The movie went well because of that, because of him"

The Marches were at their farm in Connecticut when they heard the shocking news on Friday, November 22, 1963, that President Kennedy had been shot and killed while driving in a motorcade at Dallas, Texas. They had come to greatly admire the young president and support his progressive domestic policies—even if they were a little bit leery of his Cold War rhetoric. Yet, they were heartened by the recent Nuclear Test Ban Treaty that JFK had signed with the Soviet Union. The Marches didn't have much time to overcome their own grief, when ABC television called asking them to fly to New York to participate in an hour-and-a-half "Tribute to President John F. Kennedy from the Arts" to be broadcast on Sunday, November 24, in prime time. March would act as master of ceremonies and would be joined on stage by Florence, Jerome Hines, Marian Anderson, Charlton Heston, Isaac Stern, Albert Finney, Christopher Plummer, and The Boston Symphony for an evening of songs, music, poems and readings. For his part, March would recite Lincoln's Gettysburg Address and close with a passage from JFK's Pulitzer Prize winning book "Profiles in Courage." He opened the tribute with these words:

> The wind is cold and crisp in New York this night. And outside this door, it tumbles and pursues the fallen leaves along the streets. It is what we would call 'A Fine Fall Day'. If it were not the most terrible November in history. In any normal November, we would on this night begin to turn our thoughts, our hearts, to giving thanks to God, for the goodness of life and land. But this year instead of life there is death, instead of thanks, tragedy. In place of goodness, Grief.

1964 would be a relatively quiet year. March would be on the nation's movie screens, of course, with *Seven Days in May*, but he had completed that job the previous summer. What he did do was give of his time for charitable causes, and add his stature and great voice to a string of television documentaries. May was an especially busy month, with activities ranging from recording ten to sixty-second radio spots supporting the Heart Fund, to narrating and hosting an NBC News documentary called *Small Town USA: A Farewell Portrait*, which dealt with the vanishing small town. While he narrated most of the program, he did do three days of taping for the introduction in Cimarron, Kansas, population 1100. At the time, March told reporters, "I can't tell you how much I enjoy doing this kind of documentary show. I think maybe I've reached a stage where I'm tired of make believe. I like working with things happening now, real things, real places."

One of the most significant events of that month of May 1964, was his participation in a program sponsored by the NAACP in recognition of the tenth anniversary of the landmark Brown vs. Board of Education Supreme Court ruling on May 14. The program appeared on closed-circuit television and was broadcast to forty-six cities across the United States. As the organization wrote to March in April, the "desire is for you to read the heart of the Supreme Court decision, as a keynote to the production," which is what he did; as just prior to that, on May 11, he taped a program for ABC-TV on the Supreme Court decision.

The summer of 1964 was spent in Italy visiting Penny and the family—there were now three grandchildren, two boys and one baby girl. The Marches returned to the U.S. just in time to attend the Democratic National Convention in Atlantic City, New Jersey, on August 27, where they performed a program of poetry at a reception honoring Jackie Kennedy in a ballroom before 6,000 guests. Mrs. Kennedy responded to the reading by saying, "I want to thank Mr. March and Miss Eldridge for reading so beautifully the poems that meant so much to President Kennedy." With 1964 being an election year, CBS decided to do a documentary on the presidency, titled *The Presidency: A Splendid Misery* with March narrating, and it aired on September 21. Just the day before, March was part of another CBS program celebrating the Lincoln Center for the Performing Arts in New York. Then, in late November and early December, he hosted and narrated yet another program, this one titled *The Artists Eye*, about artwork in the White House. Christmas and New Year's was spent in California with relatives.

In early 1965, the State Department contacted the Marches with a request that they represent the United States in the first theatrical exhibition sent out in four years as part of the State Department's cultural exchange program. What the department was requesting is that they spend six weeks in April and May, touring eight nations, and giving some twenty-three performances. The choice of where they would go and what their material would be was fully up to the Marches. "When they telephoned, I said, 'no,' but she talked me into it," March said. "It wasn't such a hard sell," Florence responded.

Once they were onboard, the Marches decided where they wanted to go. They knew they wanted to go to Greece, which they loved visiting and considered almost a second home. Italy was another given, if for no other reason than an opportunity to see Penny and Bert and the grandchildren. March had visited Egypt during his USO tour during the war but Florence had never been there, and she was fascinated by it and wanted to visit, so it was added. Filling out the itinerary would be visits to Iran and Turkey as well as three countries neither March had ever visited: Afghanistan, Lebanon, and Syria.

The program they had in mind was titled "An Evening with Fredric March and Florence Eldridge." And, over the course of one hour and twenty minutes, they would perform select scenes from three of the plays they had appeared in together: *The Skin of Their Teeth, The Autumn Garden,* and, logically enough, *Long Day's Journey into Night.* To round out the show, they would perform five poems by Robert Frost ("Mending Wall," "They Wait for Science," "Departmental or The End of My Ant Jerry," "An Importer" and "Home Burial.") There would also be poems by Alan Seeger ("I Had a Rendezvous with Death," which Florence explained had been a poem loved by President Kennedy and that Mrs. Kennedy had told them that JFK had made her learn it on their honeymoon!), Henry Wadsworth Longfellow ("The Building of a Ship") and as the finale "No Man is an Island" by John Donne. "I was all set," March said, "to read the poems. But she'd (Florence) already learned all of her lines, so I did too." The only prop the actors would use is having a glass of water handy, "I get a mouthful of cotton when I talk a lot," March explained.

The tour opened on April 7, in Cairo, where a leading Egyptian critic wrote, "Spellbound, that's it, The audience was too spellbound to applaud. I tried to clap myself but I said it's better not to and I sank back into my emotions." The critic went on to write, "For the first time, most of the audience was hearing American literature and American poetry done live. Many went out of curiosity to see the Marches. But from the first moment, this curiosity was replaced by the magic of their art."

When it was all finished and done with, Florence wrote out a recollection of what had happened during the tour, and it's worth quoting here:

CAIRO: "We played the residence of the American Embassy to an official audience and the second night the Pocket Theater, which led to two conclusions that we formed again and again. Whatever the tensions between governments, it does not brush off on cultural programs. We had supper after the performance in a great hand sewn tent of many colors (seating about 150), floored with magnificent Persian rugs, which gave a feeling of what the splendor of desert life must have been—I, sitting at a table with the deputy Prime Minister, the publisher and his 'Walter Lippman', who are Nasser's (the Prime Minister) mouthpieces and screams constantly at the U.S.A.—who couldn't have been more cordial. In fact, the press generally was great. The second impression was repeated in every country and that is that the young intellectuals have found common expression in avant guard plays and that our 'off Broadway' theater has its equivalent in each capital—many of the same plays being done in translation in each country. One hopes this says something about the future."

ALEXANDRIA: "From Cairo we drove at 80 miles per hour across the desert, passing Bedouins in their tents with flocks of goats and camels to Alexandria, where we played that night to a most moving audience. Alexandria was...the Cosmopolitan City, with large foreign communities, education in French and English, and an upper class that traveled a great deal in Europe...The performance in the auditorium of the museum was for 8:30, At 6:30 every seat was filled and as tickets had been counterfeited there was great confusion outside the hall. I can only say that as we walked on the upturned faces looked thirsty and the response was touching."

BEIRUT: "Have you ever tried to go 70 miles an hour on a jam-packed road of cars, water buffalo carts, camels, donkeys, etc.? ...Four hours back to Cairo, where harassment by bureaucracy almost kept us off the plane as 'our overweight might imbalance it.'...We staggered off at Beirut at 11 pm, more dead than alive; to meet flashing bulbs of photographers, an embassy welcoming committee, and reporters... One embassy wife asked if we'd like supper. I said, 'I'd like a bath most of all' as I felt so soiled. 'Why should you feel soiled, when you've just gotten off a nice clean plane?' I could have killed her. Beirut was unbelievably clean and brilliant—the hotel unbelievably well-appointed after Egypt. We gave three performances—2 at the American University, which produced a large alumni association and English speaking audiences."

DAMASCUS: "...we proceeded to the Syria border. We were always escorted by Embassy personnel to borders, where a car flying the American flag would appear from the opposite direction to take us over from there. We called them 'escort officers' but one day found them referred to as 'control officers.' Hi Ho! You'd always get a folder with their plans for you—inter-views, radio, receptions, guest lists to familiarize oneself with, etc. We stayed mostly at residences which were comfortable, did good laundry and pressing, had safe food, and where generally in a quiet moment before bed—after the excitement— we got a good idea of the political picture from the Ambassador."

ISTANBUL: "On to Istanbul for three performances and an adventure with a stark-mad American Consul. We stayed one night with him and his wife, and then using the excuse of matinee performances, which necessitated our staying in town, moved to the Hilton. For the first matinee we waited in the lobby for the car, and as we didn't know which theater the performance was at, became increasingly fidgety as no car appeared. A phone call elicited the information that the consulate was closed. They'd forgotten to send a car for us! Fortunately, they remembered once the audience had been waiting for 15 minutes. After the performance the Turkish—American Women's Club was having a reception for us. The consul swept us into his car, but we soon discovered that he had no idea where the reception was, so we went round and round in Istanbul, while the ladies cooled their heels and time cooled the refreshments."

ADANNA: "The first day's drive over pot hole roads left us broken backed, but not too feeble to load up at the P.X. of our military base there, and get Freddie a shot in the elbow for a painful arm. The pain left but he still has two numb cold fingers."

TEHERAN: "A performance at the residency the first night. We were constantly adjusting to an audience of 150 at the residencies one night, and to 600 to 800 at the theaters the next…We didn't see the Shah as he was under complete tight security because of the recent assassination attempt, but he did send Freddie a message and an autographed picture."

KABUL: "Kabul is fascinating—very beautiful bowl surrounded by snowy mountains and a mixture of camel, women in shadris (robes like Fortuny silk, descending from a kind of pillbox hat, with fine lattice work in front of the face to peer through), little boys in sweaters emblazoned with the names of American high schools, as second hand American clothes are a big item in the bazaars, and a million dollar radio station, fine arts building, etc…There a cable arrived. 'Unaccountably' they'd discovered a law that said a performance must run two hours. Since we were short, would we share the program with a couple of Italian artists? Aren't they the most? Politely we offered to cancel. A compromise was reached that we could do our stuff and they'd do a simultaneous translation."

ATHENS: "A lovely four days there with three performances— two at the Royal Theater, which is divine. The King and Queen were to come to the first one but, after we'd learned all the protocol, Makarios's (Makarios III) arrival caused a meeting of the King's Council over Cypress, so they didn't come. What with arrival flowers and theater flowers, we looked like a funeral parlor for four days and then of course the goodbye gifts, etc. at the plane. What a people they are."

ROME: "Then on to Rome, where Burt (their son-in-law) brought Gianni (their grandson who was by this time nine years old), who was described the Ambassador's butler as 'molts elegante' and who threaded his way with aplomb through a reception at the Embassy residence and a scene right out of a Marx Bros. picture after the performance. Did you ever see their picture, laid on an ocean liner, where about 100 people are crowded into one stateroom? That was our dressing room. Some friends and acquaintances, any enthusiastic stranger, and about 8 paparazzi, the free-lance photographers who trail one all over the city."

In Rome, the Marches got the following telegram from their friend Spencer Tracy:

SOME SAY YOU ARE IN ITALY OTHERS NEW YORK OTHERS WISCONSIN WHEREEVER YOU ARE CONGRATULATONS AND LOVE TO BOTH OF YOU—SPENCE.

NAPLES: "In Naples, the simultaneous translators made so much noise that after Freddie's first poem, a man in the audience screamed 'Silencio', which terrified us, until we realized he was shouting at the translators—not at us."

Bone tired after this exhausting but rewarding trip, the Marches went to a spa on the Island of Ischia in Italy, where they were to begin a regiment of mud baths, inhalations of steam, massage, brief strolls, and lots of sleep. "We were to begin yesterday," Florence wrote, "but the doctor said my blood pressure was too low and Freddie's was too high, and counseled 24 hours of rest first." While there, they received the following cable from the Secretary of State, Dean Rusk:

PLEASE ADVISE MR AND MRS FREDRIC MARCH THAT THE DEPARTMENT CONGRATULATES AND THANKS THEM SINCERELY FOR HAVING INITIATED WITH OUTSTANDING SUCCESS A NEW PHASE IN THE CULTURAL PRESENTATIONS PROGRAM. THEIR HIGHLY EFFECTIVE PERFORMANCE IN BOTH A PROFESSIONAL AND A REPRESENTATIVE SENSE HAS MADE A REAL CONTRIBUTION TO THE PROGRAM'S BASIC PURPOSE OF BUILDING RESPECT FOR OUR ARTISTIC ACHIEVEMENTS AND THEREBY TO THE CAUSE OF IMPROVED INTERNATIONAL UNDERSTANDING.

The Marches found that they were as welcome at the Johnson White House as they had been at the Kennedy White House, and on October 7, March was invited to speak at the White House's annual Salute to Congress dinner. While he was delivering his remarks, White House aide Bill Moyers jotted inside a program "When you finish, introduce the president," and had it delivered to the lectern as March was drawing towards the end of his prepared remarks, so on this night he had the honor of introducing the President to the audience. The following day, LBJ, from Bethesda Naval Hospital where he was preparing for an operation, wrote a thank you note to March:

Dear Mr. March,

Your performance set the tone of the evening at the 'Salute to Congress,' and I want you to know how deeply Mrs. Johnson and I appreciate our giving us a most memorable send-off to the hospital.

Every line was worth repeating over and over but the one I carried with me to the hospital was that we have outlined a Great Society "where the bullet in the night will be replaced by a ballot in the hand and a book under each arm."

This is truly the goal of mankind. I hope I have helped move us closer toward it.

Please convey to Mrs. March my gratitude that she came down to be part of an admiring audience of the most distinguished gentleman on the American stage.

Sincerely,
Lyndon Johnson

Later on that month, the Marches flew to Chicago where they delivered remarks celebrating the wit and humor of UN Ambassador and two-time Democratic nominee for President, Adlai Stevenson, who had died suddenly the previous summer, at an event honoring his life.

It had now been nearly three years since March had made a film, and director Martin Ritt was eager to get March back in the saddle—almost literally—for he offered the sixty-seven year old actor the opportunity to appear in a western—a first for him. March ended 1965 pondering this offer.

CHAPTER FIFTEEN
1966–1975

March was making a familiar complaint when he told LA Times Hollywood columnist Bob Thomas that "it's time to hang up my hat." He had just returned from an arduous location shoot of his very first—and last—western film, *Hombre*. "What am I doing here?" March went on. "I've got four grandchildren coming from their home in Italy to our house in Connecticut…My son is getting married this summer. Here I am making a picture, feeling as tired as I have ever been, when I should be in the East with my family. It doesn't make sense." He just returned from thirteen weeks in the Arizona and Nevada deserts and mountains.

Based on a novel by Elmore Leonard, *Hombre* tells the story of a white man (Paul Newman) brought up by Indians, who is an outcast among the group of stage coach passengers he is traveling with. But, when the stagecoach becomes the target of bandits, it's to this outcast that they turn to for protection. March was cast in one of his most unsympathetic roles, as the Indian Agent named Favor. Bigoted and corrupt, Favor has a sexually repressed much younger wife, played by Barbara Rush. At one point in the film, she says of her husband, "He reads late into the night, which is just as well because when he takes off his trousers and folds them neatly over the chair, that sharp, keen intelligence of his doesn't count for much." Among the other cast members are: Diane Cilento (at the time Mrs. Sean Connery) who runs a boarding house; Martin Balsam as a bandit; and the always reliable Richard Boone as the chief baddie. Directing the film is Martin Ritt, who had a strong association with Newman having directed the star in five films including *The Long Hot Summer* and *Hud*.

March recalled that the weather during the location shoot was "murderous, so hot that you couldn't sleep at night." At one point, the film location moved to a mountain peak that was fifty-three miles from their camp, with roads "so narrow that a jeep would have to back down...to descend." The heat and narrow roads weren't the only problems connected with the production—rain, heavy winds and illness were other culprits. At one point, Newman was out sick for six days. Martin Ritt invited an old high-school friend to the set who proceeded to keep a diary of his observations and wrote, "It's rugged, dirty work. Each scene requires many tedious hours of work and sweat in the hot, dusty outdoors." He described Ritt as a "perfectionist" who leaves "nothing to chance."

March later said that the only way he got through the film was due to the presence of Florence for the Nevada shoot, where the actors at least were allowed to stay at comfortable accommodations in Las Vegas.

"She was magnificent," March recalled. "Every morning she got up at 6:30 in the morning to make breakfast before I left on the location. She is a marvelous cook, and at night she concocted cordon bleu meals to help keep up my spirits, I don't know what I would have done without her."

Ritt wrote to March in October 1966, just after seeing the first cut of the film telling the actor, "Though I am hardly objective enough to give you a genuine opinion of the film itself, I am writing you to say how pleased I am with your performance. I think it is first rate and couldn't be happier about it." When the film was released in the spring of 1967, the reviews were generally good. Roger Ebert wrote in the *Chicago Sun Times* that *Hombre* was an "absorbing, suspenseful film" with "uniformly excellent performances." While *Variety* wrote that March, "Scored in a strong, unsympathetic—but eventually pathetic—role." When the film was released, Ritt again wrote to March telling him, "The notices were not very important, but they were the first, and as the boys say, it is better than a kick in the ass. It was a tough film to make, and while I by no means think it a great or important film, I think it well done and entertaining and that's about all I had hoped for." The film went on to be a top grosser for 20th Century Fox.

With March again seemingly announcing his retirement, he and Florence went off to Rome to spend the summer with Penny and her family, which now included the fourth grandchild: a girl named Marie. But the retirement turned out to be short-lived, for while in Italy, he was invited by ABC to narrate a documentary *The Legacy of Rome*, which was broadcast on November 25, 1966.

In 1967, both Marches were invited to appear in a CBS TV drama titled *Do Not Go Gentle into that Good Night*, based on Dylan Thomas's poem about the approaching death of his father. March plays a cantankerous retired carpenter who is sent by his grown children to live in an institution for the elderly, where he meets another resident (Florence) who attempts to sooth his soul. Eventually, the March character decides to go back to his house to live out his days. A prestigious production to be directed by George Schaefer, who was directing many *Hallmark Hall of Fame* films for CBS. The ninety-minute production was to start filming on April 27, 1967. Instead, when rehearsals had just begun, March was forced to drop out, due to circulatory problems. When it looked like March was in for a long hospitalization and recovery period, Florence dropped out of the project too. When he was released from hospital after nearly two weeks, March remarked to reporters, "All I need is some sunshine and rest and I'll be in great shape."

March had recovered well enough to join an all-star cast consisting of himself, Helen Hayes, Robert Ryan, Henry Fonda, Harry Belafonte, Andy Williams, and Richard Crenna for a glittering evening of songs, readings, and poetry at the grand opening of Ford's Theater in Washington, D.C., on January 30, 1968. A distinguished audience of dignitaries, including Vice President Hubert Humphrey, Senator Everett Dirksen, and Chief Justice Earl Warren, attended the event. The theater had been refurbished and reopened for the first time since the assassination of President Abraham Lincoln on April 14, 1865.

For much of the rest of the year, the Marches took things easy, and since March had essentially thought he might have finally retired for good—though it seems like he made the announcement of his retirement every couple of years or so, only to be lured back by some project or another—he and Florence decided to sell their apartment in New York. Since neither of them could ever see taking on the grueling task of another Broadway show, they could devote their time to the farm in Connecticut and, of course, traveling, which meant visits to the grandchildren in Italy as well as taking in the sun and waters of Greece—which had the effect of rejuvenating both Marches. Of their private pursuits, March once said, "An actor is only as good as the person behind him, only as deep and only as broad-ranging. So we keep busy with a variety of interests, we travel, we study, and I hope, grow as human beings."

In May of 1968, March received the first of a several honors that would come his way from his home state of Wisconsin over the next few years. He was selected, along with four other alumni, to receive the Distinguished Service Award from the University of Wisconsin in Madison. Florence accompanied March to the ceremony, which took place on May 19. He also met up with his older brother Jack. While visiting Madison, the brothers took a sentimental side trip to Racine, where they took in some of their old stomping grounds and looked up old friends.

On the evening of the ceremony, a party was held to honor March. According to Virginia Hall, the wife of March's old friend Larry Hall, Florence was a constant presence, which, according to Mrs. Hall, caused March to be subdued. "You didn't feel folksy with her at all," Mrs. Hall told Deborah C. Peterson. "Fred was obviously very afraid of Florence it seemed to me. She never had much to offer the group. When she did talk, she talked about world problems. My husband discussed something, I don't remember what, and she put him in his place in a hurry! It was terrible, my husband was quiet immediately. I was amazed. She was very rude and unkind. Fred didn't do anything." Florence was never popular with March's old Wisconsin friends, but it is probable that it was just different personality types. Florence was very passionate about politics and world affairs and was comfortable discussing such issues, which was probably contrary to what March's jovial old friends wanted or liked. It is likely that she felt like a fish out of water among all of these people who loved March and, realizing she wasn't quite their cup of tea, she over compensated in such instances.

In the summer of 1969, March was wooed back to the big screen to make *Tick Tick Tick* for director Ralph Nelson. Nelson had begun his career as an Emmy-award winning director during the so called "Golden Age of Television" and had moved into motion pictures in the early sixties to considerable success with such films as *Requiem for a Heavy Weight, Soldier in the Rain, Father Goose,* and had directed Sidney Poitier and Cliff Robertson to Best Actor Academy Awards in *Lilies in the Field* and *Charly. Tick Tick Tick,* produced by MGM, explores the exploding racial violence in a small southern town where a newly elected black Sheriff's (Jim Brown) authority is resisted when he has to arrest the son of a prominent white business man, whose drunken driving accident kills a child. Brown forms an alliance with George Kennedy, who plays the retiring sheriff, and March—who's cast as the town's mayor—is forced to reexamine his own lifelong racial beliefs. Kennedy was humbled and excited to be working with March, "I was only seven years old when he won his first Academy Award," he commented at the time.

"My wife had great fun kidding me," March told a reporter on the set of *Tick Tick Tick,* "about becoming unretired. But I couldn't resist the script. I've never said—like Cagney—boom—I'm finished! The old mayor I'm playing is determined that there isn't going to be any trouble. The NAACP or federal troops or anybody is going to be called in." To welcome March back to MGM, the studio wanted to give the veteran actor a cocktail party in his honor, but March declined. "It would be a dull party. At my age my favorite drink nowadays is hot cocoa." Returning to MGM didn't make March nostalgic for the old days, as he offered plenty of praise for the new generation of actors and filmmakers. "Ostrich feathers and limousines have been replaced by hard work and good acting." He went on to say that Hollywood was no longer "a make believe world. The young actors care about doing a good job rather than constantly affecting movie star poses. And studios are turning out more significant and socially conscious products than the fairy-tale fare we did for years." March was particularly excited about the technical advances that he utilized for the first time on *Tick Tick Tick.* "I was particularly delighted with the innovation called Video West, a television setup used on *Tick Tick Tick,* which enabled us to have instant replay of every rehearsal and actual scene. We corrected and improved on the spot rather than wishing we had done something differently when we saw the film the next day in the screening room. It's a wonderfully artistic and economic advance."

The cast and crew didn't have to go down south to film *Tick Tick Tick*, instead they traveled to the Northern California town of Colusa, near Sacramento. In Colusa there was a call out for 200 extras to play downtrodden southerners. Ralph Nelson recalls that the call was answered but that everybody showed up dressed in their finest. "It looked like opening night at the Met," Nelson recalled. "I had to send them home to change into Levis and gingham dresses." One of the reasons that Nelson decided not to go south to make this film was because he didn't want to go through the same thing Otto Preminger did when he shot *Hurry Sundown* on location in a small Southern community, "tires on his cars and trucks slashed, and that sort of thing."

March gives a good performance in this, his penultimate film. His cantankerous mayor is not a one-note character. He has prejudice, certainly, but he also understands that a new era has arrived in the south, and while he won't embrace it wholeheartedly, he also will not stand up against it. He has a superb scene, possibly the best one of the whole film, where he talks with—not down to—his black servant of eighteen years—a warm, funny, and poignant scene.

In January of 1970, March and Florence went to a sneak preview of the film at the Westwood Village Theater in West Hollywood, and he told movie columnist Dorothy Manners that he plans on making more movies, but that he wants to do comedies from now on. "When I said I was retiring several years ago, I meant from serious drama. With the world in the sad shape it's in we could use a few laughs—don't you think," sounding remarkably like Paul Lockridge of *Laughter*. He also told Manners that he and Florence were going to escape the cold of Connecticut for the warm sun of Mexico for a couple of months.

When *Tick Tick Tick* was released, most critics also lauded March's performance even if they felt that the film itself was a somewhat inferior version of *In the Heat of the Night*. The critic for the *Boston Globe* felt that March gave an "engaging performance" though at times a might hammy. Richard Schickel in *Life* magazine wrote, "The best thing about the film is the presence of Fredric March, too long away and certainly deserving of something more interesting to play than the crusty major of a dusty small town." The critic for the *Washington Afro-American* wrote that "George Kennedy and Fredric March deserve credit for strong type casting...Backed by a good script black and white actors come on forceful to liven Brown's lines which were made for Sidney Poitier." As it turned out, *Tick Tick Tick* was not a success for MGM, and the studio quickly sold it to television.

The Marches again got away from the snow and cold temperatures of Connecticut to spend two months over the winter of 1970 in San Miguel de Allende, Mexico. "It's a wonderful pure Spanish colonial town," Florence said. "I want to take a crash course in Spanish and Freddie wants to paint water colors."

In May of 1970, the Marches traveled to Madison, Wisconsin, for the fiftieth anniversary of the class of 1920. Naturally the class president—Fred Bickel—was expected to attend, and he didn't disappoint. At a news conference, the Marches related that they enjoyed seeing current movies and were not stuck in a nostalgia of the past. March embraced such contemporary films as *Easy Rider, Midnight Cowboy, Z,* and *They Shoot Horses, Don't They?* as films he and Florence had enjoyed. But when March added *MASH* to that list, Florence dissented, "Too bloody!" March also mentioned Steve McQueen, Elliot Gould, Dustin Hoffman, and Jon Voight as among his favorite contemporary actors. As for nudity and sex in movies and the theater, Florence maintained that, "This too shall pass—it's all so boring and dull."

On May 15, the class of 1920 alumni—some 300-plus strong, the greatest turnout of alumni for a class reunion the news ever reported—met in the Great Hall of the Wisconsin Memorial Union. March, in his role of class president, spoke. He mentioned that he always felt of the UW as "on Wisconsin" adding, "I think we need the 'on', and think that this too will pass," referring to campus disturbances. The ceremony ended with the gathering performing a rousing rendition of 'Varsity.'"

While the Marches were in Wisconsin, they were the guests of the Governor of the State, Warren P. Knowles, at the Governor's Mansion. "This house is simply exquisite," Florence told a visiting reporter. "... there is a dignified serenity to the house that I find most appealing." She added that "Freddie loves Madison and the University. He grew up in Wisconsin and knows so many people here. This reunion is terribly exciting for both of us."

On the final night of their visit to Madison, the Marches attended a farewell party thrown by March's old school friend Norman Bassett. At one point, March noticed an attractive reporter and came over to shake her hand. The reporter gushed, "I'm delighted to have a chance to meet you, Mr. March, because I've always had a terrible crush on you." Without missing a beat, March replied, "Oh! That's nice to hear. Please tell me again."

At around this time, March announced he was going to star in a new movie: a comedy-drama called *Kotch* about a cantankerous old man, to be directed by Jack Lemmon. But, in the end, March backed out due to health problems and Walter Matthau, heavily made up, made the film. Instead, the summer of 1970 brought Penny and Bert and their four children (aged six to fourteen) to the Connecticut farm for the summer—an event the Marches always treasured.

March was again honored by his home state of Wisconsin in the fall of 1971, when the seventy-four-year-old actor and Florence flew to Oshkosh to be present at the dedication of the new 500 seat Fredric March Playhouse of the Arts and Communications Center at Oshkosh State University. The Marches also attended the premiere presentation of the playhouse, the Friedrich Dürrenmatt drama *The Visit*, which had been made popular on Broadway a decade earlier with the Lunts. March was ecstatic about having a playhouse named in his honor, telling reporters that he was "thrilled beyond words. I never anticipated such an honor." He thought the $7 million center was "magnificent." The dedication ceremony took place after the final curtain of *The Visit* and was followed by a cocktail party in March's honor.

While he was in Oshkosh, he told reporters that while he loved the idea of a playhouse named after him, he had come to appreciate films more so than the stage. "I prefer the screen to the theater, although for a long time I preferred the theater. Theater, you build on sand. Pictures last. Pictures are physically tiring, while theater is more mentally tiring. I liked mixing them up, though."

By this time, March was appearing frailer, depending on a cane to keep his balance due to some small strokes he had suffered. He also conceded that he was getting a little deaf. "I'm a little hard of hearing and I don't get what it's all about sometimes, so I ask my wife to explain on the way home." Florence piped in, "What I can't explain I make up." By contrast, Florence appeared healthy and radiant, and at least ten years younger than her seventy-one years. Naturally, March was asked when he would be going back to work, and he replied, "I like to think I'm retired, that I quit while I was ahead. I had an awful good run for my money."

The Marches were still working politically for liberal causes, and that cause in 1972 was George McGovern, the anti-war democrat nominated to take on President Richard Nixon in the November elections. Writer William Styron threw a fundraising dinner at his Connecticut home and invited the Marches to be among his cohosts. The dinners honored guest was McGovern's vice-presidential running mate, Sargent Shriver. The dinner raised $10,000 for the McGovern-Shriver ticket. "Which seemed to me prodigious, but was rather disappointing to the state political pros," Styron later wrote. When asked by the *New York Times* about Nixon, Florence replied, "Doesn't your paper say it prints everything fit to print? Well, I'm afraid my comments on that subject would not be fit to print."

He was reasonably sure he was finally retired, but relatives and friends convinced him to appear as Harry Hope in the American Film Theater's ambitious four-hour production of Eugene O'Neill's *The Iceman Cometh*, directed by John Frankenheimer. Knowing that Frankenheimer was at the helm of the production was a big plus in his decision to take on the role of the cantankerous owner of the Last Chance Saloon. Also aiding in the decision was the casting of his old *Long Day's Journey* costar Bradford Dillman, as well as a seasoned and talented cast including Lee Marvin, Robert Ryan, Jeff Bridges, Sorrell Booke, and Moses Gunn. The film was a prestigious production but also one made on a limited budget. For instance, March, Marvin, and Ryan—the three key leads—all received the same salary—a miniscule $25,000.

The Iceman Cometh is historically significant, not only for being one of the great works of Eugene O'Neill, but the 1973 film version is also the last film of two great American actors, Fredric March and Robert Ryan. Both were ill during the making of the movie. Ryan would die before the film was released—though at the beginning of shooting he told Frankenheimer that he had the cancer "licked"— while March would live nearly two years following the completion of the film—with frequent hospitalizations. Rehearsals were to begin in early January, but then, just before Christmas of 1972, March suffered a mild stroke that hospitalized him. Florence contacted Frankenheimer and asked him to come to New York, "but not to tell anybody." Frankenheimer recalled that "he had just had an operation, but he wanted very much to do the film and was afraid that the fact that he was in the hospital would cause the insurance company to insist that he withdraw. We talked. He said that he would be there for the first day of shooting and that he would know the part—of course by this time I knew he would, and that's the way we left it."

March rallied what strength he had and arrived for rehearsals on time. "Freddie was dying," Bradford Dillman declared years later.

> *John Frankenheimer had to go through hoops to finally get Freddie insured to do the film. Finally they had to sign a waiver. Filming was done at 20th Century Fox studios and Florence would come in with Freddie every morning and get his seated and comfortable. He would slump down in his chair but then the minute that he had a scene to do he would jump up and become Harry Hope and roar like a lion and the minute Frankenheimer called cut! He would sit and slump down again. I thought he had courage and ego to want to go out on the top.*

Dillman contends that the only real flaw with the film was the casting of Lee Marvin in the pivotal role of Hickey. "Lee Marvin was a mean drunk and a mean son of a bitch," Dillman says. "He was the only one who was really miscast—the part called for Jason (Robards)."

Frankenheimer began three weeks of rehearsals beginning in January of 1973, before filming began. The film was shot in sequence, which was something that Frankenheimer demanded in return for his services. Robert Ryan was ecstatic about the film for two reasons. One, unlike some of the others he had a very good relationship with Lee Marvin, "Lee had tremendous respect for Bob, and the two of them worked very well together," Frankenheimer later recalled. Two, Ryan was finally working with his acting hero: Fredric March. According to Ryan's biographer, Franklin Jarlett, Ryan excitedly told friends about working with March and "in typical Bob Ryan fashion he was more delighted with Freddie March than he was with himself." Dillman recalls that "Frankenheimer was very clever in that the cast wore the same clothes every day. Rags, seldom cleaned—we stunk up the place but we were the characters and it worked."

It was not an easy shoot for March. During the course of filming, March suffered another of his small strokes. This caused him to miss four days of shooting, "and then he was back," Frankenheimer later recalled. He missed a couple of more days later on when he developed the flu, but "he was back again, working with a temperature," according to Frankenheimer. Despite his ill health, March gave it everything he had. "When Freddie arrived, knowing every line, it was as if something bigger than life took over the entire rehearsal hall. What had seemed a good scene with someone else reading someone else reading Harry Hope became unforgettable with Freddie March playing the part. He constantly surprised me. He made it always better than I had ever hoped it could be." Frankenheimer later recalled that March "inspired everyone" and that he had seen "very hand-boiled technicians break into applause at the end of a scene by Freddie March on both *Seven Days in May* and *The Iceman Cometh*."

Dillman recalls a funny episode during the making of the film.

> *Freddie had a stand-in who would be on hand to do all the camera angles, thus allowing Freddie more rest. Hildy Parker was playing a hooker in the picture and in one rehearsal she jumps in the lap of Freddie's stand-in just as she would be doing with Freddie when the scene was actually shot. She then says, "Oh, wait a minute. Do you think Mr. March would mind my sitting in his lap?" and I replied from the side, "Hildy, protect yourself! He'll love it!"*

Exhausted, sick, but elated to have completed the picture, March returned home to Connecticut. When the film opened in select theaters in October of 1973, it received respectful reviews—especially for March. The critic for the *Christian Science Monitor* wrote, "March shines brilliantly as the long-lost Harry Hope." The only real flaw he found with the performances was that of Lee Marvin (echoing Bradford Dillman), "Marvin brings little more than competence to the central role of Hickey." In the *New Yorker*, Pauline Kael paid tribute to March:

> *Fredric March can let the muscles in his face sag to hell to show a character falling apart. He interprets Harry Hope (who could be a dismal bore) with so much quiet tenderness and skill that when Harry regains his illusions and we see March's muscles tone up we don't know whether to smile for the character or for the actor. March is such an honorable actor; he's had a long and distinguished career. On the stage since 1920, in movies since 1929, and at 76 he goes on taking difficult roles; he's not out doing TV commercials or grabbing a series.*

Ill and more or less confined to a wheelchair, March and Florence joined Penny, Bert, and the grandchildren in the summer of 1973 on a two-week Scandinavian cruise. March was preoccupied during the cruise, not only by his own declining health but by the news that his brother Jack was suffering from terminal cancer and was not expected to live long. March, writing to his brother, would call this voyage his "Last Trip" and wrote that "Bert and the boys have been wonderful. Gianni (their oldest grandson, now 16) wheeled me through the Hermitage at Leningrad and Michael through the Frognes Park at Oslo (in the rain). All of them—and Flo—have been so damn kind to me, but it's a trip I should have taken ten or twelve years ago." Following the cruise, the Marches spent more time with Penny and the family in Italy where March celebrated his seventy-sixth birthday. He reported to Jack that he was gifted a shirt and tie and two magnifying glasses with battery lights "so I can read the paper." By September, the Marches spent time with Jack and his wife Mary at their home in Myrtle Beach, South Carolina. It would be the last time the brothers would be together. Jack died on November 3, at the age of eighty-one. While his passing was certainly not a surprise, it surely left March despondent, and probably helped lead to a severe stroke later that same month. This stroke left him partially paralyzed.

Due to his declining health, the Marches decided to sell a portion of their Connecticut farm in 1974. The farm was bought by Slim Hawks Hayward, who at one time had been married to director Howard Hawks, who had directed March in *The Real Glory* back in 1936 and also to Leland Hayward, who had at one time been March's agent. They sold thirty acres for $185,000 and retained a parcel of 8.6 acres on the south end of the property. They decided to move to the warmer climate of California, buying a condo.

The change of climate and location did little to help March's failing health. In June of 1974, he was hospitalized again, this time diagnosed with cancer. He spent three weeks at Good Samaritan Hospital in Los Angeles before finally being released on July 3. If this wasn't enough, he suffered another stroke in November. He spent his final Christmas at his condo where his niece Jean and her husband David visited.

As 1974 turned to 1975, March was steadily declining. On April 4, 1975, he entered Mt. Sinai Hospital for the final decline. Much of the last ten days of his life was spent sleeping, with Florence constantly by his side.

The Marches friend Hume Cronyn recalls that Florence told him the following story from March's final hospitalization:

> *When he was in the hospital and very ill, Florence spent most of her days with him. While Freddie slept, she would creep out of his room and sit in the sun-room at the end of the hospital corridor. She had been given a lot of books by friends who were aware of her painful vigil, and she'd take a couple of these with her and leaf through them as she waited. One of the books was about Carole Lombard, who had worked with Freddie in the film* Nothing Sacred. *Lombard, no puritan herself, recounted with glee that, being aware of Freddie's tendencies, she was fully prepared for him. When Freddie got his hand up her skirt, he discovered she discovered she was wearing a dildo. 'I read that and I was furious!,' said Florence. It seemed like such an indignity. I marched into his room and gave him absolute hell.' I asked her what Freddie had said. 'Oh darling, he couldn't say anything…he was dying.'*

Florence's anger had little to do with Freddie's behavior. As she told me the story she was laughing. It was the 'indignity' of the story—the light that it seemed to throw on her husband—that she resented."

Fredric March died at ten-thirty in the morning of April 14, 1975, with Florence at his side. He was four months shy of his seventy-eighth birthday. His death made front page headlines in newspapers across the country as well as leading off television newscasts. John Frankenheimer, who directed him in two of his best latter-day performances, wrote, "I know that I will never work with anyone like him again and that I will never know anyone like him again. He invented the term 'professional.' He exemplified the word 'excellence.' I loved him and will miss him." Certainly he would have greatly appreciated the tribute that was paid to him in his hometown newspaper, *The Racine Journal Times*, under the headline, "Fredric March also had Strength of Character." The editorial reminded readers of the attacks on March in the late forties and early fifties, smearing his patriotism and labeling him as a communist sympathizer, and how he fought back and eventually persevered. The editorial ended, "In the later years of his life, Fredric March didn't have strong connections to Racine. But he was born here, grew up here, and began his acting career in local schools. Racine can claim him as a native son who earned fame and fortune as one of the finest actors ever to grace the American stage and screen. March was also a gentleman of the highest order. That is the highest epitaph we can inscribe." But perhaps the most thoughtful tribute appeared in *The Baltimore Sun*. "Because, like Robert Frost, he took the road less traveled by. He could have settled for super stardom, but instead he sought to become the consummate actor. He knew to achieve one would negate the other."

AFTERWORD

March left an estate worth $830,000 and most of his possessions to his wife. Hardly a pittance but not the estate you would expect a star of more than forty years to leave. But it was enough so that Florence could live comfortably for the rest of her life—another thirteen years.

There were still honors to come his way. In the fall of 1978, the University of Wisconsin, his alma mater, renamed their playhouse "The Fredric March Play Circle" in his honor. A ceremony was held attended by Florence and Penny. Tony wasn't among those in attendance as he was estranged from the family. Penny presented the University with a large oil painting of March as Major Joppolo from *A Bell for Adano*. It is still hanging there to this day. Florence gave the university $15,000 to set up a Scholarship fund in March's name.

In 1982, Anthony March died—killed in an automobile accident in Texas.

In 1987, a special tribute was held in March's honor presented by the Academy of Motion Picture Arts and Sciences and the American Cinematheque. Clips from eighteen March movies were screened, along with recollections from many March coworkers and friends. Florence was an honored guest. "I hope they show Freddy in a scene from *The Iceman Cometh*," she told reporters. "He was so sick that it was his last movie. But, my God, he gave a performance. That movie showed his strength. He was so versatile. To me, that's what's important about his career."

The following year, on August 1, 1988, Florence Eldridge March died. "Taken while she was saying her prayers" according to Bradford Dillman. She was eighty-six years old. Her daughter, Penny, continued to live with her husband and family in Italy.

BIBLIOGRAPHY

Alonzo, Harriet Hyman, *Robert E. Sherwood: The Playwright in Peace & War*, University of Massachusetts Press, 2004

Astor, Mary, *A Life on Film*, Dell, 1967

Atkinson, Brooks, *Broadway*, The MacMillan Company, 1970

Bankhead, Tallulah, *Tallulah: My Autobiography*, Sears Readers Club, 1952

Basinger, Jeanine, *Silent Stars*, Alfred A.Knopf, 1999

Behlmer, Rudy, *Memo from Darryl F. Zanuck*, Grove Press, 1993

Behlmer, Rudy, *Memo from David O. Selznick*, Viking Press, 1972

Berg, A. Scott, *Goldwyn: A Biography*, Knopf, 1989

Bernstein, Matthew, *Walter Wanger: Hollywood Independent*, University of Minnesota Press, 2000

Birchard, Robert, *Cecil B. DeMille's Hollywood*, University Press of Kentucky, 2004

Block, Alex Ben & Lucy Autrey Wilson, *George Lucas's Blockbusters*, It Books, 2010

Bogdanovich, Peter, *Who the Hell Made It*, Ballantine Books, 1997

Bona, Damien, Wiley, Mason, *Inside Oscar: The Unofficial History of the Academy Awards*, Ballantine Books, 1986

Bordman, Gerald, *American Theater: A Chronicle of Comedy and Drama 1914-1930*, Oxford University Press, 1995

Bowen, Croswell & O'Neill, Shane, *The Curse of the Misbegotten: A Tale of the House of O'Neill*, McGraw-Hill, 1959

Brown, Jared, *Moss Hart: A Prince of the Theater*, Back Stage Books, 2006

Bryer, Jackson R & Gibbs Wilder, Robin, *Selected Letters of Thornton Wilder*, Harper Perennial, 2009

Buford, Kate, *Burt Lancaster: An American Life*, Da Capo Press, 2000

Callow, Simon, *Charles Laughton: A Difficult Actor*, Intl, 1997

Champlin, Charles, *John Frankenheimer: A Conversation with Charles Champlin*, Riverwood Press, 1995

Chierichetti, David, *Hollywood Director*, Curtis Books, 1973

Considine, Shaun, *Mad as Hell: The Life and Work of Paddy Chayefsky,* iunivese, 2000

Cronyn, Hume, *A Terrible Liar*, William Morrow & Company, 1991

Curtis, James, *Spencer Tracy: A Biography*, Alfred A. Knopf, 2011

Davidson, Bill, *Spencer Tracy: Tragic Idol*, E.P. Dutton, 1987

Davidson, Murial & Westmore, Frank, *The Westmores of Hollywood*, Lippincott, 1976

Davis, Ronald L, *Just Making Movies: Company Directors in the Studio System*, University Press of Mississippi, 2005

Dick, Bernard, *Claudette Colbert: She Walked in Beauty*, University of Mississippi, 2008

Epstein, Edward Z & Morella, Joe, *The It Girl: The Incredible Story of Clara Bow*, Delacorte, Press, 1976

Eyman, Scott, *Ernst Lubitsch: Laughter in Paradise*, Johns Hopkins University Press, 2000

Eyman, Scott, *Print the Legend: The Life and Times of John Ford*, Simon & Schuster, 1999

Eyman, Scott, *Lion of Hollywood: The Life & Legend of Louis B. Mayer*, Simon & Schuster, 2005

Flamini, Roland, *Thalberg: The Last Tycoon & The World of MGM*, Crown Publishing, 1994

Ford, Tom, *Glenn Ford: A Life*, University of Wisconsin Press, 2011

Garnett, Tay (with Fredda Dudley Balling), *Light Your Torches & Pull Up Your Tights*, Arlington House, 1973

Gazzara, Ben, *In the Moment: My Life as an Actor*, Carroll & Graf, 2004

Goodrich, David L, *The Real Nick and Nora*, Southern Illinois University Press, 2001

Gordon, Ruth, *An Open Book*, Doubleday, 1980

Gottfried, Martin, *Arthur Miller: His Life and Work*, Da Capo Press, 2004

Greenberg, Joel & Higham, Charles, *The Celluloid Muse: Hollywood Directors Speak*, Signet, 1969

Herman, Jan, *A Talent for Trouble: The Life of Hollywood's Most Acclaimed Director*, William Wyler, Da Capo Press, 1997

Hirschhorn, Clive, *Gene Kelly: A Biography*, St. Martin's Press, 1985

Houseman, John, *Front and Center*, Simon & Schuster, 1984

Jarlett, Franklin, *Robert Ryan: A Biography & Critical Filmology*, McFarland & Company, 1997

Jason, Rick, *Scrapbooks of My Mind: A Hollywood Memoir*, Strange New Worlds, 2000

Kael, Pauline, *Kiss Kiss Bang Bang*, Bantam Books, 1965

Kahn-Atkins, Irene, *Arthur Jacobson*, Scarecrow Press, 1991

Katz, Ephraim, *The Film Encyclopedia*, Collins, 2005

Kazan, Elia, *Elia Kazan: A Life*, Da Capo Press, 1997

Keyes, Evelyn, *Scarlett O'Hara's Younger Sister*, Fawcett, 1978

Kobal, John, *People Will Talk*, Alfred A. Knopf, 1985

Koszarksi, Richard, *Hollywood on the Hudson: Film & Television in New York*, Rutgers University Press, 2008

Kramer, Stanley with Thomas M. Coffey, *A Mad Mad Mad World: A Life in Hollywood*, Harcourt, 1997

LaGuardia, Robert, *Monty: A Biography of Montgomery Clift*, Arbor House, 1977

Lake, Veronica with Donald Bain, *Veronica: The Autobiography of Veronica Lake*, Citadel Press, 1970

Lambert, Gavin, *Norma Shearer: A Biography*, Knopf, 1990

Lenburg, Jeff, *Peekaboo: The Story of Veronica Lake*, Iuniverse, 2001

LeRoy, Mervyn with Dick Keiner, *Take One*, Hawthorne Books, 1974

Lobenthal, Joel, *Tallulah! The Life and Times of a Leading Lady*, Regan Books, 2004

Long, Robert Emmet (editor), *George Cukor Interviews*, University Press of Mississippi, 2001

Loy, Myrna and James Kotsilibas-Davis, *Myrna Loy: Being and Becoming*, Knopfs, 1987

Lynn, Kenneth, *Hemingway*, Harvard University Press, 1995

Mann, Theodore, *Journeys in the Night*, Applause, 2009

Mann, William, *Kate: The Woman Who Was Hepburn*, Henry Holt & Co, 2006

Martinson, Deborah, *Lillian Hellman: Life with Foxes and Scoundrels*, Counterpoint, 2011

Maychick, Diana & L. Avon Borgo, *Heart to Heart with Robert Wagner*, St. Martins, 1986

McCarthy, Todd, *Howard Hawks: The Grey Fox of Hollywood*, Grove Press, 1997

McGilligan, Patrick, *George Cukor: A Double Life*, Harper Perennial, 1991

Mellow, James R, *Hemmingway: A Life Without Consequences*, Addison-Wesley, 1992

Meyers, Jeffrey, *The Genius and the Goddess*, University of Illinois Press, 2012

Miller, Arthur, *Timebends: A Life*, Penguin Books, 1995

Niven, Penelope, *Thornton Wilder: A Life*, Harper, 2012

Peters, Margot, *House of Barrymore*, Touchstone Books, 1990

Peterson, Deborah C, *Fredric March: Craftsman First, Star Second*, Greenwood Press, 1996

Phillips, Gene D, *Conrad and Cinema: The Art of the Adaptation*, Peter Lang Publishing, 1997

Pizzitola, Louis, *Hearst over Hollywood: Power, Passion, and Propaganda in the Movies*, Columbia University Press, 2002

Quintero, Jose, *If You Don't Dance They Beat You*, Boston: Little, Brown, 1974

Quirk, Lawrence, *Films of Fredric March*, Citadel Press, 1971

Quirk, Lawrence, *Claudette Colbert: An Illustrated Biography*, Crown Publishers, 1985

Rasmussen, R. Kent, *Critical Companion to Mark Twain: A Literary Reference to His Life and Work*, Facts on File, 2007

Reid, John Howard, *These Movies Won No Hollywood Awards*, Lulu, 2010

Rollyson, Carl, *Lillian Hellman: Her Life and Legend*, in universe, 2008

Ross, Lillian & Helen Ross, *The Player: A Profile of an Art*, Limelight Editions, 1961

Russell, Harold with Dan Ferullo, *The Best Years of My Life*, Paul S. Erikson, 1981

Schatz, Thomas, *The Genius of the System: Filmmaking in the Studio Era*, Henry Holt & Company, 1988

Shafer, Yvonne, *American Women Playwrights, 1900-1950*, Peter Lang Publishing, 1998

Shafer, Yvonne, *Performing O'Neill*, Palgrave-MacMillan, 2000

Shipman, David, *The Great Movie Stars: The Golden Years*, Crown Publishers, Inc, 1970

Sperber, A.M. & Lax, Eric, *Bogart*, William Morrow & Company, 1997

Spoto, Donald, *Stanley Kramer: Film Maker*, Samuel French, Inc., 1990

Spoto, Donald, *Possessed: The Life of Joan Crawford*, William Morrow, 2010

Stenn, David, *Clara Bow: Running Wild*, Cooper Square Press, 2000

Sterling, Anna Kate, *Celebrity Articles from Screen Guild Magazine*, Scarecrow Press, 1987

Styron, William and Rose Styron & R. Blakeslee Gilpin, *Selected Letters of William Styron*, Random House, 2012

Swenson, Karen, *Greta Garbo*, Scribers, 1997

Swindell, Larry, *Screwball: The Life of Carole Lombard*, William Morrow & Co, 1975

Thomas, Bob, *King Cohn*, G.P. Putnam's Sons, 1967

Thomson, David, *Showman: The Life of David O. Selznick*, Knopf, 1992

Thomson, David, *The New Biographical Directory of Film*, Knopf, 2010

Van Patten, Dick with Richard Baer, *Eighty is Not Enough*, Phoenix, 2009

Wagner, Robert, *Pieces of My Heart: A Life*, Findaway World, 2009

Weaver, Tom, *Double Feature Creature Attack*, McFarland, 2003

Wyden, Peter, *The Passionate War: A Narrative of the Spanish Civil War*, Simon & Schuster, 1983

Young, Jeff, *Kazan: The Master Director Discusses His Films*, New Market Press, 2001

Yudkoff, Alvin, *Gene Kelly: A Life of Dance & Dreams*, Billboard Books, 2001

Zierold, Norman, *Garbo*, Stein & Day, 1969

NOTES AND SOURCES

Frequently cited archives, collections and libraries have been identified by the following abbreviations:

FM WSHSA, Fredric March Papers, Wisconsin State Historical Society Archives, Madison, WI

KB WSHSA, Kermit Bloomgarden Papers, Wisconsin State Historical Society Archives, Madison, WI

KD WSHSA, Kirk Douglas Papers, Wisconsin State Historical Society Archives, Madison, WI

JC WSHSA, John Cromwell Papers, Wisconsin State historical Society Archives, Madison, WI

MM WSHSA, Michael Myerberg Papers, Wisconsin State Historical Society Archives, Madison, WI

WK WSHSA, Walter Kerr Papers, Wisconsin State Historical Society Archives, Madison, WI

WW WSHSA, Walter Wanger Papers, Wisconsin State Historical Society Archives, Madison, WI

GC AMPAS, George Cukor Papers, Margaret Herrick Library, Academy of Motion Picture Arts & Sciences, Los Angeles, CA

GH AMPAS, Gladys Hall Papers, Margaret Herrick Library, Academy of Motion Picture Arts & Sciences, Los Angeles, CA

MR AMPAS, Martin Ritt Papers, Margaret Herrick Library, Academy of Motion Picture Arts & Sciences, Los Angeles, CA

CHAPTER ONE

"You see I was born in Racine Wisconsin...," *Pittsburgh Press*, August 20, 1939
A "swell family..." *Screenland*, "The Real Life Story of Fredric March," June/July 1932
"We sneaked from our homes after supper...," ibid
"Dreadful, sleepless night...," ibid
"Security is what I have always wanted beyond and above all else...," GH AMPAS
"I liked keeping tidy accounts of all my earnings...," *Screenland*, June/July 1932
"He always imitated the people with whom he came into contact...," *Racine Journal*, November 29, 1927
"My one and only distinguishing feature was a revolting one...," *Screenland*, June/July 1932
"Never was there such indignation...," ibid
"This was something a little different...," ibid
Fred Bickel to Cora Bickel, June 23, 1912, FM WSHSA
Fred Bickel to Cora Bickel, July 5, 1912, FM WSHSA
Fred Bickel to Cora Bickel, July 11, 1912, FM WSHSA
Fred Bickel to Jack Bickel, March 12, 1913, FM WSHSA
"First real glimpse of theater...," *Screenland*, June/July 1932
"We weren't really poor...," ibid

CHAPTER TWO

"Following in my brothers' footsteps...," *Screenland*, June/July 1932
"I was rotten!...," ibid

"A rich oratorical voice...," *Daily Cardinal*, March 9, 1917

"To help earn spending money and ease burden on his father...," *Milwaukee Sentinel*, September 4, 1965

"Even though Freddie took part in the annual 'Edwin Booth' production...," *Movie News Weekly Chicago*, June 30, 1937

"Very black hair...accentuated the clearness of her skin...," ibid

"Then my oldest brother advised me to get into the artillery...," *Screenland*, June/July 1932

"It was a grand act...," *Milwaukee Journal*, February 14, 1933

"Fred Bickel was burdened with a wordy part...," *Daily Cardinal*, May 26, 1919

"Frank Vanderlip of the National City Bank in New York...," *Screenland*, June/July 1932

"When I had been there seven or eight months...," ibid

"His attitude toward life in general was different...," Peterson, *Fredric March: Craftsman First, Star Second*

"At noon, one day (at work)...," *Screenland*, June/July 1932

"I cannot warm up to the banking business...," *Badger History*, March 1960

"Part of the mob and not very happy about it...," *Screenland*, June/July 1932

"So I switched from decorating the far backgrounds of movies...," ibid

"Don't let anyone tell you that posing for artists...," ibid

"My minor function in it was the finest training camp...," ibid

"At dress rehearsal...," ibid

Background on March's first wife, *Picture Play*, "Her Ex-husband Fredric March," February 1937

CHAPTER THREE

"Little did she know that I would one day choke her to death...," *Screenland*, June/July 1932

"Anyone who was successful there (Elitch's Garden)...,
Edwin Lewis Levy, *Elitch's Garden, Denver, Colorado: A History of the Oldest Summer Theater in the United States,* Columbia, University, 1960

Ellis also urged -her husband to go to Denver..., *Picture Play*, February 1937

"I remember the first thing I did when I arrived in Denver...," Levy

"As the leading man for the summer he received $500 per week...," Goodrich, *The Real Nick & Nora*

"As far as I was concerned, heaven had descended right on to that stage...," *Screenland*, June/July 1932

"I was pretty young then...," Article "Lyceum Days Recalled by Florence Eldridge," FM WSHSA

"Background on Florence Eldridge's career with the Theater Guild, Bordman, *American Theater*

"There was just something about him that attracted me in the beginning...," *Screenland*, "Why I Married Fredric March," June 1933

March refuses to act in *The Poor Nut*, Denver Post, "March refuses to play role in play coming to Elitch, undated, FM WSHSA

"A Genius must live alone...," *Picture Play*, February 1937

March deputized Jack Bickel to speak with Ellis regarding divorce, ibid

"This was my first honest to goodness lead on Broadway...," *Chicago Tribune*, August 7 ,1938

"No more beyond thine eyes...," *Chicago Tribune*, April 25, 1935

"Florence and I went on the road together...," *Screenland*, June/July 1932

"You had better explain that we are married...," *Montreal Gazette*, March 29, 1928

"They turn you out stamped," ibid

"I have seldom met such a group of indignant, overworked people...," Langer, *The Magic Carpet*

Background on *The Royal Family*, Peters, *House of Barrymore*

"The experience was a tremendous one for me...," Ross & Ross, *The Player*

"Fredric March played the fellow who was supposed to be me...," John Barrymore quoted in *The American Magazine*, 1933

"Don't lose your reputation, Fred...," *Milwaukee Journal*, February 17, 1933

CHAPTER FOUR

"I'm enormously interested in talking pictures...," GH AMPAS

"It's what you might term my 'break-in' part...," ibid

"Her voice was actually quite good...," Stenn, *Clara Bow: Running Wild*

"A quiet woman...," Atkins, *Arthur Jacobson*

Bow "vital and gay," *New York Times*, 1973

"The best looking young leech on the lot," Morella & Epstein, *The It Girl*

"Florence didn't hit it here...," Peterson, *Fredric March: Craftsman First, Star Second*

"Yes, I believe the psychology of Paris Bound was correct...," GH AMPAS

"Jeanne Eagels was wonderful...," *New York Times*, 1973

"Colleen Moore was perhaps a bigger star...," Basinger, *Silent Stars*

"The adoration stopped about three years after...," Kobal, *People Will Talk*

"Freddie, when I say camera...," GH AMPAS

"March brought a note of sanity to this film...," Scott O'Brien to author

"Florence was very sympathetic..," Astor, *A Life on Film*

"Florence saw that I was going to be all right...," Sterling, *Celebrity Articles from Screen Guild Magazine*

"We sat and gossiped on the couch...," Astor, *A Life on Film*

"Tremendous, smoldering sensuality to her...," Dick, *Claudette Colbert: She Walked in Beauty*

"Colbert would make $13,750...," ibid

"Laughter was a flop...," Koszarski, *Hollywood on the Hudson: Film and Television in New York*

"It was a mad, merry film...," *Silver Screen*, February 1937

"With *Royal Family* it was Cyril and Cukor...," McGilligan, *George Cukor: A Double Life*

"I was on familiar territory with *The Royal Family*..." ibid

"He was the prototype of John Barrymore...," *Arthur Jacobson: Interviewed by Irene Kahn Atkins*

"The famous scene in that picture...," ibid

"When he was making *The Royal Family*...," *Screenland*, No date, FM WSHSA

"My Sin...A mess," Bankhead, *Tallulah: My Autobiography*

CHAPTER FIVE

"I wanted someone who could play Jekyll...," Higham & Greenberg, *The Celluloid Muse: Hollywood Directors Speak*

"Alright, if you're so obstinate...," ibid

March was apprehensive about Mamoulian, Westmore & Davidson, *The Westmores of Hollywood*

"What's wrong with you? Ivy's going to steal the picture," *The Celluloid Muse*

"Difficult is an understatement!...," Weaver, *Double Feature Creature Attack*

"All the stories I hear about Miriam Hopkins, her temper tantrums...," *www.altfg.com/blog/actors/rouben-mamoulian-interview*

"A very typical European...," Rose Hobart in *Double Feature Creature Attack*

"Struss...up to every challenge I threw his way," Rouben Mamoulian to James Bawden, http://www.thecolumnists.com/bawden/bawden58.html

"My Dear Freddie...," Telegram from B.P. Schulberg to FM, FM WSHSA

"The device had to be comfortable enough for March to wear...," *The Westmores of Hollywood*.

"The Secret of the tranformation of Dr. Jekyll into Mr. Hyde...," Rouben Mamoulian in *The Celluloid Muse*.

"He (March) was very unhappy about it (the make-up)…,"
Rose Hobart to Tom Weaver, *Double Feature Creature Attack.*
"I went through the whole thing…," Mariam Hopkins to
John Kobel in *People Will Talk*, Alfred a. Knopf, 1985.

CHAPTER SIX

The Fifth Annual Academy Awards ceremony…, Wiley &
Bona, *Inside Oscar: The Unofficial History of the Academy Awards*
"Never have we been prouder of you…," Telegram from Jack
and Mary Bickel to FM, FM WSHSA
"This is the hardest thing I've ever done in my life…,"
Family Circle, March 9, 1933
"Penny-wise-and-pound foolish," *Los Angeles Evening News*,
July 24, 1934
"Fredric March had a reputation of being a ladies man…,"
fredricmarch.wordpress.com
"Two men with cardboard stirred up the milk…," *Vanity
Fair*, January 1998
"Freddie March was the worst womanizer I ever knew…," ibid
One photo, 'with Freddie's hand wrapped around…," ibid
"What a thoughtful human being you are…," Cecil B.
DeMille to Fredric March, FM WSHSA
"He worked everything out on paper…," Fredric March
interview with Guy Flatley, *New York Times*, 1973.
"Production on The Sign of the Cross…," Birchard, *Cecil B.
DeMille's Hollywood*
She allowed a concession…, Lambert, *Norma Shearer: A
Biography*
Background on Marches relationship with the Thalberg's,
Flamini, *Thalberg: The Last Tycoon & The World of MGM*
"Wonderful sincerity and poise," Quirk, *Films of Fredric
March*, Press, 1971.
"It was as famous a moniker in its day…," Bogdanovich,
Who the Hell Made It
"If he grabs me once more to show how Freddie March…,"
Eyman, *Ernst Lubitsch: Laughter in Paradise*, Scott Eyman

"The critics will not like our picture...," ibid

March liked Lubitsch..., Fredric March interview with Guy Flatley, *New York Times*, 1973.

"The problem with Cooper and March...," Andrew Sarris, *The Village Voice*, 1963.

"Mitch is 100% correct...," Chierichetti, *Hollywood Director*

Filming went smoothly except for one incident..., *Chicago Daily Tribune*, March 16, 1933.

"Stuart Walker had no idea what a camera was for...," *Hollywood Director*

"Colbert and March as 'wonderful together,' ...ibid

"He (March) was so taken with her...," Mitchell Leisen quoted in *Claudette Colbert: An Illustrated Biography*

"Maxwell Anderson and I had quite an argument...," *Hollywood Director*

"The effect of Death being transparent...," ibid

Ill during filming of *Death Takes a Holiday*, *Reading Eagle*, October 18, 1933

Background on *The Barrett's of Wimpole Street*, *Thalberg: The Last Tycoon & The World of MGM & Norma Shearer: A Biography*

"But they can't censor the gleam in my eye," Callow, *Charles Laughton: A Difficult Actor*

Background on the adoption of Anthony March, *New York Times*, August 30, 1935

House constructed in Holmby Hills, *Hartford Courant*, September 16, 1934

"I especially wanted to go to Tahiti...," GH Papers, AMPAS

Tahiti Trip, *Photoplay*, March 1935/**Background on Les Miserables, Behlmer,** *Memo from Darryl F Zanuck*

Zanuck provided March with some 'star perks'..., *Los Angeles Evening News*, July 24, 1934

"We have lost our enthusiasm for a production of Anna Karenina...," Swenson, *Greta Garbo*

"Further Fredric March will only do...," ibid

"As the saying went at the time...," Zierold, *Garbo*

In between scenes they would bounce a medicine ball..., Swenson, *Greta Garbo*

"Actually I was not overwhelmed by Garbo's beauty...,"
Zierold, *Garbo*

"I have some passionate scenes with Garbo...," *Film Weekly*,
September 20, 1935

"I can understand Oberon with Howard...," Telegram from
Sidney Franklin to Samuel Goldwyn, *Goldwyn: A Biographer*

The Dark Angel, "An old silly," Rollyson, *Lillian Hellman:
Her Life and Legend*

"Colman was superb in it...," *Film Weekly*, September 20,
1935

Background on *The Road to Glory*, McCarthy, *Howard
Hawks: The Grey Fox of Hollywood*

"At 19 it was exciting having established stars...," June Lang
to Colin Briggs, *Classic Images*, 1992

"I was covered with mud and dust...," *Sydney Morning
Herald*, November 24, 1936

Background on *Mary of Scotland*, *Kate: The Woman Who Was
Hepburn*, William Mann & *Print the Legend: The Life and Times
of John Ford*

"He's a comic, just a comic...," Fredric March interview with
Guy Flatley, *New York Times*, 1973.

"I think it's true (that) she is not as popular...," *Calgary
Daily Herald*, December 28, 1936

"Very adverse," GH AMPAS

"Their notations said that we couldn't film those forty
pages...," Leroy & Kleiner, *Mervyn Leroy: Take Two*

"I want to do light comedy roles...," *Sydney Morning Herald*,
November 24, 1936

CHAPTER SEVEN

"It is impossible for 40 or 50 productions...," *Nashua
Telegraph*, June 24, 1965

"Suggest looking at what we did in What Price Hollywood...,"
Thomson, *Showman: The Life of David O. Selznick*

Wellman moved the picture along smoothly and briskly...,
Schatz, *Genius of the System: Filmmaking in the Studio Era*

"I believe we can retain Gaynor's entire approach...," *Memo from David O. Selznick*, editor Rudy Behlmer

"I find that there is a reaction of uncertainty that March...," ibid

"I had been called the best John Barrymore imitator around...," Quirk, *The Films of Fredric March*

"Dear Freddie...," David Selznick to Fredric March, *Memo from David Selznick*

"Nothing Sacred started shooting this morning...," David Selznick to John Hay Whitney, ibid.

"As I told you in New York...," Joseph Breen to David Selznick, *Genius of the System*

"While Hecht and the director, William Wellman...," Kael, *Kiss Kiss Bang Bang*

Additional source on back ground of *Nothing Sacred*: Swindell, *Screwball: The Life of Carole Lombard*

"Unsuited for the harsh reality of war," Lynn, *Hemingway*

"Yes I guess I should say something," Wyden, *The Passionate War*

CHAPTER EIGHT

Evelyn Keyes' recollections of *The Buccaneer*, Keyes, *Scarlett O'Hara's Younger Sister*

"Freddie liked ladies...," Bradford Dillman to Deborah C. Peterson, *Fredric March Craftsman First, Star Second*

"Now, let me get this straight, I don't have anything against picture...," *New York Times*, November 7, 1937

"Monty Clift was the juvenile lead...," Fredric March to Guy Flatley, *NY Times*, 1973

"Monty had great talent...," ibid

"In the studios...," *Columbus Citizen*, November 26, 1937

"Of course you've got to be in love...," *Pittsburgh Sun-Telegram*, December 14, 1937

March landed in the hospital the same day..., *New York Times*, December 27, 1937

"I wanted to do this play every bit as much as she did…,"
Fredric March to Gladys Hall, "Film Can Be Success," undated,
GH AMPAS

"It's all Norman McLeod's fault…," *Hartford Courant*, August
13, 1938

Background on *Trade Winds*, Garnett & Balling, *Light Your
Torches* & WW Papers, WSHSA

Background on *The American Way*, Brown, *Moss Hart: A
Prince of the Theater*

"It was just the kind of thing we wanted to do…,"
Milwaukee Journal, February 1, 1939

**"At that moment I was only vaguely aware that Fredric
March was special…,"** Van Patten & Baer, *Eighty is Not Enough*

"Get your mind on your acting!…," ibid

"To Fredric March gratefully, Marian Anderson," FM Papers,
WSHSA

"When the children were small…," *Milwaukee Journal*,
November 9, 1958

Marches sued by their cook for injuries, *Milwaukee Journal*,
January 17, 1940

"Hope you've learned your lesson—F," McGilligan, *George
Cukor: A Double Life*

**Exchange of letters between George Cukor and Fredric
March in preparation for *Susan and God*,** GC AMPAS

Joan Crawford "A nice person, but…," Fredric March to Guy
Flatley, *NY Times*, 1973

"I owe a lot to Fredric March," Spoto, *Possessed: The Life of
Joan Crawford*

"Sorry you didn't like S & God better…," Peterson, *Fredric
March-Craftsman First, Star Second*

Background on Dies Committee/Communist accusations,
Pizzitola, *Hearst over Hollywood*

"They were all good liberal minded…" Loy, *Being and
Becoming*

"Margaret, doesn't he remind you of a young Hank Fonda?,"
Ford, *Glenn Ford: A Life*

Background on *Victory*, Phillips, *Conrad and Cinema: The Art
of the Adaptation*

"Finished 'Victory' on Friday and John Cromwell...," Fredric March to Jack Bickel, FM WSHSA

"Casey Robinson's screenplay was pretty wonderful...," Irving Rapper to James Bawden, http://thecolumnists.com/bawden/bawden67.html

"Irving, you're the first director who has taken the ham out of him...," Davis, *Just Making Movies: Company Directors on the Studio System*

"When Hartzel Spence saw the picture...," unsourced newspaper article, FM WSHSA

"Nobody was going to cheat me," Thomas, *King Cohn*

Background on *Hope for a Harvest* & Sophie Treadwell, Shafer, *American Women Playwrights, 1900-1950*

"Worth it...slowly declining...," Peterson, *Fredric March: Craftsman First, Star Second*

"I'd later use Freddie in films...," Michael Gordon to James Bawden, http://www.thecolumnists.com/bawden/Bawden68.html

Letters from Clara Clemens Gabrilowitsch to Fredric March re: *The Adventures of Mark Twain*, FM WSHSA

"Every day for twelve weeks...," *New York Sun*, undated, FM WSHSA

"I couldn't think of any other American actor who could do it...," Irving Rapper to James Bawden, http://thecolumnists.com/bawden/bawden67.html

"Irving's a darling...," *Christian Science Monitor*, April 15, 1944

"Dear Freddie may you always remember this birthday...," Jesse Lasky to Fredric March, FM WSHSA

March turning down Foote's *The State of the River*, Rasmussen, *Critical Companion to Mark Twain*

CHAPTER NINE

Background on Thornton Wilder & *The Skin of Our Teeth*, *Thornton Wilder: A Life*

"A tall man, without the grace some tall men have...," Kazan, *Elia Kazan: A Life*

"An erratic tactless man," Bankhead, *Tallulah: My Autobiography*
"dickering, middleman, promotion," *Selected Letters of Thornton Wilder*, editors Jackson R. Bryer & Robin Gibbs Wilder
"there was never any doubt that I was the one to do the play," Article dated December 12, 1942 titled *Bliss Incarnate*, but no source as to publication, MM WSHSA
"I was excited and eager...," *Hartford Courant*, January 3, 1943
Elia Kazan's recollections of meeting with Marches in their New York apartment, *Elia Kazan: A Life*
"March had worked with many beautiful actresses...," Lenburg, *Peekaboo: The Story of Veronica Lake*
"I moved my foot up and down...," Lake & Bain, *Veronica: The Autobiography of Veronica Lake*
"I had been called in for a portrait sitting with Freddie March...," *Peekaboo: The Story of Veronica Lake*
"She was touchy on the set...," Quirk, *The Films of Fredric March*, Lawrence J. Quirk
"I've hated only two people in my life...," *Elia Kazan: A Life*
Bankhead was always guaranteed sole billing above the title..., Lobenthal, *Tallulah! The Life and Times of a Leading Lady*
"Four stars and Monty Clift...," *Elia Kazan: A Life* (Kazan)
Bankhead "tried to have everybody fired...," *Tallulah! The Life and Times of a Leading Lady*
"Our present plans call for four and one-half weeks...," FM WSHSA
"Two star dressing rooms on the stage of the (Plymouth) theater," MM WSHSA
"The tensions between the Marches and Bankhead...," *Elia Kazan: A Life*
"Real jealousy" between Bankhead and Florence, *Tallulah! The Life and Times of a Leading Lady*
"Oh, why don't you stop being such a tight, neurotic bitch," ibid
"Don't let me ham it up," *Elia Kazan: A Life*
Kazan "didn't know how to direct a star," ibid
"Everybody was getting along splendidly," *Tallulah! The Life and Times of a Leading Lady*

Bankhead "looking for something to rant about...," *Elia Kazan: A Life*

"The fundamental basis of our plan is the free use of the stage...," MM WSHSA

"The first dress rehearsal was a nightmare of hysteria...," *Elia Kazan: A Life*

"I tell you, if we hadn't had a full house...," *New York Herald Tribune*, April 14, 1946

"Naturally I am astonished by the degree of Tallulah's difficulty...," Thornton Wilder to Michael Myerberg, MM WSHSA

"May this launch you on the top flight producing career...," Fredric & Florence March to Michael Myerberg, MM WSHSA

"The show opened...and Thornton had what he deserved...," *Elia Kazan: A Life*

Tallulah "throwing her head back over the railing...," ibid

"I watched the show in the wings...Freddie lifted the glass to his lips...," ibid

Benny Stein reports to Michael Myerberg, MM WSHSA

"Dear Mr. March..." Blair Davies to Fredric March, FM WSHSA

"The eye is mending rapidly..." Fredric March to Michael Myerberg, MM WSHSA

"You're not very popular around here at the moment...," Florence Eldridge to Michael Myerson, MM WSHSA

"Your letter is a strange mixture of a stone hatchet with feathers...," Michael Myerson to Florence Eldridge, MM WSHSA

"What was it like to work with Tallulah?..." Fredric March to Guy Flatley, *NY Times*, 1973

CHAPTER TEN

"It is really our idea of a complete home," *New York Journal American*, March 7, 1944

"I had a lot of humorous stuff...," *New York World Journal-Telegram*, January 25, 1944

"I came into one of the downstairs rooms and saw him before a battery of cameras...," *Evening Independent*, June 20, 1963

Lt. Norton Goodwin recollections of March, *Flyer tells of Narrow Escape while Flying Fredric March*, newspaper clipping, unsourced or dated, FM Papers WSHSA

Ernie Pyle quotes from *Milwaukee Journal*, January 16, 1944

"The performance by the Fredric March troupe were especially good...," Letter from Lt. Commander Dunn to Camp Shows Association, FM WSHSA

"Seeing Fredric March and the reception the boys gave him...," *LA Daily News*, December 14, 1943

"On that trip I came to have the greatest admiration for the average run of our G.I's...," "March Trained to play Joppolo" article by Helen Ormsbee *New York Times*, undated, FM WSHSA

"This soldier in Persia showed me a letter from his wife...," *New York World Telegram*, January 25, 1944

"Dear Fred...Am in absolute agreement...," Telegram from Jack Warner to Fredric March, February 3, 1944, FM WSHSA

"When Lester Cowan announced he was going to make *Tomorrow the World*...," *St. Petersburg Times*, July 23, 1944

"Upstairs in the barn, away from everybody...," *New York Sun*, December 1, 1944

"I have played dozens of characters over the years...," Helen Osmsbee, "March Trained to play Joppolo" undated FM WSHSA

"Tony and Penny have been here for their Thanksgiving holiday..," ibid

"Many come back stage to tell me not only how much they like the play...," ibid

CHAPTER ELEVEN

Background on *The Best Years of Our Lives*, Goldwyn, A Scott Berg & *Robert E. Sherwood: The Playwright in Peace & War*, Harriet Hyman Alonzo

"Stands as the epitome of married love on the screen," Teresa Wright quoted in *Myrna Loy: Being and Becoming*

"I liked the book from the beginning...," *Christian Science Monitor*, March 31, 1947

"He didn't give you anything particularly himself...," Teresa Wright, Columbia University's Oral History Research Office, 1959.

"It's very important that your figure suggest a K-ration diet...," William Wyler to Fredric March, Herman, *A Talent for Trouble*

"He adored Freddie," ibid

"This classically, tall, dark-haired and handsome actor...," Russell with Ferullo, *The Best Years of My Life*

"I was biting my nails," Fredric March to Gladys Hall, GH Papers, AMPAS

"Fredric March is quite brilliant...," *The Independent*, February 1, 2002

Background on *Years Ago*, Gordon, *An Open Book*

"That mustache...," *New York Post Weekend Magazine*, January 25, 1947

"Just once, she gave me a suggestion...," "Marches play as parents again," *New York Times*, Helen Ornsbee, undated, FM WSHSA

"Freddie's method is what he calls twenty-four-hours-a-day...," ibid

Michael Gordon's recollections of *Another Side of the Forest & An Act of Murder*, http://www.thecolumnists.com/bawden/Bawden68.html

"One thing we learned from our USO tour during the war...," unsourced and undated clipping in FM WSHSA of article titled "Fredric March and Family at Home."

Fredric March communist..., *Los Angeles Mirror*, June 8, 1949

"She had a job right there in the justice department...," *Los Angeles Times*, March 4, 2011

The report was particularly hard on March..., http://www.history.com/this-day-in-history/fbi-report-names-hollywood-figures-as-communists

"It's an unmitigated lie...," *Los Angeles Daily News*, June 4, 1949

"Mrs. March and I are not Communists…," *Boston Globe*, July 1, 1949

"Another informer reports that I received an acting award…," ibid

"Withdraws and retracts its previously published statements…," *The Hollywood Reporter*, Dcember 22, 1949

"We are glad, that we, and our children…," *Newsweek*, January 2, 1950

"We were in bed before lunch…," Florence Eldridge to Jack and Mary Bickel, FM WSHSA

"I'd wanted to do Columbus for a long time…," *Miami News*, September 18, 1949

"At last we're on a normal keel…," Florence Eldridge to Jack and Mary Bickel, FM WSHSA

"We're beginning the preliminaries…," ibid

"It was like stepping back into the fairy tales of childhood…," ibid

"We're counting the days until she arrives…," Fredric March to Jack Bickel, FM WSHSA

"Bless you, and thank you for sending…," ibid

"…Dad and I set out to wander…," Florence Eldridge to Tony March, FM WSHSA

"I missed one in a production with Lilli Palmer…," *Minneapolis Star*, December 18, 1951

CHAPTER TWELVE

"Freddy was not only a superb actor but he had great panache…," Cronyn, *A Terrible Liar*

"General Leonidas Erosa gives me a chance to play a really flamboyant character…," *Philadelphia Bulletin*, January 29, 1950

"That's one of the wonderful things that comes from acting together…," ibid

Rick Jason's recollections of *Now I lay Me Down to Sleep*, Jason, *Scrapbooks of My Mind: A Hollywood Memoir*

"I'm rooting for you…," Penny March to Fredric and Florence March, March 2, 1950, FM WSHSA

"Freddy—the epileptic scene I will never forget in my life…," Clifford Odets to Fredric March, FM WSHSA

"I know how deep is the debt I woe busy people…," Norman Thomas to Fredric March, FM WSHSA

"…he was under wraps—he was not the fun Freddie March," Virginia Hall to Deborah C. Peterson, *Fredric March: Craftsman First-Star Second*

"Interested in some response to the crucifying of left wingers…," Gottfried, *Arthur Miller: His Life and Work*

"Arthur sensed this wish to Florence's to be loved…," Meyers, *The Genius and the Goddess*

Background on *The Autumn Garden*, Kermit Bloomgarden Papers, KB WSHSA

"She began to give me notes on the second or third day…," Martinson, *Lillian Hellman: Life with Foxes and Scoundrels*

"It was an important play…," Jane Wyatt in *Movies were Always Magical*, Leo Verswijver,

Cohn was certain that the film (Death of a Salesman) was a certain loser…, Thomas, *King Cohn*

"My sole participation was to complain that the screenplay…," Miller, *Timebends: A Life*

"By the time the sets were built and dressed…," *New York Times*, December 9, 1951

"Willy is on the verge of insanity throughout the play…," *Minneapolis Morning Tribune*, December 19, 1951

"We haven't planned anything special…," *Milwaukee Sentinel*, December 20, 1951

"Fred embarrassed me…," Jackie Ramsey Macaulay to Deborah C. Peterson, *Fredric March: Craftsman First-Star Second*

"What the hell, give it to him," Reid, *These Movies Won No Hollywood Awards*

Elia Kazan recollections of *Man on a Tightrope*, *Elia Kazan: A Life & Kazan: The Master Director Discusses His Films*

Background on *Executive Suite*, Houseman, *Front and Center*

"Barbara Stanwyck screamed her head off…," Nina Foch to James Bawden, http://www.thecolumnists.com/bawden/bawden19.html

"I devised a motion just to signal to him...," Robert Wise to James Bawden, http://www.thecolumnists.com/bawden/bawden79.html

"I've seen everything he's ever done...," *Reading Eagle, AP,* November 14, 1954

March was the top choice by a 2-1 margin, *Miami News,* January 30, 1955

Background on *The Desperate Hours,* Sperber & Lax, *Bogart,* A.M. Sperber

"The audience loved him," Herman, *A Talent for Trouble*

"Dear Freddie, I have just seen THE DESPERATE HOURS...," Joseph Hayes to Fredric March, FM WSHSA

Background on Alexander the Great, Production Facts, Robert Rossen Enterprises, FM WSHSA

"You're playing a rich man...," *Reading Eagle,* July 2, 1956

CHAPTER THIRTEEN

"Carlotta was very much conscious of wanting to resurrect (O'Neill's) reputation...," Mann, *Journeys in the Night*

"We knew Freddie was perfect for James Tyrone...," ibid

"An impressive man—a great actor...," Bradford Dillman to author, August 4, 2012

"I had the guts to call him 'Freddie' from the start...," ibid

Quintero "very intense...," ibid

"Now Florence and Freddy...," Quintero, *If You Don't Dance They Beat You*

"Freddie and James had similarities in their careers..." *Journeys in the Night*

"Opening night (in New Haven) did not go well...," ibid

"As we drove along...I was dismayed to see the commercial development...," ibid

"I kept seeing Mrs. O'Neill in my mind...," ibid

"When Freddie as James gets up on a chair...," Dillman to author

"We did not expect success in New York...," ibid

"I don't know what to say...how to express it...," Bowen & O'Neill, *The Curse of the Misbegotten: A Tale of The House of O'Neill*

Quote from congratulatory letters from Joseph L. Mankiewicz, Martha Scott, Charlton Heston, & Helen Keller, FM Papers WSHSA

"It was so emotionally draining that we all went home and collapsed," Bradford Dillman to author

"The great thing about Jason was that he always surprised me...," ibid

"Freddie's vocal coach would often be in the audience...," Mann, *Journeys in the Night*

"Jason loved his father and also loved Fredric March...," Shafer, *Performing O'Neill*

"Freddie had the physical stamina but it was tiring...," Bradford Dillman to author

"How do you think Florence did tonight?...," Mann, *Journeys in the Night*

"March, "very protective of Florence...," Bradford Dillman to author

"The play is really about the wife...," ibid

"I needed to leave the show...," ibid

"I think both of us were even more taken with the play...," Walter Kerr to Fredric March, WK papers, WSHSA

"Two weak actors," FM WSHSA

"I have seen other great, great actors perform James Tyrone...," Shafer, *Performing O'Neill*

"It makes a parent wonder how he can sue when he is doing the right thing...," *Victoria Advocate*, November 9, 1958

"thumping good theater...," *Oxnard Press Courier*, November 13, 1958

Novak, "shaking. This was a new experience for Kim...," Considine, *Mad as Hell: The Life and Work of Paddy Chayefsky*

"She was extraordinary," ibid

Middle of the Night "going to be an enormous hit...," ibid

"There is one consolation about having your daughter live in another country...," *Milwaukee Journal*, November 9, 1958

"I would like to have Fredric March for the Clarence Darrow role," *Los Angeles Examiner*, March 25, 1958

"Was I out of my mind?...," Kramer & Coffey, *A Mad Mad Mad World: A Life in Hollywood*

"At first glance, March didn't quite look the part...," ibid

"Herewith a draft of INHERIT THE WIND...," Stanley Kramer to Fredric March, October 24, 1958, FM WSHSA

"God knows, we are still trying to improve and sharpen...," Stanley Kramer to Fredric March, September 8, 1959, FM WSHSA

"We had Tracy and Fredric March nose to nose...," Davidson, *Spencer Tracy: Tragic Idol*

"To be working with two of the best actors in the world...," Hirschhorn, *Gene Kelly: A Biography*

"All you could do was watch the magic and be amazed...," Yudkoff, *Gene Kelly: A Life of Dance and Dreams*

Anthony March crashing his car in a stone wall, *St. Joseph News Press*, November 22, 1959

"Dear Freddy, I have to admit to you...," Spencer Tracy to Fredric March, March 3, 1961, FM WSHSA

CHAPTER FOURTEEN

"NO. Wait a minute! One. Dr. Jekyll!," *Newsweek*

"Here was an actor in command of his craft...," Gazzara, *In the Moment: My Life as an Actor*

"The one thing that impressed me most about working with Fredric...," Dick Clark to Deborah C. Peterson, *Fredric March: Craftsman First-Star Second*

"I was a little leery about *The Young Doctors*...," *Newsweek*

"Freddie was very fond of Paddy...," Considine, *Mad as Hell: The Life and Work of Paddy Chayefsky*

"I was in the country...when Paddy told me about the play...," *Pittsburgh Press*, December 22, 1961

"I want actors to really work...," Considine, *Mad as Hell*

March decided to lose the slippers..., *Pittsburgh Press*, December 22, 1961

"Can you believe this?...," Considine, *Mad as Hell*
Background on March at Nobel dinner, An Evening at the
Kennedy White House: Fredric March Performs Hemingway's
Islands in the Stream, Marc Cirino, *The Hemmingway Review*,
Spring, 2000
**"After dinner there was a boring reading by Fredric
March...,"** *Selected Letters of William Styron,* William Styron,
Rose Styron & R. Blakeslee Gilpin
March took away one very special gift from this dinner, *St.
Petersburg Times,* May 9, 1962
**"Then in the morning I saw Freddie March's hands shaking
too...,"** May chick & Borgo, *Heart to Heart with Robert Wagner*
"Every day Vittorio would tell him...," Wagner, *Pieces of My
Heart: A Life*, Robert Wagner
"Very obviously he cropped a feel...," ibid
Background on *Seven Days in May*, KD WSHSA
March contract information, ibid
**"I didn't know what it was going to be like to direct a man
of his stature...,"** *Los Angeles Times*, April 27, 1975
Burt Lancaster in "careful awe" of March, Burford, *Burt
Lancaster: An American Life*
"One of the best I ever directed," Champlin, *John
Frankenheimer: A Conversation with Charles Champlin*
Richard Anderson recollections of Fredric March,
http://www.Americanlegends.com/interviews/Richard_Anderson
"We had to film it from many various angles...," *Los Angeles
Times,* April 27, 1975
"The New York screening...," Memo from David Horowitz to
Kirk Douglas, KD WSHSA
"He was an inspiration for everyone in that film...," *Los
Angeles Times*, April 27, 1975
Information on "A Tribute to President John F. Kennedy,"
FM WSHSA
**"I can't tell you how much I enjoy doing this kind of
documentary...,"** *Toledo Blade*, September 20, 1964
Florence Eldridge's journal of their State Department Tour,
FM WSHSA

"Some say you are in Italy...," Spencer Tracy to the Marches, FM WSHSA

"Please advise Mr and Mrs Fredric March...," Dean Rusk to the Marches, FM WSHSA

"Your performance set the tone of the evening...," Lyndon Johnson to FM, FM WSHSA

CHAPTER FIFTEEN

"What am I doing here?...," *The Deseret News*, June 16, 1966

"Murderous, so hot you couldn't sleep at night...," ibid

"She was magnificent...," ibid

"Though I am hardly objective enough to give you a genuine opinion...," Martin Ritt to Fredric March, October 31, 1966, MR AMPAS

Background on *Do Not Go Gentle Into that Good Night*, *Times Daily*, April 29, 1967

"All I need is some sunshine...," *Gadsden Times*, May 3, 1967

"An actor is only as good as the person behind him...," Quirk, *Films of Fredric March*

Grand opening of Ford's Theater, FM WSHSA, January 30, 1968

"You didn't feel folksy with her at all...," Virginia Hall to Deborah C. Peterson, *Fredric March: Craftsman First-Star Second*

"I was only seven years old...," Vernon Scott, UPI, May 23, 1969

"My wife had great fun kidding me...," *Milwaukee Sentinel*, February 21, 1970

"It looked like opening night at the Met...," *Pittsburgh Press*, June 1, 1969

"When I said I was retiring several years ago...," *The News & Courier*, January 27, 1970

"It's a wonderful pure Spanish colonial town...," *Wisconsin State Journal*, May 15, 1970

"I'm delighted to have a chance to meet you, Mr. March...," *Wisconsin State Journal*, May 19, 1970

"Thrilled beyond words...," *Reading Eagle*, October 15, 1971

"seemed prodigious but was rather disappointing...,"
Styron, *Selected Letters*

"Doesn't your paper say...," *New York Times*, 1973

"He had just had an operation, but he wanted very much to
do the film...," *Los Angeles Times*, April 27, 1975

"Freddie was dying...," Bradford Dillman to author

"Lee Marvin was a mean drunk...," ibid

"Lee had tremendous respect for Bob...," Jarlett, *Robert
Ryan: a Biography and Critical Filmology*

"And then he was back...," *Los Angeles Times*, April 27, 1975

"When Freddie arrived, knowing every line...," ibid

"Freddie had a stand-in who would be on hand...," Bradford
Dillman to author

"Bert and the boys have been wonderful...," Peterson, *Fredric
March: Craftsman First-Star Second*

"So I can read the paper," ibid

Sold 30 acres of the Connecticut farm, *Hartford Courant*,
August 2, 1974

"When he was in the hospital and very ill, Florence...,"
Cronyn, *A Terrible Liar*

"I know that I will never work with anyone like him
again...," *Los Angeles Times*, April 27, 1975

"Fredric March also had strength of character...," *Racine
Journal Times*, April 17, 1975

"Because, like Robert Frost, he took the road less traveled...,"
Baltimore Sun

APPENDIX
SELECTED RADIO PERFORMANCES OF FREDRIC MARCH

Much of this book has concentrated on the stage, film and television performances of Fredric March. But like other actors of his day March also made several radio appearances over the years and here are some selected performances from that great medium.

The Lux Radio Theater

Death Takes a Holiday, March 22, 1937, March recreates his film role with Florence Eldridge cast in the role played by Evelyn Venable in the film
The Plainsman, May 31, 1937, with Fredric March as Wild Bill Hickok and Jean Arthur as Calamity Jane
The Outsider, September 20, 1937, with Fredric March, Florence Eldridge and Donald Crisp
Bachelor Mother, January 22, 1940, Joel McCrea took ill and March replaced him in this radio broadcast with Ginger Rogers recreating her role from the 1939 film.
One Foot in Heaven, April 20, 1942, March and Martha Scott recreate their screen roles in a radio adaptation of the Warner Brothers film.

The Cavalcade of America

One Foot in Heaven, November 3, 1941, with March recreating his film role and Florence Eldridge cast as his wife. Also featuring a Norman Vincent Peale.

The Lengthening Shadow April 12, 1943, about the life of Thomas Jefferson with Fredric March, Will Geer and Arlene Francis.

Treasury Star Parade

April 4, 1942—March and Walter Huston perform a vaudeville routine. Program also features Florence Eldridge.

April 28, 1942—March hosts this program, which also features Jane Cowl.

December 25, 1942— "A Modern Scrooge"—a wartime version of *A Christmas Carol* featuring Lionel Barrymore and March.

April 29, 1943—theme of episode is "This is America" and features March along with First Lady Eleanor Roosevelt

Radio Hall of Fame

February 13, 1944—March recites the Pledge of Allegiance in a program also featuring Joan Fontaine and Jimmy Durante.

December 3, 1944—March is the host of a program also featuring Victor Borge and Paul Whitman and his Orchestra.

The Radio Reader's Digest

We Took to the Woods, January 20, 1946, March plays a blind man hoping to regain his sight. Florence Eldridge costars.

Victorian Lady, October 2, 1947, March and Florence Eldridge costar.

Suspense

Actor's Blood, August 24, 1944, March stars with Hans Conried and John McIntire.

The Night Reveals, May 26, 1949, March stars with Jeanette Nolan.

Theater Guild on the Air

No Time for Comedy, March 9, 1947, Fredric March and Florence Eldridge recreate the roles played by James Stewart and Rosalind Russell in the 1940 motion picture.

Cyrano de Bergerac, October 12, 1947, March plays the hero of Edmond Rostand's romantic play costarring with Florence Eldridge.

Dr. Jekyll and Mr. Hyde, November 19, 1950, March recreated his Oscar-winning motion picture role costarring Barbara Bel Geddes.

Other Selected Performances:

Hollywood Hotel, *A Star is Born*, April 30, 1937, March, Janet Gaynor and Andy Devine perform scenes from their then current film.

The Gulf Screen Guild Theater, *The Enchanted Cottage*, November 26, 1939, with Helen Hayes, Fredric March and Harry Von Zell.

Words at War, *George Washington Carver*, February 8, 1944, featuring March and Canada Lee as Carver.

The Lady Esther Screen Guild Theater, *The Good Fairy*, July 31, 1944, with Fredric March, Deanna Durbin and Gene Lockhart.

Frank Sinatra in Person, August 16, 1944, with guests Fredric March and Eileen Barton

The Jane Cowl Show, April 4, 1945—March discusses his play *A Bell for Adano*.

Hollywood Fights Back, October 26, 1947—The Hollywood community takes on the House Un-American Activities Committee. Among those who spoke out: March, Charles Boyer, Judy Garland, Gene Kelly, Lauren Bacall, Joseph Cotton, Danny Kaye, William Holden, Florence Eldridge, Robert Young, Lucille Ball, Humphrey Bogart, Edward G. Robinson, Audie Murphy, William Wyler and John Garfield.

The Camel Screen Guild Theater, *The Best Years of Our Lives,* November 24, 1947, March, Myrna Loy and Teresa Wright recreate their screen roles.

The Screen Director's Playhouse, *Trade Winds,* May 29, 1949, Director Tay Garnett introduces this episode, which recreates his 1939 film with March playing the role he played in the film.

The MGM Theater of the Air, *The Citadel,* October 18, 1949, with March and Florence Eldridge.

New Birth of Freedom, October 6, 1950, March appears in a scene from *A Bell of Adano.*

Best Plays, *There Shall Be No Night,* January 25, 1953, March and Florence Eldridge appear in the same roles played by Alfred Lunt and Lynn Fontanne in the 1940 play.

NBC Star Playhouse, *A Farewell to Arms,* December 13, 1953, with Fredric March and Florence Eldridge.

Cavalcade of Stars, March 27, 1955, A tribute to the Academy Awards featuring March, Bing Crosby, Bob Hope, Cecil B. DeMille, Donna Reed, Ginger Rogers, Greer Garson, Jane Wyman, Joan Crawford, Jose Ferrer, Mary Pickford, Walt Disney, William Holden, among others.

INDEX

Milton Keynes UK
Ingram Content Group UK Ltd.
UKHW051322170724
5UKWH00070B/958